INDIAN NATIONALISM AND
THE EARLY CONGRESS

INDIAN NATIONALISM AND
THE EARLY CONGRESS

———— *John R. McLane* ————

PRINCETON UNIVERSITY PRESS

Copyright © 1977 by Princeton University Press

Published by Princeton University Press, Princeton, New Jersey
In the United Kingdom: Princeton University Press,
Guildford, Surrey

All Rights Reserved

Library of Congress Cataloging in Publication Data will
be found on the last printed page of this book

This book has been composed in Linotype Baskerville

Printed in the United States of America
by Princeton University Press, Princeton, New Jersey

Contents

Preface		vii
Abbreviations		ix
Glossary		xi
Introduction		3

PART I

One	The Rulers	21
Two	Congress Leaders	50

PART II

Three	The First Years of the Congress and Allan Octavian Hume	89
Four	Congress in the Doldrums	130
Five	Moderates, Extremists, and the Congress Constitution	152

PART III

Six	Toward the Integration of Indian Elites	179
Seven	Congress and the Landlord Interest	211
Eight	The Congress, Peasants, and the Alienation of Land	243

PART IV

Nine	Cow Protection and National Politics	271
Ten	Cow Protection Riots and Their Aftermath	309
Eleven	The Hindu Martial Revival and the Chapekar Terrorist Society	332
Conclusion		359
Bibliography		371
Index		391

---—————————————— *Preface* ——————————————

This book analyzes the relations between the early Indian National Congress and the larger Indian society. The Congress was founded in 1885, before the emergence of nationalist organizations in other colonial societies which might have served as models. Because of this and the fact that most Congress leaders were both English educated and anglicized, the early Congress depended heavily upon English models and ideas. The early Congress was hobbled by the attempt to apply to India political forms and concepts from a society in a different stage of development and with a dissimilar culture. From the beginning, though, Congress leaders realized that in order to obtain reforms from their English rulers, they had to attract support from outside the small, scattered groups of graduates of English-language schools.

This study examines the efforts to reach new sections of the population—particularly elites without university education. In the pre-Gandhian period, the decisive developments affecting Congress relations with the larger society often occurred outside the Congress, in official policy, among landlords and Muslims, and in religious revitalization movements. The following pages therefore focus as much on the fringes of the Congress and beyond as on the Congress organization itself. If the first twenty years of the Congress lacked drama, they were nevertheless a vital period of experimentation and education for nationalist politicians which helped shape the later terrorist, Gandhian, and communal phases of Indian politics.

This study grew out of a dissertation written at the School of Oriental and African Studies at the University of London. My supervisor was Kenneth Ballhatchet to whom I am grateful for valuable criticism and support. I also want to thank my other teachers at S.O.A.S. who introduced me to South Asian history: A. L. Basham, Peter Hardy, and J. B. Harrison.

I benefited from advice from many other persons, too numerous to acknowledge here. I will, however, mention A.F.S. Ahmad, Amiya Barat, Bernard S. Cohn, Robert Frykenberg, Leonard A. Gordon, Stephen Hay, Briton Martin, S. R. Mehrotra, Thomas Metcalf, Mukhil Ray, Niranjan Sen Gupta, and S. R. Wasti. In addition, I owe a special debt to Barun De for his imaginative suggestions and to Tarun Mitra for his generous friendship.

Preface

Most of the research was done in the India Office Library in London. The I.O.L. staff was always cooperative. I wish also to thank the staff of the National Archives in New Delhi and the West Bengal State Archives in Calcutta.

The research was financed by grants from the American Council of Learned Societies and the Social Science Research Council, the American Institute of Indian Studies, and Northwestern University. My colleagues in the History Department were supportive, not only in granting research time but in other, more important ways. I want to express my appreciation for that support and especially for the help of my former chairman, Gray C. Boyce. Few historians can have been as fortunate in having such excellent colleagues.

Finally, I owe more to Joan than I can express. She gave invaluable advice and help. Derek and Rebecca suffered my absences good-naturedly. It was always difficult to leave their company to return to my study.

Sections of Chapter Two were published previously in my article, "Bengal's Pre-1905 Congress Leadership and Hindu Society," in Rachel Van M. Baumer (editor), *Aspects of Bengali History and Society* (The University Press of Hawaii: Honolulu, 1975).

The map of India is reprinted from Briton Martin, *New India, 1885* (Berkeley, 1970). Copyright © 1969 by The Regents of the University of California; reprinted by permission of the University of California Press.

Abbreviations

Bd.	Board
Bom.	Bombay
Ch. Sec.	Chief Secretary
Col.	Collector
Com.	Commissioner
C. P.	Central Provinces
C.S.B.	Central Special Branch
Div.	Division
Fin.	Financial
Gov. Gen.	Governor General
IHP	India Home Proceedings
INC	Indian National Congress
IOL	India Office Library, London
JAS	*Journal of Asian Studies*
Jud.	Judicial
LCP	Legislative Council Proceedings
Leg.	Legislative
L. P.	Lower Provinces
Lt. Gov.	Lieutenant-Governor
Mag.	Magistrate
NNR	Native Newspaper Report
NWP and O	North-Western Provinces and Oudh
Offg.	Officiating
P.	Punjab
Pol. and Sec.	Political and Secret
P. P.	Parliamentary Paper
Prog.	Proceeding
PSLI	Public and Secret Letters from India
Pub.	Public
R	Rajputana
Rev.	Revenue
Sec.	Secretary
S. of S.	Secretary of State
Supt.	Superintendant
T. and D.	Thagi and Dakoiti

Glossary

akhara: gymnasium
amla: subordinate officials of government or zamindar
anjuman: Muslim association
babu: originally a term of respect, but in the nineteenth century the English used it pejoratively to refer to educated Indians
bania: trader or shopkeeper
bhadralok: refined or cultured people in Bengal
cutchery: land record office where rent or revenue is collected
dakoit: robber
Devanagari: script in which Sanskrit and Hindi are written; also called nagari
diwan: leading financial officer
fatwa: a ruling on dispute in Islamic law
gaurakshini: cow protection
goonda: a criminal or tough
gurdwara: Sikh temple
hartal: a strike, usually involving the closing of shops
jotdar: holder of rights to land, often a substantial peasant
Khalifa: the successor to the Prophet Muhammad as head of the Muslim community
Khilafat: the office held by the Khalifa; the movement to have the Sultan of Turkey recognized as the Khalifa of all Muslims
khot: hereditary revenue officer in the Konkan
kshatriya: the warrior varna or status group
Kuka: a member of the Namdhari (or Kuka) movement to reform the Sikh religion
lakh: one hundred thousand
lathi: a stick, usually bamboo, which is used as a weapon
mamlatdar: revenue officer in charge of subdistrict
mofussil: rural areas, as distinct from metropolitan centers
mukhtear: legal agent without authorization to practice in district courts
nawab: Muslim title, comparable to raja or maharaja
pandal: enclosure or marquee
Parsis: Zoroastrians who migrated to India from Persia
Puranas: ancient stories of Hinduism, compiled since the fourth century, which contain legends about gods and kings as well as religious instructions
Puranic: relating to the Hinduism of the Puranas; post-Vedic
ryot: cultivator or peasant; in Madras some ryots were small landlords
sabha: assembly or society

Glossary

sadhu: holy man or monk
sahib: honorific for European in India
sahukar: money-lender
samiti: society or organization
sanatan dharma sabha: orthodox Hindu society
sannyasi: wandering religious ascetic
satyagraha: literally, truth-grasping; Gandhi's technique of civil disobedience
sepoy: an Indian soldier
Shastras: texts on Hindu law and morality
sheristadar: head Indian officer in a court or collectorate
sudra: the lowest of the four varnas or theoretical status groups, but higher than untouchables
swadeshi: of one's own country; Indian-made
swaraj: self-rule
taluqdar: holder of a taluq or hereditary estate; taluqdars in the North-Western Provinces and Oudh were comparable to zamindars in Bengal
tehsildar: subordinate collector of revenue or rent
ulama: plural of alim, or a man learned in Islamic law
vakil: originally an agent, but in the nineteenth century a pleader authorized to practice in the law courts
varna: refers to the four theoretical classes or ranks in ancient Hindu society
Veda: the earliest body of Indian religious literature, consisting of hymns, commentaries, and philosophical texts
zamindar: holder of a zamindari or landed estate; landlord
zenanna: women's apartments

INDIAN NATIONALISM AND
THE EARLY CONGRESS

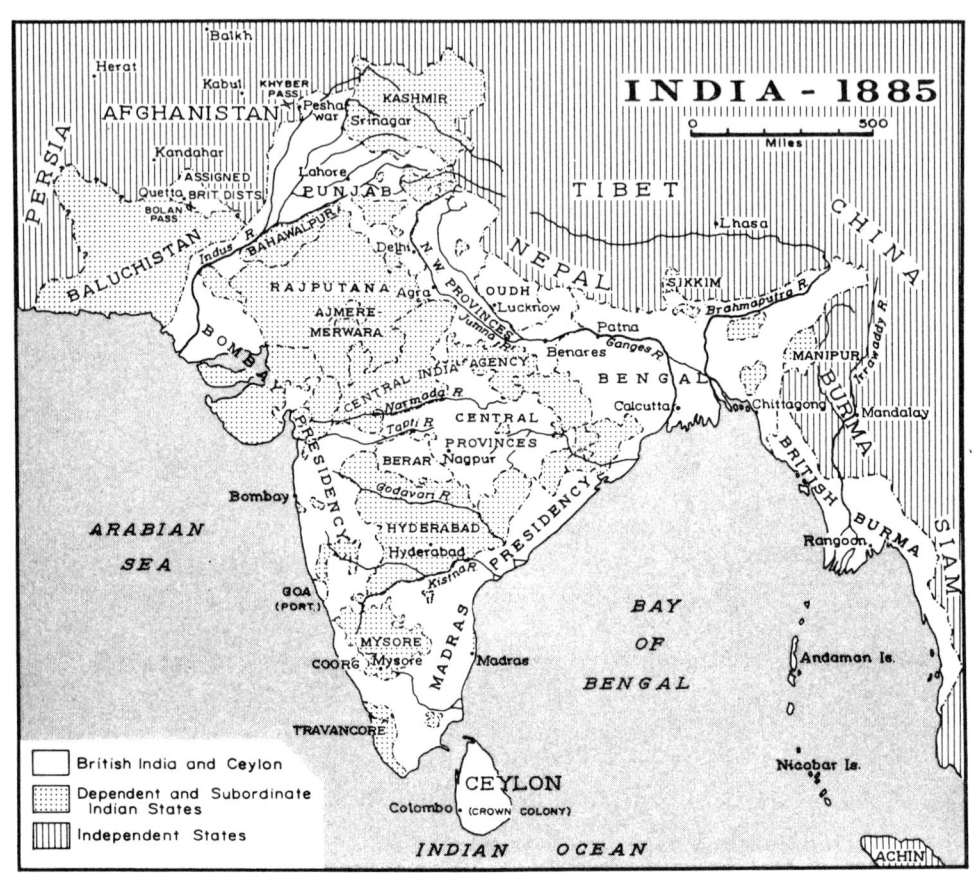

Introduction

This is a study of an early stage of the movement to build a national political community in British India. It focuses on the Indian National Congress, the party founded in 1885 to agitate for a larger role for Indians in governing their country. The Congress began modestly, without militancy and with a retired English civil servant as its chief organizer. Its membership came largely, and its leadership almost exclusively, from the graduates of colleges whose curriculum and language of instruction were English. The graduates constituted a tiny but rapidly expanding national community of their own. As many Congress leaders realized, their success in creating a community or nation of all Indians, as well as in gaining concessions from the English, depended upon their ability to win support outside the English-educated community. That capacity, in turn, would be determined by their relations with the larger Indian society.

The founders of the Congress faced formidable obstacles. Some of the obstacles were internal and included the Congress members' ambivalence toward the English who had created the modern educational and professional system through which many of them had prospered. Moreover, the Congress's many ties with landlords ruled out the possibility of seeking peasant support by championing their interests. The main obstacle outside the Congress was Indian Islam. One of every five Indians was a Muslim. Although a few Muslim leaders joined the Congress, a larger number seemed to accept the argument that Muslims and Hindus constituted separate nations.

Indian society in the 1880s was still diffuse. Modern voluntary associations had scarcely begun to undermine the more exclusive allegiances given to ascriptive groups. Western-educated Indians had formed local political associations in the major cities beginning in the middle of the century, and their organization of the Congress was a continuation of those local efforts to influence government policy. Starting political societies was part of a much larger process of realizing the potential for wider community identification where it existed, building bonds between members of traditional ethnic groups where they were absent, and mending cleavages when new ones appeared.

Introduction

Time and the integrating tendencies of modernization were on the side of the nation-builders. As more people entered a uniform school and career system, as the electoral process and interlocking webs of economic relationships expanded, the tasks of political consolidation could be expected to be correspondingly easier. In 1885, there were 160 English newspapers and periodicals with a circulation of 90,000; in 1905, there were 309 English newspapers with a circulation of 276,000. In the same period, the number of vernacular newspapers increased from 599 to 1,107 and their circulation from 299,000 to 817,000.[1] In 1886, 4,286 Indian students matriculated and 708 received their B.A.s; in 1905, the numbers were 8,211 and 1,570, respectively. In 1887, there were 298,000 persons studying English and in 1907 there were 505,000.[2] The facilities for communication underwent similar expansion. In 1887, the 15,245 miles of operating railroads carried 111 million passengers; by 1913, the mileage had doubled and the passengers had quadrupled. In the same period, the number of letters and postcards mailed tripled, reaching 892 million, and the number of telegrams increased from 3½ million to 15½ million.[3] These trends added to the potential strength of nationalism, but the size of the literate classes and other indices of modernization remained small relative to the total population. Less than 1 per cent of British India's 244 million people in 1911 were literate in English, and only 6 per cent were able to read and write in their own language. On the other hand, literacy among male adults was 11 per cent and among city-dwellers it was 30 per cent.[4]

It hardly needs to be said that these gross figures, while indicating that the opportunities for education, association, and communication were increasing, do not necessarily mean that a single, all-Indian community was being formed. Insofar as these opportunities spread unequally and led disadvantaged sections of the population to feel threatened by rival sections, and insofar as new opportunities for association were used by groups hostile to

[1] The 1885 figures include periodicals while the 1905 figures refer to newspapers alone.

[2] Govt. of India dispatch, 21 March 1907, No. 7, IHP, Pub., MSS. Eur. D. 573/29.

[3] Royal Commission on the Public Services in India, *Report of the Commissioners* (London, 1917), I, 12.

[4] East India (Constitutional Reforms), *Report on Indian Constitution Reforms* (P. P. Cd.9109 of 1918), p. 111.

all-Indian integration, they tended to hinder the making of a nation. The emerging political and legal order was one in which English education provided the surest access to new opportunities for political influence and economic success. However, the differential spread of education meant that a much larger percentage of Hindus than Muslims, of high castes than low castes, and of people from coastal provinces than from the interior were entering college. Some of the more group-conscious minorities who believed their life opportunities were decreasing relative to those of rival groups emphasized their separate identity and sought protective treatment from the English. The founding of the all-India Muslim League in 1906 and the growth of the south Indian non-Brahman movement are examples of this countermobilization and search for distinctive identities. In the case of the Muslims, the English stimulated the growth of communal consciousness by partitioning Bengal in 1905 into separate Hindu-majority and Muslim-majority provinces and by granting separate electorates to Muslims in the 1909 legislative council reforms.

The entry of Indians into political life through the religious community was by no means confined to Muslims. Groups of Hindus combined against cow slaughter, conversion of Hindus to Islam and Christianity, nonobservance of orthodox marriage and eating regulations, and British legislation to regulate the age of marriage. A few prominent Congress members were active in Hindu protest and revival movements. But the anglicized leadership kept specifically Hindu issues and symbols out of formal Congress proceedings in accordance with their own cultural preferences and in an attempt to disarm Muslim apprehensions about coexistence with the Hindu majority. This simultaneously increased Congress dependence on English political traditions and diminished the appeal of the Congress for men without English education. One of the major reasons for the Congress's arrested development before 1905 was its refusal to use Hindu culture, without which the movement lacked emotional intensity and an atmosphere congenial to most Hindus. Herein lay a major dilemma for the Congress movement. To Hinduize the Congress would risk alarming Muslims who were already skeptical, and it would endanger the ability of the anglicized leadership to perpetuate their autocratic control of the Congress. But continuing the Congress in its original acultural, elitist form threatened to render impotent its efforts to arouse a patriotic love of India and

Introduction

to gain political power for Indians. By the beginning of the twentieth century, the dimensions of this dilemma were becoming clear as increasing numbers of Indians pursued nationalist goals outside the Congress party in the movements to promote *swadeshi* (literally, of one's own country) commerce and industry, national education (schooling with Indian curricula and control), and the revitalization of Vedic and Puranic Hinduism.

The aim of this study is to analyze the competition between Indian elites with conflicting conceptions of political community, from the founding of the Congress in 1885 to the dramatic developments between 1905 and 1909. In these last five years, many of the incipient conflicts and trends of the preceding two decades manifested themselves in new cultural and political activities. Regional and religious appeals were used to mobilize large numbers of people who had previously not participated in nationalist politics; the Congress split into mutually hostile moderate and extremist branches; the all-India Muslim League was founded; Hindu-Muslim riots broke out; and guns and bombs were used by secret terrorist societies in Bengal, Bihar, and Bombay.

Analysis of Indian politics on a national scale in this period presents special problems. Cultural traditions, social structure, the distribution of castes, religions, education, and land, and the configuration of political forces in general varied so markedly from one region to the next that generalizations which apply to one part of India often do not to another. Moreover, the level of political involvement was generally so low, especially in all-Indian organizations, that gauging the strength of political identification is an uncertain undertaking. In addition, the accumulation of basic historical data concerning Indian politics, and especially political behavior, in this period is still in its infancy. In recent years, though, a number of valuable political studies have appeared which have increased our understanding of the interaction between national, regional, and local levels of politics. Three books analyze the founding of the Indian National Congress and its connections with regional and local politics.[5] Other recent studies explicitly concentrate on regional and local affairs.

[5] Anil Seal, *The Emergence of Indian Nationalism: Competition and Collaboration in the Later Nineteenth Century* (Cambridge, 1971); S. R. Mehrotra, *The Emergence of the Indian National Congress* (Delhi, 1971); and Briton Martin, *New India, 1885: British Official Policy and the Emergence of the Indian National Congress* (Berkeley, 1969).

Introduction

Some of these recent studies suggest that the Indian National Congress may have been in some major sense not really national, that the Congress functioned as a vehicle for the pursuit of parochial goals and the advancement of local careers. C. A. Bayly has argued that for "many local leaders, the Congress was essentially a secondary organization, and their association with it derived from the need to pursue within the regional and all-India skeleton of organization and aspiration the much more circumscribed local and sectional aims which derived from lower levels of politics."[6] Anil Seal has gone further and claims that "it is no longer credible to write about a [Congress] movement grounded in common aims, led by men with similar backgrounds, and recruited from widening groups with compatible interests. That movement now looks more like a ramshackle coalition throughout its long career. Its unity seems a figment."[7] The present author does not accept the argument that the Congress was without common aims or that the Congress was peculiarly a movement of self-interested individuals. The Indian founders of the Congress were impressed by the nobility of a nationalist vision of subordinating the interests of self, family, and caste to the interests of an Indian nation. The Congress vision held that Indians shared fundamental economic and political interests, that those interests were in conflict with those of Britain, and that the collective welfare of all Indians could be improved by restructuring the relations between India and her foreign rulers.[8]

[6] C. A. Bayly, *The Local Roots of Indian Politics: Allahabad, 1880–1920* (Oxford, 1975), p. 4.

[7] Anil Seal, "Imperialism and Nationalism in India," in John Gallagher, Gordon Johnson, and Anil Seal (eds.), *Locality, Province and Nation: Essays on Indian Politics 1870–1940* (Cambridge, 1973), p. 2.

[8] Anil Seal speculates on the motivation of men who joined the Congress in the following words: "The advantages of one group meant the drawbacks of the rest. The successes of the advanced regions blocked the aspirations of the backward. With all these local rivalries and the glaring national differences between east, west and south, there was still a level at which the elites of Bengal, Bombay and Madras could work together—and this was the level of all-India. In so doing, their main purpose may well have been to strengthen their position inside their local societies" (*The Emergence*, pp. 112–113).

The assumption that one group's gain is another's loss might apply to a static soicety not experiencing economic growth. But many sections of the Indian economy were growing in the late nineteenth century.

Political motivation is often complex and difficult to determine. Yet subordination of individual and group interest to the interests of the larger

Introduction

The first generation of Congress leaders was groping for a means of translating the vision into concrete political tactics. Congress leaders were sometimes diverted from this task by their personal careers. Nevertheless, the vision was potent, sincerely held, and widely shared.

But having said that, it is readily conceded that local politics occupied a much greater share of the time and energies of educated Indians than did national politics. An understanding of local and regional affairs is indispensable for analysis of nationalism. Involvement in town and regional politics first brought Indian nationalists into contact with colonial institutions and stimulated a desire to alter those institutions. It also provided the training in the skills of organization and communication necessary for future leadership in the Congress. Each Indian who attended one of the annual Congress sessions carried with him the perceptions shaped at home. If participation in local affairs revealed the potentialities for uniting Indians, local experiences often showed how easily Indians were divided. The character of local politics was such that the perceptions a man gained in his home region often limited or depressed his nationalist aspirations. As our understanding of particular localities has grown, so has the realization that local politics were extraordinarily complex, fluid, even volatile. Political alliances were continually shifting as the topics of public controversy changed and as new political arenas were created. At times, local politics polarized along lines determined by caste, linguistic, or religious ties, at other times around issues of economic group interest, and at others around the personalities or neighborhoods of faction leaders and their clients.

C. A. Bayly's study of the Allahabad region has demonstrated the vitality of patron-client relationships in the period between 1880 and 1920, and the corresponding weakness of other forms of political association. The most powerful patrons of Allahabad were the wealthy bankers and traders, some of whom owned large *zamindaris*. Their clients included relatives who "shared in the profits of the family businesses and ran subsidiary trades and services." A second group of clients included the priests, lawyers,

---

society may provide both increased self-respect and higher political status. Evidence of Congressmen's concern about the welfare of broad sections of the Indian population is presented in Section III below.

8

and other specialists who worked to maintain the family's "ritual, social, and political status." In addition, "publicists and literati attached themselves to the connections of town magnates as hagiographers and propagandists, or in the hope of gaining support for wider religious or political projects."[9] While we lack detailed studies of most other localities, there is good reason to believe that the patron-client model was common throughout India in the late nineteenth century, that clients clustered around a multitude of merchant, banker, landlord, and lawyer patrons in most cities, and that patron-client ties cut across other alliances based on caste, economic interest, and, sometimes, religion. The patron-client relationship was most fully operative at the local level, but it extended into the Congress as well. While the Congress seemed to be monopolized by lawyers, the lawyers were frequently linked through mercantile and landed patrons, as well as *vakil* clients, to a broad spectrum of society.

Another important conclusion which emerges from recent studies, especially Bayly's, is that in the period under review, ethnicity was not the most common determinant of political allegiance or alienation.[10] The divisions between Brahmans and non-Brahmans, Hindus and Muslims, and one regional linguistic group and another were far less common in the late nineteenth century than after World War I. However, as Chapters Nine, Ten, and Eleven suggest, Hindu-Muslim rivalry escalated in north India in the 1890s.

Studies by Anil Seal, C. A. Bayly, R. Suntharalingam,[11] and others suggest that several related processes were drawing educated Indians into local politics in the 1870s and 1880s. First, the rapid expansion of institutions of higher education had produced degree-holders who, in contrast to the first generation of graduates, could not find government employment which they considered suitable to their qualifications.[12] Many turned to the law, education, and journalism. Some entered the fields of medicine or business. But none of these professions was expanding fast enough in the last quarter of the century to absorb the surplus college graduates.[13] Graduate unemployment intensified Indian interest

[9] Bayly, *The Local Roots*, pp. 74–75.   [10] In particular, see ibid., p. 281.

[11] R. Suntharalingam, *Politics and Nationalist Awakening in South India, 1852–1891* (Tucson, 1974).

[12] Mehrotra, *The Emergence*, p. 245.

[13] Seal, *The Emergence*, p. 128, and Suntharalingam, *Politics*, pp. 134ff.

Introduction

in lowering racial barriers in the civil service and the legal profession and in political reform in general. Partly as a result of the new ferment among graduates, the government became more sensitive to Indian opinion. Government surveys of Indian opinions, though, accelerated the politicization, although often not the unification, of educated elites. The Education Commission of 1883 and the Public Service Commission of 1886–1887 attracted large numbers of witnesses, memorials, and editorials commenting on the differential effects of official policies on particular sections of Indian society.

English interest in diffusing and channeling the aspirations of both traditionally educated and Western-educated Indians led to reform of local self-government. Lord Ripon's 1882 Resolution on Local Self-Government enlarged the role of elected Indians in municipal and district committees. Municipal governments, with their ability to raise or lower taxes, award contracts for public works, distribute patronage, license trade, and regulate religious festivals, affected the interests of diverse groups and attracted large numbers of men into public affairs.[14]

Graduate unemployment, official solicitation of Indian opinions, and the extension of government functions stimulated the organization of local voluntary associations. During the later decades of the nineteenth century, a bewildering variety of local societies were started to pursue idealistic-sounding objectives. Whether or not their primary objectives were political, their activities served to expand political horizons and to provide their members with political skills. Even the cultural, religious, linguistic, and educational societies found that, sooner or later, government policies affected the goals they had set for themselves. In joining together to pursue a common purpose, in holding formal meetings and electing officers, in publishing newspapers or pamphlets, the local societies were introducing their members to the same organizational experiences as societies with explicit political aims. Although the multiplication of local societies appeared to stimulate competition and divisiveness at times, it also was integrating the competitors into an increasingly uniform political system, with the government generally accepted as the

---

[14] By 1895, municipal income in the North-Western Provinces and Oudh equalled a full one-eighth of the total provincial expenditure. Francis Robinson, *Separatism Among Indian Muslims: The Politics of the United Provinces' Muslims, 1860–1923* (Cambridge, 1974), p. 55.

Introduction

arbitrator and ultimate authority. Moreover, the growth of local societies was characterized by multiple membership which reduced the intensity of certain identities. Local politics were pluralistic with alliances and membership which crisscrossed the ascriptive communities based on language, religion, and caste.

There were four broad categories of local voluntary associations. The first were the local political associations which explicitly claimed to represent the interests of Indians to the government. In effect, they became the regional arms of the Congress after 1885. Located in the largest provincial towns (usually the administrative capitals), many had branch associations in the *mofussil*. Their leaders were elected to Congress offices as well as to municipal and provincial legislative councils. They included the Triplicane Literary Society (1868) and the Mahajana Sabha (1894) of Madras, the Indian Association of Calcutta (1876), the Allahabad People's Association (1885–1886), the Indian Association of Lahore (1877), the Poona Sarvajanik Sabha (1867), and the Bombay Presidency Association (1885).

Professional and economic interest associations constitute a second category of local organizations. These included associations of landholders, teachers, lawyers, and municipal ratepayers as well as chambers of commerce. It was not uncommon for Hindus and Muslims to belong to the same professional or economic interest organization. In contrast to the political societies, these organizations generally concentrated their attention on government policies which affected specific economic or professional interests.

A third, more amorphous category was the social reform societies. They set up schools and colleges, science and religious study groups, reading rooms, and debating societies; they sponsored lectures on a range of subjects from temperance to the promotion of Indian industries; and they campaigned for higher marriage age, widow-remarriage, and the amalgamation of subcastes. They tended to be the least political of local societies, in part because they sought the internal, self-reform of Indian society, in part because many of their leaders belonged to the administrative elite,[15] and in part because their educational enterprises depended on government grants-in-aid. But Congress leaders were among their most active members. Those societies

[15] Suntharalingam, *Politics*, Chapter 2.

were extending the secular, universal values of Western schooling, as well as the nonsectarian universalism of modernized Hinduism and Islam. In doing so, they were theoretically helping to create a predisposition to emphasize what Hindus or Muslims shared and to break down the isolating identifications of ethnicity and religious sect. In reality, the reformers tended in the short run to create what amounted to new sectarian divisions. The reformers' attacks on the unreformed customs of their coreligionists angered orthodox groups and split society into antagonistic groups.

The fastest growing reform society in the late nineteenth century was the Arya Samaj. The Arya Samaj was similar to the other Hindu reform societies in that it was led by university graduates who worked to reduce the influence of caste, ritual, and priests and who claimed to be returning to classical Hinduism of Vedic times. Occasionally, Arya Samaj attacks on caste and Puranic or post-Vedic Hinduism were vehement and vitriolic. In other respects, though, the Arya Samaj resembled the fourth category of local organizations: societies for the defense of traditional culture. The Arya Samaj, despite its reformism, championed cow protection and the use of the Devanagari script—issues that were highly popular among orthodox Hindus.

Societies for the defense of traditional Hindu culture await detailed study. They embraced a variety of objectives but seemed to be united by a belief that the activities of Hindu social reformers, Muslims, Christian missionaries, and the government threatened the integrity and status of Hinduism. Beyond that, generalization becomes hazardous. Although they were called *sanatan dharma sabhas* (orthodox religious societies) and although, in contrast to the Arya Samaj, they rarely criticized priestly authority, caste practices, or Puranic Hinduism, many of them in fact contributed to the neoclassical Vedic revival and de-emphasized caste as the central institution of Hinduism. For a brief period in the late 1880s and early 1890s, the sanatan dharma sabhas agitated for a ban on cow slaughter. But language reform and the promotion of Sanskrit and Hindi literature were the more permanent concerns of the sanatanists.

Language reform was promoted by Hindu sabhas in the Hindi-speaking regions of northern India. The goals of linguistic reformers were varied. Some Hindus wished to standardize Hindi in order to reduce the differences between regional dialects and between the Hindi spoken by the elites and the masses. Some

Introduction

campaigned to have Hindi, written in the Devanagari script, recognized as an official language alongside Urdu. Urdu's vocabulary and grammar were similar to Hindi's, but its script was Persian. Proponents of the elevation of Hindi to the status of an official language argued that Hindus who could not read and write Urdu would be placed on an equal footing with Muslims in competition for government employment and in the law courts. The advocates of Hindi won their objective in Bihar in 1881 and in the North-Western Provinces and Oudh in 1900.[16] In the process, they antagonized many Muslims who, as the former ruling elite, had enjoyed concrete advantages from their superior knowledge of Urdu.[17]

Hinduism was emerging as a major source of political identification in north India through the activities of linguistic reformers, cow protectors, and sanatan dharma sabhas. Their activities were politicizing persons untouched by other voluntary associations. Among Muslims, there was a parallel growth of local *anjumans* or Muslim associations. The incentive for founding anjumans was frequently a desire to promote educational opportunities for Muslims or to resist Hindu attacks on cow slaughter and on the exclusive use of the Persian script.

The spread of Hindu sabhas and Muslim anjumans contributed to, and provided evidence of, a deterioration in Hindu-Muslim relations. Yet in the late nineteenth century the deterioration seemed neither deep nor irreversible. Although the rivalry and conflict between Hindus and Muslims were increasing, the main thrust of sabha and anjuman activities was inward and noncompetitive. Probably their greater political significance, at least in the short run, was in demonstrating to Western-educated nationalists the size and political potential of traditionally educated groups. The mobilization of these people into cultural defense associations reminded university graduates of their own cultural ambivalence and revealed how isolated they were from their own society. Faced with this mobilization, social reformers were forced

[16] Paul Brass, *Language, Religion and Politics in North India* (Cambridge, 1974), pp. 129ff.

[17] Paul Brass (ibid., pp. 137–138) argues that it is less useful to treat the Hindi-Urdu conflict as "the critical factor in the development of Muslim separatism and Hindu-Muslim conflict" than as an extension of a competition between Hindu and Muslim elites "for administrative and political power and for employment." "Religion and language were the symbolic instruments in this essentially political conflict."

Introduction

to trim their goals and to search for an accommodation, intellectually if not organizationally, with religious populism. The growth of Hindu sabhas and Hindu opposition to government legislation in 1891 raising the legal age of marriage revealed the strength of what Peter Hardy called "an underworld," a level of society not ordinarily visible to the Indian barrister of Bombay or Calcutta but nevertheless exercising "a subtle pull upon" British policies as well as, he might have added, upon university graduates. Hardy's analysis of the Muslim "underworld" might have described the Hindu social strata which supported the sanatan sabhas.

> It is not easy to define the Muslim underworld, except negatively. It was poor rather than rich, respectable rather than ruffianly, school-educated rather than university- or college-educated, traditionally- rather than modern-educated. It was drawn from the lower middle class of a pre-industrial society, printers, lithographers, booksellers, teachers, retail shopkeepers, skilled craftsmen and petty zamindars, men literate in the vernacular, able and willing to read the large annual output of Muslim devotional literature in Urdu. Politically they were unorganized and lacking in sense of direction, but . . . they were quick to be seized by religious passion.[18]

The expansion of the religious sabhas and anjumans points to one of the thorniest obstacles to Congress efforts to build a nation. Congress leaders sometimes spoke as if their first objective was to bridge the gap between the elites and the masses. In fact, the division between the Western-educated elite and the traditional elites was more immediate and more threatening to the search for common identities. The Western-educated Congressman often defined his national identity in exclusively political terms, without mention of culture. The problem of cultural pluralism would be solved, he hoped, by avoiding it. But for many others in India's multiethnic society, the shift from the parochial loyalties of kinship and caste to national loyalties was not direct. Rather "intermediate loyalties," based on language and religion, "have frequently intervened and been adapted as new forms of identity and as new vehicles of participation in the modern state."[19] As language and religion were adapted by more people in northern

[18] P. Hardy, *The Muslims of British India* (Cambridge, 1972), p. 169.
[19] Brass, *Language*, p. 6.

and western India in the late nineteenth century, the Congress as an organization failed to develop a response which might have either blunted or capitalized on the new developments. At times it seemed that the politics of language and religion might paralyze Congress leadership. Congress leaders from the coastal provinces believed that they had outgrown the parochial identities of an earlier generation and that they represented the vanguard of India's historical progress. They were unprepared, collectively at least, to cope with the emergence of subnationalisms.

Individually, however, many university-educated Congressmen were attracted to the culture-strengthening aspects of subnationalist movements. Finding the Congress brand of acultural nationalism socially isolating and emotionally unsatisfying, a growing number of Congressmen were exploring avenues of political identification which the Congress had avoided. These Congressmen were unwilling to recognize the incipient contradictions between the Congress emphasis upon abstract political rights for all Indians and the separate cultural revitalization movements among Hindus and Muslims. The contradictions were not obvious. The primary objective of most religious and linguistic reform movements was to reduce internal social divisions or to remove perceived character deficiencies.

Rarely did leaders of these movements seek conflict with other religious or linguistic groups. Some of the most respected Congress leaders were being drawn into these movements at the end of the nineteenth century. Madan Mohan Malaviya was active in the movement to secure government recognition of Devanagari as an official script in the North-Western Provinces and Oudh.[20] Romeshchandra Dutt wrote Bengali novels about Hindu heroism in wars in which, almost incidentally, Hindus fought Muslims.[21] Lala Lajpat Rai championed the use of Hindi in place of Urdu and the reconversion of Muslims and Christians to Hinduism. Bal Gangadhar Tilak organized festivals in honor of the Hindu god Ganapati and of Shivaji, the seventeenth-century rebel against Muslim rule.[22] In each of these cases, the intention was to overcome divisions and deficiencies within Hindu society, not to

[20] Bayly, *The Local Roots*, p. 148.
[21] Leonard A. Gordon, *Bengal: The Nationalist Movement 1876–1940* (New York, 1974), p. 46.
[22] Richard I. Cashman, *The Myth of the Lokamanya: Tilak and Mass Politics in Maharashtra* (Berkeley, 1975), Chapters IV and V.

create antagonism between Hindus and Muslims. The consequence of their activities, though, was to strengthen a specifically Hindu rather than an all-Indian identity. In the late nineteenth century, it was unclear which of the competing identities would become paramount. Would an all-Indian consciousness of England's economic exploitation and political subjection catch people's imaginations? Or would the nationalist dream of united consciousness and action be shattered by the growth of sub-nationalisms based on religion or language? How long would the cultural and economic isolation of Western-educated groups prevent them from responding to the aspirations and fears of less privileged groups? Nationalist concern with each of these questions increased in the period under review. But the answers often seemed to be becoming less certain.

This study is divided into four sections. Part I, by way of further introduction, discusses the British government and the leaders of the Congress. Chapter One examines the political policies of the government in the context of British imperial interests and racism. The British monopolized formal governmental power and determined many of the conditions under which Indians competed for influence and economic opportunities. Chapter Two is a social portrait of the English-educated elite which benefited most from those opportunities and whose members founded and controlled the Congress until World War I. It draws upon biographical information to describe the ambiguous position Congress leaders occupied in their private and professional lives in relation to both the British and Indian society.

Part II analyzes the Congress itself during its first two decades. After its first five years, the Congress organization stopped growing in size and failed to develop new goals and activities. Chapter Three attributes part of this stagnation to the effects of Allan Octavian Hume's dominance of the Congress, his abortive attempts to draw Muslims and peasants into the Congress, and the resulting estrangement between Hume and Indian leaders. The loss of momentum, the apathy, and the financial problems of the Congress following Hume's departure from India are discussed in Chapter Four. In Chapter Five the budding dispute over the proper tactics for achieving nationalist goals is related to the demands for a democratic constitution for the Congress Party.

Introduction

The moderate Congress leadership under Pherozeshah Mehta's guidance rejected suggestions that mendicant tactics and autocratic internal organization should be replaced with direct action and open election procedures. The low-key crisis in Congress affairs was so debilitating, and the failure of the Congress leadership to represent the full spectrum of nationalist feelings so complete, that some friends of the Congress suggested that the movement should be suspended.

Part III is an attempt to define the composition and program of the Congress in terms of economic interest. Chapter Six argues that behind the rivalry between urban professionals and titled landholders for political influence, there was a counterbalancing interdependence and a mutuality of economic interest. Chapters Seven and Eight test the themes of political rivalry and economic interdependence against the Congress treatment of agrarian legislation proposed by the British. Despite the Congress's connections with landlords and money-lenders and the desire of some members to use the Congress to protect their own and their patrons' economic position, the Congress generally remained neutral in conflicts over tenancy and usury legislation in the interests of national unity. This preserved the potentiality for recruiting lower-class members, but it also left many affluent Indians indifferent to the Congress platform.

Two Hindu revitalization movements which were organizationally separate from the Congress but which nevertheless affected the Congress are the subject of Part IV. A clearer perspective of the strengths and the limitations of the Congress is sought by examining the political concerns of Indians who deliberately stood apart from or who had only marginal contact with the Congress. Some revitalization movements, such as the Arya Samaj, promoted a selective emphasis or reinterpretation of certain aspects of Hindu tradition with the effect that a revival of an ancient value was often a reform along modern lines. In other movements, Hindu revivalists sought to conserve existing Hindu culture, including its social stratification and Brahman supremacy, against English and Indian pressures for reform. But in either case, the disparate efforts to arouse pride in the cultural and political achievements of Indian civilization, the aggressive affirmation of Hinduism's superiority over Christian culture, and the attempts to tighten the bonds of Hindu community tended to isolate further the anglicized reformist leadership of the Congress.

Introduction

They also reduced the Congress's chance of persuading Muslims to join the Congress. Chapters Nine and Ten deal with the movement to prevent the English and Muslims from killing cows. The movement originally appealed to high-caste Hindus in central and north India who wanted to protect a source of nutrition and a symbol of the Hindu way of life. In 1893, however, the movement provoked serious communal riots in widely scattered parts of India. Until 1893, Hindu-Muslim disturbances had been uncommon. Chapter Eleven discusses the new and related Hindu interest in developing physical courage and overcoming a reputation for lack of bravery and robustness. It concentrates on the Maharashtrian Brahman terrorist, Damodar Chapekar, who wrote a remarkable autobiography explaining his reasons for murdering two English officials in 1897 and for his attacks on Christian missionaries and reformed Hindus. His resentment at the decline of respect for Brahmans, cows, and Hindu orthodoxy in general, combined with his personal economic frustrations, seem to have been characteristic of men who joined militant Hindu organizations and participated in communal riots.

The study concludes with a brief discussion of the transformation of nationalist politics in the period following the partition of Bengal in 1905, a transformation which followed the lines anticipated by developments within and on the fringes of the Congress in its first twenty years. The Congress was almost destroyed by the split between moderates and extremists. Nationalists adopted new militant forms of protest, some violent and some nonviolent, and they recruited support from sections of the population previously ignored. And perhaps of greater consequence for the future evolution of Indian nationalism, Muslims formed the all-India Muslim League and persuaded the British to give constitutional recognition to Muslim separateness.

PART I

─────────────── *Chapter One* ───────────────

THE RULERS

A majority of the leaders of the early Indian National Congress had been educated in England, most had had English teachers, most drew their main political ideas from English traditions. All spoke English and used it to communicate with nationalist colleagues from other linguistic regions. In their professions, many of them had English superiors as well as English rivals. When Indians sought administrative change or constitutional reform, they had to ask English officials or English politicians. And in seeking reform, they looked for allies both in England and among the small band of sympathetic editors, missionaries, administrators, and other European friends within India. The tactics and rhetoric of pre-Gandhian nationalism were profoundly affected by the leaders' multiple dependencies upon the rulers' language, culture, and political divisions.

THE BRITISH STATE

The intimate association with the English, however, should not obscure the basic conflict which existed between English national interests and the ultimate goals of the Indian national movement. The Indian National Congress was founded to gain Indians a larger share of political and economic power. That power at its higher levels was monopolized by the English. Indian demands in the 1870s and 1880s for liberalization provoked English assertions of the superiority of Western civilization and a determination not to compromise their monopoly. Few Englishmen doubted the necessity or stability of British rule. Most believed India was Britain's and would remain so indefinitely. It was, as Francis Hutchins has argued, the age of "the illusion of permanence."[1] English rejection of nationalist demands, and racist arguments

[1] Francis G. Hutchins, *The Illusion of Permanence: British Imperialism in India* (Princeton, 1967).

and behavior which accompanied the rejection, provided a powerful impetus to the growth of nationalism.

Most Englishmen in India seemed to feel the general principles guiding British administration, while subject to refinement and minor improvements, were satisfactory on the whole. As long as the natives did not rebel, and as long as India continued to be profitable for British public and private interests, the great majority of Englishmen were content with the autocratic character of the Raj. For the indefinite future, there was no need to share political power with Indians. To do so would lessen India's economic and strategic value.

The value of the Indian connection was obvious and growing in the last two decades of the century. As one official wrote in 1892, "if British rule should end, the value of the interests affected would be so great that practically no adequate compensation would be possible."[2] Englishmen had invested heavily in Indian agricultural and extractive industries, including tea, coffee, jute, indigo, and coal; they had bought shares in the Indian railways, some of which had had a guaranteed rate of profit and had been located to serve British manufacturing and military needs; they were able to sell British textiles in a sizable market in competition with the young, unprotected Indian textile industry; and they owned the largest banks, insurance companies, export houses, and shipping lines.[3] Almost one-fifth of the total British overseas investment was in India and about one-fifth of British exports went to India.[4] In return, the Government of India sent about one-fifth of its annual revenues to Britain as payment for loans, investments, administrative services, and military supplies and personnel.[5]

India was also vital to British economic and strategic interests in the rest of Asia and in east Africa. British Indian banks serv-

[2] Charles Lewis Tupper, *Our Indian Protectorate: An Introduction to the Study of the Relations between the British Government and its Indian Feudatories* (London, 1893), p. 390.

[3] See Michael Kidron, *Foreign Investments in India* (London, 1965), Chapter 1.

[4] Ronald Robinson and John Gallagher with Alice Denny, *Africa and the Victorians: The Climax of Imperialism in the Dark Continent* (New York, 1961), p. 11.

[5] See John R. McLane, "The Drain of Wealth and Indian Nationalism at the Turn of the Century," in *Contributions to Indian Economic History* II, ed. Tapan Raychaudhuri (Calcutta, 1963).

iced British trade in the Indian Ocean and further east, and Indian labor was exported to build railways, mine minerals, and work on British plantations. In strategic terms, India was Britain's most valued possession, representing her "oriental barracks," a reservoir of military manpower, a subsidy for the cost of the British military establishment, and a potential second front against Russia. The Indian Army was used for imperial and expansionist purposes which the British public tolerated because India paid a major share of the cost. In the forty years after the Mutiny, the Indian Army went to China (1859), Ethiopia (1867), Singapore (1867), Hong Kong (1868), Afghanistan (1878), Egypt (1882), Burma (1885), Nyasa (1893), the Sudan (1896), and Uganda (1896).[6] Although the Indian taxpayers' share of the costs was gradually decreased in response to nationalist complaints, India was still required to contribute to Britain's non-Indian interests. As late as 1908, the Liberal secretary of state for India, Lord John Morley, agreed to the War Office's request to increase India's annual contribution to English army reserves from £420,000 to £720,000. When Lord Kitchener objected, the War Office replied

> The principles of fair dealing enunciated by Lord Kitchener might be applicable enough to two independent states in alliance with each other. They are inapplicable to a dependency inhabited by alien races, our hold over which is not based on the general goodwill of those disunited races.[7]

India, in other words, was held as she had been taken—by the sword.

The sword, it was hoped, would remain sheathed except to awe the native population, and the ordinary work of administration was performed by the civilians of the Indian Civil Service. The largely British I.C.S. was a powerful opponent of nationalist aspiration in its own right. The more than 900 members were a well-paid elite who looked forward to a varied and exotic career and the option of retiring with a generous pension after 25 years. All but a few Indians were kept out by giving the I.C.S. entrance examinations in England in subjects which ordinarily required years of schooling in England. When British officials discussed

---

[6] Robinson and Gallagher, *Africa and the Victorians*, p. 12.
[7] Stanley A. Wolpert, *Morley and India, 1906–1910* (Berkeley, 1967), p. 216.

changing this system in the late nineteenth century, they usually considered ways of restricting, rather than expanding, the trickle of Indians entering the I.C.S. By 1902, 40 of the 1,067 I.C.S. officers were "Natives."[8]

Exclusion of Indians from high office in the allied services was even more effective than in the I.C.S. In 1907, "not a single post out of 278 paying Rs. 800 or more per year was held by an Indian in the forest, police, post office, telegraph, salt, survey, or political services of British India."[9] Taking the civil services together, and using a lower salary base, in 1887 Europeans held 4,836 of the 8,840 posts paying Rs. 200 per month or more; in 1913 they held 4,898 out of 11,064. In both years, Anglo-Indians held a third as many as Indians and Burmans, so that Indians and Burmans held a mere 34 per cent of the total in 1887 and 42 per cent in 1913.[10] The combined opposition of British administrators and British commercial and military interests to any relaxation of their privileged position continued until World War I to be an insurmountable obstacle to realization of the nationalist goal of Indianization of the Raj.

An earlier generation of Englishmen had held that preparation for self-rule was part of their mission in India. But in the last quarter of the nineteenth century, as nationalists asked to share power and as Gladstonian liberalism declined in popularity in England, justification for continuing autocracy was frequently heard. James Fitzjames Stephen, Henry Maine, and others with Indian experience were among leading Liberals who joined Conservatives in suggesting that extending forms of democracy might inhibit creative individualism and initiative, that it might produce inefficient government, and that it would weaken the Empire.[11] The strongly conservative current within the Liberal Party, which emerged clearly during the controversy over the Irish Home Rule Bill in 1886, meant that the leaders of both major British political parties were unsympathetic to the major demands of the Indian National Congress. The new conservatism was a retreat from the earlier "emphasis on moral force and the

[8] Sir John Strachey, *India: Its Administration and Progress*, 3rd ed. (London, 1903), p. 77.
[9] Wolpert, *Morley and India*, pp. 178–179.
[10] Royal Commission on the Public Services in India, *Report*, I, 26.
[11] John Roach, "Liberalism and the Victorian Intelligentsia," *The Cambridge Historical Journal*, XIII, No. 1, 58–80.

influence of the example of British character, to the less ambitious idea that India was held simply by military power."[12]

Congress demands were not rejected indiscriminately. They were formulated in the vocabulary of English liberalism, they were advanced through constitutional channels, and they were supported by Liberal backbenchers and a handful of active and retired I.C.S. officers. Most specific policy demands were moderate and would not have fundamentally compromised British political and economic interests. Public commissions on education, civil service, finance, and famine listened to lengthy testimony from Indian and British witnesses and then recommended reforms along lines suggested by the more moderate critics. Nationalist requests for Indianization of the administration, for example, were considered by the Public Service Commission which was appointed in 1886. The commission rejected the demand for simultaneous I.C.S. examinations in India and Britain. As a consolation, though, a small number of posts were transferred from the I.C.S. to the Provincial Civil Service (the examinations for which were held in India), and the maximum age limit for entrance into the I.C.S. was raised from nineteen to twenty-three, making it somewhat easier for Indians to compete. However, these were minor changes. In 1915, more than 50 years after the first Indian was admitted, only 63 Indians, or 5 per cent of the total, were members of the I.C.S. Rapid Indianization began only with World War I.[13]

The British were more accommodating to nationalist requests for representative institutions. Most district boards and municipal councils had large Indian majorities by the 1880s. Officials regarded local government as a training ground and safety valve for Indian political aspirations. However, educated nationalists were far more interested in the provincial and the Viceroy's legislative councils. Parliament enlarged the councils in 1892 for the first time in thirty years, and under the Councils Act of 1892 certain Indian political bodies were given the right to nominate members to the councils. But the role of the Indian minority in the councils remained an advisory one, and individual provincial councils met as infrequently as half a dozen times in some years.

The slight modification in the procedures for recruiting civil

[12] Hutchins, *The Illusion*, p. 186.
[13] Sir Edward Blunt, *The I.C.S.: The Indian Civil Service* (London, 1965), pp. 50–52.

servants and the Councils Act of 1892 fell far short of Congress goals. Yet the administrations of Lord Lansdowne (1888–1894), Lord Elgin (1894–1898), and Lord Curzon (1898–1905) believed that the government had gone as far as it should in meeting Indian desires for participation in the public service and legislatures. Some officials felt that it had gone too far, that it should have reserved the 900 or so highest posts for Englishmen. Curzon wrote in 1900 that the absence of an absolute racial qualification meant these posts were "being filched away by the superior wits of the Natives in the English examination." He thought this "to be the greatest peril with which British administration in India was confronted."[14] Attitudes of this sort were common. They meant that the government and the Congress had reached an impasse within a few years of the Congress's founding. It is not too much to say that between 1892 and 1907, no major reform was made in response to nationalist aspirations.

Efforts to Isolate the Congress

Although the Congress was not regarded as an immediate threat to the British, the government wanted to prevent it from becoming one. The government evolved a number of strategies for isolating and weakening the Congress. These strategies were most clearly articulated, and were apparently effective, during Lord Curzon's viceroyalty. Official control over education and the press was tightened, official pressure was applied to rural supporters of the Congress, the Congress was deliberately ignored in official speeches and documents,[15] and an effort was made to project an image of the government as the special friend and protector of the rural classes against the educated classes of the cities who supported the Congress.

At the heart of the anti-Congress policy were efforts to win rural support for the government in order to remove the possibility that either landlords or tenants might find common cause with urban nationalists. Particular attention was given to the restoration of the Indian aristocracies' fading influence as "nat-

[14] S. Gopal, *British Policy in India, 1858–1905* (Cambridge, 1965), p. 267.

[15] Curzon explained his policy of studied public indifference to the Congress in Curzon to Lord Ampthill, Gov. of Madras, 15 June 1903, MSS. Eur. F. 111/207.

ural leaders" of society.[16] This policy predated the Congress and was based on the notion that "the basis of internal order is . . . to be found in the recognition of a patrician aristocracy of indigenous growth, and trained by past associations to control and lead."[17] As an anti-Congress policy, it was reinstituted by Lord Dufferin, who complained that "at one time it was our policy to cut off the tall poppies."[18] Dufferin intervened on the side of landlords in Bengal, Bihar, and Oudh to modify some of the protection I.C.S. members had written into tenancy bills during the drafting stage.[19] Under Lord Curzon, the pro-aristocracy policy was pursued with determination on the grounds that since the government could offer little "which will fit in with the aspirations of 'young India,' it is most advisable to encourage in every way we can 'older India.' "[20] This involved favoring non-Congress landlords in awarding appointments, titles, and honors, granting army commissions in the Imperial Cadet Corps to sons of aristocratic families, insisting that aristocrats develop a high conception of public responsibility and service, and enacting laws to keep landed estates from passing out of the hands of old families. Officials wanted more than that the aristocrats feel well disposed toward the Raj; they also wanted them to enter public life and compete with urban professionals. They encouraged landlords to educate their children so they would be prepared for this competition. And they advised them how to run their organizations.

Government protection and support were extended to small landholders as well as large. The statutory rights of protected tenants[21] in Bengal, Bihar, and the North-Western Provinces and Oudh were increased in the 1880s. In both Bombay and the Punjab, legislation was passed to prevent the appropriation of

[16] The term "aristocracy" was used loosely in contemporary writings to refer to holders of major titles (rajas, sardars, nawabs, etc.) and major landlords, regardless of whether their position predated the British conquest or had been established through conquest or administrative, military, or religious service. It is used here with similar imprecision.

[17] H.J.S. Cotton, *New India or India in Transition* (London, 1886), p. 122.

[18] Gopal, *British Policy*, p. 190.   [19] Ibid., pp. 154–156.

[20] Lord George Hamilton, S. of S. for India, to Curzon, 5 Jan. 1900, MSS. Eur. F. 111/159.

[21] There were two broad categories of agricultural tenants. "Occupancy tenants" were offered protection from unfair ejection and enhancement by tenancy laws; unprotected tenants were given little help by statutes in the nineteenth century.

land by money-lenders and other noncultivating groups. Many officials perceived this strengthening of the interests of landlords and the richer cultivators as a means of retaining the loyalty of rural India and of isolating urban nationalists from a potential source of danger to the British Raj.[22]

There were periods between 1885 and 1905 during which British efforts to isolate the educated nationalists seemed to be working. The failure of the Congress to win over many Muslims and large landholders was evident by 1890. Moreover, from roughly 1890 to 1903, the Congress was beset by organizational problems and by some disappointing attendances. Curzon even predicted the collapse of the Congress. Yet each time official optimism rose, new crises developed which indicated that nationalism's appeal might easily spread beyond the university-educated classes.

Portents of Future Trouble

The comforting political placidity of the late nineteenth century was disturbed periodically by religious revival movements, by localized unrest and violence, and by natural catastrophe. None but the crisis of 1897 was major, perhaps, but each was worrisome and potentially dangerous to the Raj.

In the early 1890s, sections of "older India," with support from English-educated nationalists, were aroused against British legislation raising the legal age of marriage to twelve and against British tolerance of cow slaughter. The magnitude of Hindu feeling expressed over the Age of Consent Bill and the cow slaughter issue suggested there existed considerable latent support for anti-British movements outside the English-speaking classes. The refusal of most educated Indians to support the raising of the legal age of marriage indicated that English-educated Indians had realized their Westernized ways had alienated them from their countrymen and that they were now siding with the conservative "masses" against European civilization.[23] The Congress's refusal to permit the Social Reform Conference to use its *pandal* in 1895 was further evidence of a growing Hindu reaction among the nationalists.[24]

---

[22] For discussion of government land policies, see Chapters Seven and Eight below.

[23] J. D. Rees, *The Real India*, 2nd ed. (London, 1909), p. 255.

[24] The Hindu reaction is the subject of Chapters Nine, Ten and Eleven.

The Rulers

In the late 1890s, two major famines, judged by many to be the worst of the century, cast serious doubts on official estimates of increasing prosperity. The inability of poor Indians to survive disease during the famine was evidence of pervasive malnutrition; the death of at least six million Indians stricken with plague between 1896 and 1909 gave further confirmation. Soon after the twin disasters of famine and plague first appeared, a small group of Brahman conspirators, who perceived an erosion of Hinduism, assassinated two British officials responsible for enforcing unpopular plague regulations in Poona in June 1897, foreshadowing the larger terrorist movement which began in 1907.

In the same year as the Poona murders, Muslim tribesmen rose in a bloody rebellion along a lengthy section of the northwest frontier. This trouble on the frontier coincided with a marked increase of Indian Muslim interest in Middle Eastern affairs, stimulated by the Pan-Islamic movement and the 1897 Graeco-Turkish War. The exhortations by the Pan-Islamicists to regard the Sultan of Turkey as the political and spiritual leader of all Muslims made Englishmen apprehensive about future Muslim loyalty to British rule.

The English in India had long been accustomed to local outbreaks of violence and to periods of unrest among isolated sections of the population. What frightened them in 1897 was the convergence of disturbances and the extension of ties between groups which had previously been unconnected. The two Brahmans convicted for the Poona assassinations had had little formal education and yet they seemed to have been influenced by extremists within the Congress, including Tilak. Moreover, Poona politicians used the 1896–1897 famine to seek links with peasant groups. Peasants in neighboring districts followed the lead of educated members of the Poona Sarvajanik Sabha in a movement to withhold payment of the land revenue demand. The assistant collector of Poona district reported that "not a pie of the revenue instalment" due on 10 December 1896 had been paid to the government.[25] In Dharwar district, peasants refused to pay their revenue even in areas where there was no distress.[26]

[25] Memorandum from collector of Poona to asst. collectors in Poona Dist., 28 Dec. 1896. Enclosure to memorandum from the commissioner, Central Div., 30 Dec. 1896. Famine Prog. No. 98, Bombay Rev. Prog., Famine, Vol. 5,326.

[26] Letter from the commissioner, Southern Div., 26 Jan. 1897. Famine Prog. No. 875, Bombay Rev. Prog., Famine, Vol. 5,326.

The Rulers

The collector of Kolaba district complained that his camp was besieged by crowds of up to 4,000 people with petitions for revenue suspensions and remissions. Many of the petitions were on printed forms.[27] Correspondents of *The Times of India* reported that several of the meetings convened by agents of the Sarvajanik Sabha attracted upwards of 2,000 villagers.[28]

The Maharashtrian no-tax campaign was brief and on a small scale, but in view of the social background and political motivation of its leaders, it was unique. It was one of numerous if minor indications of a growing willingness to challenge British authority. In the Punjab and the Central Province, members of the Arya Samaj organized relief operations and orphanages during the famine to prevent Christian missionaries from making conversions among the destitute. In the Lahore Town Hall, a group of Indian schoolboys broke up a meeting of leading English and Indian citizens by insisting that money be raised for famine orphans rather than for a memorial to Queen Victoria.[29]

A month after the Poona murders, in July 1897, Muslims in Calcutta and surrounding towns rioted against a court order to demolish a small building used as a mosque.[30] For several days large groups of Muslims roamed the streets, attacked isolated Europeans, and threatened to loot and burn factories. The disturbances were unusual in that the rioters singled out Europeans and ignored Hindus. Many Europeans bought revolvers, carried loaded guns,[31] and ventured into the streets only when necessary.[32] In the following year, the number of pistols imported into Bengal, Bombay, and Madras rose sharply.[33]

The 1897 disturbances and assassinations, the frontier risings, the plague and famine, and a devastating earthquake in Assam led *The Times* of London to conclude "that India continues under British rule, very much as it was under Mughal rule, the

---

[27] Memorandum from the commissioner, Central Div., 6 Feb. 1897, Famine Prog. No. 559, Bombay Rev. Prog., Famine, Vol. 5,326.
[28] *The Times of India* (overland edition), 2 and 9 Jan. 1897.
[29] *Bengalee*, 5 June 1897.
[30] C. C. Stevens, Offg. Lt. Gov. of Bengal, to Elgin, 8 July 1897, and C. W. Bolton, Ch. Sec. of Bengal, to J. P. Hewett, Sec., Home Dept., 7 July 1897, enclosures to Elgin to Hamilton, 14 July 1897, MSS. Eur. D. 509/6.
[31] *Pioneer*, 3 July 1897. [32] Elgin to Hamilton, 14 July 1897.
[33] Ch. Secs., Govts. of Madras, Bombay, Bengal, and Burma, to Sec., Govt. of India, Home Dept., various dates. Dec. 1900. Prog. Nos. 317–320. IHP, Pub., Vol. 5,874.

arena of disruptive forces on a vast scale."[34] After an informal official survey of political feeling in India in 1897, the Viceroy, Lord Elgin, concluded that at the time there probably was not "any solidarity of interests" between the university-educated classes and other classes, "upwards or downwards," and that "the intense jealousy" which Muslims "feel of the clever Hindu" prevented any "substantial union between these two groups."[35] But he also thought that, "the dangers of the present and future to the Government were concentrated in a movement that they can no more stop than Canute could restrain the waves, the progress of education and the acquisition of knowledge."[36]

The government response to the unrest of 1897 was repressive rather than liberalizing. It moved against the educated nationalists it thought might have influenced the Poona assassins by incarcerating two extremists (the Natu brothers) without trial for over a year and by prosecuting Bal Gangadhar Tilak and the editors of four other newspapers for sedition. The government also stiffened the law of sedition in 1898 by redefining the offense to include attempts to excite "feelings of enmity" and by giving magistrates the power to require bonds for good behavior from editors suspected of publishing seditious matter. This procedural change was designed to avoid the publicity and martyrdom of an open trial.[37]

In the following six years, nationalism occupied little of the Government of India's attention. Nationalists were relatively inactive and the government was far more concerned with the advance of Russia in Central Asia and Afghanistan. The 73,600 British and 153,000 Indian troops were armed with modern weapons. The army was reorganized, frontier defenses were bolstered, and an intricate diplomatic campaign was conducted with India's neighbors to the north and northwest. However, in the process of strengthening its defenses, the government took into account the manifestations of disaffection among educated nationalists, Hindu revivalists, and Muslims who were protesting the treatment of Islamic Turkey and Afghanistan by the imperial powers. To secure its inland defenses, the government prepared armored cars, built blockhouses near rail tunnels and bridges,

[34] *The Times*, 19 July 1897.
[35] Elgin to Hamilton, 30 Dec. 1897, MSS. Eur. D. 509/8.
[36] Elgin to Hamilton, 20 July 1897, MSS. Eur. D. 509/6.
[37] The amended law of sedition was Act IV of 1898.

drew up plans to defend railway workshops from local attack, and drafted emergency bills which, in time of war, would have imposed local responsibility for the sabotage of railways. It also prepared detailed plans for the control of each district in India. And it adopted proposals for the coordination of the police and the 30,000 European volunteers with army troops in maintaining internal order.[38] The suggestion of Sir George Clarke (governor of Bombay, 1907–1913) that the number of white soldiers might be reduced in order to improve the quality of government by making English officials dependent on the good will of the governed rather than on the military[39] was not given serious attention. The deliberate show of strength in the display of military power on the northwest frontier and elsewhere, the prosecution of extremist editors, and the new sedition law had the intended, short-term effect. For a number of years editors and politicians were more circumspect about what they wrote and said in public.

BRITISH MORALE AND PERFORMANCE

The lull in nationalist activity, the appointment of Lord Curzon as Viceroy, and a series of favorable monsoons after the 1899 famine lifted the morale of Europeans living in India. Curzon's energy and confidence were infectious and gave the impression that first-class leadership had returned, after a long absence, to the top of Indian administration.

Yet part of the apparent improvement in India's condition and administration was simply the contrast with the grimness of the preceding period. Curzon's governor-generalship followed what was probably the roughest year (1896–1897) the Raj had experienced since the Mutiny. And he followed two lackluster men, Lord Lansdowne and Lord Elgin, who tended to preside over rather than lead their governments. Despite the Viceroy's 700 servants and a salary almost twice as large as the Prime Minister's,[40] British Cabinets had been having difficulty finding men of high quality. The Liberals had offered the post to Sir Henry

[38] *Summary of the Administration of Lord Curzon in the Military Department* (Calcutta, 1907), pp. 2, 10–22, and 157.

[39] Hamilton to Curzon, 1 May 1902, MSS. Eur. F. 111/161.

[40] Martin Gilbert, *Servant of India: A Study of Imperial Rule from 1905 to 1910 as Told Through the Correspondence and Diaries of Sir James Dunlop Smith* (London, 1966), p. 3.

Norman and Lord Cromer before finding the almost unknown Lord Elgin. "At last Mr. Gladstone's Government have succeeded in finding a Viceroy for India," *The Times* announcement began. Lord Elgin's "political record, if almost a blank, is blameless."[41] News of Curzon's appointment, by contrast, was received with enthusiasm by almost everyone. His first several years seemed to live up to peoples' anticipations. He was a fine administrator and he fought hard to activate the "gigantic quagmire" as he called the government.[42] But improvements under Curzon were temporary and illusory in many instances. In particular, the Congress organization's internal troubles deceived Englishmen into thinking the nationalist movement was waning. Too few realized that inside and outside the Congress nationalist feeling was hardening against the moderate leaders. And for those administrators who had come to India for more than a five-year term and who worked outside the secretariats, Curzon's vaunted reforms made little impact on their work. Moreover, the diminution of nationalist criticism of the administration turned out to be brief. Curzon's decisions to tighten official control over the universities and to partition Bengal brought the Congress movement to life. By 1905, the intensity of nationalist criticism was beginning to reach even Curzon. "It is disheartening to those of us who, like myself," he wrote, "have given their whole soul and the best years of their life to India. We go on doing our duty, because it is our duty, in a dogged way, but our hearts are chilled to the marrow."[43]

It is almost impossible to summarize the official mood which varied markedly from person to person, region to region, and monsoon to monsoon. Many officials chose to focus on British successes and "shared the pathetic 'contentment'" about the blessings of the Raj which was said to be characteristic of the I.C.S.[44] Administration of famine relief and railroad and canal construction, for example, provided grounds for pride. Others, including some of the most perceptive administrators, felt discouraged by the seemingly intractable nature of Indian problems. Whether in raising the standard of living or in improving the quality of justice and education, progress was spotty or negligible.

[41] *The Times*, 12 Oct. 1893.
[42] Earl of Ronaldshay, *The Life of Lord Curzon* (London, 1928), II, 64.
[43] Curzon to Samuel Smith, 8 Jan. 1905, MSS. Eur. F. 111/210.
[44] Sir Robert Reid, *Years of Change in Bengal and Assam* (London, 1966), p. 20.

John Beames wrote with resignation about "the apparently unconscious and unintentional, but for that reason all the more unconquerable obstructiveness of the whole population."[45] And Sir John Strachey referred to the "almost unchanged and unchangeable" character of "the vast majority."[46] What Beames called "obstructiveness" was in part a function of backwardness, of the segmented, rural, and uneducated condition of Indian society. Literacy in 1900 was not much over 5 per cent, and in rural areas, where four-fifths of the population lived, it was considerably lower. This unmodernized population was administered by a small number of Englishmen, many of whom were not fluent in local languages. In 1913, the average population per I.C.S. executive officer ranged from just over 200,000 in Assam and Bombay to over 530,000 in Bihar and Orissa. The average population per I.C.S. judicial officer was even greater, ranging from roughly 500,000 to almost 2,000,000.[47]

When an I.C.S. official stationed in a district worked through established institutions, such as the revenue collecting agencies and the courts, and where administrative procedures were established and understood, he could conduct his business with at least the appearance and feeling of efficiency. In this he was assisted by a largely Indian subordinate staff. Of the posts with salaries of less than Rs. 500 per month, the vast majority were held by Indians. But when the I.C.S. officer went outside the routine tasks of administration, in emergencies such as plague administration or even in making surveys, he was apt to encounter suspicion, obstruction, and frustration. Edgar Thurston's account of conducting his anthropometric survey in south India around the turn of the century was intended to be humorous, but it does reflect the sense of helplessness an official on special assignment might experience.

> ... it was unfortunately impossible to disguise the fact that I am a Government official, and very considerable difficulties were encountered owing to the wickedness of the people, and their timidity and fear of increased taxation, plague inoculation, and transportation. The Paniyan women of the Wynaad

[45] John Beames, *Memoirs of a Bengal Civilian* (London, 1961), p. 156.
[46] Strachey, *India*, p. 12.
[47] Royal Commission on the Public Services in India, *Report*, I, 182.

believed that I was going to have the finest specimens among them stuffed for the Madras Museum. An Irula man, on the Nilgiri hills, who was wanted by the police for some mild crime of ancient date, came to be measured, but absolutely refused to submit to the operation on the plea that the height-measuring standard was the gallows. The similarity of the word Boyan to Boer was once fatal to my work. For, at the time of my visit to the Oddes, who have Boyan as their title, the South African war was just over, and they were afraid that I was going to get them transported, to replace the Boers who had been exterminated. Being afraid, too, of my evil eye, they refused to fire a new kiln of bricks for the club chambers of Coimbatore until I had taken my departure. During a long tour through the Mysore province, the Natives mistook me for a recruiting sergeant bent on seizing them for employment in South Africa and fled before my approach from town to town. The little spot, which I am in the habit of making with Aspinall's white paint to indicate the position of the frontonasal suture and bi-orbital breadth, was supposed to possess vesicant properties, which would serve as a means of future identification for the purpose of kidnapping. The record of head, chest, and foot measurements, was viewed with marked suspicion, on the ground that I was an army tailor, measuring for sepoy's clothing. The untimely death of a Native outside a town, at which I was halting, was attributed to my evil eye. Villages were denuded of all save senile men, women, and infants. The vendors of food-stuffs in one bazaar, finding business slack owing to the flight of their customers, raised their prices, and a missionary complained that the price of butter had gone up. My arrival at one important town was coincident with a great annual temple festival, whereat there were not sufficient coolies left to drag the temple car in procession. So I had to perforce to move on, and leave the Brahman heads unmeasured. The head official of another town, when he came to take leave of me, apologised for the scrubby appearance of his chin, as the local barber had fled. One man, who had volunteered to be tested with Lovibond's tintometer, was suddenly seized with fear in the midst of the experiment, and, throwing his bodycloth at my feet, ran for all he was worth, and disappeared. An elderly Municipal servant wept bitterly when undergoing the process of measurement, and a woman bade farewell to her husband, as she thought for ever, as he entered the threshold of my impromptu laboratory.[48]

There are indications, apart from the self-doubt and apart from the exasperation with and fear of nationalists, that India no longer appealed to the British imagination as it once had. The satisfaction of work, the emoluments, the high style of living, the hunting and other sports were still attractive, but the pleasure and excitement had diminished for many officers. Perhaps "the horrid din of the temples," the cawing crows and "the perpetual chatter of our Aryan brothers" irritated no greater proportion of British officialdom than formerly.[49] Perhaps the "hectoring language" and "bullying tone" used by Englishmen serving on committees with Indians was no more common than before nationalists began to question British dominance. Possibly women's use of terms such as "those horrid natives" and "nigger" had been "almost universal" and "common" long before the birth of the Congress.[50] It does seem, however, that the compensating rewards for exile in India had been devalued in English eyes as nationalism spread, as the administrative and military frontiers had been closed, and as government became increasingly routine and bureaucratic.

The sense of discovery, of service, and of individual fulfillment is often missing from available letters and memoirs of men employed in India in the last years of the century. Work was something to be endured; the rewards came not in the work itself but in the salaries, promotions, and awards, and in the early pension.

Many observers commented on the apparent decline in the Indian Civil Service's dedication and performance.[51] The Royal Commission on the Public Services in India (1912–1914) received many complaints about the deterioration in the caliber of I.C.S. recruits, including their "lack of manners, decline in social status, want of consideration for Indians, and absence of the power of

[48] Edgar Thurston, *Castes and Tribes of Southern India* (Madras, 1908), I, xvi–xvii.

[49] Gilbert, *Servant of India*, p. 30.   [50] Cotton, *New India*, pp. 36–37.

[51] Curzon often complained of the caliber of English officials and Lord Morley received devastating reports on British administration. (Wolpert, *Morley and India*, pp. 58ff.) The under-secretary of state for India suggested in the House of Commons in 1912 that India was "only getting the leavings of the Home Civil Service." *The Cambridge History of India*, VI, ed. by H. H. Dodwell (Cambridge, 1932), 376.

The Rulers

leadership."[52] What was especially noticeable in this criticism was the charge that the officials were isolated from Indian affairs. Many reasons for this isolation were suggested. The growth in litigation and paper work kept men in their offices. When the British were few in number, civilians depended on the land for company and recreation. Now, however, British society was relatively self-sufficient. The construction of railways and the Suez Canal reduced the civilians' need to find Indian friends and activities by making it easier to escape to an Indian hill station or to England for holidays and schooling.[53] With this self-sufficiency there developed at Simla and other locations where there were large concentrations of Englishmen "the affectation of being very English, of knowing nothing at all about India, of eschewing Indian words and customs."[54] Contrary impressions notwithstanding, J. D. Rees was probably correct in stating in 1908 that "Europeans who can really carry on a conversation in the vernacular are exceedingly rare."[55]

The isolation of Europeans was reinforced by a parallel growth in the size of English-speaking Indian communities. Large numbers gave Western-educated Indians the companionship and confidence they often had lacked in the early decades of the Raj. And they increasingly viewed Englishmen not so much as their mentors but as their rivals. The growing challenge by Indians to English privilege in turn drove the European official and non-official communities into each other's arms. Whereas civilians once protected Indians in conflicts with nonofficials, this now happened infrequently.[56]

[52] Vol. I, p. 164. Lord John Morley was so concerned about the effect of official discourtesy to Indians that he spoke about it in public in 1907 and said "Bad manners are disagreeable in all countries. India is the only country where bad and overbearing manners are a political crime." Quoted by the Earl of Ronaldshay, *An Eastern Miscellany* (Edinburgh, 1911), p. 259.

[53] There was a saying that "the Suez Canal has brought England and India closer together only to separate them the more." Cotton, *New India* (1904), p. 44.

[54] Philip Woodruff, *The Men Who Ruled India*, II, *The Guardians* (London, 1953), 94.

[55] Rees, *The Real India*, pp. 263 and 335–336.

[56] Curzon emphasized that the interests of all Englishmen, official or non-official, were identical. He told a meeting of English mine-owners in Burrakur in 1903 that "My work lies in administration, yours in exploitation; but both are aspects of the same question and of the same duty." Cotton, *New India* (1904 ed.), p. 55. John Florey in George Orwell's *Burmese Days*

The Rulers

The separation of British and English-speaking Indian societies was accompanied by frequent comments on British racism. Whether or not there were more conflicts of a racial character, British and Indian awareness of them was growing. The Ilbert Bill controversy of 1884 brought into sharp relief the difference between English professions and practice of nondiscrimination. The bill would have removed the distinction between Indian and English I.C.S. judges in determining jurisdiction over cases involving Englishmen. Europeans were so upset that they organized a campaign of unparalleled proportions against the bill. Some plotted to kidnap the Viceroy, Lord Ripon, and deport him to England.[57] Others who ordinarily regarded public racial slurs as bad form, made insulting remarks. A leading Calcutta barrister, J.A.H. Branson, warned Englishmen at a public meeting against "the wily natives who creep in where you cannot walk because you cannot walk unless you walk upright."[58] The strength of English feeling and the threat of a "White Mutiny" forced the government to compromise in 1884 and to permit Europeans to be tried by juries, at least half of whose members would be European. In the Ilbert Bill controversy, nationalists saw a crude racism which was normally hidden behind the impersonality of institutions and the walls of private clubs. Some, for the first time, concluded from the government's compromise that "the justice of a cause was insufficient for its triumph in politics and that the only path of victory lay through agitation."[59] But administrators reached different conclusions. The European community's demonstration that it could prevent significant reductions in its privileges was a standing reminder to reform-minded administrators after Lord Ripon of "the risks of bidding for native popularity and stimulating native ambition."[60] These risks also included arousing strong racial animosities.

(New York, 1934), p. 40, analyzed the partnership in different terms: "The official holds the Burmese down while the business man goes through his pockets."

[57] S. Gopal, *The Viceroyalty of Lord Ripon, 1880–1884* (Oxford, 1953), p. 156.

[58] Ibid., p. 143.

[59] Quoted from unspecified source by H. P. Mody, *Sir Pherozeshah Metha: A Political Biography* (Bombay, 1921), I, 142.

[60] Quoted from Sir Alfred Lyall, Lt. Gov. of the North-Western Provinces and Oudh, by Sir Mortimer Durand, *Life of the Right Hon. Sir Alfred Comyn Lyall* (Edinburgh, 1913), p. 283.

While there were no racial controversies on the scale of the Ilbert Bill between 1885 and 1905, many minor racial incidents were brought to public attention and many more must have gone unreported. The two most common types of recorded incidents were those between villagers and British soldiers out shooting game and those involving *punkah* coolies who failed to pull the punkahs (fans) fast enough to please their sweating military employers. There were 81 recorded cases of the first type between 1880 and 1900. Some ended with British soldiers shooting into crowds of angry villagers. The second type led to the beating and sometimes the death of the coolie and, incidentally, hastened the British search for mechanical punkahs. In addition, there were 29 "serious cases in which British soldiers were accused of robbery or rape" in the same twenty years.[61]

Many British officials were unwilling to report, and British jurors were unwilling to convict in, cases which would reflect discredit on the ruling race.[62] Lord Curzon, however, believed that the common failure to prosecute and punish Englishmen for their violence to Indians held much greater danger to British rule. When he discovered that military and civilian officials had conspired to cover up the rape of a Burmese woman by a group of British soldiers, he insisted the appropriate authorities act. In the trial which followed, the accused were acquitted on a technicality. The case so infuriated Curzon that he banished the defendents' regiment to Aden for two years.[63] On another occasion, Curzon had the 9th Lancers punished for hiding the fact that two British soldiers beat an Indian cook to death after he refused to procure a woman. The European audience at the Delhi Durbar in 1903 gave the Lancers a rousing welcome to show their disapproval of Curzon's actions.[64] It was said that "for the next year or two the British soldier was constantly exposed to provocative insult from the scum of the bazaars."[65]

[61] *Summary of the Administration of Lord Curzon in the Military Department*, pp. 28–29.

[62] Europeans charged in the death of Indians they beat were often acquitted on the grounds that the deceased man's spleen was abnormally enlarged and weak as a result of malaria. This led an Indian newspaper to comment sarcastically that God had given Indians enlarged spleens so that Englishmen would not be convicted of murder.

[63] Michael Edwardes, *High Noon of Empire: India Under Curzon* (London, 1965), pp. 85–87.

[64] Earl of Ronaldshay, *The Life of Lord Curzon*, II, 247–248.

[65] Evan Maconochie, *Life in the Indian Civil Service* (London, 1926), p. 116.

In insisting that cases of this sort be brought to trial, Curzon behaved as many I.C.S. officials would have in his position. To have done otherwise might have further damaged the government's already tarnished reputation for impartial criminal justice. However, such action was not incompatible with the general feeling of British racial and cultural superiority. Curzon conducted his campaign to stop collisions between soldiers and "Natives" at the same time he erected monuments to British victories over Indians and to the British who were killed by Indians in the Black Hole of Calcutta and elsewhere. His attitude, which was probably common among officials, is shown in his comments on the monument which marked the well into which Nana Sahib's men threw the bodies of their English victims during the Mutiny. The sign on the gate said "Dogs not allowed," but in fact it was Indians who were not allowed unless they had a special pass. Curzon defended the exclusion of the "natives" by arguing it was

> one of the sacred places of Northern India, at least to the Englishman, and no one of our race can visit it without emotion. . . . We respect the sacred places of the Hindus, and no Englishman is ever permitted to enter the inner shrines of their temples. The well at Cawnpore is equally sacred to us. . . .[66]

For Curzon and others, the Mutiny was an event and a betrayal never to be forgotten. At the Delhi Durbar in 1903, the procession of the Mutiny veterans was received, one observer recalled, in a way "which none who witnessed can ever forget or recall without emotion. . . . The whole great assembly rose as one man, and with what voice it could control cherred till it could cheer no more."[67]

Comments in Indian newspapers indicate, and British memoirs confirm, that many Englishmen continued to inflict indignities upon Indians despite the efforts of concerned officials to halt them. A sampling of autobiographical writings by prominent officials shows areas of day-to-day life affected by racism as well as indications that a growing number of officials were speaking out against racism. Henry Cotton protested the exclusion of Indians from part of Eden Gardens, a public park in central Calcutta.[68]

[66] Curzon to Hamilton, 6 Feb. 1902, MSS. Eur. F. 111/161.
[67] Maconochie, *Life in the Indian Civil Service*, p. 161.
[68] Lord Beveridge, *India Called Them* (London, 1947), p. 260.

The Rulers

Henry Beveridge complained in his east Bengal station when police refused to let Indians onto the river-front pier and promenade maintained with local, Indian taxes;[69] Sir Walter Roper Lawrence saw an Englishman explode "with wrath" when an Indian entered a first-class carriage, and he heard him say "the country was going to the dogs, and that he would not submit to the indignity of having a black man pushing into his carriage";[70] Sir Montagu Gerard recounted how a subaltern boarded a railway carriage, found to his disgust two Indian gentlemen seated there, waited calmly until the train was moving, and then "fires them out of the door";[71] Sir David Barr confirmed a report that two *sahibs* returning from snipe shooting in a first-class railway compartment forced a petty raja to wash the mud off them;[72] and Sir Andrew Fraser saw a British officer "severely" beat country carters because their carts wandered all over the road and blocked the passage of his carriage.[73]

One Englishman, T. L. Pennell, experienced his countrymen's racism directly when he and an Indian companion traveled through northern India dressed as *sadhus*, sometimes on bicycles, at other times riding on trains. An English soldier rudely told him to stay out of a railway compartment occupied by Europeans; he was not permitted to visit the English cemetery at the Old Residency at Lucknow; and he was forced to wait "more than once" on the verandah or in the sun when calling on Englishmen. And when he tried to enter a railway office, an Indian Christian, seeing his Indian clothes, told him *Nikaljao!* [get out].[74] However, Pennell's sensitivity and experience were rare among the English in India.

British awareness of the effects of insolent and cruel behavior was not growing fast enough to stem the counterracism which became particularly evident after 1905. Englishmen failed to realize that Indian cruelty to Indians was judged more tolerantly by

---

[69] Ibid., p. 295.

[70] Sir Walter Roper Lawrence, *The India We Served* (London, 1929), p. 85.

[71] Quoted for *The Times* review of Sir Montagu Gerard, *Leaves from the Diaries of a Soldier and Sportsman*, by Cotton, *New India* (1904 ed.), p. 60.

[72] Ibid., pp. 60–61.

[73] Sir Andrew H. L. Fraser, *Among Indian Rajahs and Ryots: A Civil Servant's Recollections and Impressions of Thirty-seven Years of Work and Sport in the Central Provinces and Bengal*, 2nd ed. (London, 1911), p. 86.

[74] T. L. Pennell, *Among the Wild Tribes of the Afghan Frontier* (London, 1909), pp. 253–255.

Indians than British cruelty. And Englishmen were misled about the depth of Indian feeling by failures, as in the case of the petty raja on the train, to resist openly. Moreover, the Raj continued to depend upon an illusion of infallibility which almost required exclusive and superior behavior. Englishmen had not only to maintain their own belief in their permanence and invincibility, many also felt a conscious need to keep Indians convinced of their superiority. This need tended to perpetuate the arrogant and exclusive conduct of which sensitive officials complained. Sir Walter Roper Lawrence, who served for many years in western India before becoming Lord Curzon's private secretary, expressed the importance of the illusion of infallibility:

> Our life in India, our very work more or less, rests on illusion. I had the illusion, wherever I was, that I was infallible and invulnerable in my dealings with Indians. How else could I have dealt with angry mobs, with cholera-stricken masses, and with processions of religious fanatics? It was not conceit, Heaven knows: It was not the prestige of the British Raj, but it was the illusion which is in the very air of India. They expressed something of the idea when they called us the "Heaven-born" and the idea is really make-believe—mutual make-believe. They, the millions, made us believe that we had a divine mission. We made them believe that they were right. Unconsciously, perhaps, I may have had at the back of my mind that there was a British Battalion and a battery of Artillery at the Cantonment near Ajmere; but I never thought of this, and I do not think that many of the primitive and simple Mers [tribesmen] had ever heard of or seen English soldiers. But they saw the head of the Queen-Express on the rupee, and worshipped it. They had a vague conception of the Raj, which they looked on as a power, omnipotent, all-pervading, benevolent for the most part, but capricious, a deity of many shapes and many moods. . . .[75]

At the turn of the century, as doubts about the illusion spread, first Lord Curzon and then Lord Minto tried to bolster it by emphasizing the ceremonial pomp of the Raj with a view to impressing Indians with British power and grandeur. Curzon began planning the £550,000 Victoria Memorial in 1901,[76] when the

[75] Lawrence, *The India We Served*, pp. 42–43.
[76] Earl of Ronaldshay, *The Life of Lord Curzon*, II, 162.

Government's gross annual tax receipts were £20,816,000.[77] The Delhi Coronation of 1903 cost £360,000, or more than the total annual government expenditure on arts and professional colleges. The Prince of Wales' and the Amir of Afghanistan's visits in 1905 and 1907, respectively, together cost an additional £420,000.[78] If the panoply impressed Indian princes and rajas, this attempt to conform to "oriental custom" angered nationalists of varied persuasions. Lalmohan Ghose, the moderate who emerged from political retirement to preside over the 1903 Congress, told the delegates that the Delhi Durbar was a waste of "vast sums of money on an empty pageant, when Famine and Pestilence were stalking over the land." It was a good example, he felt, of "that utter recklessness of expense which you may always expect when men, no matter how highly placed, were dealing with other people's money, and were practically accountable to no one for their acts."[79]

HUME AND THE FOUNDING OF THE CONGRESS

The evidence of British racism and administrative inefficiency presented in this chapter have been taken almost entirely from reports and accounts supplied by Englishmen. Among the tens of thousands of Europeans residing in India, a sizeable minority found exclusive and discriminatory practices politically inexpedient and morally distasteful. Educators such as Professor Wordsworth of Elphinstone College and John Adam of Pachaiyappa College, businessmen such as George Yule of Calcutta and William Chambers of Bombay, lawyers such as Spring Branson of Madras, and officials such as Henry Beveridge, Lord Ripon, William Wedderburn, and Henry Cotton occasionally stepped forward to plead for the rights of Indians in racial conflicts. One of these conflicts, over the Ilbert Bill, brought Allan Octavian Hume to the forefront of nationalist activities in 1883–1884.

The Ilbert Bill, as mentioned above, would have deprived European British subjects residing in the mofussil (rural areas) of the right *not* to be tried by an Indian magistrate. The practical

---

[77] After adding the nontax receipts, the total gross revenue for 1900–1901 was £75,272,000. Strachey, *India*, p. 121.

[78] Wolpert, *Morley and India*, p. 280.

[79] Annie Besant, *How India Wrought for Freedom: The Story of the National Congress Told from Official Records* (Madras, 1915), p. 377.

effects of the bill would have been limited, since in 1883 there were only two Indian covenanted civil servants whose jurisdiction would have been extended to European subjects under the bill.[80] But the bill frightened the European community which saw it as a dangerous erosion of British privilege. The bill provoked a section of the English population to agitate for its withdrawal. In the process, English speakers and newspapers stunned educated Indians with the rudeness and virulence of their racial attacks on Indians. Their success in forcing Lord Ripon, the Viceroy, to modify the bill demonstrated to nationalists the value of public, organized agitation. Nationalists also learned how deep was English hostility to political reform in India.

The Ilbert Bill incident intensified interest in the often-discussed idea of organizing a national political conference of educated Indians. Hume brought regionally based nationalists into contact with each other. Nationalists listened to and respected Hume because, as a former member of the I.C.S. and a confidant of Lord Ripon, he could offer them informed advice about influencing the bureaucracy and Parliament. Hume acted as spokesman for nationalists with the Viceroy about the Ilbert Bill. He then took a leading role in founding the Indian National Congress in Bombay in December 1885.

Hume dominated the Congress in its early years. As its general secretary, he was the only man in most years who gave full-time attention to Congress affairs between its annual meetings. Even after he left India in 1892, he continued to hold the post of general secretary and to advise the Congress. More than any other single individual, he was responsible for the movement's early success. But his erratic and domineering behavior and his failure to give up the general secretaryship postponed the time when nationalists would feel the Congress was their own organization. By refusing to share responsibility, Hume hindered the development of an experienced leadership cadre within the Congress. Yet the fact that Indian Congressmen allowed Hume to control the Congress's affairs was a measure of their lack of confidence in their own political abilities and of the weakness of interregional ties between educated nationalists.

Hume had been a member of the I.C.S. until 1882. He served with distinction as a district officer in the North-Western Prov-

[80] Mehrotra, *The Emergence*, p. 339.

The Rulers

inces. During the Mutiny, he and his men killed more than a hundred rebels. In 1871 he became secretary to the Government of India's Department of Revenue. However, in 1879 he was superseded by a junior man, and when he retired several years later he was a bitter and frustrated man, having failed to gain the high post he had hoped for.[81]

At the time of his retirement, Hume had spent most of his adult life in positions of authority over Indians. An imposing man, "tall and erect, with . . . beady, squinting eyes" and a walrus mustache which covered his mouth, he enjoyed the opportunity to command. His superiors in the administration had found him impatient, tactless, and cantankerous.[82] Nationalists subsequently spoke of his "despotism" but usually with appreciation, implying that the nationalist movement needed a leader of his forcefulness. An Indian admirer wrote he had "the fervour of a prophet and the enthusiasm of a fanatic."[83] Both his official career and his role in the Congress suggest a powerful personality with a need to be morally superior.

Prior to 1879, it seems that Hume had had little contact with Western-educated Indians. But at the time his career was turning sour, he "became convinced," according to William Wedderburn, "that some definite action was called for to counteract the growing unrest" among the masses who suffered during the famine of the late 1870s and the Western-educated Indians who were alienated by racial exclusion and the apparent increasing poverty of their country under British rule.[84] With the appointment of the Liberal Lord Ripon as Viceroy in 1880, educated nationalists gained a sympathetic ear. By acting in 1883 and 1884 as an adviser to Ripon on Indian opinion, Hume was able to regain informally some of the influence he lost when he was superseded. At the same time, he was moving toward cooperation with educated Indians through the Theosophical Society.

One may speculate about what combination of political motives and religious inclinations led Hume into the company of Madame Blavatsky's *mahatmas* (religious masters), *chelas* (disciples),

[81] Martin, *New India*, p. 61. Also, Seal, *The Emergence*, p. 270.

[82] Martin, *New India*, pp. 53–59.

[83] Quoted from an obituary in the *Tribune* (Lahore) by Sir William Wedderburn, *Allan Octavian Hume, C. B.: 'Father of the Indian National Congress'* (London, 1913), p. 172.

[84] Ibid., p. 50.

and seances. Aging, his failure to have a son,[85] and the collapse of his official career may have deepened his interest in mysticism. Apparently, he sincerely believed that Mahatma Koot Hoomi Lal Singh, with whom he carried on mystical communication, had helped to control the masses during the Mutiny.[86] Neither the discovery that Koot Hoomi Lal Singh apparently was Madame Blavatsky herself nor the revelation that Madame Blavatsky's celebrated finding of Mrs. Hume's lost broach was a fraud[87] disillusioned Hume about theosophy. Briton Martin undoubtedly was correct in his belief that Hume found theosophy a useful "vehicle for social interaction with Indian leaders."[88]

The Theosophical Society had over one hundred branch associations in India by 1884.[89] Indians were drawn to it by its flattering views of ancient Aryan civilization and its attacks on Western civilization as materialistic, aggressive, and decadent. The European theosophists who praised ancient Indian culture and who argued for reconstruction of modern India along Aryan lines accelerated the rediscovery of the Indian past by college graduates. The theosophists facilitated the emerging accommodation between anglicized Indians who had regarded Hinduism an archaic collection of irrational superstitions and Hindu revivalists who found ample grounds for pride in Hindu values. As in the case of the founding of the Congress, European initiative gave organizational form to ideas which were "in the air." Their doubts eased by European endorsement, a number of Indian graduates joined the Theosophical Society in the early 1880s.[90] Some of them continued to work with Hume in the early Congress. Among the influential Congressmen who had been theosophists were Kashinath Telang of Bombay, Mahadev Ballal Namjoshi of Poona, Narendranath Sen of Calcutta, and P. Ananda Charlu of Madras.[91]

Hume's nationalist contacts were also expanded by the agitation to gain admission to the armed auxiliary force known as

[85] Mehrotra, *The Emergence*, p. 312.   [86] Martin, *New India*, p. 63.

[87] J. N. Farquhar, *Modern Religious Movements in India* (London, 1924), pp. 228–231.

[88] *New India*, p. 64. Seal (*The Emergence*, pp. 251–252) makes the same point.

[89] Farquhar, *Modern Religious Movements*, p. 223.

[90] Martin, *New India*, pp. 62, 64, and 295.

[91] Suntharalingam, *Politics and Nationalist Awakening*, pp. 296, 300–302, and 330.

The Rulers

the Volunteer Corps. Volunteering became a major issue for members of local political associations in Bombay, Calcutta, Madras, and other cities within months of the passage of the Ilbert Bill in 1884. The Government of India had decided to expand the Volunteer Corps in connection with the Russian advance in central Asia. The government wished to augment internal defenses while preparing to shift regular troops into Afghanistan to counter the Russian threat. The intention had been to enlist volunteers only from among the 71,000 European and Eurasian males available, and from a limited number of Indian Christians and Parsis. The volunteers had originally been organized without Indians during the Mutiny, but in 1885, educated Indians asked that they too be permitted to volunteer. Their request seemed to be on the verge of fulfillment when a sympathetic English officer in the Madras volunteer corps accepted three Madrasis who met the physical and educational requirements. However, the consequent furor among Europeans persuaded the government to decline their services.[92] The *Pioneer* of Allahabad spoke for many Englishmen when it warned against "any premature relaxation of all our safeguards." It said "The English in India are still a garrison in what was once a conquered country."[93]

Nationalist attention was diverted from the volunteering question by the fall of the Liberal government in England in June 1885, before the rejection of Indian volunteering was public knowledge. Indian political associations turned to the problem of influencing the British electorate in the forthcoming general election. Associations in major Indian cities decided to send a delegation to participate in the English campaign. Three lawyers were selected: N. G. Chandavarkar from Bombay, Manomohan Ghose from Calcutta, and S. Ramaswami Mudaliar from Madras. The Indian delegation stressed two issues during the autumn campaign of 1885. They asked for larger Indian participation in Indian legislative bodies and for a reduction in the Government of India's military spending. Nationalists considered the latter issue particularly appropriate for this general election because English foreign policy had produced an alarming increase in India's military budget.

During 1885, three major burdens were added to India's mili-

[92] Martin, *New India*, pp. 106–109.   [93] Ibid., p. 110.

tary expenditure which in 1884–1885 had reached £17,000,000 or "39.5 per cent of India's total revenues." First, after Gordon's death at Khartoum, the Government of India sent a relief expedition to Suakin on the Red Sea; second, Lord Randolph Churchill's new forward policy in Afghanistan added £2,000,000 to the Indian budget; and finally, the dispatch of an expeditionary force into Upper Burma in November 1885 further aggravated India's mounting financial problems.[94] These three expensive departures in foreign policy, coming almost simultaneously with the Ilbert Bill and the volunteer question, generated a sense of urgency for longstanding nationalist goals of expanded participation in the legislative councils, greater Indian control over financial matters, and diminished reliance on expensive foreign administrative personnel.

Hume helped plan the nationalist strategy of seeking redress from the English electorate. But even during this pre-Congress effort to influence an English general election, Hume's relations with his Indian collaborators were dogged by poor communication and disagreements over tactics. Hume and the Indian delegation traveled to England separately and, once there, had little contact with each other. The delegation placed itself in the hands of William Digby, a radical Liberal and a former editor of the *Madras Times*, and it soon became identified with the radical wing of the Liberal Party. The alliance with English radicals antagonized some influential Indian moderates, including Sir Jamsetjee Jeejeebhoy who resigned as president of the Bombay Presidency Association.[95] The nationalist divisions and disagreements over the issues were reported in the British press and damaged the credibility of the Indian mission. Most of the candidates whom the Indian delegation tried to help were defeated, including Lalmohan Ghose and William Digby, and the first major Indian intervention in British politics ended in total and unexpected failure.[96] Whether other tactics could have brought election results more favorable to Indian reform is doubtful.

When Hume and the seventy-odd delegates assembled in

[94] Ibid., pp. 186, 253, and 302.

[95] Ibid., p. 224. In resigning, Jeejeebhoy wrote "I cannot be a member of an association which apparently aims at using India and Indian interests for political purposes of one or the other political party in England." Husain B. Tyabji, *Badruddin Tyabji: A Biography* (Bombay, 1952), p. 166.

[96] Martin, *New India*, p. 267.

Bombay in late December 1885 for the first session of the Indian National Congress,[97] their mood was somber and restrained. They gathered in the aftermath of a series of failures to obtain reforms. In the recent controversies over military expenditure, volunteering, impartial justice, and Indian admission to the civil services, nationalists had made few gains. On the contrary, nationalists had aroused English hostility and had learned that two possible avenues of reform, the Government of India and Parliament through the British electorate, were blocked for the time being. Few nationalists were as yet prepared to go beyond strictly constitutional channels to seek reform.

The founders of the Congress were cautious, moderate men who were confident in the ultimate fairness of the British people. For most Congressmen, obtaining political concessions was not an urgent matter. The advances they had made in their professional careers satisfied some nationalist urges and absorbed energies which might otherwise have been directed toward politics. Congress leaders had entered an English-created educational and occupational nexus through which they had achieved prestige and high income. The cost, inefficiencies, and racial exclusiveness of English administration sometimes moved the Congress founders to anger, but that anger was tempered by dependence on political ideas, language, and occupations which were more English than Indian. Few Congress leaders appeared to harbor feelings of hate for their rulers. In too many ways, the English-educated Congressman shared values and interests with the rulers. Although only an occasional ruler would support their cause and although the English public would continue to be regarded as more sympathetic to Indian reform, Congressmen in the pre-1905 era approached politics without enough passion either to satisfy Hume or seriously frighten the English.

[97] Martin, ibid., and Mehrotra, *The Emergence* (Chapter Seven), discuss this session in detail.

──────────── *Chapter Two* ────────────

CONGRESS LEADERS

Nationalist politics were a full-time activity for only a few Indians before 1905. In most years between 1885 and 1905, all-Indian political activity was concentrated in the months of November and December. First, informal and usually uncontested elections were held to select delegates for the annual session of the Indian National Congress. In the final week of the year, delegates from different parts of India converged on the host city for three or four days of meetings.

The formal Congress meetings were devoted to speeches and resolutions on many key political issues of the day, such as volunteering, Indianization of the civil service, and expansion of the legislative councils. However, the founders of the Congress were determined to make their movement genuinely "national" and therefore they avoided discussion of controversial issues, such as cow protection and tenant rights, which would have antagonized important sections of the population. The Congress leaders sought a consensus among Indians. This meant focusing on issues about which Indian and British interests differed.

For several days, delegates listened to speeches in English which both criticized the government and affirmed their gratitude to the English for bringing order and education to India. Few of the speakers discussed the organization of the Congress as a political party. Most delegates regarded the Congress in the pre-1905 period as an annual meeting and a state of mind. The state of mind was expressed in the moderate and formal language of the resolutions which were passed by acclamation. Most of the resolutions were based on the principle that English interests in India should be subordinated to the rights and welfare of Indians and that India's constitution should gradually be rearranged so that Indians would be empowered to enforce that principle.

When delegates advocated converting the Congress into a year-round operation, they rarely took concrete action beyond reelecting Allan Octavian Hume as General Secretary and voting funds for Congress propaganda in England. They did even less about extending Congress membership outside the Western-educated groups, although in some years Muslim and lower-caste Hindus were elected delegates to give the Congress at least the appearance of being more broadly representative. Few delegates engaged in sustained political work between the annual Congress sessions. In fact, only a handful of delegates from any single province attended two consecutive Congress sessions unless the sessions happened to be held in neighboring provinces. But even though they attended irregularly, the majority of delegates seemed to regard themselves as Congressmen and seemed to share the sentiments expressed in the annual resolutions and in their local newspapers. The Indian-owned newspapers with the largest circulations generally supported Congress positions.

The concern of this chapter is with the lives of the Congress leaders between the annual meetings. That they were not full-time or even half-time politicians suggests either a low level of political commitment or a strong counterattraction. How did they spend their time? How did their experiences outside the Congress affect their political perceptions? Congress leaders wanted to share political power with the rulers, but what was their emotional feeling toward the English who had often given employment to their fathers? How did men whose educations and occupations had in important respects been shaped by Englishmen view their own culture and countrymen? How did men who overcame great odds in entering the top levels of professional life which until recently had been closed to Indians look at themselves?

In seeking answers to these questions in this chapter, we are anticipating the following chapter on the Congress itself which argues that the Congress was unsuccessful either in gaining concessions from the English or in mobilizing Indians in active support of Congress goals. Some of the reasons for the stagnation of the Congress become clear in studying the occupational and family backgrounds of the men who ran the early Congress.

This chapter is, then, a group portrait of that English-educated segment of society from which most Congress leaders came. Occasionally illustrative material is drawn from the lives of non-members, but for the most part it is limited to the officers, members of major committees, and the men who spoke most frequently at the annual meetings. It is hoped that this somewhat impressionistic analysis of the leaders' lives outside the Congress

Congress Leaders

will help explain why the Congress failed to establish a popular base, why the Congress split into moderate and extremist factions in 1907, and why other nationalists formed terrorist societies or remained outside political organizations altogether.

ACHIEVING IN THE NEW PROFESSIONS

The nucleus of Indian leadership in the early Congress was drawn from a group of nine men from Bombay and Calcutta who had formed interregional friendships while in London studying for the bar and the Indian Civil Service. The future Congress leaders who were together in London in the late 1860s were Pherozeshah Mehta, Badruddin Tyabji, W. C. Bonnerjee, and Manomohan Ghose.[1] As those young friends were finishing their studies, a second group, who also became Congress leaders, had begun to arrive. W. C. Bonnerjee met Surendranath Banerjea and Romeshchandra Dutt when they landed in 1868 to study for the civil service.[2] Before Banerjea and Dutt returned to Calcutta, they were joined by Lalmohan Ghose[3] and Anandamohan Bose.[4] All of these men seemed to have come under the influence of Dadabhai Naoroji and his efforts to start an all-Indian political organization. Naoroji was an older Parsi merchant who lived in London and acted as an informal ambassador for the nationalist cause for half a century.

Four of the students who later led the Congress (Mehta, Tyabji, Bonnerjee, and Manomohan Ghose) joined Naoroji when he founded the London Indian Society in 1865. That organization was soon succeeded by the East India Association. In 1868, Naoroji urged the new association's members to coordinate political activity in different parts of India with a view to preparing "for that great end, a Parliament of Parliaments in India." Not only were the students in London exposed to Naoroji's early vision, but other future Congress leaders such as M. G. Ranade, K. T. Telang, and William Wedderburn joined the association's Bombay branch.[5] The importance for the Congress of these

[1] Tyabji, *Badruddin Tyabji*, p. 22.
[2] Surendranath Banerjea, *A Nation in Making: Being the Reminiscences of Fifty Years of Public Life* (Oxford, 1927), p. 10.
[3] Ibid., p. 15.
[4] H. C. Sarkar, *A Life of Ananda Mohan Bose* (Calcutta, 1910), p. 54.
[5] Seal, *The Emergence*, pp. 246–249.

London contacts and experience is suggested by the fact that eight of the nine men who were in London in the 1860s and early 1870s served as president in eleven of the first twenty sessions.[6] Three (Mehta, Bonnerjee, and Banerjea) were among the half-dozen most influential Congress leaders in those twenty years. After Hume left India, Mehta emerged as the dominant figure in the Congress.

All these men except Dadabhai returned to successful careers in India. Judging from their incomes, their London training was a major asset. Mehta, Tyabji, Bonnerjee, and the Ghose brothers established exceedingly prosperous law practices, earning as much as leading English barristers and more than almost any Indian lawyers. Anandamohan Bose also practiced law with profit but gradually turned his attention to education, founding City College with Surendranath Banerjea. Surendranath taught, ran a college, and edited the English-language *Bengalee* after his expulsion from the Indian Civil Service. And Romeshchandra Dutt remained in the Indian Civil Service until 1897 when he joined the Congress.

Both the choice of career and the success of these men were typical of the pre-1905 leadership. Eleven of the sixteen Indians who served as Congress presidents from 1885 to 1909 were successful lawyers. Two others, Surendranath Banerjea and Romeshchandra Dutt, had received legal training while qualifying for the I.C.S. Not only were most Congress leaders in the coastal cities of Bombay, Calcutta, and Madras lawyers, but their counterparts in inland cities, where English education and the modern bar had shorter traditions, were often lawyers also.[7] These leaders included Pandit Ajudhia Nath and Pandit Madan Mohan Malaviya in Allahabad, Bakshi Jaishi Ram and Lala Harkishan Lal in Lahore, and R. N. Mudholkar in Amroati. It was not necessary to be a lawyer to belong to the Congress "inner circle."[8] A

---

[6] Manomohan Ghose was the one who did not. Four of the other nine sessions were presided over by Englishmen. The five Indian presidents who had not studied in London were R. M. Sayani, N. G. Chandavarkar, and D. E. Wacha of Bombay and Ananda Charlu and C. Sankaran Nair of Madras.

[7] The published *Reports* of the annual Congress contain lists of all delegates, with caste or religion, occupation, and place of residence.

[8] The "inner circle" was an informal group, consisting of the leaders of local political associations who corresponded with each other, selected the president each year, and made other decisions which the annual Reception Committee, Subjects Committee, and Congress session usually ratified.

group of journalists, educators, and businessmen also participated in making final policy. These men included D. E. Wacha (Bombay), G. K. Gokhale (Poona), Ganga Prasad Varma (Lucknow), Surendranath Banerjea and J. Ghosal (Calcutta), G. Subramania Iyer (Madras), and Dadabhai Naoroji (London). However, they were outnumbered by the lawyers.

The dominance of lawyers is evident when a broader index of leadership is used. Taking the 86 Congressmen who spoke five or more times or who were appointed to three or more *ad hoc* Congress committees from 1885 to 1914, 60 were in the legal profession.[9] Of the total number of delegates in these years, over one-third were lawyers.

While most Congress leaders were lawyers, their fathers usually had not been. An analysis of the paternal occupations of the thirty leaders for whom information was found (and this thirty includes almost all of the "inner circle"), only the fathers of W. C. Bonnerjee, Bipinchandra Pal, G. Subramania Iyer, S. Subramania Iyer, and Sachchidananda Sinha were in the legal profession. It was more usual for a Congressman's father to have held an administrative post under the British government or in a princely state. This category included the fathers of P. Ananda Charlu and C. Sankaran Nair in Madras; Ananda Mohan Bose, Aswinikumar Dutt, Norendranath Sen, and Manomohan and Lalmohan Ghose in Bengal; Sachchidananda Sinha (whose father had careers in both law and government) in Bihar; Pandit Ajudhia Nath and Pandit Bishan Narayan Dar in the North-Western Provinces and Oudh; Lala Harkishan Lal in the Punjab; R. N. Mudholkar in the Central Provinces; and G. K. Gokhale, M. G. Ranade, and B. G. Tilak in Bombay. In most instances their positions had been minor ones, such as clerk, *sheristadar, mamlatdar, khot,* or *tehsildar*. In the majority of cases, sons earned incomes which far exceeded those their fathers had earned in government service. This was most often true for Congress lawyers and judges.[10]

[9] This number was computed from lists of Congress participants in Annie Besant's *How India Wrought for Freedom*. It includes two Englishmen, at least two ex-lawyers, a "law agent," and a retired judge. It does not include Surendranath Banerjea and Romeshchandra Dutt.

[10] Strictly speaking, no judges were members of the Congress since the government forbade judges to participate openly in politics. However, appointment to High Court judgeships was part of a successful lawyer's prospects. Former Congress presidents (Badruddin Tyabji, P. Ananda Charlu, and N. G. Chandavarkar) and other leaders were elevated to the High Court bench. And

Congress Leaders

Ranade's father earned Rs. 250 per month as private secretary to the Maharaja of Kolhapur while Ranade's own salary as High Court Justice was in the neighborhood of Rs. 4,000 per month.[11]

Gandhi's law income of over Rs. 6,000 per month in South Africa[12] must have been many times the amount his father earned as a minister in a small princely estate.[13] Lala Lajpat Rai's father never earned more than Rs. 35 per month as a Persian teacher in a government school, whereas Lajpat averaged more than Rs. 1,000 per month as a *vakil* (an Indian lawyer who is not a barrister or solicitor) in Hissar between the ages of twenty-two and twenty-eight, before he joined the Chief Court bar at Lahore.[14]

At least a few Congress leaders earned less than their fathers. Generally, these were men who did not practice law. Bipinchandra Pal, who had to sell the modest zamindari estate he had inherited, earned only Rs. 150 per month in 1890 as librarian and secretary of the Calcutta Public Library.[15] A few men voluntarily limited their incomes. G. K. Gokhale and B. G. Tilak pledged themselves to salaries of Rs. 40 from the Deccan Education Society which they ran on Jesuitical lines.[16] Lajpat Rai eventually gave up most of his lucrative legal practice to work for national causes. However, these men were exceptions. The average pre-1910 Congress leader rose to heights in his profession which had been out of reach for his father.[17]

Probably all the Congress leaders who had successful profes-

Ranade was active in Congress affairs from behind the scenes while serving as High Court judge.

[11] Ranade rose to the High Court through government service, not through the legal profession. Ramabai Ranade, *Ranade: His Wife's Reminiscences* (Delhi, 1963), p. 42.

[12] Louis Fischer, *The Life of Mahatma Gandhi* (New York, 1962), p. 67.

[13] Gandhi was not a Congress leader before 1910, although he had attended Congress meetings and was well known for his South African activities.

[14] *Lajpat Rai: Autobiographical Writings*, ed. by Vijaya Chandra Joshi (Delhi, 1965), pp. 15–16 and 42.

[15] Bipin Chandra Pal, *Memories of My Life and Times (1886–1900)* (Calcutta, 1951), pp. 97 and 111.

[16] Stanley A. Wolpert, *Tilak and Gokhale: Revolution and Reform in the Making of Modern India* (Berkeley, 1962), p. 29.

[17] Among well-to-do fathers were those of Badruddin Tyabji, D. E. Wacha, and Kashinath Telang (Bombay merchants); of Pandit Ajudhia Nath (administrator and then merchant); of Norendranath Sen and Anandmohan Bose (administrators); of Pandit Bishan Narayan Dar and Sachchidananda Sinha (administrators and lawyers); and of Surendranath Banerjea (doctor).

sional careers received help from Englishmen at important stages in their academic and occupational development. S. Subramania Iyer studied English under William Williams, the principal of the New Zilla School, who had him learn grammar by analyzing the writings and speeches of famous parliamentary figures. When Iyer was seventeen years old, an English district official gave him a job in the Collectorate and allowed him frequent leave to study for the bar.[18]

C. Sankaran Nair developed a series of close relationships with his teachers in Cannanore, Calicut, and Madras. For almost fifty years, Nair "always had free access" to the house of Colin MacIsaac's widow in Edinburgh. It seems that both in school and at the bar, his English seniors took a particular interest in him, perhaps in part because he was a Malayalum-speaking Nair entering a world dominated by Tamil and Telegu Brahmans. During his apprenticeship with Horatio Shepherd, a future High Court judge, they used to read together the latest books from England.[19]

It is evident from the biographies of Indians born in the 1840s, as most early Congress leaders had been, that the ratio of English teachers to students in the schools was high and that teachers took a personal interest in the development of their better students. They voted these students scholarships, entertained them in their homes, advised them about their careers, and helped them go to England or the local university for further study.

English kindnesses did not stop with college, although they seem to have diminished considerably as Indians moved nearer to the point of direct competition with Englishmen. Many nationalists who went to London in the nineteenth century, before the number of Indians in England was large and before English-speaking Indians ceased to be a novelty, boarded with English families, continued to learn the ways of their rulers, and returned with positive feelings about the English as individuals. Romeshchandra Dutt, Surendranath Banerjea, Pherozeshah Mehta, and Gandhi are examples.

Whether they completed their schooling in England or in India, Indians graduating in the 1860s and 1870s were equipping themselves to move into professions still manned by Europeans. And part of their success depended upon having learned how to

---

[18] Anon., *Heroes of the Hour: Mahatma Gandhi, Tilak Maharaj, Sir Subramanya Iyer* (Madras, n. d. [1918?]), p. 221.

[19] K.P.S. Menon, *C. Sankaran Nair* (Delhi, 1967), pp. 13–17.

win the confidence, and how not to antagonize, European teachers, lawyers, and administrators. At least a minority of Englishmen in the legal profession, as in the schools, were willing to assist promising Indians. Possibly that assistance was often contingent on how English a young man's bearing and accent were. However, while this might explain why English lawyers did accept W. C. Bonnerjee,[20] Bhupendranath Basu,[21] and C. Sankaran Nair[22] as apprentices, it would not account for the apprenticeships of less anglicized men such as S. Ramaswami Mudaliar.[23]

Gaining access to the highest positions in the bar was a lonely and arduous process for most men who made it, with or without English help. Most Indians did not make it. The majority of those who enrolled in law classes either dropped out or failed the exams, and many others who passed did not find employment in the major cities and had to look for work in the mofussil (the districts outside the major metropolitan areas). Legal education and apprenticeship suffered from lack of system. Few English professors of law seem to have given the close attention to the education of their students which teachers in the schools gave. Law college students found that their courses were only marginally related to their examinations or future work. P. S. Sivaswami Iyer and V. Krishnaswami Iyer, subsequently prominent Congress lawyers, used to sign the register for their law class at Presidency College, Madras, and then spent their class time at the beach.[24] K. N. Katju confirmed that many students did not attend classes or read the assigned texts. He wrote that while preparing to take the High Court Pleader's exam in 1906, "everyone used cribs and aids to scramble through no matter how poor his grounding in legal principles or how meagre his reading of those classics."[25] Law classes were crowded, teachers were poorly

[20] Sadhona Bonnerjee, *Life of W. C. Bonnerjee: First President of the Indian National Congress* (Calcutta, n. d. [1944?], p. 10.

[21] *Who's Who In India* (Lucknow, 1911), Part VIII, p. 121.

[22] Menon, *C. Sankaran Nair*, p. 17.

[23] G. Paramaswaran Pillai, *Representative Indians*, 2nd ed. (London, 1902), p. 210.

[24] K. A. Nilakanta Sastri (ed.), *A Great Liberal: Speeches and Writings of Sir P. S. Sivaswami Aiyar* (Madras, 1965), p. 227.

[25] Samuel Schmitthener, "A Sketch of the Development of the Legal Profession in India," *Law and Society Review*, Vol. III, Nos. 2 and 3 (Nov. 1968–Feb. 1969), pp. 363–364. Many of the references and arguments in this analysis of the legal profession were suggested by Schmitthener's article.

paid; sometimes young English lawyers were appointed to teach until they could find a private practice, and some law classes were operated chiefly for profit.[26]

After graduation, the more successful law students usually entered an apprenticeship in the High Court which was also likely to be unsupervised and unstructured, regardless of whether they apprenticed with an English or Indian lawyer. Apprentices attended court and observed the performances of the best known lawyers. Judging by the frequent references in memoirs and biographies, the High Court lawyers had a keen appreciation of the verbal aptitudes of their colleagues. This was reflected in speeches at the annual Congress sessions, for which some men spent weeks preparing, knowing that delegates valued highly a ringing speech. Apart from attending cases in court, apprentices tried to make themselves useful by taking notes and preparing briefs for their lawyers. In general, though, apprentices were ignored and their education was largely a matter of self-help.[27] It may be that the haphazard and unprofessional character of nineteenth-century legal training in India contributed to the early Congress's failure to develop businesslike procedures and a permanent organization.[28]

Indian efforts to break the English monopoly of the highest positions in the bar took three forms. First, Indians qualified themselves as barristers and tried to attract clients who traditionally took their cases to English barristers. Pherozeshah Mehta made one of the earliest attempts in Bombay. He soon discovered that in spite of his London education, he was unable to obtain many briefs.

> The entire practice was more or less concentrated in the hands of a few eminent counsel, such as Anstey, Scoble, Green, Latham, White, Mariott and one or two others. It was a very difficult thing either to dislodge them from their position, or even to carry away a few crumbs from their richly-laden table. . . . The litigant public hung upon [these counsel], and took no notice of the knot of hapless juniors hungrily looking

[26] Ibid.
[27] See Sastri (ed.), *A Great Liberal*, pp. 228–229.
[28] However, the nineteenth-century Indian bar was not unique in its lack of professionalism. See Robert H. Wiebe, *The Search for Order, 1877–1920* (New York, 1967), pp. 116–117, on the late professionalization of the American bar.

for briefs.... There were hardly any firms of Indian attorneys to give the young men a lift in the profession. A deal of patronage rested in the hands of managing clerks, whose smile was to be courted....[29]

Mehta complained publicly in 1873 that Indian barristers were not receiving a fair share of the legal business. The Bar Association of Bombay responded by demanding an explanation from Pherozeshah for this "breach of professional etiquette." Eventually he gave up hope of finding sufficient work in the High Court and instead concentrated his practice in the mofussil, where he prospered. Badruddin Tyabji, the third Congress president, was more fortunate in finding work in the Bombay High Court after he returned from England, largely because his brother had already staked out a large practice as solicitor. Tyabji's cases came mostly from Indians. He found that the English lawyers did not like having Indian rivals and that English solicitors gave "all the work of the Government, the Municipality, public works, railways, post offices, telegraphs and the great mercantile firms" to English barristers.[30] Even with friendly Indian solicitors and vakils who were willing to send clients to Indian barristers, it took years to overcome a widespread assumption among Indians that even a London-trained Indian was less likely than an Englishman to win in the High Courts.[31] However, by the 1880s, Indian barristers were making deep inroads into the practice of Englishmen.

The second direction of Indian efforts was toward alteration of the rules restricting practice before the High Courts. High Court vakils fought for the right to appear without a barrister on the Original Side.[32] Victory came first in the 1870s in Madras where vakils formed their own association to press for changes in the rules. The English barristers fought back and were supported by Judge Bittleson, a former barrister, who said he could not support new regulations which would "take the bread out of the mouth of a Christian and put it in the mouth of a pagan." Eventually, the Vakils' Association, applying pressure with arguments and a vote

---

[29] H. P. Mody, *Sir Pherozeshah Mehta* (Bombay, 1921), I, 27–28, 33, and 37.
[30] Tyabji, *Badruddin Tyabji*, pp. 28–29.
[31] M. C. Setalvad, *Bhulabhai Desai* (New Delhi, 1968), p. 11.
[32] The High Court had an Original and an Appellate Side. It was the more lucrative practice on the Original Side which English barristers hoped to preserve for themselves.

not to act as junior counsel to any European barrister, persuaded the High Court justices to equalize the vakils' status.[33] The Calcutta High Court vakils, under the leadership of Rash Behari Ghose, soon followed the example of the Madras Vakils' Association and won similar changes in the rules of the Calcutta High Court.[34]

The third issue which concerned Indian lawyers was the appointment of Englishmen to government legal offices. Again, it was the Madras vakils who led the way. They agitated not only to have Indians appointed to government legal offices but also to have vakils considered along with barristers for these offices. They won their campaign when V. Bhashyam Iyengar became the first vakil in India to be appointed an advocate-general.[35] Up to that time, Europeans in Madras had held the offices of advocate-general, government pleader, government solicitor, crown prosecutor, and administrator-general.[36] By 1900, a number of Indians in each of the four High Courts had been appointed to government legal offices and High Court judgeships.

Thus by the end of the century, Indian lawyers had broken European monopolies. Institutional changes in court procedures had been accomplished by acting in concert through Indian bar institutions. Moreover, Indian lawyers had combined informally to redistribute legal business by channeling clients to fellow Indians. At times, this cooperation had been highly effective as in the case of J.A.H. Branson. Branson was the Calcutta barrister mentioned in the previous chapter as having made offensive remarks about Indians during the Ilbert Bill controversy. The subsequent Indian boycott was so effective that Branson was forced to return to England.[37] On occasion, collective pressure was exerted on Indian lawyers as well. C. Sankaran Nair, a beneficiary of several English friendships, was the only member of the Madras Vakils' Association to vote against the resolution

[33] Menon, *C. Sankaran Nair*, pp. 17–18.

[34] Sastri (ed.), *A Great Liberal*, p. 213.

[35] Iyengar, unlike most of the lawyers mentioned in this section, was hostile to the Congress. C. P. Ramaswami Aiyar, *Biographical Vistas: Sketches of Some Eminent Indians* (Madras, 1966), p. 132.

[36] Sastri (ed.), *A Great Liberal*, p. 233.

[37] Schmitthener, "Sketch of the Development of the Legal Profession in India," p. 377.

calling on Indians not to assist English barristers, and in consequence his practice suffered for a while.[38]

Yet cooperation in the Indian bar was limited and fitful. In contrast to the common partnerships found between English lawyers, Indian partnerships were infrequent and unstable. The Indian bar did not provide many of the corporate experiences of teamwork and specialization which ordinarily characterize modern professions and which might have been utilized within the nationalist movement. One reason the legal profession was highly individualistic was the "chronic oversupply" and the consequent competition which limited "solidarity and the capacity for corporate action."[39] The great success of a small number of Indian lawyers and their prominence as Congress leaders should not obscure the intensity of the competition between Indian lawyers and the numbers of people who did not reach the top. Able men such as Gandhi[40] and C. R. Das[41] were total failures in their first years of law practice in the 1890s. Muhammad Ali Jinnah spent three years in Bombay, after his return from England, "without a single brief."[42] These three men ultimately built up successful practices. But the wealthy Indian lawyers represented only the peak of a broad-based pyramid.

The majority of Indian lawyers practiced in courts in the mofussil. The main concern of this discussion has been the High Court bar, to which most Congress leaders belonged. However, lawyers who were unable to qualify for or find a practice in the High and Chief Courts in the provincial capitals generally went to the mofussil. P. S. Sivaswami Iyer estimated that only 32 out of the 80 students in his Presidency College class in 1882–1883 passed the law examination, and of these 32, only about one-fifth went to the Madras High Court as apprentices.[43] Most of the others turned to mofussil practice. This practice could be highly

---

[38] Menon, *C. Sankaran Nair*, p. 18.

[39] Marc Galanter, "Introduction: The Study of the Indian Legal Profession," *Law and Society Review*, Vol. VIII, Nos. 2 and 3 (Nov. 1968–Feb. 1969), p. 208.

[40] Fischer, *The Life of Mahatma Gandhi*, p. 46.

[41] Hemendranath Das Gupta, *Deshbandhu Chittaranjan Das* (Delhi, 1960), p. 24.

[42] Matlubul Hasan Saiyed, *Mohammad Ali Jinnah (A Political Study)*, 2nd ed. (Lahore, 1953), pp. 5–7.

[43] Sastri (ed.), *A Great Liberal*, p. 228.

profitable for an able individual, such as Pherozeshah Mehta, with the proper qualifications and contacts. The prospects in law were so attractive, and the occupational alternatives so limited, that 2,898 or over 11 per cent of Indian university students in 1906–1907 were studying law.[44]

Little has been written about the mofussil bar. English officials believed that the success of lawyers in being elected to the provincial legislative councils, even when most of the voters were landholders, was partly due to the network of contacts lawyers established in the course of their practice which made canvassing easy. Perhaps only the nationalist press had a more extensive system of communications than the bar. It is likely that the bar association was the most visible and active voluntary association in many mofussil towns, and that it was the place were mofussil men were most likely to exchange political ideas. Many mofussil pleaders occasionally attended Congress sessions and together with school teachers represented the Congress's chief link to the mofussil.

The struggle to reach the top levels of the Raj's occupational structure in the mofussil and the larger cities had nationalist implications, especially when it brought down racial barriers. But most of all, the new professionals were helping themselves. Few used either their money or their professional expertise in the service of their country before 1905. Once they had reached the top, not surprisingly they made no attempt to dismantle or level the structure. The structure recognized and rewarded ability and diligence, and, as the very success of the new professionals demonstrated, presented no insurmountable barrier to Indian talent. For those men who wanted to join them, the new professionals recommended self-improvement, assiduous study ("never two words when one was enough, clearness of thought and diction"),[45] regular work habits, frequent exercise, and so on. Few of them were levelers. Despite English efforts to portray them as parvenus, most of them came from high-caste families. They had not been trying to bring down or displace other Indian elites as much as to

---

[44] Galanter, "Introduction," p. 213.
[45] These are the words used by Dadabhai Naoroji to describe what he learned from Watts' *Improvement of the Mind* while a student at Elphinstone Institution. R. P. Masani, *Dadabhai Naoroji* (Delhi, 1960), p. 11. The didactic, self-improving attitude is obvious in Surendranath Banerjea's *A Nation in Making*.

open the modern professions to proven Indian talent. Most of them were adding individual professional achievement and wealth to a previous, ascriptively based, high social status.

LIFE STYLES

Most Hindu Congress leaders were high caste. Among the 86 most active delegates[46] between 1885 and 1914, Brahmans outnumbered non-Brahman Hindus two to one (38 to 19). Among the 19 non-Brahmans, commercial, writer, and warrior castes predominated. All these men were part of a new status hierarchy composed for the most part of families with more than one generation in English administrative and professional occupations. The new hierarchy was parallel to the traditional social order, but many members near the top of the new hierarchy themselves occupied an indefinite place in traditional society. It may have been the indefiniteness of their position vis-à-vis the old order which helps explain their preoccupation with making money. Perhaps many of them felt they had lost respect in the eyes of traditional Hindus when they abandoned ancestral customs in favor of English education and habits. Perhaps they were trying to compensate for loss of status in the old order by achieving in the new.

In any case, the English-educated elite lived in a society in which some form of social hierarchy was taken for granted. Neither Indian custom nor Anglo-Indian social and official practices provided a serious challenge to assumptions that people were ranked in an order of lesser and higher beings. Englishmen treated Indians as inferior and excluded them not only from high office, but from their private clubs, barber shops, city parks, and railroad cars. It was not uncommon for members of Indian elites to treat their inferiors in similar fashion. Henry Nevinson, the *Manchester Guardian* correspondent, wrote about the visit he made with Madhusudhan Das, the Uriya leader, upon a Bengali deputy magistrate during a famine in Orissa. The Bengali magistrate "had evidently determined not to fall below the standard of European dignity. Consequently he received us with his legs on the long arms of his deck-chair—an attitude which, I suppose, he observed as customary among English officials when they re-

---

[46] That is, the delegates who were appointed to three major committees or who spoke five times.

ceive 'natives.' " Madhusudhan Das tried in vain to persuade the magistrate to listen to the widows outside the door who said their husbands had starved to death. After failing to arouse a sympathetic response from the magistrate about the villagers' problems, Madhu Sudhan and Henry Nevinson had no choice but to leave, "waving good-night to his boots" as they went.[47]

Before 1905, the desire to display status and wealth was part of the effort to become acceptable to English society and even to be superior to most of that society. Renunciation of wealth was not yet a common way of establishing superiority. Vishnu Narayan Mandlik, a leading Bombay lawyer and politician until his death in 1889, once hired a separate train to get to a court case he was working on, and Pherozeshah Mehta "engaged a special saloon for himself" on his way to the Calcutta Congress of 1901.[48] Occasionally a member of the English-educated elite appeared in public with such a large entourage that he might be mistaken for a raja. This happened to Ranade, who usually lived in modest style, when he was in Simla in 1886 with the Indian Finance Committee and took his family for walks each evening to enjoy the mountain air.

> There would be about fifteen of us, four or five servants and an equal number of jinricks or hand-rickshaws. Each jinrick was drawn by four coolies. That made about twenty to twenty-five coolies. . . . Quite often some Europeans would ask our peons, who were local persons, to which Rajah the party belonged.[49]

Lala Harkishan Lal, the English-trained lawyer and entrepreneur who was a major Congress leader in Lahore, flaunted his financial success. He lived in a palace and drove about in one of the two automobiles in Lahore. When not in his automobile, he traveled in a phaeton pulled by two pair of horses, knowing that his rivals used only one pair. He was determined not to be outdone or put down by either Indians or Englishmen. According to his son, when another traveler entered his railroad carriage and moved his luggage,

[47] Henry W. Nevinson, *The New Spirit in India* (London, 1908), pp. 148–149.
[48] M. K. Gandhi, *An Autobiography or the Story of My Experiments With Truth* (Ahmedabad, 1948), p. 273.
[49] Ranade, *Ranade*, pp. 111–112.

he would retaliate by throwing the intruder's luggage out of the window. His advice to his friends and members of his family was "My experience has been that the less polite you are on a journey, the more polite you will find others. The most effective way of reaching your destination in time, or in catching connections, or in obtaining assistance from the station staff, and due attention in the restaurant cars, is to put on the airs of a prize fighter, to carry a heavy stick, to pronounce your wants in a voice of authority; get your bearer to remove your shoes in the middle of the platform, and insist on your rights. Above all, right or wrong, never give in."[50]

Motilal Nehru's life style was only slightly less flamboyant. He lived in Anand Bhavan in the European section of Allahabad. A photograph taken about 1895 shows him wearing a European suit, high collar, and key chain. He furnished Anand Bhavan, the future Congress headquarters, with purchases made during several trips to Europe in 1899, 1900, 1905, and 1909.[51] The story that he sent his laundry to Paris[52] may have been apocryphal, but, by importing the first automobile to Allahabad, by employing European governesses, and by weighing his son, Jawaharlal, with bags of grain on his birthday and then distributing them to the poor, he seemed to be saying that he was not inferior to Indian rajas or successful Englishmen.[53] In the same fashion as Lala Harkishan Lal, he removed doubts about his right to be respected and obeyed by treating inferiors arrogantly. His personal servant recalled that at one dinner party as his guests were being seated, Motilal spotted a servant wiping a plate with his sleeve. Motilal was so furious that he "beat up the poor wretch so violently that the other servants ran for their lives and the guests—embarrassed and hungry—quietly retired."[54]

Only a handful of nationalists were wealthy enough to live as lavishly as Mandlik, Mehta, Harkishan Lal, and Motilal Nehru,

[50] K. L. Gauba, *The Rebel Minister: The Story of the Rise and Fall of Lala Harkishen Lal* (Lahore, 1938), pp. 27 and 29.

[51] B. R. Nanda, *The Nehrus: Motilal and Jawaharlal* (London, 1962), frontispiece and pp. 27–31.

[52] See S. J. Perelman, "No Starch in the Dhoti, S'il Vous Plait" [*The Road to Miltown or, Under the Spreading Atrophy*] (New York, 1957) for an imaginary exchange of letters between Motilal and his Parisian launderer.

[53] Nanda, *The Nehrus*, pp. 31, 40, and 42.

[54] Ibid., pp. 62–63.

but their life style was shared by Badruddin Tyabji, W. C. Bonnerjee, Romeshchandra Dutt, and other early Congress leaders. Less affluent Congressmen could not match the display of affluence of these leaders, but many also had large numbers of servants, large houses, and first-class travel accommodations, and in general they lived on a scale which set them apart from most other Indians. The luxurious life style and the elitist attitudes it encouraged were visible in the operations of the Congress itself. They inhibited efforts to build a popular base and became a source of dissatisfaction in and around the Congress.

Younger nationalists were most sensitive to elitism within the Congress. Gandhi, for example, who had himself recently lived in a "fine bungalow" outside Bombay and had "frequently felt a certain pride in being the only first class passenger in my compartment" on the train,[55] reacted to the behavior of the Congress leaders at the 1901 Calcutta session. He remarked that J. Ghosal, a Bengali Brahman merchant, zamindar, and member of the leadership's inner circle, had his bearer button his shirt.[56] Gandhi noticed that while some speakers were permitted to exceed their time by half an hour or more, he was cut off by the president's bell in less than five minutes.[57] He also commented on Gokhale's use of a horse-carriage to travel about Calcutta and his frequent trips to the India Club to play billiards.[58] This type of criticism was not limited to men who had lived outside India. The Maharashtrian terriorist, Damodar Chapekar, had only scorn for the behavior of another Congress leader, Manomohan Ghose "or some such other name which I do not remember." "Though a Hindu by religion he dresses like a European from top to toe and shaves his moustache like a eunuch. . . . He had a European to drive his carriage, and had to pay him a salary of Rs. 500 a month."[59] The Congress leaders' investment of energy and income in attempts to live like sahibs or maharajahs diverted their attention from the

[55] Quoted from *An Autobiography* by Erik H. Erikson, *Gandhi's Truth: On the Origins of Militant Nonviolence* (New York, 1969), p. 190.

[56] Gandhi's attitude toward this seems to have been ambiguous for he saw it as an opportunity to do service. He "volunteered to do the bearer's duty, and I loved to do it, as my regard for elders was always great." *An Autobiography*, p. 278.

[57] Ibid., p. 281.   [58] Ibid., pp. 283 and 287.

[59] "Autobiography of Damodar Hari Chapekar," in Govt. of Bombay, *Source Material of the Freedom Movement in India, 1885–1920* (Bombay, 1958), II, 983–984.

Congress and led Lala Lajpat Rai to remark that only Naoroji and Gokhale permitted the movement to interfere with their income and way of life.[60]

While complaints similar to those of Lajpat Rai, Gandhi, and Chapekar increased, especially after the turn of the century, many nationalists did not share these views. To earn as large an income as a *burra sahib*, to speak English as well as an Englishman, to have as good taste as the Victorians who shopped on Tottenham Court Road, was to demonstrate equality with Englishmen. This was important not only to that handful of men who assimilated British values and habits but also to a much larger number who could share these triumphs only vicariously. Until a substantial number of Indians demonstrated to themselves and their admirers individual achievements in law, government, education, and business equal to those of Europeans, personal careers would continue to absorb energies which otherwise might have been channeled into the Congress. Preoccupation with personal achievement may have been a necessary stage of nation-building because it contributed to Indian self-esteem and helped overcome the negative feelings about fellow Indians which English education and political subordination inculcated. Many people took pride in the election of Dadabhai Naoroji and M. M. Bhownaggree to Parliament in 1892 and 1895, respectively, in Ranjit Sinhji's exploits in English cricket matches, in the promotion of the first Indian, Romeshchandra Dutt, to the position of acting commissioner, and in the elevation of Indian lawyers to the High Courts. Nevertheless, as success in the I.C.S. examinations, industry, and letters became common, a new generation of nationalists began to question the value of individual achievements to the Congress cause. Although Aurobindo Ghose, Lajpat Rai, and other young men appealed for sacrifice and a selfless approach to politics, they had little impact on the Congress before 1905. The older generation remained firmly in control of the Congress and continued to enjoy large incomes.

Elite Attitudes

The efforts of Congress leaders to adapt to British Indian professional life did more than absorb their energies. It also led some

[60] Lajpat Rai, *Young India: An Interpretation and a History of the Nationalist Movement from Within* (New York, 1916), p. 146.

to identify with the institutions of the Raj in a way that isolated them from the bulk of the Indian population. Surendranath Banerjea was probably sincere when he told a group of English passengers on his ship en route to the 1894 Madras Congress that "we have everything to lose, nothing to gain by the severance of our connection with England. We owe whatever position or prestige we have acquired to our English education and culture. If you were to leave the country, our English education and culture would be at a discount. We are not particularly anxious to commit political suicide."[61]

Not only would the advantages of English education be lost, but probably also the physical security of the life and property of the English-educated elite. Anxiety about violence is difficult to document because to have discussed it publicly would have played into British hands. As it was, Englishmen enjoyed reminding Indians of the "anarchy" of the eighteenth and early nineteenth centuries. We may imagine the relish of Lord Welby, chairman of the Royal Commission on Indian Finances, suggesting to Dadabhai Naoroji in London that "the history of India is that the people have been continually slaughtering each other" and then proceeding to quote Sir Madhava Rao's alleged statement to Lord Roberts to the effect that if the British were removed from India, "it would be like loosing the bars of the cages of the Zoological Gardens and letting out the animals, that very soon they would all be dead except the tiger—the tiger was, I believe, the warlike people of Northern India."[62] Few nationalists would have agreed with this observation. However, there is enough evidence about the experiences and attitudes of early Congress leaders to indicate that some distrusted the volatility of the lower classes or at least had so little contact with them that they really did not know what to expect. A fear or apprehension of popular violence seems to have been common among at least a minority of early Congress leaders, just as efforts to use it were common among the extremists of the next generation.

The carnage of the 1857 Mutiny was part of the memory of the first-generation Congress leaders. Pandit Ajudhia Nath, Surendranath Banerjea, W. C. Bonnerjee, P. Ananda Charlu,

[61] Daniel Argov, *Moderates and Extremists in the Indian National Movement, 1883–1920* (Bombay, 1967), p. 56.

[62] Masani, *Dadabhai Naoroji*, pp. 126–127. Lord Roberts published that remark in his *Forty-One Years in India: From Subaltern to Commander-in-Chief* (London, 1897), II, 388–389.

Congress Leaders

Manomohan Ghose, Pherozeshah Mehta, and Mahadev Govind Ranade were born in the 1840s and were in schools run by Englishmen during or soon after the Mutiny. Whether any of them sympathized with the mutineers is not known. It is likely, though, that they were thoroughly exposed to a British view of the mutineers as cruel and rapacious barbarians.

It is interesting how little empathy is revealed in Dinshaw Wacha's account of the execution of two mutineers in Bombay city. Wacha was a Parsi, a close associate of Pherozeshah Mehta, and Congress general secretary after Hume's resignation. He remembered coming out of his school in Bombay with his classmates and finding two mutineers had been tied across the mouths of cannon in the usual military fashion.

> So far as my recollection goes, the European troops, Infantry and Artillery, took up a position by way of a square. The Indian regiments were located within the squares. There was a thrill of excitement all round and our pulse throbbed faster and faster till at a given word of command the cannons were fired and the pinioned criminals were blown. The burnt flesh sent an unpleasant odor which we all could easily sniff. All was over.[63]

Similarly, Surendranath Banerjea wrote about "the lower classes of the rural population" of Bengal as if they were not his own countrymen. He described his investigation of the sale of country liquor in Hughli district in 1887. He had heard reports that drunkenness was spreading among "the lower classes," although he had apparently never before visited the liquor shop "within a stone's throw of my house."

> I was not content with these reports. I visited a liquor shop at Haripal, and the sight I witnessed there was one that I shall never forget. I saw half a dozen men and women lying dead drunk on the floor of the shop. Another band of about a dozen men and women, all belonging to the lower classes, in varying stages of drunkenness, began dancing around me in wild delirious excitement. I apprehended violence and I slowly and cautiously retraced my steps from the shop....[64]

[63] Wacha, *Shells from the Sands of Bombay*, p. 67, quoted in Govt. of Bombay, *Source Material*, 1, 296.
[64] Banerjea, *A Nation in Making*, p. 87.

After this, Surendranath campaigned to reform the drinking habits of poor people. For the first time in twelve years of public life since returning from England, he lectured in Bengali rather than in English. Although his campaign was within his own Hughli district, he described the rural areas as if they were alien. "It was indeed hard, rough work—tramping along trackless areas, living in malarial countries, and eating strange food."[65] It may be that Surendranath's isolation from rural and lower-class life in his own province was different only in degree from a contemporary, wealthy Londoner's separation from the people of English slums and farms. Yet the isolation was genuine and it was recognized, especially after 1905, as a major hindrance to the making of a nation.

Other members of the Congress leadership had had unpleasant encounters with groups less privileged than themselves. Ranade was in the Poona procession in honor of Swami Dayananda in 1875 when it was attacked by *goondas* with sticks and stones at the instigation of orthodox Brahmans. In spite of the presence of the police, several members of the procession required hospitalization.[66]

Pherozeshah Mehta described his confrontation with anti-Parsi Muslim rioters in Bombay in 1874 in these terms:

> . . . our buggy was surrounded by the rioters shouting and yelling at us, as if the very sight of a Parsee was a sort of red flag to them and we were assailed with a perfect storm of missiles, amongst which stones and broken bricks were the most conspicuous . . . we were compelled to bring out a gun and two revolvers which we had taken care to provide ourselves with before starting. The effect was electric; like the veriest dastards that they really were, the very sight of the fire-arms sent them flying in all directions, clearly proving to us that only a bold front and a firm hand were required to quell this beggarly rabble and scum of the Mohamedan population.[67]

In both communal and grain riots, well-to-do Indians found they were often more vulnerable than Europeans to mass violence. During disturbances, they depended upon the Europeans

---

[65] Ibid., p. 90.
[66] James Kellock, *Mahadev Govind Ranade: Patriot and Social Servant* (Calcutta, 1926), p. 65, and Ranade, *Ranade*, pp. 54–56.
[67] Mody, *Mehta*, I, 84.

to protect them with police or *sepoys*. This was true of the communal riots in Bombay city in 1874 and 1893 and of the attacks on *bhadralok* by goondas and up-country men in Calcutta in 1907. It was also true of the grain riots in the Central Provinces in 1896. In the Nagpur grain riots, the house of a leading Congressman, Gangadhar Madho Chitnavis, was singled out by a mob for looting and was saved by the intervention of sepoys. The rioters chose Chitnavis's house apparently because they believed that, as a wealthy money-lender and landowner and president of the municipality, he could influence the price or supplies of grain.[68] Even when Europeans were the main targets of rioting, as in the 1897 Muslim riots in Calcutta and in the 1898 Bombay Muslim plague riots, the effect on Congress leaders must have been to reinforce the impression of lower-class volatility.

In normal times, the threat of violence to the new urban professionals was slight. And in the disturbances which accompanied plague, famine, and communal trouble, only a small section of the urban population was prone to violence and then most violence was directed against property rather than human life. Lower-class violence, then, was an episodic rather than a regular occurrence in city life. If its effect was to make some wealthy Indians anxious about their security, that anxiety was eased by having large numbers of servants and dependents who were sensitive to their pride in their new status. It is likely that in normal times the more successful among the new professional elite were treated at home and in their work with great respect and deference. Badruddin Tyabji's son wrote of an incident concerning the family full-time *dhobi* (washerman) which occurred after Badruddin had been appointed to the High Court bench and had moved into a house in Bombay behind that of Sir Lawrence Jenkins, the Chief Justice. It suggests how servants might adjust to their master's view of himself. What happened was that some of Sir Lawrence's clothes appeared with Badruddin's clean laundry. The *dhobi* was summoned for an explanation.

> Badruddin asked him what he had to say to the charge against him of washing the Chief Justice's clothes as well. With sparkling eyes, wild gesticulation and great indignation the *dhobi* protested: "I wash Cheap Sab's clothes? Not I! I don't wash

[68] Sir Andrew H. L. Fraser, *Among Indian Rajahs and Ryots* (London, 1911), p. 120.

his clothes. My son does! He does not know *dhobi's* work properly. He is learning. I tell him *khabardar*, dare not wash our Sab's clothes! You wash Cheap Sab's and when you have learnt your business you can wash our Sab's!"⁶⁹

This was closer to the usual experience with the urban lower classes than encounters with rioters. Yet occasional violence did intrude into the normally peaceful cities where Congress leaders lived and worked, and reminded at least some of them of their common interest with the British in the emerging social and political order and of their separation from sections of Indian society. It happened frequently enough so that British and Indian enemies of the Congress were able to play on fears among Western-educated Indians of sectional and lower-class violence. Lord Welby's remark about letting the animals out of the zoo has been mentioned; Sayyid Ahmad Khan taunted the Congress in a similar vein in his December 1887 speech. He suggested that if the Congress demands were met, Bengalis would rule India.

> Over all races, not only over Mahomedans but over Rajas of high position and the brave Rajputs who have not forgotten the swords of their ancestors, would be placed as ruler a Bengali who at sight of a table knife would crawl under a chair. (uproarious cheers and laughter).... Do you think that the Rajput and the fiery Pathan who are not afraid of being hanged or of encountering the swords of the police or the bayonets of the army, could remain in peace under the Bengalis? (Cheers).⁷⁰

The *Pioneer* of Allahabad publicized this speech, the Pioneer Press published it in pamphlet form, and Sir John Strachey quoted from it approvingly in 1888, adding "that the most essential of all things to be learnt about India" was that without England to keep the peace between conflicting peoples, "anarchy and bloodshed would spread themselves over the land."⁷¹

Sayyid Ahmad referred specifically to Bengalis, but the term "Bengali," if it had not become a code word, had come to stand for a member of the new professional elites in the eyes of Indians

---

⁶⁹ Tyabji, *Badruddin Tyabji*, pp. 330–331.

⁷⁰ Speech of 28 Dec. 1887, *Sir Syed Ahmed on the Present State of Indian Politics, Consisting of Speeches and Letters Reprinted from the 'Pioneer'* (Allahabad, 1888).

⁷¹ *India: Its Administration and Progress*, pp. 499–501.

Congress Leaders

and Englishmen who disliked the competitive society that was emerging. Those few Englishmen who publicly predicted or emphasized communal and interregional violence were accentuating real divisions in Indian society and were making their prophecies more likely to fulfill themselves. They were also contributing to the estrangement felt by some Western-educated Indians from their own society.

Social Reforms Among Hindu Elites

A more significant cause of the Congress leaders' isolation from Indian society was the conflict over social reform within their own families, castes, and ancestral villages. A sizeable minority of the 86 most active members were social reformers—men who advocated reforms in their own family's social practices. Probably a majority of the 86 members were "reformed" in the sense of having abandoned some of the major constraints or prescriptions concerning eating, marriage, ritual, or social intercourse. Congressmen who no longer observed the full range of family custom were subjected to a multitude of pressures from their own largely unreformed social groups. These pressures strained family unity and diverted some Congress leaders' energies and emotions from politics.

Many men who went to England to study faced excommunication by their caste, ostracism by sections of the larger society, and disapproval within their family. For Parsis, Muslims, Punjabis, Brahmos, and others who tolerated overseas travel, the return to India seems to have been relatively easy. There were also precautions a man might make to relieve his community's apprehensions. Ramaswami Mudaliar, for example, was said to have been received back in Madras and his home town of Salem "without a murmur" after campaigning in the 1885 general elections because he took a servant with him to cook his vegetarian meals.[72] But many men were less fortunate and, if not ostracized, were suspected of taking forbidden food and being corrupted by the fleshpots of Europe. When Surendranath Banerjea, Romeshchandra Dutt, and Behari Lal Gupta prepared to go to England to study for the I.C.S., they had to keep their plans secret, and

[72] Mudaliar was a vakil who served on the Public Service Commission and turned down an offer to be president of the Congress. Pillai, *Representative Indians*, pp. 214–216.

the latter two sneaked out of their houses at night to avoid being stopped.[73] Enough men returned from England with changed habits or views to give credence to orthodox fears. For example, Motilal Nehru's elder brother, Bansi Dhar, had carefully observed the commensal rituals of Kashmiri Brahmans until he went to London for Queen Victoria's Jubilee in 1897. But his trip to England "broke the shackles of a lifetime," and he returned with anglicized eating and other habits.[74]

A few men came back thoroughly alienated from Indian society. An extreme case was W. C. Bonnerjee who wrote home from England in 1865:

> I have discarded all ideas of caste, I have come to hate all the demoralizing practices of our countrymen and I write this letter an entirely altered man—altered in appearance, altered in costume, altered in language, altered in habits, altered in ways of thought—in short altered and altered for the better too, in everything, I should say in all things, which have contributed towards making our nation the (most) hateful of all others in the world.[75]

In later years, Bonnerjee and his family spent much of their time in London where he maintained a house. Three of his children converted to Christianity and most if not all of them spoke and thought in English rather than Bengali. W. C. Bonnerjee was referred to disparagingly as "a Sahib and a Christian" by other Bengalis.[76] Bonnerjee's anglicization was exceptional in its completeness. Other leaders, including Ranade and Pandit Madan Mohan Malaviya, remained Indian in large areas of their lives and were respected for it. Nevertheless, Bonnerjee's membership in the Congress high command was a measure of its character. Bonnerjee was the first man to be elected twice as Congress president in spite of the fact that his behavior closely resembled that of the rulers. His admiration for England and his doubts about Indian culture were shared in varying degrees by other Congress leaders. Surandranath Banerjea, Anandamohan Bose, Romesh-

---

[73] J. N. Gupta, *Life and Work of Romesh Chander Dutt* (London, 1911), p. 17.
[74] Nanda, *The Nehrus*, pp. 37–38.
[75] Bonnerjee, *Life of W. C. Bonnerjee*, pp. 14–15.
[76] Ibid., pp. 99ff.

chandra Dutt, and many others were also open to charges of "sahibism."

Society's disapproval of those Indians who had crossed the *kali paani* (black water or the ocean), married widows, or otherwise violated Hindu customs was registered in domestic as well as public life. This placed heavy burdens on reformed Hindus, for however anglicized they were, members of the new professional elite continued to value traditions of family loyalty and unity. It is difficult to find examples of parental disapproval or family division which did not cause distress. Sea voyages and new habits interfered with basic filial responsibilities. Performance of the *sradh* (Hindu death ceremonies) is a case in point. Conceivably the common desire to perform orthodox sradh for their parents was an effort to atone for the grief caused by their challenge to family traditions and to reestablish a measure of harmony with a society they had affronted. In any case, carrying out family rituals was sometimes difficult. Bipinchandra Pal found that when his father died, "as a Brahmo and an outcaste I could not even touch his dead body nor perform the last duties of a Hindu son to his father at the cremation ground. It was my step-mother who had to light his funeral pyre while I had to stand by."[77] Wealthier men than Pal were able to overcome some Brahman objections to participation in the sradh. W. C. Bonnerjee, for example, more of an apostate than Pal, spent "thousands of rupees" on his mother's sradh at Benares. "Brahmans from various provinces were invited to come, and lands were given away to them."[78] However, few men had such means for easing Brahman consciences.

The income and prestige of the new professionals won a certain tolerance from orthodox society for their reformed behavior. Still more freedom was gained when reformers broke away from their family traditions and formed new social groups within which marriages occurred, such as the Brahmo, Prarthana, and Arya Samajes, or new subcastes such as the Kashmiri Brahman Moti and Bishan Sabhas of Allahabad.[79] These groups were somewhat self-contained, with their own priests and social life. Even Ranade, who did not break with his caste, maintained two Brah-

[77] Pal, *Life and Times*, p. 2.
[78] Bonnerjee, *Life of W. C. Bonnerjee*, p. 101.
[79] Nanda, *The Nehrus*, p. 37.

man priests in his home to officiate for his acquaintances whose reformed lives had caused them to be boycotted.[80] However, none of these new social cells was able to give full protection from society's disapproval.

As a Brahmo, Bipinchandra Pal could not find any servants to work for him in his father's home town, nor could he enter his father's kitchen or dining room.[81] W. C. Bonnerjee could not live in his family's ancestral house because he knew that "the servants would refuse to wash any dishes that he used."[82] Motilal Ghose's marriage arrangement was endangered by rumors in his village that he and his brothers were meat-eaters. His neighbors assumed this because at the time Motilal was a Brahmo and because witnesses claimed a large bull had entered the Ghose house and had not come out.[83]

Chittaranjan Das's biographer says that he experienced "social obloquy and opprobium" and "the indignation of the whole country" because he arranged his widowed step-mother's remarriage. Das was a Brahmo, but he found himself in trouble with the Samaj on account of his "atheistic and bohemian views." Because of these views, the leading Brahmo ministers refused to officiate at his wedding in 1897.[84] Das was relatively well protected from society's pressures. The majority of reformed Hindus in the Congress did not have even the limited security of Brahmo Samaj community.

Most of the examples mentioned are from Bengal. However, the biographies of Ramabai Ranade, Lakshmi Tilak,[85] D. K. Karve,[86] and Gandhi,[87] among others,[88] confirm the impression that, in western and southern India also, reformed Hindus in the late nineteenth century lived under severe domestic and social strains. A brief review of one reformer's married life is useful because it suggests how reformers' domestic experiences impinged upon their public careers and perceptions. This review also in-

[80] Ranade, *Ranade*, p. 138. [81] Pal, *Life and Times*, pp. 368–369.
[82] Bonnerjee, *Life of W. C. Bonnerjee*, p. 100.
[83] Paramananda Dutt, *Memoirs of Moti Lal Ghose* (Calcutta, 1935), p. 21.
[84] Prithwis Chandra Ray, *Life and Times of C. R. Das: The Story of Bengal's Self-Expression* (London, 1925), pp. 18 and 25.
[85] Lakshmibai Tilak, *I Follow After: An Autobiography* (London, 1950).
[86] D. D. Karve (ed.), *The New Brahmans: Five Maharashtrian Families* (Berkeley, 1963).
[87] Gandhi, *An Autobiography*.
[88] See Suntharalingam, *Politics*, pp. 79ff., on south India.

dicates that reformers in and outside the Congress were highly vulnerable to society's mechanisms for enforcing conformity to its norms.

Mahadev Govind Ranade's wife, Ramabai, wrote a sensitive autobiography about her life with one of the most influential men in both the Congress and social reform movements. Ranade's father, like the fathers of most Congress leaders, was a member of the new Anglo-Indian bureaucratic-professional order. He rose to the rank of mamlatdar (revenue officer in charge of a subdistrict) under the Bombay government, and then became the private secretary of the Maharaja of Kolhapur. At a young age, Ranade surpassed his father in education, income, and professional rank, as many other Congress leaders had. Yet his father guided his life well into adulthood. After Ranade's first wife died when he was thirty-two, his father intercepted letters addressed to Ranade from Bombay, fearing that they would persuade him to marry a widow. Within a month, his father prevailed on Ranade to have an orthodox marriage, although according to his new wife, Ramabai, his failure to live up to his professed belief in widow remarriage brought "the ridicule and lasting calumny of society."[89]

On the night of their marriage, Ranade asked his eleven-year-old bride if she could read or write. Ramabai recalled that "I could do neither. So that very night I was given a slate and a pencil and the first lesson of syllables, 'Shriganeshayanamah.' It was my first chance to handle a slate and a pencil and my first glimpse of the alphabet."[90] Ramabai's education was tortuous. Ranade found that he did not have enough time for her lessons, so he engaged a tutor. Once Ranade suggested in Ramabai's presence that the tutor was making poor progress and the tutor replied that Ramabai was "an utter rustic. She does not understand a thing. All labour is wasted upon her." Ramabai then "burst into tears."[91]

Ramabai's difficulty was less her background or lack of desire than the other women in the Ranade household. Although some of them knew how to read Marathi, they resented Ramabai's ef-

[89] *Ranade*, p. 33.   [90] Ibid., p. 37.

[91] Ibid., p. 40. Lakshmi Tilak's inital attempt to read ended even more unhappily than Ramabai's. Lakshmi's husband, who was not a Congressman, became so angry at her incomprehension that he tore all the books he had bought into shreds and burned them. Tilak, *I Follow After*, p. 66.

forts to learn. And as Ramabai began to attend public meetings and to learn English from an English missionary lady, their hostility increased. When Ranade was out of the house, they mocked and harangued Ramabai, and they made her eat alone. Ramabai often wept. But she followed the advice given her by her father before her marriage and did not tell Ranade what was happening. Occasionally he noticed her melancholic, tear-streaked face and asked her what was wrong. Ramabai "would evade it all or say that I was thinking of my mother or my little brothers and sisters."[92]

Even when Ranade returned home during a scolding by the eldest woman in the household, he did not intervene. Nor did he reply when that woman turned on him and said

> People have given up all sense of honour these days. In the good old days, women did not even come into the presence of men, let alone talk to them. . . . Were you not ashamed to see your wife reading English in the presence of two thousand people? How did your *pugree* not fall off! In the old days, people valued their good name above all. Now things are all changed.

What is interesting and revealing are Ranade's words to Ramabai once they were alone. He admitted to Ramabai that the attack on her behavior was likely to continue for many days. But, he said,

> we must be equally well prepared. Let us make our minds to withstand it, with equal courage and patience. We shall give no room for adding to the fury. She cannot be blamed, because she talks according to the notions of her day. But please do not hurt her or answer back. I can quite understand how painful it must be for you to swallow everything without a word in your defense. But the endurance we acquired today will be a life-long asset to us. . . . So, do remember this—never say anything but never fail to do what you consider to be correct and proper.[93]

Change would come, in other words, but it would require patience, endurance, courage, understanding of the feelings of conservatives, and the preservation of existing social units such as

[92] *Ranade*, p. 49. [93] Ibid., pp. 88–90.

the family. Ranade did not want a confrontation or split with his family and society. He pressed his beliefs to a point just short of irrevocably dividing his family. With his income, Ranade could easily have made himself independent. However, that was not his way. He wanted to preserve Hindu society. He carried his recognition of the importance of Hindu corporateness into the Social Reform Conference where he tried to reconcile reform with the *Shastras*.

Ranade's approach to social reform anticipated Gandhi's in two respects. By not turning his back on Hindu customs and by not separating himself from orthodox Hindus, he was showing his respect for them even when he made clear his disagreement with them. Second, in his response to the pressures exerted on him by his family, he used a dogged, quiet, and spirited resistance which Gandhi applied to politics in the shape of satyagraha.

Ranade's path was a lonely one, requiring self-discipline and character of exceptional dimensions. The companiship of marriage helped alleviate some of the feeling of isolation. In fact, the reformers' efforts to educate their wives was partly intended to bring a new mutuality into married life and to relieve the loneliness that was often the reformer's lot. Yet relations between husband and wife in some of the most reformed homes of Victorian India remained distant and difficult. Companionship was limited by wide differences in age and education, by the absence of expectations of companionship, as well as by the jealousies and intrigues of relatives. In addition, some wives may have resented their husband's reformed behavior, for they often bore the brunt of the orthodox pressure from the family and neighbors.

Modernizing the marriage relationship often took several generations. Ramabai rarely seems to have discussed her feelings with Ranade. Direct communication was rare in the married lives of two other famous reformers, Maharshi Dhondo Keshav Karve[94] and Gandhi, who tried to educate their wives. Gandhi wrote that he gave reading and writing lessons to Kasturbai "against her will and that too at night. I dared not meet her in the presence of the elders, much less talk to her."[95] Moreover, in the early years of their marriage, his jealousy prevented him from accepting her freedom to come and go as she pleased. Eventually, Gandhi came

[94] See Karve (ed.), *The New Brahmans*, p. 78.
[95] Gandhi, *An Autobiography*, p. 24.

to respect and accept her independence. But intellectually they shared little, and Gandhi could write around 1925 that "it is likely that many of my doings have not her approval even today. We never discuss them, I see no good in discussing them."[96]

Reformers' marriages were thus subjected to heavy burdens. Not only did the couple stand against the censures of people with a more traditional view of family honor and propriety but the husband-wife relationship had to carry the combined weight of emotional tensions inherent between lover and lover, teacher and pupil, and sometimes even guardian and child. It was likely that the emancipation of women would come quickly only as girls entered school and received their education away from the domestic pressures of jealous women or paternal husbands.

Some of the most liberated wives of Congressmen were Bengali women who had attended Banga Mahila Vidyalaya, Benthune School, and Dacca Adult Female School. Bengali women were the first to participate in the Congress. Kadambini Ganguli, wife of Dwarkanath Ganguli, an active Congressman, spoke at the Bombay Congress of 1889, which she attended with Svarnakumari Debi, daughter of Debendranath Tagore.[97] During the partition agitation, Svarnakumari's daughter, Sarala Debi, who was married to Rambhuj Dutt, a Punjabi Congressman, emerged as a nationalist leader. However, these were exceptional cases, as was Ramabai Ranade. Most Congressmen's marriages seem to have been traditional, even though husbands were often "reformed."

FACTIONALISM

The foregoing discussion has suggested that participation in modern professional life, the common interest in English education, and the special, ambivalent relationship to the English rulers were creating a new set of bonds among the Western-educated classes. The Indian National Congress was a product of these bonds. However, the sense of community among the educated was limited by both the crowding and competition within the professions and the counterpull of traditional allegiances. Indians who entered the new professions remained members of families, castes, religious sects, and regions. Although the older

---

[96] Ibid., p. 340.
[97] Nirmal Sinha (comp. and ed.), *Freedom Movement in Bengal, 1818–1904. Who's Who* (Calcutta, 1968), pp. 417–418.

identities may have become less intense in many cases, they never disappeared. A man might become a lawyer and a Congress leader, but his social, professional, and political contacts were determined by whether he was a Hindu, a Muslim, or a Parsi, by whether or not he belonged to a reformed branch of his religious community, by what region he came from, and so on. Finally, cooperation within the new class was impeded by cultural habits affecting group interaction, by the novelty of voluntary forms of organization which required subordinating concern for traditional social boundaries and individual status to the interests of a broader society.

As a result of these factors, cooperation in late nineteenth-century Indian politics tended to be sporadic, both in and outside the Congress. In the next chapter we will examine the effect of these factors on the Congress organization. Here we wish to describe and suggest reasons for the divisiveness and diffuseness of Indian politics at the local level. Nationalist leaders who went to the all-India Congress sessions in December participated in local and provincial controversies, political associations, professional organizations, and cultural enterprises at various times during the rest of the year. Congressmen's involvement in bitter controversies in their home town limited their ability to work together on behalf of the national movement.

A major source of local strife was disagreement over matters of fundamental principle. Social reform issues, as much as any other, divided Congressmen from one another. In the Age of Consent Bill debate, for example, Congressmen took strong positions, supported with logical arguments, on opposite sides of the issue. One section of educated opinion had urged the English to pass legislation regulating the age of marriage and another section vehemently denied the right of a foreign government to interfere in the domestic affairs of Hindus. That disagreement was part of the more basic issue between those who felt that Indians should reform their society in preparation for independence and those who thought that attacks on existing social customs would divide Indians and hinder the struggle to obtain more political freedom.

A second source of division grew out of rivalry between administrative and political elites. In 1885, government was still the single largest employer of college graduates in most provinces, although the legal, educational, and journalism professions were attracting a growing share of graduates. The administrative and political elites overlapped substantially because they were recruited from the same castes and often from the same families. Yet members of the administrative elite viewed themselves as bringing the British rulers and the common people closer together. They resented the tendency of new political elites to polarize public issues around questions of racial or national interest, to recruit support from less educated groups, and to usurp their claim to represent the interests of the common people. "The administrative elite regarded its younger rivals as upstarts, or in the words of Seshia Sastri 'penniless patriots,' whose extravagant rhetoric and radical posturing betrayed their youthfulness, inexperience in public affairs, and an impatient idealism."[98] Individual members of the administrative elite families joined Congress leaders in social reform movements and occasionally in the Congress itself, but cooperation between the two groups was strained.

It is much less easy to explain the splintering into rival factions of like-minded men within the same profession and the same political organizations. Some factions formed without significant disagreements over principles. Other factions, when they argued about principles, seemed actually to be engaged in a more personal competition motivated by jealousy and concern for individual prestige.

It has been suggested that a small group or faction, within and sometimes in opposition to the larger group or organization, eased the transition from traditional to modern forms of cooperative enterprise, that it helped bridge the gap between membership in the small social unit such as the family, caste, and patron-client network, and membership in a larger, less personal society[99] The political faction often resembled the family in its limited membership, the intensity of its members' loyalty to the group, and the domination of that group by a single individual or patron. On the other hand, membership in a faction was voluntary and often temporary, and it frequently included persons from different castes. Although factions were generally restricted to men who shared views on such matters as social reform and political tactics, a common ideology was almost never the sole

[98] Suntharalingam, *Politics*, p. 97.
[99] On the functions of political factions, see Myron Weiner, *Party Politics in India: The Development of a Multi-Party System* (Princeton, 1957), pp. 234ff.

basis of such a group. There were far more factions than significant differences in ideology. Groups formed around strong personalities. The personal rivalries and jealousies of the faction leader, more often than ideology or economic interest, determined conflict between factions. Because a faction resembled traditional social units in both scale and attachment to a leader, faction membership was often the transitional route to participation in modern political parties.

Probably no province had more extensive factionalism in the organizations to which Congressmen belonged than the Punjab. The Lahore Brahmo Samaj split into three factions, the Arya Samaj divided into separate branches (the Mahatma and College branches), each with its own officers and schools. The Indian Association of Lahore, the main political association in the province, was badly divided. Perhaps the failure of the Congress to take root in the Punjab before 1905 was more the result of the contentiousness of public controversy than of indifference to the Congress itself. Many nationalists seemed to feel that cooperation in local politics would have been impossible in view of rancor over both political and religious issues.[100]

Congress leaders were often the leaders of rival factions. Lala Harkishan Lal feuded with Arya Samajists in the Punjab, whose leader was another prominent nationalist, Lala Lajpat Rai. In Poona, Tilak and Gokhale struggled for control over the Deccan Education Society and the Sarvajanik Sabha although their differences rested in part on philosophical disagreements. In Calcutta, Motilal Ghose often feuded with Surendranath Banerjea and his supporters (Krishnakumar Mitra and Pandit Kaliprasanna Kavyavisharad). The bad feeling between Motilal Ghose and Surendranath was so great in 1896 that some doubted if the Congress could be held in Calcutta that year.[101] In 1898–1899, the rivalry erupted in three defamation suits between Pandit Kaliprasanna and Motilal.[102]

Certain Congressmen seemed to relish conflict. Motilal was such a person. His personality was colorful and controversial, but he seemed incapable of lasting cooperation with other nationalists. An account of Motilal's effort to be elected to the Calcutta

[100] See *Lajpat Rai: Autobiographical Writings* for a frank discussion of factionalism in the Punjab.
[101] Dutt, *Memoirs of Moti Lal Ghose*, p. 86.
[102] Ibid., p. 115.

Municipal Corporation in 1892 has been preserved, and it suggests the intensity that intragroup rivalry could reach. The group in this case was the Kayasths of Ward No. 1 in north Calcutta. Eight candidates had started the campaign, but by election day the field had been reduced to three: a wealthy zamindar (Pasupatinath Bose), a young Congress lawyer (Bhupendranath Basu), and a Congress editor (Motilal). The following description of the campaign, probably by Motilal himself, appeared in the *Amrita Bazar Patrika* shortly before the election.

> The three candidates who have presented themselves this year (from Ward No. 1) for the honour of a seat on the Municipal Board are all Kayasthas. Now these Kayasthas like others marry and give in marriage and thus form relationships. In Ward No. 1, therefore, the Kayasthas, as a rule are related to each other.
>
> When therefore (would-be) Commissioner No. 1 appears in the field his affectionate father-in-law as a matter of fact canvasses for him. The spectacle fires the relations of other candidates with emulation and they thus plunge themselves into the vortex of the whirlpool. The voters and candidates being all Kayasthas are related to each other. The voter who is the uncle-in-law of a candidate is the grand-father of another, and thus the candidates find themselves in the midst of voters, who are generally their relatives.
>
> The usual rule for candidates in all countries is to base their appeals to voters upon their own merits. In Ward No. 1 it is based, with very few honourable exceptions upon relationship. One candidate pleads to a voter:—"Is not my brother your son-in-law?" and thus secures the support of a voter. This voter is immediately after beseiged by another candidate, who tries to convince him that the brother of a son-in-law can never have so much claim as the brother of a maternal uncle, which relation he bears to him. When such is the way the votes are canvassed for, it is no wonder that the candidates and voters should all lose their proper senses.
>
> It was very calm in the beginning. At that time the candidates met and shook hands like friends. This was succeeded by squibs, lampoons and satires. And now it is foul abuse—abuse which fouls even the mouth of a fisherwoman.

> It was very dull in the very beginning, when the candidates and their friends bowed to each other whenever they met, formally and politely. It was very exciting and exhilirating when lampoons and satires were hurled upon their rivals. Now that abuses have been resorted to the matter has become more nauseating than putrid human flesh.[103]

The campaigning and canvassing became increasingly tense and unfriendly. The day before the election, Pasupatinath Bose had his English lawyer apply for a ruling from the High Court to remove Motilal's name from the ballot on the grounds that Motilal's family, but not Motilal individually, was the registered rate-payer. Justice Trevelyan rejected the application. On election day, goondas appeared to intimidate voters. "Voters were physically restrained from voting." Mounted police were finally called to restore order.[104]

Enjoyment of strife, touchy independence, eccentric personality—these and other characteristics contributed to what seems to have been an unusually rapid fragmentation of organizations and partnerships. Many nationalists responded to the divisiveness of public life by avoiding strong commitment to political organization. Given a choice between abstention and the messiness of factional politics, many men preferred the former. As a result, politics were atomized as well as fractious.

In conclusion, people entered the new organizations of nineteenth-century India with differing views of their rights and responsibilities as individuals in group enterprise. There was seldom general agreement on the degree of subordination required to make an organization function. Men who had recently established a measure of freedom in relation to their families, elders, and castes were reluctant to surrender any of that freedom to a different group. That was as true for their participation in the Congress as it was for their activities in local organizations.

[103] Ibid., p. 81.   [104] Ibid., p. 82.

PART II

Chapter Three

THE FIRST YEARS OF THE CONGRESS AND ALLAN OCTAVIAN HUME

INTRODUCTION

The Indians who helped found the Indian National Congress relied heavily upon Allan Octavian Hume for guidance. Hume had a knowledge of the British bureaucratic mind and British politics which seemed invaluable to men who hoped to persuade their rulers of the reasonableness of their demands rather than to mobilize their countrymen for political activism. Moreover, there is reason to believe that many Congress members felt easier with Hume at the helm than if the leadership had been vested more exclusively with the anglicized Bengalis and Parsis who were his chief collaborators. The early Congress lacked well-defined procedures and it therefore needed a leader with clear vision and a forceful personality. The autocracy of an Englishman was more palatable than that of W. C. Bonnerjee and Pherozeshah Mehta in the early years. Many Congressmen were accustomed to depending upon Englishmen in areas or stages of their lives. Theoretically, the Congress aimed at lessening that dependence. In the actual working of the Congress, the annual reappointment of Hume as the general secretary was one of many indications that Congress leaders were not inclined to separate themselves culturally or racially from Englishmen.

The purpose of Congress politics was the modest goal of enlarging Indian participation in government decision-making and administration, rather than reshaping political institutions in a way which would express India's essential being or national character. Consequently, Congress political emotions were not deep. Early Congress sessions produced little evidence of passionate love of country or revulsion against foreign people or ways. A reading of Congress proceedings suggests an indifference to the question of what was and was not culturally Indian.

The previous chapter argued that the Indians who led the Congress occupied positions of ambiguity in Indian society. Their material success in the new occupations, their dependence upon the English language and political idiom, and their urbanized lives meant that in many respects they were closer to their foreign rulers than to the majority of their own countrymen, despite their intellectual recognition of a conflict between Indian and British interests. It was in the debates over the purposes and organization of the Congress that anomolies in the position of Congress leaders became clear. This and the following two chapters analyze the ways in which those anomalies affected the functioning of the Congress.

Hume's leadership contributed to nationalist understanding of the inadequacies of the early Congress movement. It did so in two ways. First, Hume's vision of Congress goals was more comprehensive and was drawn from a more advanced stage of historical evolution than that of his fellow leaders. While Hume tried to expand the social bases of the Congress to include all sections of the Indian nation by making a special effort to win Muslim and peasant support for the Congress in the late 1880s, his fellow leaders gave him little more than rhetorical help. Instead of addressing the specific interests of Muslims and peasants, other Congress leaders tended to concentrate on gaining increased government employment and representation in consultive bodies —objectives which would most directly benefit their own economic and social groups or religious community. Partly as a result of Hume's activities, a growing number of men outside the leadership came to see the Congress as insufficiently selfless. Second, and somewhat ironically, Hume's attempts to implement his progressive vision were so highhanded, his treatment of his fellow Congress supporters so imperious and condescending, that his period of leadership persuaded Congress members that the Congress ought to be run by Indians themselves.

Within a decade of the founding of the Congress, Hume had returned to England and many educated men had realized that neither the goals nor the organization of the Congress were adequately serving the cause of Indian nationalism. There was little agreement, however, on what changes should be made. Some men wanted to expand the social base of the Congress to include people without English education; others wished to seek support from socially conservative Hindus by ending Congress ties with the Social Reform Conference; others tried to increase people's sense of participation by writing a democratic constitution for the Congress, while still others wished to shift the main Congress emphasis from political participation to questions of poverty and industrialization. Perhaps the greatest disagreement arose over the efforts of extremists and cultural nationalists to redefine Congress purposes and procedures in ways that would move achievement of independence and identification with Indian culture to the heart of Congress activities. However, these men stopped short of forcing a break with the original Congress leaders until the Surat split of 1907. Many extremists remained in the Congress, at least nominally, and tried to persuade the organization to adopt more democratic procedures. Rather than divide the Congress, they allowed it to continue as it had begun: a noble idea which took concrete form for several days at the end of each calendar year before dispersing until the next annual meeting.

This and the following two chapters aim to explain the conflicts between men with varying conceptions of Congress purposes during its first years. They concentrate on the organization of the Congress, for the debates over the Congress's constitution and organizational activities reflect the deeper problems of Indian nation-building. If the failures of the early Congress seem to dominate this account, it should be remembered that both the Congress itself and its original goal of representative government did survive its painfully slow, early development. The disappointments and disagreements of the pre-World War I Congress were educational. The cautiousness of the founders of the Congress contributed to the eventual success of the movement in gaining independence along the lines advocated by its first members. Few other nationalist parties in the world survived as long as the Indian National Congress, and few others had to contend with such extreme linguistic or religious diversity.

Organizational Beginnings and Hume

In the Congress's first five years, hesitancy and uncertainty gave way to cautious optimism as attendance grew steadily, rising from 72 delegates in 1885 to almost two thousand in 1889. But almost from the beginning it was evident that the Congress was failing to win or keep sections of the population its English-speaking leaders had hoped would support it. The realization that the Congress rested on a narrow base contributed to the deep malaise which settled over the movement in the 1890s in the form of dispirited leadership, poor attendance, abstention of Muslims, internal division, a reluctance of its financial backers to pay for its activities in England and India, and a widespread indifference to the Congress organization and platform among nationalist-minded Indians in general. Its own leaders were beset with such severe doubts about the future of the Congress that they seriously considered discontinuing it. The third president, Badruddin Tyabji, suggested in 1888 that its sessions be suspended for five years.[1] Hume in 1891 said he felt the Congress "should not be held in India for some time to come." The next year Hume, who was still general secretary, suggested that the Congress be suspended until after the next English general election. He admitted that he had "almost begun to despair," and he left India to reside in England.[2] On a number of occasions during the next twelve years, leading Congressmen publicly raised the possibility of temporarily disbanding the Congress because of its failure to command the confidence of educated Indians.

Government officials also envisaged the Congress's disappearance or collapse. Lord Dufferin and his advisers considered suppressing it,[3] but after observing its early sessions, Dufferin dismissed it in 1888 as a "microscopic minority" and initiated proposals for enlarging the legislative councils which he thought would give Indian conservatives more prominence. Lord Hamilton, the secretary of state, wrote in 1900 that "there is little doubt that the Congress is losing its popularity and influence,"[4] and a year later he was contemplating its total collapse.[5] The governor-general was no less sanguine. Lord Curzon believed "that the Congress is tottering to its fall, and one of my greatest ambitions while in India is to assist it to a peaceful demise."[6] The reception given to Lord Curzon's partition of Bengal in 1905 showed that Curzon was confusing organizational weaknesses inside the Congress with the strength of nationalist sentiment in general. But nationalists would have agreed with Hamilton and Curzon that the Congress organization was divided and listless.

[1] Govt. of Bombay, *Source Material*, II, 81.
[2] Daniel Argov, *Moderates and Extremists in the Indian National Movement, 1883–1920* (Bombay, 1967), pp. 47–49.
[3] Martin, *New India*, pp. 328–329.
[4] Hamilton to Curzon, 22 Feb. 1900, MSS. Eur. C. 126/2.
[5] Hamilton to Curzon, 24 Jan. 1901, MSS. Eur. C. 126/3.
[6] Curzon to Hamilton, 18 Nov. 1900, MSS. Eur. D. 510/6.

First Years and Hume

The Congress clearly failed in its first two decades to express the intensity and range of nationalists aspirations. There was a wide discrepancy between the strength of the Congress organization and other measurements of nationalist feeling. For example, in the first twenty years in which the Congress developed but little, the circulation of Indian newspapers was doubling, with much of the new circulation going to militant nationalist papers such as *Kesari, Kal,* and *Bangavasi*. In the same period, the unemployment problem for college graduates grew more severe, and the two famines accentuated the appalling poverty of the rural lower classes. While these developments affected the Congress platform, they did not, apparently, increase Congress membership or political activity. Nor did the Congress provide an outlet for the new energy being given to patriotic cultural activities, such as religious revival, linguistic reform, nationalist theater, revival of martial traditions, or the creation of a nationalist historiography. In short, the Congress was static during a period when nationalist sentiments were spreading and deepening.

Hume's dominance in the Congress during its first decade was a major reason why many nationalists did not feel the Congress was an adequate embodiment of Indian aspirations. At first, there was general agreement between Hume's conception of the role of the Congress organization and that of many Indian leaders. As time went on, though, Hume retained so much of the initiative that many nationalists seemed to feel that the Congress was not theirs. The primary purpose of the Congress, as conceived by Hume, W. C. Bonnerjee, and its other founders, was as much organizational an anticolonial. The founders were impressed by the practical difficulties of building a cooperative movement among men who were strangers to one another. The March 1885 circular which announced the first Congress session stated that the Congress's first object would be "to enable all the most earnest labourers in the cause of national progress to become personally known to each other." Its authors were anxious that the delegates should actually "reside *together* for a week" so that they would get to know each other better than if they were "scattered about in dozens of private lodging houses all over the town."[7] When W. C. Bonnerjee explained the first objective of the Congress in his 1885 presidential address, he used words similar to

[7] Besant, *How India Wrought*, p. 4.

First Years and Hume

the announcement circular about "the promotion of personal intimacy and friendship," and then he said the second goal was "the eradication by direct friendly personal intercourse of all possible race, creed, or provincial prejudices amongst all lovers of our country. . . ."[8] The Congress founders, in stressing first the need for communication and friendship between provinces and religious groups, were tacitly recognizing the arduous task which lay ahead of the Congress before it could wrest concessions from the English.

The major stated external objective was to obtain "representative institutions" for India. The March circular said that the Congress would "form the germ of a Native Parliament and, if properly conducted," it would prove India's fitness for parliamentary institutions.[9] Accordingly, the Congress adopted procedures which resembled those of representative government. Each year, delegates from different parts of India were nominated and elected in what might be described, because they were informal and rarely contested, as mock elections; resolutions were drafted, debated, amended, and approved in closed meetings of an elected Subjects Committee at the annual session; and the resolutions and nomination of officers were finally moved, seconded, and voted on in the open session of the Congress itself. Hume, W. C. Bonnerjee, and others regarded these parliamentary forms as preparation for representative government, but the whole process had an air of artificiality and make-believe about it which invited scorn from Congress enemies. The Congress was a political party, not a parliament, and, more importantly, it was a party without a constitutional arena in which to compete for electoral support and political power. The absence of institutions through which Indians might gain significant political power meant that the early Congress was without the incentives a political party normally "provides to retain the support and loyalty of its memmers." It was not able to distribute patronage, pass or alter legislation, provide full-time party offices and organizational tasks, or create a sense of continuing political participation.[10] Only the constitutions of 1909 and 1919, combined with the post-World War leadership of Gandhi, brought those incentives. Yet, even though the Congress's democratic procedures were more symbolic

[8] Ibid., p. 7. [9] Ibid., pp. 3–4.
[10] These incentives are listed by Myron Weiner, *Party Building in a New Nation: The Indian National Congress* (Chicago, 1967), p. 8.

First Years and Hume

than substantive, they indicated a commitment both to representative institutions and to an accommodation of India's pluralism in a future Indian constitution. This commitment was enunciated clearly at the first session of the Congress in 1885, and it remained central in Congress thinking through the drafting of India's constitution after independence in 1947.

Hume, with W. C. Bonnerjee's help from the chair, guided the Congress through its first proto-parliamentary session in 1885, intervening to keep the proceedings moving, to clarify issues, and to find compromises when delegates disagreed on resolutions.[11] The first Congress made no formal arrangements for a permanent organization, apparently because it was understood that Hume would continue in 1886 as he had in 1885 to work for the nationalist cause. Hume followed up the Bombay meeting with a campaign to draw into the Congress those nationalists who had missed the first session. He arranged an alliance between Surendranath Banerjea's Indian Association and the landholders of the British Indian Association. These two Calcutta associations had recently been divided over the Bengal Tenancy Bill, and Hume's diplomacy meant that two important groups which had missed the first Congress would participate in the 1886 Congress at Calcutta.[12]

In the first few years, Hume acted as the catalyst and brought together men who previously were strangers or rivals. Other men, such as W. C. Bonnerjee or M. G. Ranade, might have performed this function, but, as a foreigner, Hume was not subject to the jealousies and rivalries which emerged when various Indians broached plans for an all-Indian body.[13] In addition, it was still thought—mistakenly as it turned out—that he possessed influence with the administration. This was a major qualification for leadership among men who hoped to gain their goals by reasoned appeals to authority and demonstration of their basic loyalty rather than by agitation or confrontation.

Hume also helped the Congress achieve an harmonious beginning by persuading delegates to avoid discussion of issues such as tenants' rights and to concentrate instead upon questions "in which we are . . . at one *versus* the administration."[14] This became a Congress rule which, although it was not always followed, removed much of the potential excitement and controversy from

---

[11] Martin, *New India*, pp. 305–306.   [12] Ibid., p. 314.
[13] Ibid., pp. 45ff.   [14] Seal *The Emergence*, p. 295.

Congress meetings. However, the absence of debate in the first years did not seem to detract much from nationalists' interest in the Congress. The very act of coming together to criticize the British for their racially exclusionary policies in matters such as jury trials, military volunteering, and civil service employment, for their refusal to conduct a Parliamentary inquiry into Indian affairs, and for the considerable expense of their war in Burma was sufficient to arouse widespread interest in the Congress.

In its early years, the Indian National Congress continued to be a loose affair without well-defined procedures or a written constitution. Apart from the Reception and Subjects Committees, which were selected each year to plan and run the annual meeting, its organization was skeletal, consisting of little more than the president, the general secretary (Hume until 1906) and joint general secretaries, and, beginning in 1887, the Congress standing committees in the major cities. As a result, the Congress was less an organization than an annual meeting, a group of demands directed toward the British, and, most importantly, an attitude of mind which held that Indian interests should prevail over British interests in the conduct of Indian affairs.

The casualness of Congress procedures may be seen in the selection of delegates. Almost anyone could have himself elected to the Congress in its early years, before the Reception Committees found ways of checking on the credentials of delegates. Some delegates were elected at public meetings of interested citizens, some were self-elected, others were chosen by the people's associations, bar associations, and the plethora of voluntary groups which came into existence in the 1870s and 1880s. Even opponents entered the Congress on occasion and made hostile remarks. In 1888, Raja Shiva Prasad, chief adviser to the Maharaja of Benaras (who disliked the Congress), startled the assembled delegates by rising and moving an amendment which would have called attention of the government to the political danger the Congress represented to the British Empire. The other delegates hissed and the president, George Yule, intervened to silence him.[15] Some years delegates were elected in order to achieve a different class or religious balance, as in 1899 when 289 of the 388 Lucknow delegates were Muslims. However, it is doubtful that many people believed that the high proportion of Muslim

[15] *Report of the 4th INC*, pp. xviii, 24, and 25.

or peasant delegates was a genuine measure of Muslim or peasant feelings about the Congress.

A minority of delegates probably attended because they were curious or because, as it was often alleged, they were paid. As a result, delegate lists give only a rough indication of what social groups supported the Congress. But they leave no doubt that most men who attended the Congress were distinguished from the majority of Indians by their educational and professional achievements, urban backgrounds, and high ritual and social status. Of the 13,839 delegates who attended the Congress from 1892 to 1909, 40 per cent were in the legal profession, and another 9 per cent were divided almost evenly between journalism, medicine, and teaching. Almost 40 per cent were Brahmans, although Brahmans represented less than 6 per cent of the total Indian population. And less than 7 per cent of the delegates were Muslim, despite special efforts to swell the proportion.[16] Roughly one of every five Indians was Muslim.

Regional variations in the distribution of castes among delegates corresponded generally to differences in the spread of English education. Where Brahmans had proportionately higher literacy in English than other castes, as in Madras and Maharashtra, they not only attended the Congress more frequently but dominated it and its supporting associations. In Bengal, where Kayasthas and Baidyas shared high literacy rates with Brahmans, they also contributed a major proportion of the members and leaders. In the Punjab, Brahmans were not well educated as a group and had little contact with the Congress. Instead, English-educated Agarwals, Aroras, and Khatris predominated. In the North-Western Provinces and Oudh, local and Kashmiri Brahmans provided leadership, with the major following coming from Kayasthas. In general, the Congress attracted Hindus who had found English education and the modern professions either an alternative or an additional source of position and prestige in a society which for the most part was still ascriptively hierarchical.

Congress conceptions of Indian political community usually did not envisage participation by people without education or property. When the electoral franchise was discussed, Congressmen usually assumed that educational and income qualifications would be continued. Participation by uneducated Indians in the

[16] Ghosh, *The Indian National Congress*, pp. 23–25.

Congress or in a system of representative government was scarcely an issue for most Congressmen. A much more pressing issue was the role of those Indians who were not literate in English but who could read their vernacular or who had other measures of elite status such as wealth or high caste. Less than 10 per cent of literate Indians were literate in English. The anglicized life style of Congress leaders and the need to communicate in English were, it is safe to assume, a deterrent to non-English speakers who might otherwise have supported a nationalist organization and who read the nationalist vernacular newspapers such as *Kesari* and *Bangavasi*.

From the beginning, Congressmen were uneasy about the narrowness of their constituency. Although that constituency was expected to grow with the spread of English education, immediate attempts were made to enhance the movement's popularity and to establish Congress identification with the interests of a wider group than the English-speaking classes. The attempts took different forms. The Subjects Committees arranged for occasional delegates to speak in their vernacular. The Reception Committee maximized the annual session's appeal as a *tamasha* or entertainment. The pandals were decorated with gay bunting, flags, and plants. Stalls were set up to sell refreshments and Indian-made goods, giving some sessions the atmosphere of a bazaar or rural fair. Sometimes patriotic songs were sung. At the 1901 Calcutta Congress, a choir sang Sarala Debi Ghosal's "Hindustan" with several hundred student volunteers joining in the chorus. The visiting delegates were an attraction in themselves with a seemingly endless variety of Indian and European clothes and hat or turban styles. An average of 316 delegates came from outside the host province annually from 1885 to 1909, and their presence probably helped swell the large number of curious visitors to the Congress sessions. Five thousand or more nondelegates attended the 1888 Allahabad, 1890 Calcutta, 1903 Madras, and 1907 Surat sessions, and 20,000 persons visited the 1906 Calcutta Congress.

The ancillary activities associated with the Congress sessions also attracted the attention of many nondelegates. Large crowds visited the industrial exhibitions which became a regular adjunct to the Congress after 1900. The arrival of a visiting dignitary, such as Charles Bradlaugh (1889), or the president-elect was often a well-attended event. In some years the president-elect's approach to the host city was the occasion for political demonstra-

First Years and Hume

tions which looked like triumphal processions as crowds gathered at the railway stations to cheer and hang garlands on the president-elect. Sometimes he was accompanied by local politicians, as in 1895 when Bal Gangadhar Tilak, at that time lionized by anti-reform Hindus for his fight to prevent the social reform conference from using the Congress pandal, went up the line to board the train carrying the president-elect, Surendranath Banerjea, and rode into Poona with him. In some years, after the train arrived in the host city, large cheering crowds gathered along the president's route as he traveled by carriage, sometimes pulled by the student volunteers. When anti-British feeling was high, the welcome of the president was the occasion for an emotional display of nationalist feeling and unity. Lala Lajpat Rai described the "splendid reception" given to Gokhale by the people of Benaras in 1905: "One thought the evil days of the nation would soon be over. Gokhale was very happy. . . . Tears were seen in his eyes. It was a wonderful sight indeed."[17] In 1907, it took more than two hours for the presidential procession to move about two miles from the Surat railway station to the Congress camp. "At every few yards more garlands were offered [to Rashbehari Ghose], more bunches of flowers and sweet-smelling seeds. Thick fell the showers of rose-water sprayed from silver bottles. On every side rose the great cheer of 'Bande Mataram!' "[18] These ritual occasions closed some of the distance between the English-language proceedings and those who did not understand English.

Presidential Speeches

The high point of most Congresses was the president's speech. It followed the welcoming speech of the chairman of the Reception Committee and the unanimous election of the president. The selection of the president and the president's speech were both used to reassure the British and Indian admirers of the Raj of the essential loyalty of the Congress. Three of the first ten presidents actually were British: George Yule, president of the Calcutta Chamber of Commerce; Sir William Wedderburn, retired I.C.S. officer; and Alfred Webb, Irish M. P. The Indian presidents were chosen from among men with reputations for

---

[17] Joshi (ed.), *Lajpat Rai: Autobiographical Writings*, p. 110.
[18] Nevinson, *The New Spirit*, p. 237.

loyalty and high achievement in Anglo-Indian professional life. The repeated encomiums to British rule by Indian presidents were criticized as abject by extremists, but they were in part a calculated effort to dispel suspicion of the Congress. Suppression of the Congress was seriously contemplated by Lord Dufferin's government, a series of obstacles was placed in the way of the 1888 Allahabad Congress organizers' efforts to find a site for the Congress pandal, and the Congress was subjected in subsequent years to open as well as secret police surveillance. The sometimes effusive references to British gifts to India, then, were in part an effort to win government tolerance of the Congress. This is not to suggest that statements of appreciation were insincere. English education had given Congress leaders their commanding position in Anglo-Indian professional life. The leaders wanted to reform the system they had benefitted from, not to overturn it, and they wanted their rulers to understand that. Many of the early Congress leaders, having been born before the Mutiny, were close enough to a period of disorder and arbitrary rule under both Indian and East India Company regimes to find the notions of personal liberty, representative institutions, and impartial justice exciting, fresh concepts. By contrast, a younger generation of nationalists regarded Congress salutes to English liberalism as irrelevant, unoriginal, and uninspired, and instead of thanking the English for introducing reforms, criticized the English for not fully implementing them. From the beginning of the Congress's history, the older generation of leaders tried to prevent their more extreme colleagues from giving the Congress an appearance of disloyalty.

Few delegates criticized the moderate and loyalist tone of the leadership in the open sessions of the Congress. The general Congress positions were developed in the presidential addresses which repeated the same arguments year after year, at least until 1905 when Gokhale's analysis of economic problems broke new ground. These Presidential speeches were listened to with patience and respect, even though they tended to be lengthy—often over two hours. D. E. Wacha's prepared speech in 1901 was so long (Gandhi described it as "a book by itself") that he could only read excerpts,[19] and Pandit Madan Mohan Malaviya was reported to have concluded his two-and-a-quarter-hour speech in

[19] Gandhi, *An Autobiography*, p. 280.

First Years and Hume

1909 "with an apology for its brevity."[20] In some years, presidential speeches were published prior to delivery, an act which might have diminished the delegates' interest in hearing it. However, the cries of "question" and "vote" during and after Pandit Malaviya's 1889 speech in support of a resolution seem to have been one of the few times delegate impatience was openly expressed.[21] Surendranath Banerjea's 1895 presidential speech took six weeks to prepare and over four hours to deliver, and such was the audience's appreciation of his fine oratory that Surendranath may not have exaggerated when he wrote that he held the attention of the five thousand people in the audience. At the end, young members of the audience rushed to the platform to take the dust from Surendranath's feet.[22] If many delegates objected to the repetitiveness of the speeches or to the absence of discussion of how Congress goals could be translated into political action, they did not express these opinions in the first twenty open sessions of the Congress. Speeches and newspaper articles criticizing British imperialism seemed to satisfy the political needs of many early nationalists.

GETTING TO KNOW EACH OTHER

Most delegates who traveled long distances to attend a Congress session probably had left their home regions on previous trips. Nevertheless, the experience of attending a meeting with people from a wide variety of backgrounds was a novel one. Visiting delegates generally ignored Hume's early efforts to persuade delegates to reside together. Instead, they preferred the familiar and stayed with people from their own region where they could eat the kinds of food to which they were accustomed and mix with delegates they knew. Separate living quarters limited the contact between people from different regions, but given the importance people placed upon food, segregated quarters were inevitable. Even a man who traveled as often as Tilak was orthodox about his meals. Tilak sometimes stayed with Motilal Ghose when he visited Calcutta and he shared Motilal's room "and sometimes even the same bed." But he would not eat with Motilal or accept food

[20] Valentine Chirol, *Indian Unrest* (London, 1910), p. 163.
[21] *The Hon. Pandit Madan Mohan Malaviya: His Life and Speeches*, 2nd ed. (Madras, n. d.), pp. 207–208.
[22] *A Nation*, pp. 129 and 133.

from his kitchen. He insisted on cooking his own meals on a verandah.[23] The more usual practice was, apparently, for delegates both to eat and sleep with men from their own region. When Tilak attended the 1893 Congress at Lahore, he stayed in a house with Ranade and Gokhale,[24] even though he had recently quarreled bitterly with them over the Deccan Education Society and the Age of Consent Bill. Only an occasional critic found fault with the separate living arrangements. Gandhi, for example, remarked upon the special cooking facilities required by the Tamils at the 1901 Congress, and he deprecated "such untouchability between the delegates."[25]

South Indian Brahmans were particularly caste conscious. The 1897 president, C. Sankaran Nair, wrote in his memoirs that the position of non-Brahmans in the Congress

> was not very agreeable. On our journey to the north to attend the Congress meetings our Brahmin friends would often ostentatiously avoid our company when taking meals. This is done by Brahmins in the north only in the case of low castes. They would also tell us we were Sudras, which in North India meant a low caste. To us, who belonged to the old ruling race in this Province, this was repellent; and as we did not want to create a scene, we stayed away from the Congress.[26]

South Indian Brahman exclusivity did not always extend to non-Brahmans from the north. Nagendranath Gupta, for example, ate breakfast with the Brahmans in "the Madras camp" in 1893 "without any protest from any one."[27]

In fact, delegates often visited other regional camps and established lasting contacts. Delegates caucused about Congress business both before and after the daily sessions, they settled most of the differences which arose between regional groups, and in some cases they formed social friendships. Through the annual Congresses, nationalists were learning to communicate with their counterparts in other regions and were gaining an understanding of the social and political geography of India. Early contacts were sometimes strained, no doubt, but by 1905, interregional travel and communication were far more common than before 1885.

[23] Dutt, *Memoirs of Moti Lal Ghose*, p. 258.
[24] Gupta, *Reflections and Reminiscences*, p. 161.
[25] *An Autobiography*, p. 275.   [26] Menon, *C. Sankaran Nair*, p. 35.
[27] Gupta, *Reflections and Reminiscences*, p. 157.

First Years and Hume

The exploratory encounters between peoples of different regions were occurring with increased frequency outside the Congress as well as in and were contributing to the national unification the Congress sought. Often these encounters brought a sense of discovery and relief. Surendranath Banerjea found on his trip to Lahore in 1879 that he "was received with the utmost kindness by my countrymen of all denominations, Hindus, Mohamedans and Sikhs. It was an exhibition of friendliness that was a revelation to me."[28] Surendranath spoke English and he had lived outside of India so that communicating with non-Benalis was relatively easy. Ranade's wife, though, provides an insight into the potential awkwardness of initial meetings between people who did not share customs or wide travel experience. Ramabai Ranade was staying in a *sarai* (caravansary or roadside hostel) in Amritsar in 1886 and she went to bathe in the women's enclosure.

> I went into the water with my saree on. The [Punjabi] women did not seem to approve of that and some of them laughed at me.
> One or two of the elderly women said, "Do you feel clean after a bath with saree on? Are we not women? Why need you be so shy? Do you always bathe like this in your country?"
> "Yes, we are not at all used to bathing in the way you do," I replied and came away quickly.

Her meeting with a group of Bengali pilgrims near Ajmere ended in a more reassuring manner. After asking one of the women in Hindustani why the women were dressed the way they were, whether they were married, etc., she said "Please don't be angry. I come from another region and I would like to know all these things." And she learned.[29] Later, when Ranade and his wife arrived in Calcutta for a stay of several months, they found they could not speak or read Bengali. But within six weeks they had taught themselves to read Bengali newspapers. Ramabai Ranade seemed to be surprised and pleased with her ability to pick up Bengali. She was also amused to find Justice Ranade learning pronunciation and vocabulary from his barber. "In the old days the pupil had to serve the guru in a humble way if he wanted

---
[28] *A Nation*, p. 43.
[29] Ramabai Ranade, *Ranade*, pp. 119–121.

to learn from him," she told her husband. "Here the guru, poor man, is serving you."[30]

The overall trend in regional interactions was in the direction of unity and homogeneity. Within that trend, the direction was far from uniform. Individuals and sometimes large groups recoiled from the process of integration after preliminary contact with people from unfamiliar backgrounds. Madhusudan Das, who founded the Utkal Union Conference in 1903, is an example of a person whose early contacts with another region reinforced his identification with and loyalty to his own special region. As an Oriya in a Bengali school, he had been the object of Bengali "sarcasm and ridicule." His Bengali schoolmates, who wore their hair short and who considered his long hair "a sign of my being a girl," cut his hair off.

> During the years of Bengali persecutions at school I looked back with a sigh, a regret sometimes with tears, on the days I spent in my village before I was transported to Cuttack for English education. I thought of the days when I was loved, respected, and blessed as the scion of an old family of zamindars. I was reconciled to a life where contempt and insult would be my share.[31]

Madhusudhan Das attended and spoke at occasional Congress sessions, but the protection of Oriya rights and culture engaged a much larger part of his energies. One would guess that his school experiences might have prevented enthusiastic participation in an organization which, in eastern India, was dominated by Bengalis. As we have seen, C. Sankaran Nair, a non-Brahman from Malabar, was another man who, because of treatment at the hands of Tamil Brahmans, gave only limited support to the Congress. It was precisely this type of experience, aloofness, and mistrust which Hume, Ranade, Bonnerjee, and other early Congress leaders were working to overcome. On the whole, they were making progress.

HUME'S MUSLIM STRATEGY AND ITS FAILURE

When Indian Congress leaders returned to their careers and local political associations after each sessions, they left to Hume

[30] Ibid., pp. 125–127.
[31] F. G. Bailey, *Politics and Social Change: Orissa in 1959* (Berkeley, 1963), pp. 161–162.

the main work of the Congress between the annual meetings. Because the annual sessions failed to assign specific duties to the general secretary, Hume had considerable latitude in what he did. Soon after Hume saw that English-speaking nationalists were becoming acquainted through the Congress sessions, he turned to the task of bringing Muslims and peasants into the movement. Hume seemed to feel more strongly than his Indian colleagues that Muslim and peasant support was necessary to justify the Congress's claim to represent the Indian people. Or at least he was less awed by the difficulties and pitfalls in trying to win that support. In the late 1880s Hume tried to enlarge Muslim and peasant participation in the Congress. His efforts to attract educated Muslims provoked the first significant Indian opposition to the Congress while his peasant campaign brought official wrath upon the Congress and strained his relations with other Congress leaders. The result of Hume's Muslim and peasant strategies was to frighten some of the more cautious sympathizers away from the Congress and to impress upon many Congressmen the limited nature of the movement's appeal.

Initially, there seems to have been no disagreement among Congress leaders about the desirability of recruiting more Muslims. However, they started with the handicap of not having influential Muslim allies in the Punjab, the North-Western Provinces and Oudh, and Bengal where the Muslim population was concentrated. Their principal Muslim associate was Badruddin Tyabji, the barrister who belonged to the minute Khoja sect of Bombay. Despite his friendship with Congress leaders, Tyabji let his legal work keep him from attending the first Congress, and he turned down W. C. Bonnerjee's invitation to preside over the second session before accepting Hume's request that he be president of the third Congress. Bonnerjee and Hume hoped that the presence of prominent Muslims such as Tyabji and Nawab Sayyid Muhammad of Madras, a descendant of Tipu Sultan of Mysore, would overcome the misgivings of educated Muslims throughout India. Tyabji's presidency and the sizeable Muslim attendance at the 1887 Congress in Madras gave Congress leaders grounds for hope.

The apprehensions of English-educated Muslims centered upon Congress demands for more elections and competitive examinations for positions in the schools and civil services. They feared that since Muslims were a minority in every province except the

First Years and Hume

Punjab, they would be outvoted. In the case of competitive examinations for government positions and education, educational deficiencies left Muslims proportionately ill-prepared to compete with Hindus except in the North-Western Provinces and Oudh. Public consciousness of the unequal distribution of education among various regions, religious groups, and castes had been raised by the tours, taking of testimony, and reports by the Education and Public Service Commissions of 1882–1883 and 1886–1887. The Congress goal of a more open and competitive society, if implemented, seemed likely to favor educated Hindus and to accentuate existing disparities between religious communities.[32]

Significant Muslim opposition to the Congress emerged in 1887 and 1888. It was led by Amir Ali's Central National Muhammadan Association which had its headquarters in Calcutta and branches in fifty or so other towns by 1888, by the Muhammadan Educational Congress which met annually from 1886, and by Sayyid Ahmad Khan and Aligarh College and the United Indian Patriotic Association, both of which he helped found.[33]

Sayyid Ahmad's views of the Congress received the greatest attention because of his prominence and because they were published in two pamphlets and reported in the newspapers. Sayyid Ahmad believed that the future of Indian Muslims lay in preserving their separate identity and community solidarity, and he had sought English help in achieving this. In his *Causes of the Mutiny*, he had criticized the Government of India for encouraging "a feeling of friendship and brotherhood" by mixing Hindus and Muslims in the same army regiments.[34] In the early years of the Anglo-Muhammadan College, he apparently did not feel it necessary to stress publically to the government the advantages of a "counterpoise" strategy. But with the founding of the Congress, his communalism became more open. His first highly publicized attack on the Congress was made in a speech at the time of the 1887 Madras Congress. In his 1887 attack, he spoke as a Muslim and a north Indian. If Congress demands for the expansion of the competitive principle in the civil services and representative bodies were conceded, he said, the Muslims would lose places to Hindus. He taunted the Congress Hindus, implying that they were mostly Bengalis. If they wanted to compete

[32] Seal, *The Emergence*, pp. 314ff.   [33] Ibid., pp. 313 and 336.
[34] Quoted by Ram Gopal, *How India Struggled for Freedom: A Political History* (Bombay, 1967), p. 79.

First Years and Hume

with the Muslims, the Hindus could use their weapon—the pen —and Muslims would use their traditional sword. Unlike Bengalis, he said,

> we do not live on fish; nor are we afraid of using a knife and fork lest we should cut our fingers. Our blood is the blood of those who made not only Arabia, but Asia and Europe to tremble. It is our nation which conquered with its sword the whole of India.

He told his listeners that

> if you accept that the country should groan under the yoke of Bengali rule and its people lick the Bengali shoes, then, in the name of God! jump into the train, sit down, and be off to Madras, be off to Madras!35

In the following year, the Congress entered into a trial of strength with the Aligarh Muslims by holding the annual meeting in Aligarh's own province, at Allahabad. The 1888 session was the first to be held outside Bombay, Calcutta, and Madras with their relatively large numbers of nationalist college graduates. The organizers of the Allahabad Congress succeeded in overcoming obstacles placed in their way by local officials in finding a suitable site for the meeting, and they drew more than twice as many delegates as any previous session. But they also met a renewed and broader opposition led by Sayyid Ahmad Khan. The Aligarh Muslims joined with Hindu *taluqdars* and other titled landholders and formed the United Indian Patriotic Association. The main thrust of the association's attack on the Congress was not that Hindus and Muslims were distinct nations, nor that Bengalis would capture the spoils distributed according to achievement in English education. Rather, members of the Patriotic Association stressed that the Congress's brand of democracy was unsuited to India's aristocratic and caste-based social structure. Sayyid Ahmad's contribution to the association's pamphlet denigrating the Congress argued that the Congress demand for elections to the legislative councils should be opposed because men might be elected who were of such inferior social stature that mixing with the British and Indian nobility

---

35 Lucknow speech of 28 Dec. 1887 in *Sir Syed Ahmed on the Present State of Indian Politics*.

on the councils would be awkward. Similarly, civil service examinations should not be held simultaneously in India and Great Britain because lower-class Indians might pass who would not be accepted by Indian aristocrats to rule over them.[36] Other members of the Patriotic Association gave equally antidemocratic reasons for rejecting the Congress and its demands for more representative government. The Maharaja of Benaras, for instance, dismissed democracy as a Western institution, unsuited to Hinduism whose basis was the *varna* (caste) system. "How would you care to have Kalvars and Mochis as our legislators?" he asked.[37] Sayyid Husain Bilgrami, Secretary of the Nizam of Hyderabad's Council of State, thought that:

> Those who have a stake in the country and have something to lose in the general upheaval apprehended from the spread of democratic tendencies which have no home in this country, ought to appreciate the full importance of keeping supreme power intact and untouched, and hedging it round with as much of the elements of awe and reverence as can be saved out of the wreck of old ideas and traditions which are in the process of being ruthlessly destroyed by a blind, ill-judged, and ill-digested imitation of European radicalism.[38]

It is interesting that the organization founded with Sayyid Ahmad Khan's help to combat the Congress based its opposition on the interests of the aristocracy rather than on those of the Muslims, because Sayyid Ahmad had been defending the specific interests of the Muslims for many years. Now he was trying to rally the Hindu landed classes behind his attack on the Congress. Possibly he was advised to adopt this tactic by one of his British friends, such as Theodore Beck, the principal of the Aligarh Muhammedan Anglo-Oriental College. Each time prominent Muslims or titled landlords in the North-Western Provinces and Oudh voiced objections to the Congress and its affiliated organizations, Englishmen seized the opportunity to emphasize the division of interests between Indian elites. Most often they employed

---

[36] Rajendra Prasad, *India Divided* (Bombay, 1946), p. 102.

[37] *Pamphlet No. 2 Showing the Seditious Character of the Indian National Congress and the Opinions Held by Eminent Natives of India Who Are Opposed to the Movement*, pub. by the United Indian Patriotic Association (Allahabad, 1888), p. 45.

[38] Letter to Sayyid Ahmad Khan, 20 Aug. 1888, ibid., p. 55.

the columns of the *Pioneer* for this purpose. British allies of Aligarh were usually cautious about stating in public that Hindus and Muslims constituted separate nations because that would expose them to charges of divide and rule. But few were reticent in arguing that parliamentary forms were alien to Indian conditions. Beck used this argument, as did another Engilshman (probably Arthur Strachey, an Allahabad barrister) who wrote a pamphlet called *Democracy Not Suited to India* which was published under the name of Udai Pratap Singh, the Rajput Raja of Bhinga.[39] Parallel views were also held by Sir Auckland Colvin, the lieutenant-governor of the North-Western Provinces and Oudh. In a note written in June 1889, Colvin said that the Congress in his province drew its membership mainly from the Kayasth caste. The Kayasths and others of the literary class, which under previous rulers had been "the mere rubble of the political building," were trying "to level up" with the other classes and the English. They were using English institutions such as representative government to gain an ascendancy over their social superiors. Colvin claimed that the Muslims were in great fear of the rise of the new literary class of "obscure antecedents," and he advised against appearing to help the classes who are growing so powerful and who are regarded "as a source of daily humiliation and annoyance."[40]

Hume recognized the seriousness of the challenge from the Patriotic Association. If Sayyid Ahmad persuaded the Muslims to stay away from the Congress, Congress claims to be a national body would sound hollow. Hume's main hope was Badruddin Tyabji who might, he thought, persuade Muslims not to follow Sayyid Ahmad. Hume wrote to Tyabji in January 1886 and said perhaps you are "marked out for the work of suppressing Syed Ahmed." The Congress had decided to invade "our opponents' own dominions" by having the 1888 session at Allahabad. Unless there were a Muslim president, and that Muslim should probably

[39] It was widely assumed that the pamphlet was ghostwritten because the Raja of Bhinga's English was inferior to that used. The *Hindu* of Madras reported that Sir Auckland Colvin had dictated it. (Hira Lal Singh, *Problems and Policies of the British in India, 1885–1898* [Bombay, 1963], p. 235.) But Colvin himself "credited" the pamphlet to Arthur Strachey. Martin, *New India*, p. 330.

[40] A. Colvin's Confidential Note on Provincial Councils, 11 June 1889. Enclosure to Landsdowne to Cross, 28 June 1889, No. 31, MSS. Eur. E. 243/26.

be Tyabji, the Muslims would be likely to stay away from the Allahabad session.[41] Tyabji refused to serve as president again, but he did write letters to Sayyid Ahmad, Sayyid Amir Ali, and Nawab Abdul Latif in an attempt to persuade them not to oppose the Congress.[42] The response to these letters was utterly discouraging and in October 1888 a dejected Tyabji wrote Hume about the increasing hostility of the Muslims toward the Congress. The goal of the Congress had been to unite the communities of India. Instead, he said, "an overwhelming majority" of Muslims opposed the movement and the Muslims in general had "been divided from the Hindus in a manner they never were before." Tyabji was so disheartened by what Anil Seal calls "the Muslim breakaway" that he thought the Congress should be suspended for "at least five years."[43]

It had been Hume, with Tyabji's help, who had tried to draw Muslims into the Congress. Hume had emphasized in his introduction to the Congress's second report that it was a secular body.

> The Congress is a community of temporal interests and not of spiritual convictions that qualify men to represent each other in the discussion of political questions; we hold their general interests in this country being identical, Hindus, Christians, Muslims and Parsis may fitly as members of their respective communities represent each other in the discussion of public secular affairs.[44]

Hume and Tyabji had worked out the minority rule in 1887 which stipulated that if the overwhelming majority of Congress delegates belonging to a single religious community objected to a resolution, that resolution would be dropped, providing the resolution had not been adopted by a previous Congress. This rule may have eased some Muslim apprehensions about the Hindu majority, but the very circumstances which necessitated the rule may have more than offset its reassuring effect. The rule was adopted after Raja Sashi Sekhareswar Roy of Tahirpur (Bengal) had announced his intention to move a resolution urging the prohibition of cow slaughter.[45] No issue could have been

[41] A. O. Hume to Badruddin Tyabji, 22 Jan. 1888. Govt. of Bombay, *Source Material*, II, 69.
[42] 13 Jan. 1888. Ibid., p. 68.   [43] 27 Oct. 1888. Ibid., pp. 81–82.
[44] Quoted by Donald Eugene Smith, *India as a Secular State* (Princeton, 1963), p. 88.
[45] Banerjea, *A Nation*, p. 108.

First Years and Hume

better calculated to illustrate the danger to Muslim rights posed by a Hindu legislative majority than a proposal to interfere with Islamic religious practices. The Congress itself refused to discuss the cow question, but the cow protection movement spread in the following year, with support from more than a few Congressmen, and culminated in serious riots in 1893.[46]

It was characteristic of the early Congress that Hume, rather than Hindu leaders, had taken the initiative in assuring Muslims that the Congress understood their concern about the position of a minority in a representative system. Muslim apprehensions might have been lessened if Hindus, instead of a foreigner, had assumed that role. Hindu Congress leaders might have gained a fuller understanding of Muslim anxieties and ways to meet them if they had approached Muslim spokesmen directly instead of relying on a third party.

Neither the minority rule, the refusal to discuss cow slaughter, nor Tyabji's letters dispelled Muslim doubts about the Congress. Because the minority rule prohibiting discussion of issues to which a religious group objected applied only to matters on which the Congress had not taken a position, it did not cover the key issue of expansion of the legislative councils. That issue was raised at the 1889 Congress during discussion of the legislative reform scheme which Charles Bradlaugh, who was present, intended to put before the House of Commons. Once again, Hindu Congress leaders missed an opportunity to confront the problem, while Europeans and Muslims argued about how best to have the Muslim minority represented. Eardley Norton, who moved the legislative council resolution, asked for proportional representation of Muslims in each electoral division.[47] Reverend R. A. Hume of Ahmednagar argued against this suggestion, saying that minority representation should be secured through tolerance and public spirit rather than by statute.[48] Norton replied that this was utopian as well as unacceptable to Parliament.[49] Before the Congress passed Norton's original motion, one Muslim delegate moved an unsuccessful amendment which asked for 50 per cent Muslim representation in the reformed councils,[50] and another Muslim argued that Muslims should have three times as many seats as Hindus since they were the superior race.[51]

[46] See Chapter Nine below.
[48] *Report of the 5th INC*, p. 30.
[50] Ibid., p. 39.
[47] Resolution II.
[49] Ibid., pp. 31–32.
[51] Ibid., p. 36.

Although the impending council reform was the major topic of discussion at the 1889 Congress, the question of minority representation did not engage educated Indian opinion as it later did. It was anticipated that government officials and their supporters would remain in the majority in the reformed councils and that the councils would continue to be essentially advisory. The Congress went on record as favoring proportional minority representation[52] without taking an explicit stand on the awkward question of whether Muslim legislators should be elected by joint or separate (i.e., Muslim) electorates or whether Muslims should receive weighted representation to compensate for their minority status. In fact, public discussion of the position of Indian minorities under an elective system had barely begun. Not even the Aligarh Muslims had yet settled on a demand for either separate electorates or weightage. In 1889, the Aligarh Muslims were still resisting the general proposition that democracy or majority rule was suitable for India. Public discussion of communal representation had not become focused and was only beginning to produce concrete, detailed constitutional proposals. It is not surprising, therefore, that Congress leaders avoided taking a more comprehensive position on an issue as divisive as minority representation.

Between 1889 and the Muslim delegation's request at Simla in 1906 for separate electorates, the Congress made no major effort to attract or open discussions with the Aligarh Muslims, who continued to be the best organized Muslim opposition to the Congress. This also is understandable in view of Sayyid Ahmad's and Aligarh College's identification with government and aristocratic opposition to the Congress. Sayyid Ahmad defended precisely those things which Congress leaders considered archaic: ascribed privilege and the two-nation theory. The possibility of the Congress reaching an agreement with Sayyid Ahmad was therefore small. Moreover, few Congress leaders were in close touch with the areas of Indian life which gave rise to Muslim fears of Hindu communalism. W. C. Bonnerjee, Surendranath Banerjea, P. Ananda Charlu, Ranade, and Pherozeshah Mehta were men with universalistic outlooks, and it is doubtful that they appreciated the working of communalism outside the cos-

[52] Resolution II of 1889 said that where "Parsis, Christians, Muhammadans or Hindus" were in a minority, they should have at least proportional representation.

mopolitan circles they lived in. They seemed to feel that by building elaborate safeguards into India's constitution in order to alleviate Muslim minority fears, they would institutionalize religious differences. They looked to elective procedures, "without distinction of race, creed, caste or colour,"[53] as a means of overcoming bias, of training people to think of themselves as part of a single political community.

In addition, Congress leaders knew that the Aligarh College spokesmen did not represent the opinions of many politically conscious Muslims. Muslims from both ends of the reformist-traditionalist continuum disagreed with Sayyid Ahmad. The head of the orthodox Islamic school at Deoband, Maulana Rashid Ahmad Gangohi, issued a *fatwa* soon after the Congress was founded warning Muslims "not to associate themselves with the activities" of Sir Sayyid and stating "that in worldly matters co-operation with the Hindus was permissible provided it did not violate any basic principle of Islam."[54] While the Deoband *ulama*'s indirect support for the Congress was perhaps motivated less by sympathy for Congress goals than by rivalry with the more secular and Westernized Aligarh intelligentsia,[55] individual Muslims who were not ulama continued to be active in the Congress after the Allahabad session of 1888. The largest number of Muslim Congress activists in the pre-1909 period were lawyers, most of whom probably had professional relations with Hindu lawyers in the Congress. These included Ali Muhammad Bhimji, Muhammad Rahimtullah Sayani (president in 1896), and Muhammad Ali Jinnah in Bombay, Abdul Rasul in Bengal, Sayyid Muhammad Sharfuddin in Bihar, Hamid Ali Khan in Oudh, Hafiz Abdul Rahim in the North-Western Provinces, and Fazl-i-Husain in the Punjab. Other active Muslim Congressmen in this period included Nawab Sayyid Muhammad in Madras, Abdul Kasim in Bengal, Sajjad Husain (editor of the *Oudh Punch*), and Muharram Ali Chisti (editor of the *Rafiq-i-Hind*) in the Punjab.

The participation of these Muslims was similar in character to that of most Hindu and Parsi Congress enthusiasts: they did not attend regularly and in some cases withdrew due to a particular controversy or to career considerations. Badruddin Tyabji and

[53] Resolution IV (5) of 1886.
[54] Ziya-ul-Faruqi, *The Deoband School and the Demand for Pakistan* (Bombay, 1963), pp. 43-45.
[55] See ibid., p. 40.

Sayyid Muhammad Sharfuddin, both distinguished barristers, were active in the first five years but then drifted away from the Congress prior to being appointed High Court judges. Sharfuddin turned against the Congress and presided over the 1906 Muhammadan Educational Conference at which the Muslim League was founded. Hamid Ali Khan and Muharran Ali Chisti seem to have lost interest in the Congress during the Hindi-Urdu and Punjab Land Alienation Bill controversies, respectively. Yet within a few years of the withdrawal of one Muslim, usually another had taken his place. It is difficult to discern a clear trend in Muslim participation prior to the partition of Bengal.[56] Overall, proportionately fewer Muslims than Hindus attended, spoke, or served on Congress committees, and the Muslims who did participate did not claim to represent the majority of educated Muslims. Muslim participants were exceptions to the general Muslim indifference and hostility to the Congress. Thus, the Congress had failed in its short-term objective of winning widespread Muslim support. Both Hume and Tyabji were discouraged by the results of their 1888 campaign. But Hindu and Parsi leaders did not despair over their future relations with Muslims. There was no Muslim consensus about India's future constitution and there was little sustained, organized Muslim opposition to the Congress outside of Aligarh. In almost every province, some able Muslims were active in the Congress, at least sporadically. As a result, Congress leaders were content to wait. There was little inclination to rethink Congress goals or tactics with Muslims specifically in mind. That rethinking did not come until after the Muslim League was founded and insisted upon separate electorates.

Hume's Peasant Strategy

In the Congress's efforts to attract Muslims and peasants in the late 1880s, Hume had taken the initiative. It has been suggested that had Hindu Congressmen, rather than Hume and Tyabji, approached Muslim leaders, the Congress might have overcome some of the Muslim indifference or hostility to the movement. However, in appealing for Muslim support, Hume

[56] An exception to this generalization which is discussed in Chapter Ten below is that the average number of Muslims attending the annual Congress session was lower after the Hindu-Muslim riots of 1893 than before.

acted with the approval of his closest Hindu and Parsi colleagues. It was otherwise with Hume's 1887 campaign among villagers. His distribution of two vernacular pamphlets in rural areas led to a serious *contretemps* with other Congress leaders in 1888. His appeal for peasant support heightened the concern about Hume's autocratic personality and his practice of acting without consulting other leaders. The concern came to a head in 1892 when he predicted a peasant insurrection in a manner which some people thought was a seditious threat.

Hume's decision to distribute pamphlets in the villages in 1887 was aimed at expanding the social base of the Congress. This was necessary, he explained, in view of the government's autocracy and unresponsiveness to educated Indians. It was time, he argued, for the Congress to adopt the methods used by Bright and Cobden after the House of Commons had declined to hear the Corn Law League. The Congress should now look to the people, "so that every Indian that breathes upon the sacred soil of this our Motherland may become our comrade and coadjutor, our supporter, and, if needs be, our soldier in the great war that we, like Cobden and his noble band, will wage for justice, for our liberties and rights."[57]

Hume's appeal for peasant support of the Congress was presented in two pamphlets published in twelve different languages. One was written by Viraraghava Chariar, the other by Hume himself. Many thousands were distributed. The general message was nonrevolutionary: it said that if genuinely representative institutions were given exclusive power to pass laws and impose taxes, government in India would be less callous toward popular needs and therefore less impoverishing. However, the tone of the two pamphlets was harsher than that of most speeches in the Congress and the audience was different.[58] Viraraghava Chariar's pamphlet denounced existing legislative councils as a sham and dismissed most Indian councilmen as "more or less foolish big men, who will just do what they are told by Government." The second gave a concrete, vivid example of arbitrary and oppressive authority in a village under British rule.[59] Members of the Congress who

[57] Wedderburn, *Hume*, pp. 62–63.

[58] Hume was quoted as saying that about 50,000 copies of the two tracts were distributed in the first year and that half a million would be circulated in the second. *Audi Alteram Partem* (London, n. d.), p. 8.

[59] *A Congress Catechism* by M. Viraraghava Chariar and *A Conversation*

helped Hume distribute the pamphlets organized mass meetings, some of which were drawn together by traditional village entertainments. Wedderburn said that more than a thousand meetings were held, some attended by 5,000 or more people.

Hume had failed to obtain advance approval from the top Congress leadership for his short-lived campaign. Although local associations, such as the Sarvajanik Sabha of Poona and the Indian Association of Calcutta, had conducted similar activities, they had not provoked as strong a government reaction as the Congress received in 1888. The government responded with a sharp attack on Hume and the Congress. Both Lord Dufferin and Sir Auckland Colvin, the lieutenant-governor of the North-Western Provinces and Oudh, objected publicly to the pamphlets on the grounds that they misrepresented government policies and were designed to arouse hatred of British officials among the masses.[60] Colvin wrote of "the extreme unwisdom and unfairness of writing and circulating [the pamphlets] among ignorant and excitable people, foreign to us in blood."[61] The Congress only represented "the wishes of a class, and that a minute and exceptional class."[62] Colvin said that it was absurd for this class to claim to represent the interests of the peasantry when, for the most part, it had, through its representatives in the Legislative Council, opposed the government's tenancy legislation in Bengal, in 1885, and Oudh, in 1886.[63]

These views were made public in October 1887, when Hume's and Colvin's correspondence on the Congress was published,[64] and again on 30 November 1888 by Dufferin in a farewell speech. Dufferin asked, with reference to the Congress, how reasonable men could "be content to allow this microscopic minority to control their administration." He stressed the unrepresentative nature of the Congress, whose selfish platform was defended by "no Native statesman of weight or importance." He regretted the circulation among the masses of the pamphlets which, he said, "were animated by a very questionable spirit, and whose

---

between *Molvi Farid ud Din, M. A., Vaquil (Barrister) of the High Court, Practicing in the Zillah Court of Hakikatabad, and Rambaksh, one of the Mukaddams (Chief Villager) of Kambakhtpur*. English translations appear as an appendix to the *Report of the 3rd INC.*

[60] Wedderburn, *Hume*, p. 63.   [61] *Audi Alteram Partem*, p. 17.
[62] Ibid., p. 24.   [63] Ibid., p. 11.
[64] Ibid.

First Years and Hume

manifest intention is to excite" hatred of the government. He also alleged that Hume had made a "silly threat" when he said that members of Congress "hold in their hands the keys not only of a popular insurrection but of a military revolt."[65]

The government showed its growing suspicion of the Congress in other ways. In November 1887, the Government of India added an intelligence department, called the Special Branch, to the Department for the Suppression of Thagi and Dakoiti to watch religious, social, and political movements.[66] The head of this new department, Col. P. D. Henderson, along with the head constable of Allahabad and the Madras commissioner of police, were reported to have been seen near the Congress pandal at Bombay in 1889.[67] The efforts of the previous year's reception committee at Allahabad to find a suitable site for the Congress pandal had been frustrated by the municipal authorities until the Maharaja of Darbhanga came forward and purchased Lowther (later Darbhanga) Castle and its grounds for the use of the 1888 Congress.[68]

Apparently Hume did not know that Dufferin considered suppressing the Congress[69] and that others suggested deporting Hume.[70] He was aware, though, that his peasant campaign was controversial. He defended his tactics in Allahabad in April 1888 by saying that the Congress was trying to keep "the coming flood" nonviolent. "We of the Congress . . . are labouring—labouring almost frantically—to provide in time channels through which this surging tide may flow, not to ravage and destroy but to fertilize and regenerate." He admitted, however, that "friends" had told him "you are stirring up feelings, you are exciting passions, the issues of which you cannot foresee; you are letting loose forces that you cannot control."[71] Later that year, a small group of Congress leaders at Allahabad rebuffed Hume by passing a resolution "disclaiming all responsibility for what their officers and members did or said outside" the annual

---

[65] Dufferin's Speech at St. Andrew's Dinner, Calcutta, 30 Nov. 1888. Enclosure to Dufferin to Cross, 3 Dec. 1888, No. 121, MSS. Eur. E. 243/25.

[66] Govt. of India Despatch to S. of S., No. 179, 15 Nov. 1887, cited in Govt. of India, Home Dept., Jud., to S. of S., No. 6, 28 March 1901, PSLI, Vol. 131.

[67] *Report of the 5th INC*, p. 19.

[68] A. C. Mazumdar, *Indian National Evolution*, 2nd ed. (Madras, 1917), p. 73.

[69] Dufferin to Cross, 17 Aug. 1888, No. 107, MSS. Eur. E. 243/25.

[70] Wedderburn, *Hume*, p. 67.   [71] Ibid., pp. 64–66.

Congress session,[72] although they rejected a suggestion that the Congress session should formally repudiate the pamphlets.[73]

The rebuff to Hume was indirect and not widely publicized, and it came after he had shifted his attention to the management of the approaching Allahabad Congress which faced a formidable opposition from officials, Muslims, and Hindu notables. But in 1892 Hume again raised the specter of peasant insurrection and this time official bodies of the Congress specifically disassociated themselves from his view. Hume's special perspective, which made other Congress leaders uncomfortable and which led to a partial break between the Congress and its general secretary, seems to have been related to his career disappointments. His cataclysmic foreboding of impending rebellion seemed to grow with his failures to influence British officials and to broaden the Congress movement.

HUME'S DEPARTURE

By 1892, it had become clear that Hume had been shut out of official circles. He was regarded as a dangerous troublemaker rather than a man whom viceroys consulted with profit on Indian attitudes. It was also evident that prior to the 1892 general election, Hume had not succeeded in his efforts to build a body of Liberal Members of Parliament to work effectively on behalf of Indian reform. And under Hume's direction the response of Muslims to the Congress had been mostly negative and of educated Hindus often halfhearted. The attendance at the 1890 Calcutta Congress was 677, barely one-third of the previous year's, and at the 1891 Nagpur session only 812 delegates appeared. Surendranath Banerjea was moved to ask the Nagpur Congress "Shall the Congress exist as it has existed in the past, or shall it pronounce its doom?"[74] Naoroji wrote Wacha in December 1891 about how discouraged Hume was and added "it will be disastrous to India if he give up."[75] But at the Nagpur session later that month, Hume did announce his intention to resign as general secretary. He reportedly issued a statement saying that if the next Congress session was not held in London, he would

[72] Seal, *The Emergence*, p. 294.
[73] Lansdowne to Cross, 11 Dec. 1888, No. 1, MSS. Eur. E. 243/26.
[74] Argov, *Moderates and Extremists*, p. 48.
[75] Masani, *Naoroji*, p. 312.

step down. He felt "it is desirable that the session should not be held in India for some time to come."[76] The Nagpur Congress rejected Hume's advice to transfer the main Congress effort to England and unanimously endorsed a resolution postponing the projected London session until after the 1893 session in India.[77] The Nagpur Congress also voted Hume to the general secretaryship again. But he did leave India in 1892.

Before Hume moved to England and before he turned over most of his responsibilities to his Indian friends, he sent out a confidential circular to Congress leaders telling them that "a very large number of you seem almost as behind as the Government" in failing to realize that "the existing system of administration . . . is inevitably preparing the way for one of the most terrible cataclysms in the history of the world" in the form of a peasant revolution.[78] This circular, dated February 16, 1892, produced a major rupture between Hume and many Congress leaders and almost ended Hume's effectiveness as a Congress leader in India. After that, he confined most of his Congress activities to London. Hume's perception of the danger of agrarian revolt was a private one, shared by few of his colleagues. Hume had explained it in a memorandum which William Wedderburn saw among Hume's papers but which has since disappeared. It seems to have been written in the 1888–1891 period as a justification for the path he wanted the Congress to follow. He claimed that in the late 1870s, while still an official, he had seen seven large volumes containing English translations of reports from "over thirty thousand different reporters," many of whom told of the secret collection of weapons and predicted violent outbreaks by the lower classes. In the beginning, there would be sporadic killing and looting of bazaars and bankers, they said.

> It was considered certain also, that everywhere the small bands would begin to coalesce into larger ones, like drops of water on a leaf; that all the bad characters in the country would join, and that very soon after the bands attained formidable proportions, a certain small number of the educated classes, at the time desperately, perhaps unreasonably, bitter against Government would join the movement, assume here and there

[76] Argov, *Moderates and Extremists*, p. 47.
[77] Resolution XV.
[78] Govt. of Bombay, *Source Material*, II, 116.

the lead, give the outbreak cohesion, and direct it as a national revolt.[79]

Among the unanswered questions about Hume's memorandum is why did Hume not show the seven volumes, if they actually existed, to his superiors in the government.[80] He seems to have convinced few persons in the government or the Congress of the danger of rebellion, although Bal Gangadhar Tilak and Gopal Ganesh Agarkar supported his 1892 analysis[81] and many persons agreed with him about India's miserable economic condition. His "belief that the reports in the seven volumes must necessarily be true because they were the reports of *Chelas* to their *Gurus*" and because no true *Chela* would deceive his *Guru* does not add to his credibility.[82] It is difficult not to conclude that Hume probably had a mystical experience, the nature of which was shaped by his frustration with the pervasive indifference to India's poverty and suffering, and by his anger over his person failures.

Hume's circular of February 16, 1892, contained arguments similar to those in the lost memorandum. It was a "private and confidential" communication to Congress leaders which reads as if it had been intended to shock them into activity by persuading them that they would be victims of lower-class violence. He warned them not to be misled by apparent peasant passivity. French peasants had also been humble before the French Revolution when they "murdered their Sovereign and practically, the bulk of the better classes." He told the Congress leaders that the wealthy were particularly in danger.

> Do not fancy that Government will be able to protect you or itself. No earthly power can stem an universal agrarian rising in a country like this. My countrymen will be as men in the desert, vainly struggling for a brief space, against the simoom. There will be no foe to meet in the field, but rail and road will become [impassable], bridges will be wrecked, telegraphs cease to exist, supplies be arrested, thousands of rioters may

[79] Wedderburn, *Hume*, pp. 80–81.

[80] His qualified pledge of secrecy would seem an insufficient answer: "I have promised . . . never to give out, without permission, anything I have been informed of or shown, unless it should appear to me a distinct moral duty not to hold my tongue." Ibid., pp. 83–84.

[81] G. P. Pradhan and A. K. Bhagwat, *Lokamanya Tilak: A Biography* (Bombay, 1959), p. 79.

[82] Wedderburn, *Hume*, pp. 82–83.

First Years and Hume

be killed, but to what avail, when there are millions on millions who have nothing to look forward to but death—nothing to hope for but vengeance; as for leaders—with the hour comes the man—be sure there will be no lack of leaders. This is no hypothesis—it is a certainty.[83]

The circular went on to explain how the Congress could avert a holocaust by working for representative institutions. But Hume's prediction of a *jacquerie* seemed to express his bitterness toward "the better classes" from which the Congress leaders came for not giving Hume the support he wanted.

The circular caused a sensation in India and England. Its appeal for increased efforts to persuade the British electorate that Indian reforms were imperative was largely ignored and discussion centered on the "incendiary" language. In India the circular revealed the incipient differences between moderates and extremists. The Allahabad Standing Congress Committee objected publicly to Hume's language, and the Bombay and Madras committees refused to distribute it. Other Congress committees would almost certainly have censured Hume if Dadabhai Naoroji and the rest of the British Committee of the Congress had not published in *The Times* "their entire repudiation of the wild language and the unjustifiable conclusions drawn by Mr. Hume."[84] In the House of Commons, James M. Maclean suggested that Hume "under any less mild rule than our own would have been hanged or shot as a traitor."[85] When Maclean's remarks were reported by the *Bombay Gazette*[86] and by Tilak's *Kesari*, Maclean was said to have stated that Hume "deserved to be hanged or shot as a traitor."[87]

Despite his many services, Hume's departure for England after the 1891 Congress probably evoked feelings of relief from many Congressmen. Hume's pamphleteering, his warnings of popular rebellion, his suggestion that well-to-do Congressmen would be among the first victims of hunger-induced anarchy, his needling reminders that nationalists were not making sufficient sacrifices, and his refusal to seek or accept advice from other Congressmen

[83] Quoted by J. M. Maclean in the House of Commons, *Parliamentary Debates*, 4th series, III (25 April 1892), 1,354–1,355.
[84] Govt. of Bombay, *Source Material*, II, 122–123.
[85] *Parliamentary Debates*, 4th series, III (25 April 1892), 1,354–1,355.
[86] Govt. of Bombay, *Source Material*, II, 125.
[87] Pradhan and Bhagwat, *Lokamanya Tilak*, p. 79.

all must have qualified the regret felt about his leaving. There was a sense that Indians must now work on their own. At the 1892 Allahabad Congress, Pandit Bishambar Nath said "the children of the soil have learnt to stand upon their feet"[88] and the president, W. C. Bonnerjee, declared the Congress "had outgrown its dependence on one individual."[89]

If Hume had regarded the Congress leadership as a collectivity, it was an extremely narrow one, and on some strategic questions he had failed to consult many other leaders. Apparently, he had been acutely aware that he alone had been working full time for the Congress. In public and in private he had given the impression of feeling superior to his colleagues who made lesser sacrifices. His references to Indian Congressmen in his letters to Dufferin were condescending. In one he had written of them as his "children" and in another as "childish" people who had not yet learned to work hard.[90] The tone of his communications to nationalists was moralistic and guruish. Sometimes he chided or tried to shame them for their inaction. In his 1883 manifesto to the graduates of Calcutta University he had written: "If you, the picked men, the most highly educated of the nation, cannot, scorning personal ease and selfish objects, make a resolute struggle to secure greater freedom for yourselves and your country . . . then we your friends are wrong and our adversaries right."[91] He delivered similar, hectoring messages after the Congress was founded. Whether his censures, his prodding, and his tireless efforts on behalf of the Congress made nationalists more or less likely to assist is uncertain. Anandamohan Bose wrote in his diary in April 1886 that he supposed Hume was doing more work "than all of us put together," and Naoroji told Hume he wondered "what would become of the Congress if you did not keep them up."[92] The gratitude and guilt, though, were often mixed with resentment. Some Bengali and Maharashtrian delegates objected to the fact that a small number of leaders met at Hume's house prior to the 1886 and 1887 Congresses and decided what would and would not be discussed and what resolutions would

[88] Besant, *How India Wrought*, p. 142.
[89] Argov, *Moderates and Extremists*, p. 50.
[90] Martin, *New India*, pp. 130 and 164.
[91] S. K. Ratcliffe, *Sir William Wedderburn and the Indian Reform Movement* (London, 1923), p. 58.
[92] Seal, *The Emergence*, p. 287.

be passed in the open session. Mahadev Ballal Namjoshi complained to Hume at Madras in 1887 about the lack of a representative executive committee. Hume, however, did not give it his "serious attention" but rather treated it "with ill-concealed contempt." When Bipinchandra Pal threatened to carry the fight for more democratic procedures to the Congress floor, Ranade intervened and persuaded Hume and others of the need for a representative Subjects Committee.[93] After that, the Subjects Committee offered a check, although a limited one, on the autocracy of Hume and later of Pherozeshah Mehta.

Complaints about Hume's imperiousness continued. Naoroji felt it necessary to urge Wacha in May 1889 not to "feel annoyed at Mr. Hume. . . . We must not forget what we owe him. . . . Trust him as one with whose scoldings we must put up as we would do of an elder brother or father."[94] But even as loyal and self-effacing a man as Wacha found Hume difficult to accept. He wrote back that Hume "ought not to behave as a tryant. . . . He thinks in all matters he must have the upper hand."[95]

ENGLISHMEN IN THE CONGRESS

Hume was not the only non-Indian to play a key role in the early Congress. Nor was he the only one to embarrass the Congress and to provoke divisions within its ranks. Their were two types of British participants in the early years. In the first and less controversial category were those who attended one or two sessions as president or prominent guests. Their presence was highly valued for the effect it was thought to have of reassuring skeptical Indians and Englishmen about the clout and basic loyalty of the Congress. George Yule, president of a large Calcutta commercial house, Alfred Webb, an Irish M. P., and Sir Henry Cotton and Sir William Wedderburn, retired I.C.S. officers, each presided. William Gladstone and other prominent English politicians were invited to preside but declined.

More important than the occasional English participants were the men who participated in the Congress for extended periods in India and London. At times, they served, as Hume did, as com-

---

[93] Bipin Chandra Pal, *Memories of My Life and Times (1886–1900)* (Calcutta, 1951), pp. 35–41.
[94] R. P. Masani, *Dadabhai Naoroji* (Delhi, 1960), p. 117.
[95] Seal, *The Emergence*, p. 288.

munication links between different regional groups. Perhaps some Congressmen found it easier or more comfortable to approach an Englishman than the Congress leaders from another province. Some may have turned to Englishmen out of habit. Whatever the explanation, on important occasions Indian Congressmen used English delegates to convey their feelings to men from other areas. Motilal Ghose's memoirs describe an illustrative case involving four Europeans and the 1888 resolution demanding that simultaneous civil service examinations be held in India and England. This perennial resolution was introduced in 1888 by Eardley Norton. However, John Adam, principal of Pachaiyappa's College and a sometime vice president of the Madras Standing Congress Committee, moved an amendment asking that successful Indian candidates be required to receive subsequent schooling in England on the assumption that an English education was necessary for membership in the I.C.S. Motilal Ghose recognized that by endorsing this amendment, the Congress would in effect be advocating the breaking of caste by sea voyage. He believed that such action might alienate important conservative supporters of the Congress, including the Maharaja of Darbhanga and Maharaja Jatindramohan Tagore. Motilal feared that "the Congress would at once be characterised as a non-Hindu organisation by its opponents and then the whole Hindu nation . . . would disavow the Congress." Therefore, he sought out Norton, Hume, and Captain Banon and explained why he felt Adam's amendment was dangerous. Norton, Hume, and Banon (an English landowner from Kulu valley), who had influence with delegates from Madras, Bombay, and the Punjab, respectively, agreed to help defeat the amendment.[96]

When Adam's amendment was debated in the next day's session, Manomohan Ghose supported it, saying that Indian candidates for the I.C.S. should be imbued with Western culture and be familiar with English social and political institutions. He said that most delegates from Bengal, Bombay, and Madras supported the amendment. However, in the interests of unity he advised that the amendment be dropped. The delegates, presumably having also received Hume's, Norton's, and Banon's advice, acceded to Monomohan's suggestion,[97] thereby ending a division

[96] Dutt, *Memoirs of Moti Lal Ghose*, pp. 65–66.
[97] *Report of the 4th INC*, pp. 36–38.

First Years and Hume

which followed generational lines, with younger delegates generally backing Adam against older delegates.[98]

On this and other occasions, Englishman helped smooth out difficulties between Indian Congressmen. However, English friends of the Congress sometimes embarrassed and divided the nationalist movement. Hume's comments on peasant insurrection did that. Particular activities of William Digby and Eardley Norton were also publicly disapproved by the Congress. In fact, in its first decade the Congress disassociated itself, it seems, only from the behavior of English members: Hume for his 1892 circular, Digby in 1892 for his Indian Political Agency, and Norton in 1894 for his extramarital affair.

Digby was the former editor of an English newspaper in Madras who, after returning to England about 1880, became a businessman, an active radical Liberal, and a champion of Indian reform. He repeatedly sought money from Indians to support his political activities and this left him vulnerable to unflattering accusations and insinuations. He was reported in Bombay in 1885 to have "requested £1,500 for election expenses and £1,000 a year for five years for arguing India's case in the Commons if elected."[99] He was defeated in the 1885 general election, but in 1889 he became secretary of the British Committee of the Congress, for which the Congress paid him about £1,000 a year.[100] Digby's trouble with the Congress arose not over the British Committee but over the Indian Political Agency which he, W. C. Bonnerjee, and Motilal and Shishirkumar Ghose had started as a non-Congress effort, *inter alia*, to defend the interests of the Native States and their rulers. In 1889 Digby, with Charles Bradlaugh's help, took up the cause of the Maharaja of Kashmir who had been forced to resign by the British after allegedly intriguing with Russian agents against the British. The Ghoses were active in India in arousing support for the Maharaja, and in October 1889 they published in the *Amrita Bazar Patrika* an edited version of a confidential Foreign Office Minute on Kashmir by Sir Mortimer Durand. Sections of the *Patrika* version were misquoted and rewritten in such a way that the intention

[98] Ibid., p. xxvi.
[99] Lord Reay, governor of Bombay, wrote that this information was reported by a member of the Bombay Association whom he did not identify. Martin, *New India*, p. 224, note 2.
[100] Argov, *Moderates and Extremists*, p. 49.

First Years and Hume

of the Government of India seemed to be to annex Kashmir; the original Minute gave no such impression. Lord Lansdowne publicly characterized the *Patrika* version as a "sheer and impudent fabrication";[101] it is difficult to believe, in reading the original and *Patrika* versions side by side, that the intention was not to deceive.[102]

Soon after the *Amrita Bazar Patrika* published its copy of the Minute, the Government of India drafted and enacted a Bill to Prevent Disclosure of Official Documents and Information, providing penalties up to transportation for life for wrongfully obtaining or communicating information of state importance. Lord Lansdowne used the occasion of its introduction in the Imperial Legislative Council to expose the differences between the true copy and the *Amrita Bazar Patrika*'s copy.[103]

The confidential Minute on Kashmir was one of three highly confidential matters leaked by the Congress press. The *Bengalee* made public Lord Dufferin's despatch outlining his proposals for the expansion of the Indian legislative councils;[104] and subsequently, the *Hindu* of Madras printed a letter from its London correspondent divulging the contents of one of Lord Lansdowne's letters on council reforms.[105] The government never discovered how these latter two items were obtained, but William Digby was thought to have secured the Kashmir despatch from the India Office,[106] and it is possible that he got hold of the other two items as well. This hypothesis is supported by the fact that Digby was the London correspondent for the *Patrika*, the *Bengalee*, and the *Hindu*.[107]

After the Kashmir affair, Pandit Ajudhia Nath, the joint general secretary of the Congress, made a special point of dissociating the Congress from Digby's Political Agency.[108] Digby ended his

---

101 Speech of 17 Oct. 1889, India LCP, p. 272.

102 The original and *Patrika* versions are enclosed in Lansdowne to Cross, 17 Oct. 1889, No. 46. MSS. Eur. E. 243/27.

103 India LCP, 17 Oct. 1889, pp. 271–276.

104 Lansdowne to Cross, 14 Oct. 1889, No. 46. MSS. Eur. E. 243/27.

105 Lansdowne to Cross, 19 May 1889, No. 76. MSS. Eur. E. 243/28.

106 T. and D. Dept. to Bradford, 16 Sept. 1889, Demi-Off. Corresp., Pol. and Sec. Dept., Vol. 3.

107 A. C. Lethbridge, Gen. Supt. for Sup. of T. and D., to D. M. Stewart, Council of India, 12 Oct. 1892, Enclosure to Memorandum on Digby, Demi-Off. Corresp., Pol. and Sec. Dept., Vol. 4.

108 *Report of 6th INC*, p. 60.

First Years and Hume

formal connection with the Congress in 1892 when he resigned as secretary to the British Committee of the Congress, although he continued to use his Indian Political Agency. He made himself *persona non grata* with the Government of India in 1892 by writing to the Diwan of Mysore State, asking to settle certain claims with a Madras client of Digby's Agency. Digby allegedly hoped to receive 30 per cent of the claims.[109] According to the government's informant, Digby implied to the Diwan that he possessed great influence with the India Office, and he expressed the hope that he would not be compelled to publish the details of the claim in the newspapers. In an interview with Digby in December 1892, Lord Lansdowne informed Digby that the Government of India would not tolerate any attempt to exploit the native chiefs.[110] To the probable relief of Indian leaders, Digby had little further connection with the Congress.

Congress disenchantment with Eardley Norton, the Madras barrister, resulted from entirely different circumstances than the political adventurism of Hume and Digby. The Norton case illustrates not only the failure of English Congressmen to keep in step with prevailing values of their Indian colleagues but also another dimension of the plurality of Indian values which the Congress was straining to contain and harmonize. Early in 1894, Norton was named as co-respondent in a divorce suit in England and as an adulterer in another suit in Madras.[111] In consequence, newspapers in Madras, Bombay, and Calcutta protested his continued presence on the executive committee of the Reception Committee of the forthcoming Madras Congress. The Calcutta Standing Congress Committee voted unanimously that the Congress "should not keep any concern with Mr. Norton." On board the steamer to Madras, 18 of the 26 delegates from Bengal and northern India endorsed a similar statement.[112] By the time delegates arrived in Madras, it was evident that Norton's conduct had offended social purists among both reformist and orthodox groups in the Congress.

However, as so often happened in the early Congress, once in

[109] Lethbridge to Stewart, 12 Oct. 1892.
[110] Memorandum on an Interview between the Viceroy and Mr. William Digby on the 16th Dec. 1892, Demi-Off. Corresp., Pol. and Sec. Dept., Vol. 5.
[111] This account is taken from the *The Tenth Indian National Congress. Purity and Politics. An Appeal to All Friends of India* (Madras, 1895).
[112] Ibid., pp. 5 and 20.

Madras, traditions of deference and good manners temporarily stilled the opposition. Surendranath Banerjea dissociated himself from the statement of other Bengali delegates asking for Norton's expulsion. When the Subjects Committee met, only one member objected to placing Norton on the agenda as a speaker.[113] None of Norton's critics, and they were present, would second the objection. Therefore, Norton was placed on the agenda to move a resolution.

The opposition which had been muted during the Subjects Committee meeting surfaced during the open Congress session. Norton was seated on the dais next to Mrs. Sullivan whose identification card called her "Mrs. Norton." Alfred Webb, the Irish M. P. who presided over the 1894 session, disallowed efforts to have Norton removed from the Subjects Committee. But the controversy continued. After Webb ruled out of order a motion by an English woman that would have denied Norton the right to speak, a number of important delegates walked out of the pavilion, including conservative Hindus such as V. Bhashyam Iyengar, Hindu reformers such as Raghunath Rao, the Indian Christians Alfred Nundy and Kalicharan Banerji, and Mr. Stuart, principal of Madras Presidency College. S. Subramania Iyer not only walked out, he formally resigned from the Congress Standing Committee.[114] Norton never recovered his position within the Congress leadership, although he was elected without opposition to the Madras Legislative Council by the Madras municipal commissioners in 1899,[115] and he spoke briefly at one more Congress (1903).

The controversies in the early 1890s over the behavior of English Congressmen led to a diminution of the English role in the leadership within India. Even W. C. Bonnerjee, who had promoted that English role, objected to the election of Alfred Webb to the presidency in 1894 on the grounds that only Indians should serve as president.[116] But the full assertion of Indian control of the Congress was delayed by divisions between aspirants for leadership and developments in England which drew nationalist attention to Parliamentary politics. As a result, there was a hiatus between Hume's withdrawal to London and the emergence of strong Indian leadership. In theory, Indian Congress-

[113] Ibid., p. 25.   [114] Ibid., pp. 7–11.
[115] *Friend of India and Statesman*, 24 Aug. 1899.
[116] Sinha (ed.), *Freedom Movement*, pp. 324–325.

men agreed that the time had come for Indians to lead the nationalist organization. However, without anything approaching a consensus about who should succeed Hume and about what direction the Congress should move in, the continued reappointment of the reluctant Hume as general secretary was a useful way of avoiding an open split in the Congress.

―――――― *Chapter Four* ――――――

CONGRESS IN THE DOLDRUMS

AFTER HUME, WHAT?

Hume's departure did less to solve the Congress's problem of finding its own direction and identity than to remove a distraction from that process. Congressmen were now freer from the erratic, unpredictable, and domineering influence of a paternal Englishman. Hume's leadership had become a problem in itself; now Congressmen could concentrate on defining India's national interests and on the means of realizing them. Hume had contributed to the process of definition or discovery in a negative way by revealing the limits of the movement's appeal among Muslims and peasants. His stewardship had also shown that few Congress founders were prepared to pursue goals which brought sanctions or even strong disapproval from the government.

The setbacks of the late 1880s were followed by a period of drift and uncertainty. Most of the major political controversies in the 1890s were not the result of Congress initiatives. In succession, the Age of Consent Bill, the cow killing question, British policies to combat plague, and famine stirred controversy. In each case the Congress faced issues for which it had no prepared response. The age of consent and animal slaughter questions were deliberately avoided by Congress leaders because of the contentious domestic and communal issues which were involved. Adoption of a partisan position on the age of marriage would have alienated one or the other important segments of Hindu society, just as a resolution on cow protection would have disappointed many Hindus or Muslims. Plague and famine were discussed in the Congress, and the famines of 1897 and 1899–1900 accelerated the shift of nationalist thinking toward economic issues. However, the immediate effect of plague and famine was to disrupt the lives of millions of Indians to such an extent that politics temporarily became a peripheral concern for many Congress supporters. For these reasons, the period between 1890 and 1904 was a time of uncertain purpose for the Congress, a time in which it rarely dominated the headlines of even the nationalist press. But even if the Congress leadership had not been kept off balance by social reform, communal problems, and natural disasters, the organization itself was in no position to provide effective leadership to Indian discontents. It was still groping for operational procedures which could harmonize its leaders' autocratic instincts and timidity with the expectations of democracy and militancy among many rank and file members.

One of the earliest indications that the Congress was drifting or marking time was the inability to agree on a successor to Hume after his departure in 1892. Throughout the 1890s, the Congress continued the annual ritual of appointing Hume to the post of general secretary despite his absence and his avowed desire to be replaced.[1] Ranade was the man with the forcefulness, prestige, and support of other leaders who had seemed a likely successor as a full-time Congress worker and coordinator. Ranade was reported to have said in 1892 that he intended to retire from the High Court after a year or two in order to devote most of his time to Congress work.[2] However, he did not, perhaps because of the strong feeling aroused against social reformers during the Age of Consent Bill controversy and the rise of Tilak's influence in Ranade's home area. Tilak's success in forcing the Social Conference, in which Ranade was the central figure, out of the Congress pandal in Poona in 1895 may have finally discouraged him from picking up the reigns of the Congress. For whatever reasons, Ranade remained on the High Court from where he could only advise the movement, and the Congress continued without a single directing figure between 1892 and the emergence of Pherozeshah Mehta around 1899 as the dominant (and domineering) leader. In the interim, the leadership was a shifting, collective affair with W. C. Bonnerjee, Surendranath Banerjea, P. Ananda Charlu, and Mehta making major decisions, sometimes with Ranade's advice. Most years the Congress appointed prominent Indians, such as Pandit Ajudhia Nath, P. Ananda Charlu, and annually beginning in 1895, D. E. Wacha, to be joint general secretary. However, in 1893 and 1894 the Congress

[1] Govt. of Bombay, *Source Material*, II, 129.
[2] P. Ananda Charlu, "The Indian National Congress: A Retrospect," *Hindustan Review and Kayastha Samachar*, Vol. VIII, Nos. 1 and 2 (July-Aug. 1903), 20–21.

did not designate any Indian to carry on Congress work between sessions. The lack of a full-time worker or organization in India was one reason the 1894 Congress resolved "that the time has come when the Constitution of Congress should be settled."[3]

The 1894 resolution calling for a written constitution reflected the growing impression that the Congress had ceased developing. Some men attributed the arrested growth to Hume's absence. J. Ghosal told the 1893 Congress delegates that "you know very well how helpless we all Indians are without the help of Englishmen of position."[4] Similarly, P. Ananda Charlu, looking back from the year 1903 and assessing the failures of the Congress, wrote that "the withdrawal by Mr. Hume of the loving and loveable despotism . . . told upon our efficiency."[5] The opposite may have been nearer the truth. If Hume and Wedderburn had left the Indian leaders to their own devices, or if Ananda Charlu and other leaders had cut themselves free from their British friends, perhaps the nationalist organization would have recovered its vitality before 1905. Instead, the Congress continued to confer the general secretary's office on Hume.

Congress in England

The bestowal of the general secretaryship on a man who lived in England signified more than inability to agree on an appropriate replacement for Hume. In the two or three years before Hume left India, many Congressmen, as a result of their early failures, had come to believe that the main hope for reform lay in England, with Parliament and the British electorate. The forceful advocacy of Indian interests by Charles Bradlaugh (who died in 1891) and the lengthy Parliamentary debates leading to the India Councils Act of 1892 contributed to the revived tendency to look to England for change. And since Congress leaders were yet unwilling to adopt confrontation tactics in India, they were attracted, as in 1885, by what William Wedderburn called a "flanking movement" or an appeal direct to the British electorate, to whom the government of India was constitutionally responsible.[6]

[3] Resolution XXVII.
[4] Govt. of Bombay, *Source Material*, II, 130.
[5] Charlu, "The Indian National Congress: A Retrospect," pp. 20–21.
[6] Wedderburn, *Hume*, p. 86.

In the Doldrums

The official organ of the Congress in London was known as the British Committee. The British Committee of the Congress was formed on 27 July 1889 with Wedderburn as its chairman and William Digby as its secretary. The first move toward reviving the Indian Parliamentary Committee was also made in 1889 when a meeting was held at the National Liberal Club under the presidency of George Yule.[7] This committee of M. P.s had been founded in 1883 with the assistance of John Bright "to secure combined Parliamentary action in matters affecting Indian public interests," but it hardly functioned before July 1893.[8]

In 1890 the Congress, as part of its flanking movement, sent a delegation on a speaking tour of England and resolved to hold the 1892 Congress in London. The cost and fear of caste excommunication prevented holding the London session and instead the Congress relied on Wedderburn, Hume, Dadabhai Naoroji, and the British Committee to represent it in England. The British Committee supplied the small number of M. P.s active in the Parliamentary Committee with information on Indian affairs and assisted them in their election campaigns. It also organized public meetings and lecture tours for Indians visiting England and for other people interested in Indian reform. It published a newspaper, *India*, which was intended to be a "storehouse from which arms and materials are supplied to all those who are willing to strike a blow on behalf of India."[9] The existence of *India*, the British Committee of the Congress, and the Indian Parliamentary Committee helped preserve a substantial role for Englishmen in Congress affairs and perpetuated the illusion that the main hope for Indian reform resided in a public relations campaign in England rather than political mobilization in India.

Confidence in the British electorate reached its height in 1892–1893 with the passage by the House of Commons of the legislative council reforms and a resolution calling for Indian Civil Service examinations to be held simultaneously in India and England,[10] and with the election of Dadabhai Naoroji, William

[7] *Report of the 5th INC*, p. 8. George Yule was a Calcutta merchant who presided over the 1888 Congress.

[8] *India*, Vol. VII, No. 5 (May 1896), 133.

[9] Wedderburn, *Hume*, p. 97.

[10] This resolution was passed by a vote of 84 to 78 and was not implemented.

Wedderburn, and the Liberal majority to Parliament. After 1893, however, interest in British politics faded somewhat as it became evident that neither the election of the Liberals nor the expansion of the Indian legislative councils was going to produce enactments favored by the Congress. The defeat of W. C. Bonnerjee and Dadabhai Naoroji in the 1895 general elections further discredited the reliance on British public opinion to liberalize the Raj. Then in 1896 the Conservative government required the Government of India to impose excise duties on Indian cotton exports in response to Lancashire fears of competition from the Indian textile industry. Probably no single act in the early decades of the Congress contributed as much to the belief that India was governed primarily for the benefit of England. P. Ananda Charlu expressed nationalist feeling in the Viceroy's Legislative Council when he said that while Britain defended India from foreign powers, India "is defenceless where the English and Indian interests clash and where (as a Tamil saying puts it) the very fence begins to feed on the crop."[11]

Congress Financial Troubles

The British Committee is of interest not so much for its successes, which were modest and infrequent, as for what its relations with the Congress in India reveal about the Congress's development. Instead of helping to unite the nationalist movement, instead of contributing to a sense of pride and patriotic achievement, the British Committee became a source of chagrin for nationalists. Tension between the British Committee and the Congress grew because of Congressmen's unwillingness to contribute the amounts of money the leadership arranged to have committed by each year's Congress. The continued failure of the Congress to finance the British Committee bears out as well as any other factor the truth of Lajpat Rai's observation that Indians did not feel their existence as honorable men depended on the success of the Congress as it was then constituted.

The amount of money budgeted for the British Committee each year was often larger than that spent by the Reception

[11] Quoted by Bipan Chandra, *The Rise and Growth of Economic Nationalism in India: Economic Policies of Indian National Leadership, 1880–1905* (New Delhi, 1966), p. 247.

Committee of the annual Congress session. The newspaper *India* was the chief expenditure, costing about £2,000 a year from the time it became a regular monthly, in 1892, until 1898 when it was converted into a weekly.[12] After that the expense was even greater. *India* contained little advertising and it was distributed free of charge in England to M. P.s and other people interested in India.[13] The activities of the British Committee itself cost another £1,000,[14] and included political breakfasts, lecture tours, and the preparation of material for Parliamentary debates, British newspapers, and witnesses appearing before such bodies as the Welby Commission on Indian Finance.[15]

Theoretically, the £3,000 budgeted for the British Committee and *India* was to be supplied by the Congress in India. For this purpose the annual sessions passed resolutions assigning Rs. 60,000 or less to the British Committee and *India*.[16] The bulk of this sum would have been collected if the annual subscription fee of Rs. 6 had been paid for each of the copies of *India* sent to India, and, indeed, at one stage, when 10,000 copies of each issue were sent, the whole Rs. 60,000 should have been gathered. But most people who received *India* did not pay, and the money that was remitted to the British Committee often consisted, in part, of surplus funds from the Reception Committee[17] or donations from zamindars and chiefs of native states. In the seven years between 1894 and 1900, the total amount transmitted to the British Committee by the Congress was Rs. 2,25,800, or Rs.

[12] Speech of Surendranath Banerjea, *Report of the 10th INC*, p. 155.

[13] Wedderburn, *Hume*, p. 98. In each of the three years preceding 1892, Rs. 40,000 was voted for work in England.

[14] Banerjea, *Report of the 10th INC*, p. 155.

[15] See monthly issues of *India*; Masani, *Naoroji*; and Wedderburn, *Hume*.

[16] Rs. 60,000 equaled £3,250 at the 1894 exchange rate of 1s. 1d. In 1894, the Rs. 60,000 was assigned exclusively for work in England. After 1894, the exchange rate rose slightly and in 1899 it was fixed at 1s. 4d. From 1895 to 1898 the Rs. 60,000 pledged for Congress work was also to cover the expenses of joint general secretary's office in India. However, the joint general secretary seems to have had few expenses and the bulk of the money was intended for England. In 1899 and 1900, the Congress pledged, respectively, Rs. 54,000 and Rs. 30,000 for work in England and did not mention the joint general secretary's office.

[17] Rs. 25,000 of the surplus of Rs. 28,000 from the 1896 Congress were sent to the British Committee. (*Bengalee*, 13 Feb. 1897.) There was a surplus of about Rs. 30,000 from the 1894 Congress, also. (*Bengalee*, 13 Apr. 1895.)

32,257 per annum.[18] This was Rs. 1,58,200 less than the amount pledged for Congress work in those years.

Hume, Wedderburn, and Naoroji periodically sent letters to the Congress standing committees reminding them of the Congress promises, but they had little effect.[19] The reluctance of people in India to contribute to Congress activities in England after 1895 was related to the improbability of their Liberal and Radical friends achieving success in Parliament against the Liberal Front Benches and the large Conservative majority. There was also a feeling in India that the British Committee was extravagant and often inactive, and that *India* was not well conducted.[20] Furthermore, the only direct communication to Congress supporters from the British Committee was more often than not the occasion of another appeal for payment of outstanding debts. Alfred Nundy, the Indian Christian from the North-Western Provinces who was appointed assistant secretary of the Congress, found during his fund raising tour in 1900 that "more than one Secretary adopted the plan of never opening the cover of a letter from the British Committee from fear it may contain a demand for money; and by far the larger number of them after reading the letter, either throw it away or file it, instead of circulating it to members of a Committee where one exists."[21]

The failure of the secretaries of the Congress standing committees to collect subscriptions for *India* became a crucial problem only after the death of the Maharaja of Darbhanga in 1898. The Government of Bengal reported that he had given Rs. 10,000 annually to *India*,[22] and he was also said to have paid for the conversion of *India* into a weekly.[23] But even before Darbhanga's death, a major portion of the British Committee's funds was coming from England. W. C. Bonnerjee, who lived with his family near London, gave "ten to twenty thousand rupees" every year,

[18] Letter from Alfred Nundy, assistant secretary of the Congress, reviewing report of the British Committee, *Bengalee*, 29 May 1901.

[19] Ibid., 13 Feb. 1897.

[20] For instance, Speech of Pandit Madan Mohan Malaviya, *Report of 17th INC*, p. 80; *Mahratta*, 6 Aug. 1899, T. and D. Selections, 14 Aug. 1899, para. 590, PSLI, Vol. 116; *Bengalee*, 20 Jan. and 26 Dec. 1900 and 24 and 29 May 1901.

[21] Ibid., 24 Dec. 1900.

[22] C. W. Bolton to C. S. Bayley, 18 July 1899, enclosure to Curzon to Hamilton, 2 Aug. 1899, MSS. Eur. D. 510/2.

[23] Hamilton to Elgin, 19 Aug. 1897, MSS. Eur. C. 125/2.

according to Pyarelal.[24] Hume and Wedderburn also gave extensive help to the British Committee in lieu of contributions from India, and neither was willing to continue to supplement Congress funds from his own resources. In the first years of the Congress, Hume had spent "ten or fifteen thousand rupees out of his own pocket" for work in England and India.[25] In later years, Wedderburn bore the greater burden, and by 1904 he had spent £10,000 or about Rs. 150,000 on the Congress.[26] In 1900, when Wedderburn decided not to stand for reelection to Parliament, it was said that he was retiring because he had been physically and financially overtaxed by his work for the Congress.[27]

By 1899 the strains between the British Committee and the Congress were beginning to show in public. When the nagging letters from Hume, Wedderburn, and Naoroji became public, they encouraged the Anglo-Indian press and officials such as Curzon in their belief that the Congress was losing strength.[28] In October 1899, Wedderburn and Hume sent a tart letter to the Congress standing committees, saying "it is almost incredible but is none the less the fact, that of the Rs. 60,000 voted annually ... only Rs. 16,205 have as yet been received on account of 1898 and only Rs. 2,064 on account of the current year, now in its last quarter."[29] Ten weeks later, at the Congress session, Surendranath Banerjea made his third appeal for funds for *India* and the British Committee. He repeated the familiar argument that "your voice will be like that of one crying in the wilderness" unless it was heard in the British Parliament, platform, and press. He reminded the Congress that the Irish agitation for Home Rule had little success until it was transferred to England, and

[24] Pyarelal, *Mahatma Gandhi*, Vol. 1, *The Early Phase* (Ahmedabad, 1965), p. 129.

[25] Annually, it seems. Speech of Surendranath Banerjea, *Report of the 5th INC*.

[26] Speech of D. E. Wacha, *Report of the 20th INC*, p. 227. Naoroji and Bonnerjee also gave money to *India*. According to Alfred Nundy, Wedderburn, Hume, Naoroji, and Bonnerjee all helped raise the special deficit fund in 1896, but then none of them contributed from 1897 until 1901. *Bengalee*, 29 May 1901.

[27] "Manifesto" sent by Wedderburn, Hume, and Naoroji to secretaries of the Congress standing committees. *Bengalee*, 22 Nov. 1900.

[28] Curzon to Hamilton, 2 Aug. 1899, and its enclosure, C. W. Bolton to C. S. Bayley, 18 July 1899, MSS. Eur. D. 510/2.

[29] Enclosure to Curzon to Hamilton, 28 Dec. 1899, MSS. Eur. D. 510/3.

this, he said, demonstrated that "we must follow the same methods."[30] However, the argument that reform would come only from appealing to the British electorate seemed to be losing its appeal: in 1899 it brought a mere Rs. 3,000[31] while Banerjea's similar appeal in 1892 had attracted almost Rs. 13,500[32] and his 1889 appeal had produced Rs. 65,000.[33]

If there was any doubt that the niggardly Rs. 3,000 contributed by the 1899 Congress for arrears was a mark of the Congress's loss of confidence in the British Committee, that doubt was removed by an 1899 resolution. This resolution said that a new agency should be established in London to carry on Congress propaganda work "in concert with the British Committee."[34] Significantly, the new agency was to be under the direction of that year's president, R. C. Dutt, who had not joined the British Committee after arriving in London in 1897. As this resolution was not followed up,[35] the British Committee alone continued officially to represent the Congress effort in England.

However, there was another organization, called the London Indian Society, which claimed to represent Indians resident in the United Kingdom. Whereas the British Committee was a closed body largely controlled by Englishmen, the London Indian Society, with its open meetings and predominantly Indian composition, was the more natural focus of allegiance for Indian students. The society made special arrangements to meet students arriving in England and to help them find lodgings. The India Office had the society's annual conference in December 1898 "specially reported" and found that the proceedings, which were intended to correspond to the Indian National Congress session, were "violent in language."[36]

Wedderburn and the British Committee must have been discouraged by the 1899 Congress's diminished contribution and its resolution calling for a new agency in London. But the committee continued its efforts to raise more money. The harder it tried the greater the gulf became between nationalists and their British sympathizers. In 1900 the committee reduced the number of copies of *India* allocated for India, raised the subscription

[30] *Report of 15th INC*, pp. 104–105. [31] Ibid., p. xxvi.
[32] *Report of the 8th INC*, p. 115. [33] *Report of the 5th INC*, p. lxv.
[34] Resolution XII. [35] Banerjea, *A Nation*, p. 165.
[36] Unc͡ted foolscap signed by W. Lee-Warner, attached to T. and D. Selections, 19 June 1899, PSLI, Vol. 114.

rate, and offered a commission on collections to the local Congress bodies.[37] Alfred Nundy toured India the same year for the purpose of collecting funds and improving Congress morale. In neither task did he have much success. During the first six weeks he raised only Rs. 4,000 for the British Committee.[38] In 1901 the British Committee and the Indian Congress Committee had an open disagreement over their respective functions. The Indian Congress Committee, which was appointed to coordinate the movement under the 1899 constitution, ordered local standing committees to channel future funds and correspondence for the British Committee through Wacha, the joint general secretary. The British Committee, however, contradicted this order in a circular of its own to the standing committees. When the British Committee stopped sending *India* to defaulters, the secretaries of the standing committees found that they were unable to collect any of the outstanding subscriptions, and almost none of the current ones.[39]

The British Committee became so exasperated by the delinquency of Congressmen in India that it announced it would give up its rooms and discontinue *India* if the outstanding balance of Rs. 37,500 was not received by the end of June 1901.[40] At the last moment, Dadabhai Naoroji deposited Rs. 25,000 with Wedderburn as a guarantee against losses, and W. C. Bonnerjee and "others" made contributions. The British Committee was able to continue operations and to turn down R. C. Dutt's offer to take over *India* in his private capacity.[41] However, relations between Indian and British Congressmen remained strained. The 1901 Congress pledged nothing for the British Committee or *India*, the 1902 Congress appointed regional secretaries who were "to be held responsible" for fixed numbers of subscriptions to *India*, and the 1903 and 1904 Congresses each pledged only about Rs. 10,000 for the British Committee. Starting in 1905, the Congress began voting thanks instead of money.[42] By this time, both

[37] R. C. Dutt's circular letter to the provincial Congress committees, *Bengalee*, 16 Feb. 1900.

[38] Ibid., 24 Apr. 1900.

[39] Alfred Nundy's circular letter to secretaries of the Congress standing committees, dated 25 June 1901, *Bengalee*, 28 June 1901.

[40] Ibid.

[41] Ibid., 21 June 1901. Also, Masani, *Naoroji*, p. 315.

[42] Resolutions XX of 1902, XIV of 1903, XVII of 1904, XIII of 1905, XII of 1906, and XVII of 1908.

Hume and Wedderburn had serious health problems, the flanking strategy had been turned over to Gokhale, and nationalist activity was focused on the partition of Bengal and the swadeshi movement in India.

The financial troubles of the Congress were by no means limited to support of its activities in England. Although more publicity was given to the sources of funds in its early years, before the government began making inquiries and exerting pressure on major benefactors, it is clear nevertheless that Congress operations within India were underfinanced. Starting in 1897, the year of Rand's assassination and Tilak's sedition trial, the Congress had to struggle to pay for its annual session and for the joint general secretary's office when it was maintained.[43] Each of the annual sessions between 1897 and 1903 cost the reception committees in the host cities between Rs. 30,000 and Rs. 50,000.[44] This included the cost of the pandal, decorations, and sometimes lodging and food for selected delegates. Some of this expenditure was recouped from fees collected from delegates and visitors, although the practice of waiving fees for certain groups, and for Muslims in particular, restricted that income somewhat. The difficulty experienced in finding funds for the Congresses of 1898 (Madras), 1899 (Lucknow), and 1900 (Lahore) was specifically attributed to lack of help from "the aristocracy" or large landholders, which in turn was blamed on government pressure. Congress leaders therefore decided to rely more heavily on the lower and middle classes.[45] This was hailed as a worthy object in any

[43] After Hume left India, from 1892 to 1894, no money was assigned by the Congress to the joint general secretary and his clerical staff, and from 1895 to 1898, a lump sum was designated for the British Committee, *India*, and the joint general secretary's office. The evidence suggests, however, that in these years there was very little activity or expenditure by the joint general secretary. See Resolutions XXIII of 1895, XXII of 1896, XIX of 1897, and XXV of 1898.

[44] An effort was always made to appoint as chairman of the Reception Committee a man possessing influence with a wide range of people. In 1905, the prototype of this person was found. He was Munshi Madho Lal. He was a Brahman, a lawyer, a banker, a landholder, an ex-judge, and a member of the U. P. Legislative Council. He donated Rs. 5,000 to the Congress and industrial exhibition funds. *Hindustan Review and Kayastha Samachar*, Vol. XI, No. 3 (March 1905), 283. Also, C. H. Rao, *Indian Biographical Dictionary, 1915* (Madras, 1915), p. 261.

[45] *Report of the 14th INC*, p. iii; also, *Report of the 15th INC*, pp. v-vi; *Report of the 16th INC*, p. 2; and *Bengalee*, 1 Jan. 1901.

In the Doldrums

case. Adversity was turned to advantage and a renewed emphasis was placed on the political education of the lower classes.[46] In 1899, the Congress distributed 30,000 copies of an appeal for funds,[47] and in 1901, the Calcutta Reception Committee printed 15,000 Bengali, Uriya, and Urdu pamphlets.[48] Congressmen also suggested various economies, including the reduction of the costly decorations and celebrations which had become a customary part of the annual session.[49] In 1899, under the pressure of financial need, it was decided to have the chairs for the Congress made in India instead of following what was apparently the usual course of importing them from Australia.[50]

The 1899 Congress also tried to revive the Permanent Fund to pay for nationalist activities. The Permanent Fund had originally been established in 1889, when Rs. 59,000 was voted to it by the Congress. Actually, only Rs. 5,000 was collected in the first year of the Permanent Fund, and this was lost when the Oriental Bank of Bombay went into liquidation in the Bombay financial crisis of 1890.[51] More money was voted to the fund by the Congresses of 1890 and 1892,[52] and in 1893, an "Indian Friend," believed to be the Maharaja of Darbhanga, gave Rs. 15,000 to the fund.[53] At one point the fund contained as much as £4,000 but by 1895, £1,000 had been borrowed to pay back debts which the Congress standing committee had failed to remit to the British Committee.[54] It seems that by 1899 the fund was wholly depleted, for in that year the Congress appointed a committee to take, among other things, "such steps as they may deem fit to raise a permanent fund for carrying on the work of the Indian National Congress."[55] This proposal was not acted on.

Bombay was the only province which seemed to have no diffi-

---

[46] Ibid., 12 Apr. 1901; also, *Report of the 15th INC*, p. vi.

[47] *Statesman*, 7 Sept. 1899.   [48] *Bengalee*, 25 Dec. 1901.

[49] See for instance, the speech of Kali Prasanna Roy, chairman of Lahore Reception Committee, 1900. *Report of the 16th INC*, p. 8.

[50] *Bengalee*, 16 Sept. 1899.

[51] Mazumdar, *Indian National Evolution*, p. 300.

[52] Resolutions XII of 1890 and XVII of 1892.

[53] Note by C. S. Bayley, 18 June 1899, enclosure to Curzon to Hamilton, 28 June 1899, MSS. Eur. D. 570/2.

[54] Report of the British Committee of the Indian National Congress for 1894–1895. *Bengalee*, 7 Dec. 1895.

[55] Resolution X (ii) of 1899.

In the Doldrums

culty in attracting funds. In Bombay city, Wacha[56] Telang,[57] Pherozeshah Mehta, and Naoroji[58] may have been influential in persuading Hindu and Parsi industrialists to assist the Congress. Among the mill-owners who gave were V. Dipchund,[59] G. G. Tejpal,[60] and J. N. Tata.[61] In the Bombay Deccan, the Maratha Brahman Congress leaders were closely associated with the money-lenders, bankers, and merchants through their caste, the Sarvajanik Sabha,[62] and the Congress itself.[63]

Another source of funds in western India were the Indian chiefs, including the rulers of Kolhapur, Baroda, Junagadh,[64]

[56] Wacha was a mill agent and was an active member of the mill-owners association.

[57] Telang was responsible for getting "the wealthy shettias of Bombay, his friends" to subscribe to the 1889 Congress. See Wacha's speech at the 1903 Telang Anniversary, Bombay, quoted by the *Bengalee*, 7 Oct. 1903.

[58] He was a partner in Cama and Co. from 1855 to 1858 or 1859, and then he started a firm of his own in England with two other Parsis. Masani, *Naoroji*, pp. 71–78.

[59] Rs. 1,275 in 1889. *Report of the 5th INC*, p. 80.

[60] Rs. 1,000 in 1889, ibid., p. 80.

[61] Rs. 1,000 in 1895. Letter from H. Kennedy, Com. of Bombay Police, to E. C. Cox, 20 July 1899. Enclosure to Curzon to Hamilton, 27 Sept. 1899, MSS. Eur. D. 510/3. Tata also gave money to Behramji Malabari for his *Indian Spectator* which often differed with the Congress. (Unsigned article by Malabari, "The Native Press–Then and Now," *East and West*, Vol. III, No. 34. [Aug. 1904], 853.) Tata was often criticized for his failure to support Congress finances. His 1895 contribution seems to have been his only one. His biographer is wrong in saying that "his participation in politics was confined to regular attendance at the Congress": he did not even attend the Congress except upon rare occasions. F. R. Harris, *Jamsetji Nusserwanji Tata: A Chronicle of His Life* (Bombay, 1958), p. 258.

[62] See occupations of Sarvajanik Sabha members attending the 1892 Congress, appendix to *Report of the 8th INC*.

[63] When the Congress was held in Poona in 1895, an exceptionally large proportion of the delegates (437 out of 1,584) belonged to the commercial classes. Most of them came from Poona and the surrounding area. See Table, P. C. Ghosh, "The Development of the Indian National Congress, 1892–1909," Ph.D. thesis, University of London, 1958, pp. 50–51; also *Report of the 11th INC*, Appendix ii. G. P. Pradhan and A. K. Bhagwat (*Tilak*, pp. 20, 97–98) say that Mahadeo Ballal Namjoshi "was largely instrumental in establishing a contact between the merchants and trading class and the extremist party led by Tilak." Namjoshi helped start the Poona Metal Factory and the Poona Industrial Exhibition, and he purchased the *Kesari*'s first printing press. He died in 1896.

[64] The governor of Bombay wrote in 1906 that Junagadh state was giving Mehta and Naoroji about Rs. 600 a month "for the exercise of their *moral*

In the Doldrums

Bhownagar, and Gondal.[65] The Gaekwar of Baroda and the Thakur of Gondal were especially helpful to Dadabhai Naoroji in London in the 1890s.[66] Naoroji, in fact, was given so much money that he was able in 1895 to turn down an offer from J. N. Tata of Rs. 5,000 toward his Parliamentary campaign expenses.[67] The question of the way in which Naoroji used his money arose in 1892 when certain British newspapers claimed that he had received £28,000 from the Indian princes.[68] John Biddulph, the Government of India agent at Baroda (1893–1895), reported that more than Rs. 100,000 had been removed from the Baroda treasury without the minister's knowledge and that Naoroji was heard to boast during a visit to Baroda "that he could do what he liked with the Irish members."[69] However, a number of officials were willing or anxious to believe the worst about the nationalists, and such hearsay is worth little without independent confirmation.

The reception committees of the Congresses held in the Bombay Presidency not only raised the necessary funds with seeming ease, but the Bombay leaders, at the 1903 Congress when the movement was in the doldrums and no other province was willing to take its turn as host to the next session, invited the Congress to Bombay for the 1904 Congress—the second time Bombay Province had held a session in three years. Even more excep-

---

influence in behalf of the State at headquarters." Lamington to Morley, 26 Dec. 1906. Microfilm Reel No. 675, MSS. Eur. B. 159.

[65] H. Kennedy, Com. of Bombay police, to E. C. Cox, 20 July 1899. Enclosure to Curzon to Hamilton, 27 Sept. 1899, MSS. Eur. D. 510/3.

[66] The Gaekwar admitted in 1899 in an interview with Lord Curzon that he gave £1,000 to Naoroji's campaign funds and Rs. 1,000 annually to the Congress. "Memorandum of Conversation with the Gaekwar of Baroda." Enclosure of Curzon to Hamilton, 12 July 1899, MSS. Eur. D. 510/2. William Lee-Warner, secretary of the Pol. and Sec. Dept., India Office, was told that the Thakur of Gondal gave Rs. 500,000 to Naoroji's campaign. W. Lee-Warner to C. S. Bayley, 30 Aug. 1897, p. 195, Demi-Off. Corresp., Pol. Dept., Vol. 12. See also Masani, *Naoroji*, p. 373.

[67] Ibid., p. 372. [68] Ibid., p. 322.

[69] Note by C. S. Bayley, 18 June 1899. F. H. O'Donnell (*History of the Irish Parliamentary Party*, II, 428) wrote that in 1878 the Irish members were offered financial assistance from the Indian nationalists if Ireland would return some Indian members to Parliament. Cited by Dr. Mary Cumpston, "Some early Indian Nationalists and their allies in the British Parliament, 1851–1906," *English Historical Review*, Vol. LXXVI, No. 299 (Apr. 1961), 282–283.

In the Doldrums

tional, the 1902 Congress was held in Ahmedabad which previously had been little affected by nationalist politics and where the local political association, the Gujarat Sabha, had a total of 23 members in 1901. The reason that Ahmedabad was willing and able to act as host to the 1902 Congress was the decision to stage an industrial conference in conjunction with the annual Congress. Starting in 1901, there were displays and demonstrations of industrial equipment and handicrafts. This helped ease the Congress's financial problems, and at the same time attracted new groups, such as the Gujarati commercial classes, to the Congress. Many Ahmedabad cotton mill-owners attended and contributed to the 1902 Congress.[70] A majority of the 195 Ahmedabad delegates were mill-owners, mill agents, mill engineers, mill managers, bankers, Seths, Shroffs, and merchants.[71] Government officials welcomed the new Congress interest in industrial development. Important officials attended and patronized the Congress industrial conferences in 1902, 1903, and 1904. This, one would guess, would have given the Congress added respectability and would have partly dissipated the fear of official disapproval among potential contributors. The reception committee of the 1904 Congress at Bombay, after financing the Congress session and contributing to the industrial conference, was able to deposit a further, unspent Rs. 69,895 in the Congress account in the Bank of Bombay.[72] This surplus was more than the cost of most previous sessions.

The sources of Congress income in Madras were more diffuse than in Bombay and Bengal. Madras lacked an Indian industrial class as wealthy as Bombay's and a zamindari class as large and lightly taxed as Bengal's. Nor did it have patrons as generous as Baroda and Darbhanga. In the early years of the Congress, funds were received on one or more occasions from the rulers or zamindars[73] of Mysore,[74] Travancore, Cochin, Ramnad, Vizi-

[70] *Report of the 18th INC*, p. 1.

[71] Actually 261 persons were elected to attend the Congress at a meeting in Ahmedabad on 6 Dec. 1902, but 67 of these came from outside Ahmedabad. Ibid., appendix.

[72] *Bengalee*, 29 Dec. 1905.

[73] The annual incomes of the largest zamindari estates in 1904 in Madras are given in Chapter Seven below.

[74] The Maharaja of Mysore gave Rs. 1,000 to the 1887 Congress and was later told that the Government of India did not consider it advisable for native chiefs to take any part in politics in British India. The Nizam of

In the Doldrums

anagram, Bobbili, and Venkatagiri.[75] Contributions also came from successful lawyers such as P. Ananda Charlu, Eardly Norton, P. Rangia Naidu, and S. Subramania Iyer; and from merchants such as Sir Savalai Ramaswami Mudaliar and Sabapathy Mudaliar.[76] Of all these people, the Raja of Ramnad seems to have given the most.[77] In 1894 alone he donated Rs. 10,000,[78] and in 1897 he invited the Congress to meet at Madura, offering his "means and services" if it did.[79] It may only be an accident of the greater publicity given to Congress finance in Madras, but one receives the impression that Congress members of the professional class in that province gave more frequently from their own pockets than members in either Bombay or Bengal and relied less on large landowners, chiefs of the Indian states, or industrialists. Door-to-door canvassing was used in Madras before it was adopted in other provinces. In 1887, when 30,000 Tamil copies of Viraraghava Chariar's *Congress Catechism* were circulated, Rs. 5,500 was collected from 8,000 persons in amounts ranging from one anna to Rs. 1–8, and Rs. 8,000 was given in sums of Rs. 1–8 to Rs. 30.[80] The Reception Committee of the 1894 Madras Congress boasted that almost half of its Rs. 40,000 came in small amounts and that door-to-door collections had been made.[81] Once again in 1898, the Madras Reception Com-

---

Hyderabad, who had given a much larger sum to the United Indian Patriotic Association, was advised similarly. Dufferin to Cross, 8 Oct. 1888. No. 114. MSS. Eur. E. 243/5.

[75] The Raja of Venkatagiri gave Rs. 500 to the 1887 Congress and Rs. 200 to the 1898 Congress. (*Bengalee*, 31 Dec. 1898.) Such small contributions do not necessarily signify active sympathy with the Congress, although the Raja of Venkatagiri may have been grateful to the Congress for its demand that the Permanent Settlement be extended. Venkatagiri was president of the Madras Landholders' Association from its founding in 1890 until his death in 1916. Venkatagiri, like his brother, the Raja of Bobbili, represented the Madras landholders on the Madras Legislative Council. Alladi Jagannatha Sastri, *A Family History of Venkatagiri Rajas* (Madras, 1922), pp. 127–131. Also, Maha-Rajah of Bobbili, *A Revised and Enlarged Account of the Bobbili Zemindari* (Madras, 1900).

[76] *Report of the 3rd INC*, p. 13, and *Report of the 5th INC*, pp. 79–82.

[77] Raja Bhaskara Sethupathi, like previous rajas of Ramnad, often faced financial embarrassment from the uneconomic management of his estates. He died in 1903. The only obvious similarity between Ramnad, Baroda, and Darbhanga was that each was educated by an English tutor.

[78] *Report of the 11th INC*, p. 57. [79] *Report of the 14th INC*, p. 96.
[80] *Report of the 3rd INC*, p. 11.
[81] *Report of the 10th INC*, pp. 9 and 14.

mittee collected "funds in driblets from the mass of people instead of in hundreds and thousands from a few rich individuals." At that time it was predicted that this system would become general in view of "the forced coldness of the money aristocracy due to official influence," and the success of this system was cited as proof that the Congress was "striking its roots in the hearts of the people."[82]

Financial details of the Congress in other provinces are not readily obtainable. In the Punjab, the death of Sirdar Dyal Singh Majithia in 1898 removed one of the nationalists' more generous benefactors. Dyal Singh was a successful businessman and landlord, in addition to being chairman of the Reception Committee of the 1893 Congress, president of the Lahore Indian Association, and proprietor of the *Tribune*, the leading Congress newspaper in the Punjab. However, spending in the Punjab as well as in the Central Provinces and the North-Western Provinces and Oudh cannot have been large except when these areas were host to the annual meetings.

PROVINCIAL APATHY

The difficulty in financing Congress operations in England and India was a symptom of the low-key crisis through which the Congress was passing in its second decade. Not only was there negligible all-India agitation and organization: within each province political life seemed tepid compared to the 1870s and 1880s when most of the local nationalist associations and newspapers were founded. On almost all side there were reports of apathy and inactivity or, as in Marathi-speaking areas where there was less torpor, of severe factionalism. "What has come over our local associations?" one Bombay writer asked.

> From every province comes the cry—no attendance, no funds, no regular work—in short, no corporate activity to speak of. . . . They seem to have suffered almost concurrently with the rise of the Congress movement.[83]

The Congress movement was especially subdued in the Central Provinces and the North-Western Provinces and Oudh. Neither

[82] *Report of the 14th INC*, p. iii.
[83] Behramji Malabari, "Ranade and His Times," *East and West*, Vol. II, No. 25 (Nov. 1903), 1,299.

province had continuously active local political associations. The Central Provinces, with Berar, had its first provincial (Congress) conference in 1905 and the North-Western Provinces and Oudh (by then the United Provinces) not until 1907.[84] Each year a contingent from these two provinces appeared at the Congress, but apart from this there was little Congress political activity outside the press.

In the Punjab the first provincial conference was organized in 1895 and attended by 40 persons.[85] But after a few years the conference was discontinued.[86] The Indian Association of Lahore, the main spirit behind the Congress in the Punjab, had only 24 members in 1897 and subscriptions amounting to Rs. 144 per annum.[87] After the death of Bakshi Jaishi Ram in late 1900, "political life disappeared altogether from the Punjab," according to Lajpat Rai. There were disputes between Lala Harkishen Lal, who controlled the *Tribune*, and the Arya Samajists, most of whom disliked the Congress. Kaliprasanna Roy, chairman of the 1900 Reception Committee, and others suspected that Congress funds had been misappropriated, a question never satisfactorily settled.[88] Not only was the Congress membership small, fractious, and inactive, it was confined to the areas in and around Lahore, Amritsar, and Amballa. In fact, in the years 1894 to 1904 only 13 Punjabi delegates from other districts traveled to a Congress outside the Punjab. In no other province except Assam was the Congress membership limited to such a small area.[89]

In Bengal the lack of enthusiasm for the Congress cause was also marked. As early as 1895 the *Bengalee* had warned that the Bengalis were in danger of being left behind by the more energetic Bombay politicians.[90] The *Sanjivani* in 1898 implored the

[84] *Kayastha Samachar*, Vol. VI, No. 5 (Nov. 1902), 490, and *Modern Review*, Vol. I, No. 5 (May 1907), 456.

[85] *Bengalee*, 28 Dec. 1895.

[86] *Kayastha Samachar*, Vol. VI, No. 5 (Nov. 1902), 490.

[87] Its membership was larger previous to the government decision in 1890 to forbid officials from participating in political movements. L. W. Dane, Offg. Ch. Sec. to Govt. of Punjab, to Sec. to Govt. of India, 20 Apr. 1897. June Prog. No. 13, IHP, Pub., Vol. 5,180.

[88] Joshi (ed.), *Lajpat Rai: Autobiographical Writings*, pp. 91–95.

[89] See L. R. Gokhale, *The First Twenty Years of the Indian National Congress*, Vol. 1 (Bombay, 1906), Part II, Table III.

[90] 27 Apr. 1895.

Bengalis to shake off their lethargy and "take part in the sacrifice for the mother."[91] And in 1899 Ambicacharan Mazumdar, the president of the provincial conference, acknowledged that the Congress had "ceased to exhibit any tendency towards further development and expansion."[92]

In 1900 the Bengal provincial conference was held in Bihar (Bhagalpur) for the first time in an effort to interest Biharis in the Congress once again. Some of them had become resentful of the position of the Bengalis in the bar, the civil services, and education in Bihar[93] and, in consequence, had withdrawn from the Bengali-dominated movement in eastern India. There was an anti-Congress demonstration in Bhagalpur, and some of the Bengali leaders refused to make the long trip from Calcutta, including J. Ghosal, A. M. Bose, and W. C. Bonnerjee. Nevertheless, the 1900 conference at Bhagalpur was a qualified success.[94] But when the Bengali leaders decided to hold the 1902 provincial conference in Cuttack, Orissa, the combination of anti-Bengali sentiment[95] and political apathy was too great, and the conference was canceled. In April 1904, four months after the plans for the partition of Bengal had been announced, the provincial conference had to be postponed due to lack of preparation and organization.[96]

After the first few years of the Indian National Congress, there was a falling off of activity by the Indian Association of Calcutta.[97] In the first fifteen years of its existence (1876 to 1891), the Indian Association had been active in a number of directions: in organizing the national conferences of 1883 and 1885 at Calcutta,[98] in organizing mass meetings in the mofussil to explain

[91] 10 Dec. 1898, T. and D. Selections, 2 Jan. 1899, PSLI, Vol. III.

[92] Quoted in *Bengalee*, 20 May 1899.

[93] See speech of Dip Narain Singh, ch'mn of Reception Committee, Bhagalpur, Bengal Provincial Conference, *Bengalee*, 21 Apr. 1900.

[94] Ibid., 14 Apr. 1900.

[95] Ibid., 7 Dec. 1904. On Bengali-Uriya antagonism, see Brajendranath De, "Reminiscences of an Indian Member of the Indian Civil Service," *Calcutta Review*, Vol. 133, No. 2 (Nov. 1954), p. 92. For an interesting sidelight on the divisions within the Bengali community in Orissa, see Radha Krishna Bose, *The Present Situation of the Domiciled Bengalees of Orissa and the Way Out of It* (Cuttack, 1917).

[96] *Bengalee*, 15 June 1904.

[97] J. C. Bagal, *History of the Indian Association, 1876–1951* (Calcutta, 1953), p. 139.

[98] Ibid., p. 80.

to the *ryots* their "real needs,"[99] in forming "rent unions" among the ryots as protection against zamindari oppression, and in establishing night schools for adult education.[100] It also sent agents to famine areas to collect information during the grain scarcities of 1884, 1886–1887, and 1889; and in 1884, in conjunction with the Sadharan Brahmo Samaj, it opened relief centers in distressed villages.[101] Dwarkanath Ganguli, the assistant secretary from 1882 until his death in 1898, was particularly enthusiastic about this line of work, and although his successor, Dwijendranath Basu, visited scarcity areas in Howrah district in 1901,[102] the activities of the Indian Association were confined almost entirely to Calcutta after Ganguli's death.

The number of branches of the Indian Association had declined also. After Banerjea's tour through northern India in 1877, there were 10 branch associations,[103] by the end of 1885 there were 80 branches in northern India and Bengal,[104] and in 1886, 21 branches sent delegates to the Congress.[105] During subsequent years, most of these branches disappeared or were succeeded by organizations with different names.

Political activity in Madras, too, was said to be sluggish.[106] In 1900 the Mahajana Sabha, whose name was more synonymous with the Congress movement in Madras than the Indian Association was in Bengal, had a membership of 200 and required a quorum of 15 members to conduct its business.[107] The Madras provincial conferences were held annually, except in 1903 when the experiment of convening four district conferences was made.[108]

[99] Ibid., p. 109.
[100] Ibid., pp. 46–49.
[101] Ibid., pp. 78–108.
[102] *Bengalee*, 28 Aug. 1901.
[103] Bagal, *History*, p. 21.
[104] Ibid., p. 79.
[105] Appendix, *Report of the 2nd INC*.
[106] Speech of John Adams, president of Madras Provincial Conference. *Bengalee*, 16 Apr. 1898. Also, *Madras Mail*, 30 Dec. 1898, T. and D. Selections, 2 Jan. 1899, PSLI, Vol. III.
[107] Curzon address to Mahajana Sabha, 11 Dec. 1900. *Speeches by Lord Curzon of Kedleston*, I, 395.
[108] *Bengalee*, 20 June 1903. The district conference at Bezwada in May 1903 was the twelfth annual Kistna district conference. The existence of district conferences in Madres—while other provinces were having difficulty in organizing even a provincial conference—confirms the impression that more attention was given to organizational activities in Madras than elsewhere. *Report of the Twelfth Kistna District Conference Held at Bezwada on 23rd and 24th May 1903* (Bezwada, 1904).

In Bombay, political activity was temporarily suspended in 1897 after the Rand murder, the sedition trials, and the detention of the Natus. The Bombay provincial conference was not held in 1897 and 1898 when plague was rampant and many politicians were respecting the self-imposed moratorium on politics.[109] The three main local political organizations in the province were also inactive. The Presidency Association of Bombay city was reported to have declined in activity and influence, perhaps because many of Mehta's and Wacha's earlier associates had quit politics.[110] In Poona the moderate Deccan Sabha discontinued its work in order to demonstrate its condemnation of Rand's assassination, and it began to function again only in January 1900 after the Natus had been released.[111] Its principal leader, Gopal Krishna Gokhale, suffered a temporary political eclipse after he apologized publicly for his allegation that British soldiers had raped two Poona women. It must have been mortifying for a man as scrupulous as Gokhale to discover he could not substantiate his charge. But many nationalists thought that Gokhale had been too abject in his apology, that "he went far beyond such a legitimate expression of regret" as the occasion required.[112] He had to face the hostility and resentment of fellow nationalists for months after making the apology. The feeling against him was so strong that he was called a traitor and was prevented from addressing the 1897 Congress at Amraoti. It seems the open opposition came from Bengali delegates but was instigated by the Maharashtrian followers of Tilak.[113] In any case, Gokhale complained of the manner in which he was treated in a letter to the press soon after the Amraoti session.[114]

Tilak's organization, the Sarvajanik Sabha, also ceased to function and its *Journal* was discontinued while he was in jail. Al-

---

[109] *Bengalee*, 2 Feb. 1900.   [110] Ibid., 16 June 1900.
[111] Ibid., 2 Feb. 1900.
[112] N. C. Kelkar, *Life and Times of Lokamanya Tilak*, trans. by D. V. Divekar (Madras, 1928).
[113] V. S. Srinivasa Sastri (*Life of Gopal Krishna Gokhale* [Bangalore, 1937], p. 25) wrote that "it would appear it was the Bengali delegates that made themselves specially prominent in this demonstration" against Gokhale. Also, B. R. Nanda, "Gokhale's Year of Decision," *Journal of Indian History*, Vol. XLIII, Part II (Aug. 1965), 560.
[114] See the *Pioneer*, 14 Jan. 1898, and T. V. Parvate, *Gopal Krishna Gokhale: A Narrative and Interpretative Review of His Life, Career and Contemporary Events* (Ahmedabad, 1958), pp. 71–87.

though Tilak was released from jail in September 1898, he did not return to a full political life for some years. In the months immediately following his release, he worked on the manuscript of *The Arctic Home in the Vedas*.[115] In 1901 he became involved in a prolonged and tangled law suit concerning an estate for which he was a trustee. During the next three years, Tilak was forced to spend many months and Rs. 25,000 defending himself against charges of forgery, fraud, perjury, and illegal confinement. The High Court ruled in his favor in March 1904, but only after the government reportedly had spent Rs. 60,000 in pressing the suit and had diverted Tilak's energies from politics.[116]

While political organizations languished and while the catchphrases of the early Congress no longer stirred enthusiasm, no one suggested the cause was a change in British policy. If anything, British rule seemed more burdensome in the Congress's second decade than it had in the first. The famines, the harshness of the plague measures, and the later reforms of Lord Curzon provoked nationalist newspaper comments that were unmatched in the early years of the Congress for their vilification of British rule. But the Congress was reflecting only a small segment of nationalist sentiment. The Congress, most nationalists agreed, needed reforming.

[115] Wolpert, *Tilak and Gokhale*, p. 124.
[116] T. V. Parvate, *Bal Gangadhar Tilak: A Narrative and Interpretative Review of His Life, Career and Contemporary Events* (Ahmedabad, 1958), pp. 258–259.

Chapter Five

MODERATES, EXTREMISTS, AND THE CONGRESS CONSTITUTION

The Congress represented a broad consensus behind the objective of increasing Indian power over Indian affairs. But there was no consensus about how that power could be achieved. The sluggish performance of the Congress in its second decade resulted from disillusionment with the early failures and from uncertainty about how to proceed. The initial tactical efforts to move the British had scarcely dented the Raj's armor. The attempt to recruit Muslims had not only failed, it had revealed a hollowness in Congress claims to speak for the whole nation. Hume's effort to arouse peasant interest in the Congress was disowned by embarrassed Congress leaders with such speed that it seemed to be an admission that the Congress did not represent the peasantry either. The campaign to arouse British public opinion was followed by the Conservative electoral victory of 1895 and a weakening of the pro-Congress forces in the House of Commons.

The most serious and difficult tactical debate in nationalist circles was over the Congress's handling of the small minority of men who were sympathetic to violent tactics. Prior to 1905, civil disobedience was not widely discussed and, therefore, opinion tended to polarize around the extremes of exclusive reliance on platform politics and the use (or advocacy) of violence. Each time a Congress member seemed to condone or advocate the use of violence, the moderate leaders tried to disassociate the Congress from him either by reasserting their basic appreciation of English rule or by denouncing extremist methods. Congress leaders had publicly censured Hume for his 1892 circular predicting agrarian rebellion. Tilak escaped a similar reprimand in 1897 for his *Kesari* articles because Congress leaders apparently feared a reprimand would imply acceptance of the official suspicion of a causal connection between his justification of patriotic killing and the assassination of Rand and Ayerst. But Tilak's close associate, Shivram Mahadeo Paranjpe, was not as fortunate. In March 1899, Paranjpe published an article in his newspaper, the Poona *Kal*, which raised again the question of what tactics the Congress would adopt and whether the Congress could control its members' actions. It also made evident the generational and regional nature of the emerging division within the Congress, because Paranjpe received his greatest support from younger Congressmen and from Maharashtra.

Paranjpe was a thirty-two-year-old Chitpavan Brahman who was an officer of the Poona Sarvajanik Sabha and a member of the Poona Standing Congress Committee. He had participated in Tilak's no-rent campaign in 1896–1897. He started the *Kal* in 1898 as a Marathi weekly, and his militant nationalism immediately gained it one of the largest circulations in India. The Goverment of Bombay warned him in 1899, 1900, 1904, 1905, and 1907 that his writing was seditious.[1] He was finally prosecuted and convicted of seditious libel in 1908.[2] The *Kal* article of 17 March 1899 discussed the action of the Chapekars and Ranade in murdering Rand, Ayerst, and the Dravid brothers, and it suggested that their deeds should be looked at "not from the point of view of the laws made by Councils, but from the point of view of the law of God, and the injunction of religion. They are, in a word, not murderers, but martyrs." Paranjpe compared India's grievances to Russia's and he praised the assassination of Plehve.[3]

Paranjpe's justification of terrorism, which echoed the argument used by Tilak in 1897 to exonerate Shivaji's killing of Afzal Khan, set off a controversy about the Congress's control over the conduct of its members. The Congress Committee of Calcutta, acting on the advice of a member of the Bombay city Standing Congress Committee, issued a condemnation of the *Kal* article and sent a telegram to the Standing Committee of Bombay, urging it to take similar action. The Bombay Committee complied by adopting a resolution recommending that Paranjpe should "be excluded from all connection with the Congress."[4] In London, the London India Society met to consider a resolution condemning "the recent statements in the (Poona) *Kal* with

[1] *Sedition Committee, 1918. Report*, p. 3.
[2] Ibid., pp. 3 and 5.
[3] Pol. Dept. Minute Paper, Registry No. 420, PSLI, Vol. 112.
[4] *Statesman*, 20 Apr. 1899.

The Congress Constitution

regard to the Poona murders." Unexpectedly, a majority of the members present rejected the arguments of Dadabhai Naoroji who presided, and they defeated the motion by a single vote. What was surprising was not that many young members agreed with Paranjpe's views or at least his right to express them but that they should vote their convictions against the respected and venerable Dadabhai. In the past, younger Congressmen had generally deferred to the wishes of the elder leaders, even when they disagreed strongly. After the vote of the London India Society, Naoroji decried the action of the majority who, he said, "had virtually expressed their concurrence" with the *Kal*'s justification of assassination. He threatened to resign the chairmanship of the society if it did not change its decision at the next meeting.[5]

In India many Congress newspapers expressed disapproval of the *Kal* article, but a few questioned the right of any Congress committee, and in particular the Bombay and Calcutta committees, to censure or expel a person from the Congress. It was suggested that without a written constitution, the right did not exist.[6] The *Amrita Bazar Patrika*, which welcomed an opportunity to attack the Calcutta-Bombay leaders, who in effect ran the Congress, commented

> So you Bengalis are now controlled by a certain clique of Bombay! An open quarrel between the Poona Party and the Bombay clique is imminent, and the action of the Calcutta committee has made it almost inevitable. An open split seems to be at hand. Unless the differences are soon amicably settled, the next Congress will have to decide either to lose the Bombay clique or the Dekhan sympathy. The crisis in fact is serious.[7]

The *Kal* controversy gave added urgency to the adoption of a constitution. Consideration of a constitution was scheduled as the first item of business for the 1899 Congress. The interest in adopting a written constitution had spread beyond those men

[5] Summary of unspecified newspaper comments. T. and D. Selections, 26 June 1899, PSLI, Vol. 114.

[6] *Advocate* (Lucknow), 7 Apr. 1899, T. and D. Selections, 10 Apr. 1899; also *Indian Mirror* (Calcutta), 22 Apr. 1899, and *Tribune* (Lahore), 22 Apr. 1899, T. and D. Selections, 1 May 1899, PSLI, Vol. 113.

[7] *Amrita Bazar Patrika*, 8 Apr. 1899, T. and D. Selections, 10 Apr. 1899, PSLI, Vol. 113.

concerned with extremism and the right of the Congress to control the behavior of its members. It appealed to those who wanted the Congress to conduct its affairs in a more systematic and efficient manner. Moderates such as D. E. Wacha of Bombay and Kaliprasanna Roy of Lahore regarded the Congress criticism of government policies as either inadequate or superficial. Instead of mere speechmaking, they wanted committees of experts to prepare the Congress case in detail on each subject before submitting it to the annual session.[8] It was pointed out that the Congress had for years demanded an inquiry into police corruption but when the police commission was appointed, the Congress sent neither witnesses nor evidence. Similarly, it sent no witnesses to give evidence before the universities commission.[9] A need, too, was felt for a Congress literature that would systematically present the nationalist argument about the "drain," the Indianization of the civil service, and similar subjects.[10] The British Committee had published various pamphlets and so had individual Indians. But the Congress in India as a body had almost entirely limited its agitation to the platform ever since it had abandoned the attempt to recruit peasants to the nationalist movement. A constitution might assign responsibility for these functions to a specific body.

There was a body of thought which held that the Congress should regularize the selection of delegates to the annual session. Lala Lajpat Rai, for instance, thought the practice of bringing people who had no qualification "except in increasing the number of delegates from a particular class" ought to be abolished so that "the honour, the dignity and the prestige of the Congress" could be preserved.[11] Norendranath Ghose and Ananda Charlu would have kept out the "nobodies,"[12] others would have

[8] See speech of Kali Prasanna Roy, chairman of the Lahore Reception Committee, 1899, *Report of the 15th INC*, p. 6; also, interview with D. E. Wacha from the *Kayastha Samachar* in the *Bengalee*, 15 Oct. 1901, and speech of A. M. Bose, *Report of the 14th INC*, p. 35.

[9] See quotations from the *Indian Nation* in the *Kayastha Samachar*, Vol. VI, No. 6 (Dec. 1902), 609.

[10] See speech of N. Subba Rao Pantulu, chairman of the Madras Reception Committee, 1898, *Report of the 14th INC*, p. 14.

[11] Lajpat Rai, "The Coming Indian National Congress—Some Suggestions," *Kayastha Samachar*, Vol. IV, No. 5 (Nov. 1901), 377–378.

[12] P. Ananda Charlu, "The Indian National Congress: A Retrospect," *Hindustan Review and Kayastha Samachar*, Vol. VIII, Nos. 1 and 2 (July-Aug. 1903), 14.

adopted more democratic procedures for the election of delegates.[13] Systematic election might strengthen Congress claims to be representative of the Indian nation. For those people, then, who thought a political party advocating democracy should conduct its affairs on a democratic basis, and for those who thought the Congress resembled an "annual Christmas *tamasha* (festival) of only three days' duration,"[14] a written constitution providing a permanent organization and orderly procedures seemed a logical solution.

Moderates were divided over the constitution issue. There is little doubt that moderate leaders anticipated that they might lose their hold on the Congress if a democratic constitution were adopted. The extremists were the younger, faster growing group who already appeared to represent a majority of Congress supporters, at least within the Marathi-speaking areas of Bombay. The moderates' dilemma was that without more democratic procedures, the legitimacy of their leadership would increasingly come under attack. Yet with a new constitution, the extremists might simultaneously displace them and alter the loyal and "responsible" purposes for which the Congress was founded. Some moderates responded to the dilemma by accepting the need for a constitution while insisting that the constitution specify that the Congress should work "by constitutional means" and "on lines of general appreciation of British rule."[15] Others, including the dominant leader, Pherozeshah Mehta, refused to accept the new constitution, thereby preventing it from becoming operative.

The extremist challenge to the leadership of Pherozeshah Mehta, Surendranath Banerjea, and other early leaders represented more than a struggle over the control and tactics of the Congress. The extremists' conception of politics differed funda-

[13] The method of election was, it seems, one of the matters which "agitated the Madras and Punjab delegates." The *Report* of the 1903 Congress, after mentioning the demand for a written constitution, says that "it is not disputed that, in sending up delegates, there have been proceedings which should have been avoided . . . [but] nothing to indicate any systematic abuse in the election proceedings. After all it is common knowledge that the best regulated elections do not invariably result in the return of the best man. A good deal has to be left to the good sense and patriotism of the educated men of the various localities." *Report of the 19th INC*, p. xvi.
[14] Speech of P. Rathnasabapathy Pillai, *Report of the 14th INC*, p. 126.
[15] Clause (1) and (7) of Resolution X of 1899.

mentally from that of most of the Congress founders who, as Chapter Two showed, were men of high worldly attainments. Extremists often began their analysis of the Congress's weakness with an assumption that the basic problem was the moral character of nationalist leadership. Aurobindo Ghose, who published in 1893 one of the earliest extremist attacks on the Congress, wrote from Baroda that the "actual enemy [of the nationalist movement] is not any force exterior to ourselves, but our own crying weaknesses, our cowardice, our selfishness, our hypocrisy, our purblind sentimentalism." The failure of the Congress to fulfill its early promise was, he felt, a consequence of the essentially self-interested character of the Congress movement which appealed to the British for more places in the civil service instead of arousing a sense of patriotism and concern for the lower classes.[16] Lajpat Rai's criticisms, which reached an all-India audience a decade later in Sachchidananda Sinha's *Hindustan Review* (Allahabad) and Behramji Malabari's *East and West* (Bombay), ran in a similar vein. He argued that few Congress leaders could be called patriots because patriotism required an ascetic, self-denying life. The present Congress leaders were making few sacrifices. They were inactive for most of the year and they were unjustifiably confident in the ultimate success of Congress agitation. He appealed to Indians to realize that politics "is a religion, and a science, much higher both in its conception and in its sphere, than mere political agitation."[17] Implicit in Aurobindo's and Lajpat's criticisms was that successful nation-building required that the leaders commit not merely their spare time but their careers and their full being to the political and cultural regeneration of India.

While Aurobindo and Lajpat Rai made their attacks from the fringes of the Congress (neither man was continuously active in the Congress before 1905), Tilak challenged the founders as a regular participant and as a member of the Poona Standing Congress Committee. Tilak provided concrete examples of how nationalists might overcome the social isolation, cowardice, and selfishness of which Aurobindo and Lajpat complained. Tilak's Ganapati and Shivaji festivals, his land-tax boycott, and his justi-

[16] Haridas and Uma Mukherjee, *Sri Aurobindo's Political Thought (1893–1908)* (Calcutta, 1958), pp. 71–74.

[17] Rai, "The First Principles of Political Progress," *East and West*, Vol. I, No. 10 (Aug. 1902), 1,038–1,040.

fication of violence plunged him into rancorous controversy and risked danger to his personal career. The Ganapati festival provoked Hindu-Muslim violence in 1894, and his newspaper articles and tax boycott in 1896–1897 led to prosecutions and jail sentences. Arguing that "we will not achieve any success in our labors if we croak once a year like a frog,"[18] he experimented with a variety of political activities and ideas which went far beyond those most Congress leaders were willing to contemplate. After serving his prison term for justifying political assassinations, he was more circumspect in writing about violence. However, by 1902 he was openly hinting at civil disobedience, a tactic which Aurobindo and Bipinchandra took up after 1905. Tilak told a Poona audience:

> You must realize that you are a great factor in the power with which the administration in India is conducted. You are yourselves the useful lubricants which enable the gigantic machinery to work so smoothly.
>
> Though downtrodden and neglected, you must be conscious of your power of making the administration impossible if you but choose to make it so. It is you who manage the railroad and the telegraph, it is you who make settlements and collect revenues, it is in fact you who do everything for the administration though in a subordinate capacity. You must consider whether you cannot turn your hand to better use for your nation than drudging on in this fashion.[19]

The politics of sacrifice and selflessness was by no means limited to the extremists. Many moderates paid lip service to it, and G. K. Gokhale and Aswinikumar Dutt were as impressively self-denying as the extremist spokesmen. Yet there were two important qualitative differences between moderate and extremist approaches to political activity. Many moderates seemed to shy away from harsh controversy. In some cases they may have had an aversion to the emotional strains involved, and they may have avoided disharmony because they were tempermentally ill-equipped to deal with anger and disorder. Many moderates, as Chapter Two suggested, feared the potential for violence in In-

[18] Wolpert, *Tilak and Gokhale*, p. 152.
[19] Quoted by Theodore Shay, *The Legacy of the Lokamanya: The Political Philosophy of Bal Gangadhar Tilak* (Bombay, 1956), pp. 94–95.

dian society. This fear extended into the younger generation of Congressmen. Gokhale expressed a moderate viewpoint well when he said "whatever the shortcomings of [English] bureaucracy, and however intolerable at times the insolence of the individual Englishman, they alone stand today in the country for order." It followed that the Congress should not attempt to disrupt the existing system until some distant time when Indians could "substitute another form of order."[20] Extremists, by contrast, were more likely to accept or even welcome confrontation, even when it led to civil disorder. They saw political fights as a means of developing inner strength.

A second way in which Congress moderates differed was in their complacency. Surendranath Banerjea was representative of the older, self-satisfied generation whose memories extended back to the Mutiny and the days when there were no Indians in the I.C.S. or the legislative councils. Banerjea's view was that "in due time we shall want Home Rule and get it too. But for the present we shall be satisfied with much less. . . . We are making steady progress, and we are bound to win in the long run."[21] Banerjea resisted all suggestions that peaceful legal political agitation should be abandoned for other methods. The reform of the legislative councils, the modification of the educational commission's recommendations—these were concessions obtained by traditional methods. And even when these methods—their critics called them the methods of mendicancy—did not succeed, Banerjea thought the very act of trying brought "a distinct moral gain—do we not feel all the better and nobler for it?"[22] The difference in outlook was between those believing in individual self-improvement of the Samuel Smiles variety and those impatient for Indian self-rule, between those impressed with the privileges already gained and those emphasizing the poverty and degradation of society under the British, and between those supplicative temperaments which shunned friction and rancorous controversy and those aggressive and combative instincts of the extremists.

The extremists, as they grew in number and confidence, were cautious in their relations with Pherozeshah Mehta, Surendranath

[20] Quoted by Bisheshswar Prasad, *Changing Modes of the Indian National Movement* (New Delhi, 1966), pp. 50–51.
[21] *Bengalee*, 15 June 1895.   [22] Ibid., 26 July 1904.

Banerjea, and the Congress old guard. Although they were willing to risk the government's wrath, few were trying to eject Congress leaders. To have done so would have violated behavioral norms regulating relations with elders and social superiors which were still strong in most families, schools, and other institutions. Many extremists avoided the Congress and were content to allow Tilak to feel his way in the amorphous and loose Congress organization. Tilak's approach was generally legalistic and gradual. In the Subjects Committee at the 1899 Lucknow Congress, Tilak moved a resolution condemning Lord Sandhurst's Bombay administration for its repressive character. The president, R. C. Dutt, ruled the resolution out of order on the grounds that it was of provincial interest only. After Tilak correctly pointed out that previous Congresses had adopted resolutions on provincial subjects, Dutt threatened to resign if Tilak persisted. Characteristically, Tilak withdrew his resolution.[23] Tilak and other extremists had based their case on the principle of majority rule and democracy. But if pressing the issue meant splitting the Congress, Tilak usually recognized another principle respected by both moderates and extremists: the principle that it was better to "have capitulated to the seniors rather than jeopardise that unity which was still dearer to the most hot-headed of us than his own opinions." Acceptance of this path was said to derive from the traditional "deferential and patriarchal habits of the undivided family."[24]

A similar incident occurred some months later at the 1900 Bombay provincial conference which was held in Satara, a stronghold of Tilak's supporters. Gokhuldas Parekh, the president, said he would resign if Tilak's anti-Sandhurst resolution was placed on the agenda by the Subjects Committee. Tilak then produced a petition asking for the inclusion of the resolution signed by 125 of the 175 or so delegates. Tilak was relying on a rule adopted by the 1891 provincial conference which said if one-third of the delegates wished to discuss a subject rejected by the Subjects Committee, then the matter would be discussed. When Parekh, like Dutt at Lahore, refused to accept the petition, there was an uproar from Tilak's supporters and the conference

[23] Ram Gopal, *Lokamanya Tilak: A Biography* (Bombay, 1956), pp. 205–206.
[24] Editors' "Notes," *Modern Review*, Vol. I, No. 2 (Feb. 1907), 208.

The Congress Constitution

seemed likely to break up. So Parekh agreed to adjourn the conference until they had worked out a compromise.[25]

Later in 1900 there was more dissension over procedure, this time over the selection of the president of the Congress. Bishambar Nath, P. Ananda Charlu, G. M. Chitnavis, Wedderburn, Caine, and Norton were all mentioned as possible presidents,[26] but in the end N. G. Chandavarkar was chosen. He was a controversial choice because, as president of the Prarthana Samaj, he was closely identified with the social reformers in Bombay, to whom Tilak and other militant Hindus were vehemently opposed, and because he had not been a delegate to a single Congress session in ten years. For these reasons his selection as Congress president "disgusted" a portion of the Indian press.[27] The selection was also controversial because Chandavarkar had been designated to fill a vacancy in the Bombay High Court, pending the secretary of state's sanction. Chandavarkar conferred with the governor of Bombay, Lord Northcote, before accepting the presidency and Northcote approved, hoping to use Chandavarkar to split the moderates of Bombay from the more extreme Congress members. Lord Hamilton was skeptical about giving the appearance of rewarding political agitation[28] but finally consented after hearing Lord Curzon's argument in favor of confirming the appointment. Curzon felt that the Congress, in selecting Chandavarkar as president, "wanted to hold out the olive branch to me." If Hamilton failed to approve Chandavarkar's appointment, Curzon warned that the moderates would be thrown back "into an attitude of hostility and revenge." As it was, the Congress was "rapidly sinking into insignificance."[29]

Chandavarkar presided over the 1900 Congress without incident. But the controversy over his selection was another indication that the relative harmony of the early Congress had disappeared and that as factionalism grew, a constitution would be

[25] *Kesari*, 20 May 1900, T. and D. Selections, 28 May 1900, PSLI, Vol. 123. Also letter signed "A Voice from Bombay," *Bengalee*, 17 June 1900, and Karandikar, *Tilak*, p. 174.

[26] *Bengalee*, 25 Oct., 6 Nov., 17 Nov., and 22 Nov. 1900.

[27] Curzon to Hamilton, 21 Feb. 1901, MSS. Eur. D. 510/7. See also comments of *Mahratta*, 30 Dec. 1900, *Vyapari* (Poona), n. d. and *Moda Vritta*, n. d., T. and D. Selections, 31 Dec. 1900, PSLI, Vol. 128.

[28] Hamilton to Curzon, 7 Feb. 1901, MSS. Eur. C. 126/3.

[29] Curzon to Hamilton, 21 Feb. 1901, MSS. Eur. D. 510/7.

The Congress Constitution

needed to decide how disputes would be solved. In fact, increasingly the main fight between moderates and extremists took place over the constitution rather than over the methods of political agitation.

THE 1899 CONSTITUTION IN OPERATION

The dispute over Chandavarkar's nomination to serve as president occurred within a year of the adoption of a constitution. The dispute suggested that Congress affairs would be no more harmonious with a constitution than without one. The Congress had adopted resolutions about drafting a constitution at the sessions of 1887, 1894, 1895, and 1898. The constitution which was finally drafted and ratified during 1899 is not of particular importance in itself—it functioned ineffectively for less than two years—but the reasons for its failure are interesting. It provided an organizational framework on three levels which was supposed to restore vitality to the Congress movement. At the top, there was to be an Indian Congress Committee, consisting of 45 members with an honorary secretary and a paid assistant secretary. This committee was to meet at least three times a year to nominate the president, draft resolutions, and make rules for the election of Congress delegates. At the provincial level, provincial Congress committees, whose rules and bylaws were subject to the approval of the Indian Congress Committee, were to carry "on the work of political education, on lines of general appreciation of British rule and of constitutional action for the removal of its defects, throughout the year, by organizing standing Congress committees, holding provincial conferences, and by such measures as they may deem proper." The functions of the third-level bodies, the standing Congress committees which in theory already existed, were not defined.[30]

The most notable feature of this constitution is that it laid down an important departure from previous practice by providing for an *elected* committee to exercise general control over the Congress. Forty of the 45 members of the Indian Congress Committee were to be elected upon the recommendation of the different provincial Congress committees[31] in a set proportion: 8 from

[30] Resolution X of 1899.

[31] In the absence of provincial committees, the assembled Congress delegates of the respective provinces would elect the committee members.

Bengal, 8 from Bombay, 8 from Madras, 6 from the North-Western Provinces and Oudh, 4 from the Punjab, 3 from Berar, and 3 from the Central Provinces. It is true that there was nothing in the constitution to guarantee that the provincial committees would be representative of nationalist opinion in any one province, because provision had not been made for election to the committees. Nevertheless, the new constitution was likely to end the virtual monopoly of the Calcutta and Bombay city leaders over the Congress. This was a major objective of some of the delegates who had been pressing for a written constitution.

The Punjabis, in particular, had been seeking a constitution since 1893.[32] In 1895 the foremost Punjabi leader, Bakshi Jaishi Ram, suggested that all officeholders in the Congress should be elected and that each province ought to be represented on "a cabinet or council" of the Congress.[33] This view was opposed by some of the better known leaders from that time until the Surat split in 1907. These leaders, especially those from Bombay and Calcutta, maintained that the Congress was too young for set rules,[34] and that some of the oldest parliamentary bodies in the world functioned without a constitution. The real issue probably was whether the men who helped organize the Congress in its first years and who continued to give it financial help had a sort of proprietary right to continue to run the Congress as they saw fit. They enjoyed their power and they sincerely believed they had earned and deserved it, especially as the Congress would likely become more extreme and communalist under alternative leadership.[35]

---

[32] Speech of Surendranath Banerjea, *Report of the 11th INC*, p. 17. Also Joshi (ed.), *Lajpat Rai: Autobiographical Writings*, p. 90.

[33] *Report of the 11th INC*, p. 60.

[34] For instance, speech of J. Ghosal, ibid., p. 59, and *Report of the 19th INC*, p. xvi.

[35] *Hindustan Review and Kayastha Samachar* (Vol. IX, No. 1 [Jan. 1904], 77) said that the present leaders were obliged to take responsibility for the Congress on themselves and probably would continue to do so until there was an organization to relieve these "few leaders of the heavy pecuniary responsibility which they bear almost alone at present." The *Indian Spectator*, 6 Jan. 1901 (T. and D. Selections, 14 Jan. 1901, PSLI, Vol. 129) reported that "the handful of veteran leaders" were not representative of the majority of the Congress members "who would like to see the Congress take a radical or religious colour." The *Indian Spectator* did not think that anything "can prevent the present numerical preponderance from being translated into a moral one."

The Congress Constitution

The first meeting of the Indian Congress Committee was held at Delhi on 10 October 1900. It was a disappointment for those who wanted the new constitution to be a success. Only 7 out of the 45 members attended: the joint general secretary (Wacha) from Bombay, 4 members from the North-Western Provinces and Oudh,[36] and 2 from the Punjab.[37] Bengal, Madras, Berar, and the Central Provinces were not represented.[38] But at least a start had been made toward giving the Congress a governing body responsible to and representative of its members.

The delegates from the Punjab and the North-Western Provinces and Oudh still were not satisfied with the distribution of places on the Indian Congress Committee, so the next Congress, at Lahore in 1900, reapportioned the seats on the committee at their request. Bengal, Bombay, and Madras each gave up a seat while the Punjab gained two and the North-Western Provinces and Oudh gained one.[39] The Lahore Congress also elected a new Indian Congress Committee for 1901.

The new committee met at Allahabad in September 1901 and again the attendance was poor. When none of the Bengali members came, it seemed probable that the Bengalis were intending to abolish the committee at the Calcutta Congress at the end of the year. It seemed that they had not brought the subject up at the Lahore Congress of 1900 because they knew that the Punjabis, with their majority, would reject such a move. As expected, just before the Calcutta Congress of 1901, it was announced that the Indian Congress Committee would be done away with. But the opposition to this was so strong, especially among the Punjabis, that the question was not formally raised. Instead, the Bengal and Bombay delegates, acting in concert, prevented the election of a new committee. Furthermore, according to one delegate, the three men who "entirely ruled" the proceedings—Mehta, Wacha, and W. C. Bonnerjee—neglected to notify the delegates of the decision taken by the Indian Congress committee to reduce the expenditure on the British Committee of the Congress in order to make *more* funds available for "propa-

[36] Pandit Madan Mohan Malaviya, Bishan Narayan Dar, Ganga Prasad Varma, and Alfred Nundy.

[37] Bakshi Jaishi Ram and Lala Harkishen Lal.

[38] *Mahratta*, 21 Oct. 1900, T. and D. Selections, 29 Oct. 1900, PSLI, Vol. 128.

[39] Resolution I.

gandism" in India.⁴⁰ That this decision of the Indian Congress Committee should have been unpalatable to Wacha, at least, is understandable because he wanted *to cut* Congress expenditure in India so that the Congress work in England could be extended.⁴¹ Whether or not this was one of the reasons for suppressing the Indian Congress Committee, discontent was widespread.⁴² The Punjabis let it be known that they would quit the Congress if the next session did not obey the 1899 Constitution and restore the Indian Congress Committee.⁴³

The next session (1902) was to be held in Ahmedabad. If the Indian Congress Committee had still been in existence, it would have selected the next president, as the 1901 committee had picked Wacha. But as no committee was elected at the 1901 Congress, some people expected a reversion to the pre-1899 practice whereby the Reception Committee consulted the standing Congress committees, or where they existed, the new provincial Congress committees. However, in 1902, no committees outside Bombay were consulted. Wacha simply wrote to Surendranath Banerjea, asking him to preside.⁴⁴

This incident brought more disapproval on the Congress inner circle. The *Hindu* and the *Madras Standard* of Madras, the *In-*

⁴⁰ A Discontented Congresswallah, "The Indian National Congress," *Kayastha Samachar*, Vol. v, No. 1 (Jan. 1902), 57–58.

⁴¹ Interview with D. E. Wacha, quoted from the *Kayastha Samachar* by the *Bengalee*, 15 Oct. 1901.

⁴² Alfred Nundy wrote of the "total demoralization" of the Congress ranks due to the abolition of the Congress Committee. Nundy asked W. C. Bonnerjee why he and P. M. Mehta objected so vehemently to the committee, and Bonnerjee replied that the committee was too cumbersome to accurately reflect the views of most members, that its members would not always attend or feel a proper responsibility for such a large committee, that some of the "young and comparatively inexperienced members" would be given more responsibility than they could handle, and that the existing committee had taken a stand on a particular issue to which the older leaders had objected. Nundy did not reveal what the issue was. Alfred Nundy, "The Troubles of the National Congress," *East and West*, Vol. II, No. 26 (Dec. 1903), 1,404–1,407.

⁴³ "Squabbles in the Congress Camp and the Forthcoming Congress," *Kayastha Samachar*, Vol. vi, Nos. 3 and 4 (Sept.–Oct. 1902), 343–345.

⁴⁴ Banerjea wrote in his autobiography with his usual lack of false humility that when Wacha invited him to preside over the Ahmedabad Congress, he "replied begging to be excused. . . . Sir Dinshaw wrote back to say that there was the great Delhi Durbar of 1902; a counter-attraction and a counter-influence had to be set up" and Banerjea therefore accepted. *A Nation*, p. 173.

dian Social Reformer of Bombay, the *Advocate* of Lucknow, the *Kayastha Samachar* of Allahabad and the *Indian Nation* of Calcutta all complained of the unconstitutional method used to select Banerjea.[45] It was less Banerjea himself than the arbitrary method to which exception was taken, although John Adam, Eardley Norton, R. N. Mudholkar, and Kalicharan Banerji were mentioned as candidates possibly deserving notice before choosing a man who had already served as president.[46] Furthermore, Banerjea, following A. M. Bose, R. C. Dutt, Chandavarkar, and Wacha, would be the fifth consecutive president from the Bombay-Calcutta coterie. Nevertheless, Surendranath Banerjea presided at the 1902 Ahmedabad Congress and the session went smoothly. But the Punjabis deliberately stayed away in protest against the despotism of the leadership.[47]

THE DESPOTISM OF PHEROZESHAH MEHTA

After 1902, the attack on the leaders' conduct of the Congress was centered on the most influential moderate of all, Pherozeshah Mehta. Mehta had come to represent a style of leadership that was distasteful to a growing number of Congressmen. He was also the major obstacle to moderate and extremist efforts to place Congress operations on a more businesslike and democratic basis. Mehta had an extraordinarily powerful and prickly personality. Few Englishmen or Indians were able to match his acumen, vigor, and thoroughness in debate. Few men were as quick to take affront to an insult to their personal dignity and status. He expressed his opinions with such certainty and contrariness that many persons regarded him as arrogant. If few people loved him, few doubted his ability. He not only dominated the Congress when he took time off from his lucrative law practice to attend, but he also was elected by his fellow English and Indian municipal councilors to four terms as chairman of the Bombay Corporation. In addition, on three occasions, the Bombay Legislative Council chose him as their representative on the Imperial Legis-

[45] *Kayastha Samachar*, Vol. VI, No. 5 (Nov. 1902), 477–479; also in same issue: "President of the Coming Congress," reprinted from the *Madras Standard*.

[46] Ibid., pp. 478–479.

[47] A Madras Delegate, "The Coronation Congress," *Hindustan Review and Kayastha Samachar*, Vol. VII, No. 1 (Jan. 1903), 31.

lative Council where he was one of four "elected" members under the 1892 Councils Act. Although he resigned from the council due to poor health in 1896 and 1900, soon after his second and third selections, his blunt criticisms of government policies angered English members who denounced him for the "new spirit" he had introduced.[48] In 1901, he led a walkout of five Indian members from the Bombay Legislative Council to protest the manner in which the officials on the council treated their efforts to amend a land revenue bill. Moderate though he was, he was no mendicant.

Mehta considered English rule in India an act of divine providence, but neither this nor his Tory instincts prevented him from vigorously opposing particular aspects of British rule, especially in his younger years. He had been an outspoken opponent of racial discrimination in the bar and volunteers and in debates over legislation such as the Vernacular Press Act of 1879 and the Ilbert Bill of 1884. He had parted company with other moderate leaders over the Arms Act of 1878 and suggested to the 1888 Congress that to forbid Indians to carry guns was to "emasculate a whole nation."[49] He had been personally disarmed by a British police constable when he "sauntered out" into the streets of Bombay during the Parsi-Muslim riots of 1874.[50] His outspoken criticism of racially exclusionary policies had won him the respect of fellow politicians.

During the 1880s, Mehta had attained a political eminence through the Indian elective process which no other nationalist had equaled. However, he seemed to look upon his political and professional success as a triumph of individual effort rather than as a collective Indian victory. He tended to personalize his struggles. He had large houses in Bombay and Matheran, a hill station favored by wealthy Parsis. He flaunted his success with his extravagant dress (including his velvet coat collars), his use of private railway cars, and his personal retinue "which often included a barber."[51] He was noted for his indifference to charitable causes and the poor.[52]

[48] Mody, *Mehta*, I, 329ff.
[49] Ibid., p. 238. Briton Martin divided the men who attended the first Congress into three political categories (conservative, moderate, and radical) and placed Mehta in the third. *New India*, p. 306.
[50] Mody, *Mehta*, I, 86. [51] Ibid., p. 207.
[52] P. Kodanda Rao, *V. S. Srinivasa Sastri: A Political Biography* (Bombay, 1963), p. 420.

His political views were as elitist as his life style. He was contemptuous of the more extreme democratic ideas of his day. He once complained of "the self-constituted leaders of popular movements" who "give loud utterance to the confused and incoherent popular cries," who "proclaim the popular indiscriminate wailings and inconclusive analyses of public grievances." The proper function of political leaders, he thought, was to provide firm, principled guidance to popular movements.[53] Translated into practice, this meant that he often scorned or ignored opinions contrary to his own, even when they were held by a majority of the members of a meeting or organization.

Mehta helped found the Congress and was elected president of the Congress in 1890, the fourth Indian to be so honored and the third from Bombay city. After 1890, however, his direct participation temporarily diminished. During the 1890s he failed to attend many sessions, and between 1894 and 1899 he did not speak at any session, nor was he appointed to any major all-Indian Congress committee. His biographer wrote that Mehta dominated the Congress "from a distance."[54] He seems to have done this through Dinshaw Wacha, his close associate who became joint general secretary in 1895. Mehta's presence was not strongly missed until other Congress leaders began to fear the popularity of Tilak and the extremists. Then Mehta's forcefulness, political acumen, and persuasiveness, which were unrivaled in the early Congress except by Hume and Ranade, were sought by other moderates. Sankaran Nair pleaded with Mehta to come to the 1898 Madras Congress to counteract the extremists. "In smooth waters, the Congress does not, perhaps, need Mr. Bonnerji or you. But if in critical times you are absent, the Congress will drift into the hands of men we may not like." Although Mehta did not attend in 1898, he did respond in 1903 to a similar appeal from Viraraghava Chariar who argued that Congress had not been "moving in the right direction" since Hume, " 'whose word was law,' " had left.[55]

Throughout the Congress's history, nationalists argued about how to reconcile the ideal of democracy with the practical requirements of authoritative leadership within the movement. As Gandhi was to do later, the early leaders on a number of occasions insisted upon Congress members' submission to their will

[53] Mody, *Mehta*, I, 68–69.   [54] Ibid., II, 445.
[55] Ibid., pp. 439–440.

as a condition of their continuing leadership. At all times, some groups within the Congress resented the leaders' authoritarianism while others regarded it as necessary for discipline and cohesion. When Hume was directing the Congress, resentment against his strong hand had been confined almost entirely to private correspondence and conversation. During Pherozeshah Mehta's period of leadership, resentment was openly expressed at the 1903 Madras Congress and then each year until it exploded in 1907 in the form of a physical attack upon the moderate leaders at the Surat Congress.

That Pherozeshah Mehta was a Parsi may have been a factor in the mounting opposition to his handling of Congress affairs. Two other prominent Parsis had drawn the ire of many nationalists in the 1890s. Behramji Merwanji Malabari had led the campaign to persuade the government to raise the legal age of marriage for Hindus. Some nationalists had complained that Parsis and Englishmen had no business legislating for Hindu domestic life.[56] The other Parsi whose activities had irked nationalists was Muncherji Bhownuggree, Conservative M. P. for Bethnal Green. To the delight of Conservatives, Bhownuggree called Gokhale "a despicable perjurer" in the House of Commons in 1897[57] and denigrated the whole Congress. As a group, Parsis—with a few notable exceptions—appeared to identify themselves more closely with England and English business interests than with the cause of Indian nationalism. Pherozeshah Mehta on at least one occasion suggested that Parsis were more loyal to English rule than other groups.[58] It was sometimes alleged that Parsis were trying to distinguish themselves from other Indians by abandoning Gujarati in favor of a separate language.[59]

However, there is little direct evidence that extremists objected to Mehta because he was a Parsi. Dadabhai Naoroji, after all, was a Parsi and he enjoyed an almost universal respect among Congressmen. The primary issue was clearly Mehta's authoritarian ways and his leadership of the moderate faction in the Congress. He had angered the extremists by ignoring the 1899 Constitution and by overriding their opposition to his conduct of

[56] Wolpert, *Tilak and Gokhale*, p. 50.
[57] Parvate, *Gopal Krishna Gokhale*, p. 117.
[58] J.R.B. Jeejeebhoy (ed.), *Some Unpublished and Later Speeches and Writings of the Hon. Sir Pherozeshah Mehta* (Bombay, 1918), p. 8.
[59] *Modern Review*, Vol. I, No. 2 (Feb. 1907), 224–225.

Congress affairs. That opposition was voiced strongly at the 1903 Madras Congress in the Subjects Committee and the open session.

That the criticism of Mehta was not limited to the extremists was revealed in Lalmohan Ghose's 1903 presidential speech. Lalmohan returned to the Congress to preside over the Madras session after a long absence. He had been the leader of an unsuccessful attempt to start a new moderate party in Bengal in 1895, although at the time it was suggested that he was motivated less by disagreement with Congress policies than by personal resentment at his failure to be recognized as a Congress leader.[60] He used his 1903 presidential speech to insinuate that Pherozeshah Mehta was despotic, and he reminded the delegates "that as the very aim and object, the *raison d'être*, of this National Congress is to introduce some little popular element into the autocratic constitution of the Indian Government, so if they aspire to be the leaders of our people, they should be especially careful that their own acts may not be condemned as autocratic by the rank and file of our party."[61]

In the Subjects Committee, Pherozeshah Mehta made a long speech defending his conduct against allegations of despotic behavior. Discussion in the committee was agitated.[62] Krishnaswami Iyer and G. Subramania Iyer led the attack on the Congress leadership and argued with Punjabi delegates that the Congress should adopt and abide by a constitution. In the end, however, Mehta, who chaired the meeting, "pounded to pieces his opponents," according to P. S. Sivaswami Iyer.[63] The 1903 Subjects Committee not only refused to implement or replace the 1899 Constitution, it also passed "a vote of censure" of G. Subramania Iyer for the intemperateness of his criticism of the old-guard leaders.[64]

The 1903 Congress would have been notable for Lalmohan Ghose's presidential speech alone, for it was the most explicit challenge to the leadership before an open session of the Con-

[60] *Bengalee*, 29 June 1895. Lalmohan Ghose was a successful criminal lawyer, as his brother, Manomohan, had been. They came from a prominent zamindari family and Lalmohan was a member of the British Indian Association. He was the unsuccessful Liberal candidate for Greenwich in the 1885 general election.
[61] *Report of the 19th INC*, p. 11.
[62] *Bengalee*, 29 Dec. 1903; *Report of the 19th INC*, p. xvi.
[63] Sastri, *A Great Liberal*, p. 263.
[64] Nundy, "The Troubles of the National Congress," p. 1,404.

gress. But the 1903 Congress was marred by low attendance[65] and a storm which flooded the meeting place, making it necessary to shift the meeting to a verandah where speakers shouted against the noise of falling rain before a small audience.[66] The *Hindustan Review* declared that the 1903 Congress was distinguished from all its predecessors as "a distinct and dismal failure."[67] Altogether, the Congress reached a low point in that year, so low, indeed, that some nationalists suggested "that the movement might with advantage be stopped for a time."[68]

Gopal Krishna Gokhale, the rising politician in the moderate ranks, tried to heal the developing rift. He was appointed joint general secretary for the first time by the 1903 Congress, and in the succeeding July he returned to Madras to dissipate the resentment of Pherozeshah Mehta. Gokhale suggested to the Madrasis that Japan's great achievements were due to the willingness of the Japanese to follow their leaders. He argued that Indians also "must be prepared to subordinate their judgment to that of" their leaders.[69]

Gokhale's appeal for discipline seemed to have little effect. The rumblings against Mehta continued. Tilak facetiously suggested that Mehta, Surendranath Banerjea, and Ananda Charlu should go to England for several years to carry on political work. In the 1904 Subjects Committee at Bombay, Tilak's allies re-

[65] The Madras Congress of 1894 had been attended by 1,163 delegates, the Madras Congress of 1898 by 614, and the 1903 Congress by only 538 delegates.
[66] *Report of the 19th INC*, p. xvii.
[67] *Hindustan Review and Kayastha Samachar*, Vol. IX, No. 1 (Jan. 1904), 76.
[68] Bonnerjee, *A Call to Arms*, p. 5. The possibility that the Congress might collapse had been mentioned before, by the *Indian Mirror*, 14 Dec. 1898 (T. and D. Selections, 19 Dec. 1898, PSLI, Vol. 110) and by the *Kesari*, 11 Dec. 1900 (T. and D. Selections, 31 Dec. 1900, PSLI, Vol. 128). The *Amrita Bazar Patrika*, 13 Dec. 1898 (T. and D. Selections, 19 Dec. 1898, PSLI, Vol. 110) reported that a minority of the delegates at the 1897 Congress had suggested that the Congress should close its operations. The *Bengalee*, 9 Dec. 1899, admitted that it did "not indeed regard the Congress as a permanent institution." And the *Poona Vaibhav*, 28 Dec. 1899 (T. and D. Selections, 15 Jan. 1900, PSLI, Vol. 120) advised the Congress to disband since its lavish expenditure had achieved nothing.
[69] Gokhale qualified this by adding "unless questions of conscience are involved." Speech of 25 July 1904, *Speeches and Writings of Gopal Krishna Gokhale*, ed. by D. G. Karve and D. V. Ambekar (Poona, 1966), II, 178–179.

The Congress Constitution

sumed the "revolt" against Mehta.[70] Lala Murlidhar "complained bitterly about Pherozeshah ... carrying everything his own way." Mehta, who again was chairman, defended himself and asked why, if they felt that way, his opponents did not vote against him. Lala Murlidhar answered "your personality carries everything before it," to which Mehta replied, "I can't help my personality, gentlemen, can I?" At this point the extremists became quiet and sullen,[71] perhaps constrained by Dadabhai Naoroji's recent private appeal to Tilak not to split the Congress.[72] Tilak must have known that Mehta would have quit the Congress, taking other respected leaders with him, if they had carried a constitution or resolutions over Mehta's objections. Neither moderates nor extremists had yet reached the point at which they were willing to decide an issue of this magnitude on the basis of a contested vote.

Mehta avoided a further confrontation with his challengers at the 1905 Benaras Congress by staying away and by sending Wacha to "deputize for him."[73] In 1905, however, there was a new mood in the Congress because of the partition of Bengal, and it is doubtful that even Mehta could have prevented that session from approving the boycott in Bengal. While Mehta opposed the adoption of new tactics, many other moderates, especially in Bengal, were willing to endorse at least a limited boycott. Moreover, the mantle of moderate leadership seemed to be passing to Gopal Krishna Gokhale. Gokhale had won great respect by his thoughtful and effective speeches in the Imperial Legislative Council as Mehta's successor. Gokhale's decision in 1905 to start the Servants of India Society to give full-time, unpaid work to the nation implied a criticism of the older Congress leaders for whom patriotic activity was secondary to their private careers. It may be that Mehta's disapproval of the Servants of India Society and his failure to attend either the welcome for Gokhale upon his return from England in December 1905 or the 1905 Congress over which Gokhale presided were marks of Mehta's jealousy or recognition of the threat Gokhale posed to his leadership of the moderate wing of the Congress.[74]

[70] Wolpert, *Tilak and Gokhale*, p. 152.
[71] Mody, *Mehta*, II, 451.
[72] Wolpert, *Tilak and Gokhale*, pp. 152–153.
[73] Parvate, *Gopal Krishna Gokhale*, p. 184.
[74] Ibid., pp. 183 and 189.

A CALL TO ARMS

In the meantime, friends of the Congress in England were trying to rally the movement away from its drift toward disunity and inactivity. In 1903, Wedderburn, Naoroji, Bonnerjee, and Hume contributed "A Call to Arms" to the *Hindustan Review*.[75] In it each urged the nationalists to overcome their despair. Wedderburn, writing in a vein in which he and Hume had written before, spoke of the failure of the British mission to awaken "this great and ancient race to a higher national existence." But unlike Hume, Wedderburn professed optimism about the future.[76] "For the last eight years this country has been dominated by the party of aggression abroad and selfish class interests at home." Now the pendulum was about to swing toward the Liberals. "With a fresh Parliament, and an awakened national conscience, the Court of Appeal will be open."[77] W. C. Bonnerjee, too, expected much of the Liberals.[78] On the other hand, Naoroji and Hume tended to minimize the significance of a change of government in England. Naoroji thought the struggle against a "blindly selfish power" would have to be continued until "Self-Government under British Paramountcy" was attained, and, until then, "there is no chance of the evil bleeding, of the plunder of an unceasing foreign invasion, the cause of all our sufferings, ever ending."[79]

Hume's bitter message broke a long period of silence which his associates had urged him to end so that no one would interpret it as indicating a loss of sympathy with or faith in the Congress. He advised Indians not to anticipate much help from the Liberals. Nor should Indians think that their position was comparable to that of the Irish who had some 90 M. P.s and who had been "fighting tooth nail . . . for nearly a century." The Indians,

[75] *A Call to Arms* (Allahabad, 1903), reprinted in pamphlet form from the *Hindustan Review*, Dec. 1903.

[76] The differences between Hume and Wedderburn had, of course, been demonstrated before, and they were recognized in an article in 1901 by a member of the British Committee [R. C. Dutt?] who described Wedderburn as "a firm believer in the sweet persuasiveness of reason" while Hume, he said, "has within him the blood of revolutionists." "Indian Politics in England: A Peep behind the Scenes," *Kayastha Samachar*, Vol. III, No. 5 (May 1901), 395.

[77] *A Call to Arms*, pp. 2–3.   [78] Ibid., p. 5.
[79] Ibid., pp. 3–4.

The Congress Constitution

he said, had no M. P.s "and you are, most of you, alas! it seems to me, never more than half in earnest in *your* fight! You meet in Congresses; you glow with a momentary enthusiasm"; and then, few people devoted earnest thought or work to India's cause. He placed the blame for India's unhappy political position on the Indians themselves who showed neither self-sacrifice nor mutual trust. "You have indeed ever eagerly clamoured for and vainly clutched at the *Crown*, but how many of you will touch the *Cross* with even your finger-tips?"[80]

The Congress had little to show for its existence in 1903, nineteen years after it was founded. It had no money, no permanent organization, no sustained activity. It had failed to find any significant support among the masses and the Muslims. It was a house divided, with little confidence in itself and enjoying the confidence of few others. It was ignored or ridiculed by British officials. It received moralistic and condescending lectures on its shortcomings from its British friends. Yet in its own torpor and demoralization lay the seeds of revival. Change was in the air. An unrepresentative leadership, pursuing ineffectual tactics against an increasingly autocratic government had poor prospects for survival. Nevertheless, the likely nature of the change was unclear in 1903. No leader in either the moderate or extremist camp was willing to split the Congress over the constitution question. Few were even willing to hold discussions about the constitution in full public view. Instead, the debate was muted and was conducted in private meetings and oblique editorials. In this way an open division of the Congress was postponed. Yet the Congress remained a weak instrument of the nationalist cause. As Gokhale said in July 1904, "it seems a kind of despondency is settling over the national mind."[81] Until the summer of 1905, Congress leaders did not know that Lord Curzon's partition of Bengal would give the Congress an opportunity to close its ranks and revitalize itself. The partition brought an

[80] Ibid., p. 9. Eardley Norton similarly told an audience of Indian friends in Bombay in 1892 that Indians lacked "grip" or "moral courage." When a European friend of the nationalists was faced with danger or difficulty, he said, "The invariable rule was that his native friend deserted him at a vital moment, and pushed him to the front to bear what blame and odium there was." *Statesman*, 30 Apr. 1892.
[81] Wolpert, *Tilak and Gokhale*, p. 154.

The Congress Constitution

unexpected and abrupt transformation of nationalist politics at a time when the Congress apparently lacked the internal resources for rebirth. Although the Congress did split at Surat in 1907, this was by no means a total defeat for the Congress or its moderate leaders. The partition had the effect of persuading the leadership to adopt *swaraj* or self-rule as the official goal of the Congress. This in turn insured the retention of much of the moderates' following. And the adoption of violence and other extreme tactics by nationalists in and outside the Congress gave the moderates a much greater influence on the government than they had enjoyed before. The moderates were in an excellent position to harvest the fruit of the extremists' sacrifices.

PART III

Chapter Six

TOWARD THE INTEGRATION OF INDIAN ELITES

The abstention of almost all titled landowners from the Congress, dominated as it was by lawyers, suggests a sharp political division between the hereditary landed classes and the achievement-oriented university graduates of the cities. Landholder associations generally disapproved of the anti-British attitudes of Congress partisans, and they disagreed with many Congressmen over specific issues, particularly agrarian legislation and Legislative Council reform. Inherent in the Congress movement was a threat to reduce the influence of landholders in Indian life. Yet in examining disputes between landholders and urban professionals during the first two decades of the Congress, it becomes apparent that numerous Congressmen and major landholders regarded each other with mutual respect, a respect born of interdependence. In fact, it would not be too much to say that because of close relations outside the Congress between urban professionals and major zamindars, cooperation was more significant than conflict, at least in Bengal, Bihar, Bombay, and Madras. This chapter examines the general areas of compromise and adjustment, while the next chapter analyzes specific controversies which threatened to wreck the late nineteenth-century landlord-urban professional accommodation.

Several developments drew particular urban professionals close to both titled landlords and chiefs of princely states. The landlords and chiefs needed and made frequent use of the professional expertise of lawyers, administrators, and journalists. Second, a growing number of successful Indian professionals and businessmen were entering a social life and elite status once reserved more exclusively for titled landholders and Europeans. The tendency was for social integration of the top ranks of Indian elites regardless of differences in economic function. Third, the effect of British policies was to encourage the mixing of landed and urban elites through both the educational and honors systems. The British intended to strengthen the landed aristocracy by educating their children, by recognizing with considerable publicity even modest achievements among the landlords, and by linking them with the majesty of the Queen Empress's sovereignty by means of the Raj's elaborate pageantry. Officials hoped thereby to preserve a highly visible and loyal buttress to their rule. But a side effect of educating a minority of landlords and princes and of associating them with the all-Indian political order was to expose them to values embraced by Congressmen. And in distributing honors for achievement, the British inevitably were obliged to give awards to many nonlandholding professionals. In the process, the British validated the entry of professionals into the status hierarchy of title-holders.

Landlord-professional relations are important for an understanding of Congress nation-building efforts. Considering the loyalty and even gratitude of titled landholders to the British, intimate ties between landlords as a group and the Congress could only reduce Congress willingness to adopt extremist political methods and goals. Moreover, a major landlord influence within the Congress would have precluded championing tenant rights or recruiting peasants into the Congress. This in turn would have undermined the force of the Congress contention that it spoke for all Indians. At stake were both the economic interests and the political status of the Indian peasantry. In many ways, peasants had yet to achieve citizenship. For example, settlement officers, in determining fair rents in the North-Western Provinces and Oudh, used one rate for low castes who cultivated with their hands and a reduced rate for the high-caste tenants whose traditions prevented them from doing manual labor and necessitated hiring menial workers. In addition, the franchise throughout British India was narrowly restricted, and most peasants were excluded from voting, as they were from education. If the Congress was to confer full citizenship upon the peasantry, it could not embrace landlords or even be neutral when landlord economic and political interests came into conflict with the interests of tenants and landless laborers. Finally, the integrity and self-esteem of Congress leaders were involved. Officials were eager to taint the Congress with the label of a selfish, class-based organization. It seems to have been important for Congress morale to demonstrate the contrary, to show to itself and the British that it was as responsive to the interests of the poor as to the rajas'. The problem was that many Congress leaders regarded the allegiance of titled landholders an easier and more rewarding objective.

Relations Between Agrarian Classes

Making generalizations about relations between classes in late nineteenth-century India is a hazardous enterprise. Articulated class consciousness or the recognition of shared economic interests in opposition to those of another class existed in peasant aphorisms, and it was demonstrated in rent and occupancy disputes. But it rarely led to the formation of formal interest-group organizations outside the towns. Concentration of habitation, separation of work from domestic life, and employment in large-scale enterprises are preconditions for class formation in most societies, and in rural India these were rarely met. In India, rural society was even more likely than in most preindustrial countries to accept sharp differences in income and status as natural; even university graduates in Indian cities in the nineteenth century seemed comfortable with the dependency and steeply graded hierarchies of professional and political life. Class jealousy and the leveling instinct were less common than the acceptance of a client's subordination, or loyalty, to a patron. In addition, nascent class consciousness was frequently diffused by factional, caste, religious, and linguistic rivalries among members of the same occupation or income level. Furthermore, the multiple tiers and overlapping interests within economic enterprises discouraged efforts to analyze property relations in simple class terms. What was the class or class interest of a *jotdar* who cultivated some of his rented land himself while renting other parts to subtenants to whom he also lent money? Who were his "class enemies"? How was it possible for a tenant to focus his anger on the taluqdari class for the *abwabs* (cesses imposed in addition to the rent) and bribes demanded by a taluqdar's *amla* (landlord's agents) when a taluqdar delegated the entire management of his estate and when a taluqdar's most visible role was support of religious activities, feeding the poor on ceremonial occasions, and suspension of rents in years of famine?

Antilandlord combinations in the nineteenth century may have been a much more common phenomenon than historians have acknowledged, but most combinations were among the relatively prosperous peasants on a sporadic, informal, and local basis. Smaller tenants and landless laborers rarely acted in concert or risked antagonizing their landlords or employers. Most, it seems, followed the classical path of survival in small-scale, despotic social groups and censured their feeling to avoid the possibility of insubordinate behavior and the painful consequences that would have entailed. The values of caste conditioned poor people to expect extreme inequality. There are indications in the reports of the famine commissions and elsewhere that the poorest sections of the rural population in the late nineteenth-century were becoming poorer, relative to other groups, and perhaps absolutely. But this deterioration did not stimulate combinations among agricultural laborers and the smaller tenants. The economic threat to rural landed elites, insofar as it existed, came from the wealthier peasants and from money-lenders and lawyers.

There are also indications that in the decade prior to the founding of the Congress, small-sized landholders who either cultivated themselves or directly supervised the cultivation (jotdars, superior ryots, tenants with occupancy rights)[1] were gaining economically relative to zamindars, taluqdars, and noncultivating tenure holders above them in many parts of India.[2] In the 1870s and 1880s, these small landholders became more assertive in their relations with superior landlords and creditors, resorting to passive resistance and the law courts to resist enhancements, illegal cesses, and transfers. Occasionally, as in east Bengal and Bombay in the 1870s, they turned violent against rent-collectors and creditors.

The agrarian violence of the 1870s and the finding of the 1880 Famine Commission that rents were exhorbitant hastened the passage of new laws regulating landlord-tenant relations. New

[1] There is some evidence about the improved position of occupancy tenants in Pradip Sinha, *Nineteenth Century Bengal: Aspects of Social History* (Calcutta, 1965), pp. 26–27; L.S.S. O'Malley, *Bengal District Gazetteers, Jessore* (Calcutta, 1912); Ravinder Kumar, *Western India in the Nineteenth Century: A Study in the Social History of Maharashtra* (London, 1968), p. 330; and Elizabeth Whitcombe, *Agrarian Conditions in Northern India*, Vol. 1, *The United Provinces Under British Rule, 1860–1900* (Berkeley, 1972), 216–217.

[2] Act X of 1859, covering Bengal, Agra, and the Central Provinces, had strengthened that group of peasants classified as "occupancy tenants" while leaving nonoccupancy tenants without significant protection from ejectment or enhancement. A Madras act of 1865 afforded some protection to tenants of zamindars.

tenancy acts were passed for Bombay in 1879, for the North-Western Provinces in 1881, for the Central Provinces in 1883, for Bengal in 1885, and for Oudh in 1886.[3] The legislation and the test of strength which preceded it had a temporary settling effect upon agrarian relations. Creditors and debtors, as well as landlords and tenants, seemed to understand better what their relative strengths were and what was permitted by law. After the passage of the Bengal Tenancy Act of 1885, landlords seemed less concerned about economic conflict with their tenants than their rivalry with urban professionals. The founding of the Congress and the legislative council reforms of 1892 encouraged landlords throughout India to pay more attention to their political future. The debates over the Bengal Tenancy Bill and the Deccan Agricultural Relief Bill had demonstrated the central role that the legislative councils would play in regulating agrarian relations. The prolonged discussions in Bengal also revealed a strong undercurrent of hostility among college-educated Bengalis to zamindari interests and to aristocratic privilege in general.

The British, as has often been said, regarded the superior landholders and chiefs of the Indian states as pillars of their rule, pillars increasingly important with the rise in the numbers of college graduates in the cities. With the educated *babus* in mind, Lord Lytton had written in 1876 that "to secure completely, and efficiently utilise, the Indian aristocracy is . . . the most important problem now before us."[4] The main vehicle for strengthening the major landowning families was the court of wards.

THE COURTS OF WARDS

Each province had a court of wards which managed the estates of certain minors, females, lunatics, and indebted landlords. The Mutiny had underlined the need for an institution to protect major estates from mismanagement. The post-Mutiny successes in placing the estates of wards under the control of district collectors and special managers persuaded officials in the 1870s to expand the operations of the courts of wards. An 1878 analysis of 59 estates which had been under the court of wards in Bengal, Bihar, and Orissa for five or more years revealed that government management had reduced their debts from Rs. 121 lakhs to Rs.

[3] Seal, *The Emergence*, p. 134.   [4] Ibid.

11 lakhs and that their investments had been increased from Rs. 3 lakhs to Rs. 63 lakhs.[5] A more limited survey in the North-Western Provinces in 1889 showed similar financial success.[6] Because many landlords died when their natural or adopted heirs were very young, the provincial governments took over a substantial portion of the larger estates in India for varying periods of time. Among those managed under the courts of wards during the nineteenth-century were the giant estates of Balrampur, Burdwan, Darbhanga, and Vizianagram. By 1899, the court of wards in the North-Western Provinces and Oudh had expanded its operations to cover 190 estates paying more than 5 per cent of the provinces's land revenue. At times the Bengal court of wards managed an even greater proportion of Bengal, Bihar, and Orissa. A survey in 1880 showed that the average divisional commissioner and district collector in the Lower Provinces of Bengal, Bihar, and Orissa was spending one-eighth of his time on court of wards' work and that in certain districts the time rose to over one-fourth.[7]

The effect of court of wards management was more evident while the estate was under government supervision than after it reverted to the owner. Although the cost of court management was high, in most cases its financial results were beneficial to the ward. Government managers rationalized and improved estate records, they developed irrigation works, they reduced debts through stricter collection of rents and through consolidation of debts by taking out new loans at lower interest rates, they kept tighter control over the subordinate staff and the personal expenditures of the raj families. In many instances, estates were returned to the wards upon attaining majority age with sizeable investments in government securities, large cash balances, fuller and more accurate rent-rolls, and perhaps a more subservient tenantry.

The court of wards' legislation of the 1850s and 1870s also

[5] *Report on Wards' and Attached Estates in the Lower Provinces of the Year 1877–1878* (Calcutta, 1879), p. 3.

[6] Sec., Bd. of Rev., NWP, to Ch. Sec., NWP, 25 Aug. 1889. May 1891 Rev. Prog. No. 18, Bengal Rev. Prog., Vol. 3,871.

[7] H.J.S. Cotton, Offg. Sec., Bd. of Rev., L. P., to Sec., Govt. of Bengal, Rev. Dept., 9 Sept. 1880. Dec. 1880 Prog. No. 33–35, Bengal Rev. Prog. Wards', Attached, and Govt. Estates, Vol. 1,488.

provided for the preparation of the wards to manage their estates once they came of age. The wards were sent either to ordinary government schools or the special wards' institutions at Agra, Benaras, Calcutta, Lucknow, and Madras, or, as in the case of heirs to the largest estates, they were given private, usually European tutors. They were taught English and their vernacular language, mathematics, history, and geography—a curriculum similar to that experienced by most Congress supporters. In the last year or two of the wardship, an effort was also made to teach them zamindari accounting and rent law.

The education of wards, or at least that education which involved cultural and physical separation of minors from their families, was often opposed by the wards' relatives. A major purpose of the courts' educational system was to remove the wards from the influence of the *zenanna* and amla during childhood. It was assumed that widow-mothers were overindulgent and eager to spare their sons from any hard work, while the estate amla were believed to have a vested interest in keeping landlords ignorant of land management and therefore incapable of interfering in their misappropriation of funds and land.[8] It was for that reason the courts of wards removed most children of major raj families from their homes and placed them under the guardianship of either a tutor or one of the wards' institutions.

Family opposition to wards' education was one cause of the limited success of the courts' educational efforts. The wards at Benaras, Calcutta, and elsewhere lived at the wards' institutions with their tutors, servants, and separate cooks, and attended classes at a local school. The experience at Benaras[9] and Calcutta in the 1860s and 1870s was that the wards did very poorly in competition with ordinary students. Because they repeatedly failed their examinations, many studied in classes with students four or five years younger than they were. A special committee appointed by the Government of Bengal, and including Maharaja Jatindramohan Tagore and Kristodas Pal, criticized this system because the zamindar's son "thus begins his school career with a sense of

[8] These were common assumptions. See Rajendralal Mitra, Dir. of Govt. Wards, to Sec., Bd. of Rev., L. P., 3 Jan. 1881. March 1881, Head No. 2, Prog. No. 23–25, Bengal Rev. Prog., Vol. 1,640.

[9] S. C. Bayley, Offg. Com., Patna Div., to Offg. Sec., Govt. of Bengal, Rev. Dept., 15 Aug. 1872. Sept. 1872 Rev. Prog. No. 35, Bengal Rev. Prog., Vol. 233.

humiliation at his inferiority."[10] After this report, the Calcutta Wards' Institution was abolished in 1881, partly on the grounds that adequate schools had been created in the mofussil. It was hoped that family opposition would be diminished by educating wards closer to home, away from the Westernizing and immoral influences associated with metropolitan life.

The early disappointments of provincial governments with the educational progress of the wards produced no relaxation of efforts to teach them English and prepare them to manage their estates. The Hunter Education Commission acknowledged that "little has resulted from" government education of its landed wards but urged continued attempts and expansion of special institutions for chiefs and nobles.[11] By the 1880s, an increasing number of government wards were becoming fluent in English and were attending college at Aligarh, Lucknow, Raipur, Ajmere, and Madras. There was no other group of Indians for whom the government made a comparable effort to assure an English education. The educational gap between the major zamindars and urban professional families remained wide at the end of the nineteenth-century, but the court of wards' special schooling had started to narrow it.

What effect the wards' institutions, the educational trips around India, and the separation from family for most of the year had upon the values of major landowners is less certain. The regulations of the wards' institutions specifically forbade any "distinction of rank among the boys," and most wards educated outside the wards' institutions attended schools for varying periods with nonlanded children. However, wealthier wards had available to them sums of money many times greater than what their tutors earned, they were flattered and pampered by personal servants, and they spent months each year with their families, most of whom were hostile to the moderate egalitarianism of the schools. It was not surprising that after attaining the age of majority, many wards ignored the values inculcated by their Indian and English tutors.

[10] Report of the Committee to enquire into the working of the Wards' Institution in Calcutta, 5 May 1880. Enclosure to H.J.S. Cotton, Offg. Sec., Bd. of Rev., L. P., to Sec., Govt. of Bengal, Rev. Dept., 17 June 1880. Jan. 1881, Head No. 2, Prog. No. 3, Bengal Rev. Prog., Vol. 1,640.

[11] *Report of the Indian Education Commission* (Calcutta, 1883), pp. 481–482.

LANDHOLDERS AND EDUCATION

Part of the problem was that landholders' children lacked the same economic incentive for educational achievement and new values as children without inherited wealth. No doubt, officials tried to create an alternative incentive by playing upon the anxieties of their wards, other landlords, and the chiefs of the Indian states by warning them that if they did not educate *their* children, college-educated *babus* and vakils of the type that joined the Indian National Congress might one day dominate the country. Officials tried to arouse class feeling against the English-speaking graduates by pointing to, or listening sympathetically to complaints about, their success in the competitive institutions introduced in recent years and the nonlanded origins of most graduates. Official efforts did persuade a considerable number of rajas to provide education for their sons, to participate in landholders' associations, and to avoid nationalist political organizations. Yet those efforts never aroused rajas to the degree officials would have liked. Most responded halfheartedly to official attempts to interest them in education. Officials commented ruefully upon their failure to stir major landlords and suggested that compared to English university students, Indian students increasingly came from nonmonied and nonelite families. A survey of Presidency College in Calcutta, published in 1884, indicated that only 11 of 280 students had annual family incomes of Rs. 3,000 or more, and almost half the students came from families with incomes of less than Rs. 100 per month.[12] Of the 110 college students in the Central Provinces in 1887, only 5 had annual family incomes of over Rs. 5,000, only 7 owned landed estates, and roughly one-third came from families with incomes of under Rs. 200 a year.[13] The situation was similar in all other provinces, it seems, except Madras.[14] For example, in 4

[12] *Education Commission: Report by the Bengal Provincial Committee* (Calcutta, 1884), pp. 343-344.

[13] C. Browning, Insp. Gen. of Educ., C. P., to Sec. to Ch. Com., C. P., 12 Apr. 1888. *Selections from the Records of the Government of India, Home Department, No. CCLXV. Papers Relating to Discipline and Moral Training in Schools and Colleges in India* (Calcutta, 1890), p. 186.

[14] Madras was exceptional in that more than one-third of the students enrolled in nonprofessional colleges in 1883-1884 were children of landholders. *Report of the Indian Education Commission*, p. 286.

of the 7 colleges in the North-Western Provinces and Oudh, only 36 of 227 students enrolled in 1883 were sons of landholders and cultivators.[15] Even after the government persuaded the Oudh taluqdars to agree to a permanent and compulsory levy upon their *jummas* (revenue payments) to support Canning College in Lucknow, which had a special class for the sons of taluqdars, few taluqdars sent their sons to the college.[16]

Explanations for landholders' avoidance of secondary and higher education included arguments that the home life of many landholders was licentious, indulgent, and undisciplined, that major landholders refused to allow their children to mix with students of lower status, that landowners lacked the economic incentive possessed by poor students, and that the education provided in Indian schools and colleges was of minimal practical value in running a landed estate.

URBAN ATTITUDES TOWARD THE ARISTOCRACY

Beyond these explanations is another factor which suggests why landholders viewed their educational backwardness with complacency and why they were not easily aroused by the potential political threat of university graduates. With the partial exception of Bengal, university graduates generally expressed little class antagonism toward landowners, and therefore they frightened landed aristocrats less than they did the British. Sir Walter Roper Lawrence, once head of the Government of India's Revenue Department and later private secretary to Lord Curzon, commented on the attitude of educated Indians toward aristocracy in relation to rulers of Indian states:

> I often watched . . . Rajas when they visited British India, and the profound respect and reverence shown by the leading citizens of the various capitals for a ruling chief impressed me. These leading men—leaders of what was spoken of by the Chiefs as the *Vakil Raj*—so free and easy in the British and official circle, were humble and deferential in the presence of a real Raja. Their manner and attitude changed at once—

---

[15] *Education Commission: Report by the North-Western Provinces and Oudh Provincial Committee* (Calcutta, 1884), pp. 94–95.

[16] *Review of the Management of Estates in the Court of Wards or Under the Taluqdars Relief Act in Oudh for the Year Ending 30 Sept. 1883.*

Integration of Indian Elites

instinctively they recognized their natural leaders and were glad and proud to see them.[17]

The "profound respect" shown to chiefs of Indian states was given with somewhat diminished intensity to the most important zamindars and taluqdars of British India, such as the maharajas of Balrampur, Burdwan, Darbhanga, Venkatagiri, and Vizianagram.[18] The major zamindars, unlike the chiefs, held no formal territorial power. But many once had enjoyed a measure of political autonomy and military strength and this alone entitled them to respect. More than that, the vast estates and fortunes still at their disposal made them powerful people. The taluqdar of Balrampur, for instance, had half a million people and over one hundred elephants in the thousand villages of his 1,500-square-mile estate.[19] In the hands of efficient managers and public-spirited zamindars, landed fortunes could, and often did, support a multitude of civic institutions and private needs. In the late nineteenth century, perhaps no individual in India was better known for charitable giving than Maharani Svarnamayi of Kasimbazar. From the income of six to eight lakhs of rupees she received from an estate scattered over 15 districts in Bengal and the North-Western Provinces, she gave to nationalist activities, colleges, Brahmans, paupers, and many other causes.[20] Numerous other zamindars and chiefs achieved similar reputations without causing themselves personal discomfort in the form of fewer palaces or elephants or loss of armies of servants. Fortunes were so ample when carefully managed, public vigilance so undiscriminating, that distribution of a modest fraction of a major landholder's income sufficed to win paragraphs of praise for benevolence.

[17] Lawrence, *The India We Served*, p. 203.

[18] Most generalizations about landholders in this chapter apply only to major zamindars and taluqdars. Petty rajas occupied a different position altogether. J. R. Reid, who served in Azamgarh district from 1868 to 1883, commented on the changed status of warrior families: "There is everywhere a tacit refusal of all tribute and homage which cannot be enforced by law. The Raja bitterly complains that the peasant, who pays him rent, no longer bows to him; the lowly salam of the grain-dealers, the shopkeepers, the pilgrims, the dancing-girls, is reserved for the English Magistrate who guards the property and punishes the crimes of all." Whitcombe, *Agrarian Conditions*, p. 140.

[19] *Who's Who in India* (Lucknow, 1911), Part IV, pp. 10–11.

[20] Banerjea, *A Nation*, pp. 49 and 97. Also C. E. Buckland, *Bengal Under the Lieutenant-Governors* (Calcutta, 1901), II, 1,064.

In Anglo-Indian usage, the chiefs of the "native states," together with the titled landholders and a few former rulers and officials of pre-British states, constituted the aristocracy. It was predominantly an aristocracy of land, for which neither non-Brahman ritual status, lack of education, nor recent origin was a disqualification. Caste position, as Louis Dumont has said, is an unreliable guide to the Indian politico-economic scene, and this was especially true of Madras and Bengal. In Madras almost all major zamindars were non-Brahmans.[21] In Bengal, major zamindaris were created during the first century of British rule, often by men from castes ranked below the majority of Congress leaders. The estates of the Tagores, Mukherjis of Uttarpara, the Debs of Sovabazar, the Lahas, and the Kasimbazar raj were all of recent origin. The Lahas were Subarnabanik (goldsmith and merchant caste), the Kasimbazar family was Teli (oil-pressing caste), the Burdwan raj family was Khatri (Punjabi money-lending caste), while the Tagore and Deb families' castes, although high, were subjects of dispute and gossip. If these families felt any stigma about their origins, it may help explain the care with which they educated their children and managed their economic affairs in most cases. Those zamindars in Bengal who were educated tended to find common interests with the urban professionals which were missing in northern India.

In the North-Western Provinces and Oudh, the division between the landed aristocracy and the urban educated classes was sharper than in Bengal, Bombay, and Madras. The educated classes were small and divided between fairly distinct ethnic groups: Kashmiri Brahmans, Kayasthas, Muslims, Bengalis, and Punjabi commercial castes. Their smallness and internal divisions made them more vulnerable to government pressure and more dependent upon merchant, banker, and landlord patrons than their counterparts in the coastal provinces. And compared to educated nationalists outside of northern India, they were less likely to come from the same castes as the major landlords, most of whom were Rajputs and Muslims. The Rajputs held twice as much land as any other single group.[22] Rajput pride in their feudal

---

[21] Eugene F. Irschick, *Politics and Social Conflict in South India: The Non-Brahman Movement and Tamil Separatism, 1916–1929* (Berkeley, 1969), p. 12.

[22] In 1907–1908, Rajputs owned 16,341,000 acres in the U. P., Muslims owned 8,963,000, Brahmans, Bhuinhars, and Tagas together held 8,095,000

traditions and warrior origins remained strong, and, consequently, they and other major taluqdars in the North-Western Provinces and Oudh responded slowly to British efforts to persuade them to send their children to school. They contributed money to modern education but generally failed to send their own children to school, just as they bought modern agricultural implements and allowed them "to rust unused."[23]

Perhaps only the elderly Rajputs of Rajputana had a greater abhorrence of the effects of education upon their traditions of riding, hunting, and fighting than the taluqdars of the North-Western Provinces and Oudh. When one old Rajput chief heard his heir tell the English political agent he did not care for riding, "the old Chief boomed out a litany of contempt and malediction, of which the refrain ran:

> Kitab Purh
> Buggi men Baith.
> (Read books
> sit in a buggy.)"

Some Rajputs even opposed the building of roads because they feared that artillery would replace Rajput cavalry.[24] However, Englishmen commented upon this strict adherence to *kshatriya* life styles because it was no longer universal. Kshatriya ways had been diluted in many families by the absence of opportunities to fight, the slow extension of education, and the decline in family incomes through partitions and debts. While the British hoped to unify the Indian aristocracy, their attempts to educate notables were lengthening the spectrum of attitudes toward custom and tradition. The Maharaja of Jaipur, with a law degree from the University of Edinburgh, may have had as much in common intellectually with a Calcutta barrister as with fellow Rajputs who deplored road building and reading.

The major landholders of British India and the chiefs of Indian states occupied different positions in relation to the Indian

---

acres, while "nonagricultural castes" held 6,948,000 acres. E.A.H. Blunt, *The Caste System of Northern India* (New Delhi, 1969; reprint of 1931 edition), p. 270.

[23] Thomas Metcalf, "From Raja to Landlord," in R. E. Frykenberg (ed.), *Land Control and Social Structure in Indian History* (Madison, 1969), p. 159.

[24] Lawrence, *The India We Served*, pp. 71–72.

National Congress. Zamindars, as citizens of British India, were participants in the same political system as Congressmen, and therefore they stood to be immediately affected by the programs and activities of the Congress. Chiefs, on the other hand, were restricted politically to their states where they were free to choose their own form of government, subject to the loose supervision of the Indian Political Service. Nationalists were generally less interested in whether chiefs lived up to the representative and liberal political principles of the Congress than whether the British honored the independence of the states. Congress resolutions asking for expansion of British Indian legislative councils were silent about the princely states. Nationalists who reacted with righteous indignation to despotic action by alien officials in British India and who regarded kingship as an archaic form of government approached the absolutism of most chiefs with the tolerance and respect owed to an elderly relative with outmoded views. When British Residents interfered with the administration of Baroda, Hyderabad, and Kashmir in the last third of the nineteenth century, nationalists protested, regardless of whether the state was well governed or not. The 1896, 1897, and 1898 Congresses passed resolutions asking that no chief be deposed without a public tribunal, and the 1901 and 1902 sessions approved the creation of the Cadet Corps which gave aristocratic families special opportunities for military training. Outside the Congress, individual nationalists defended the Maharaja of Kashmir and other chiefs from British interference in their internal affairs. British officials might have regarded the states as the breakwaters which kept the tide of the 1857 Mutiny from sweeping them into the sea; nationalists tended to look upon them as the place where "the heart of India beats,"[25] where Indians exercised real power unfettered by the racial barriers of British India. And although British policies toward the states served to magnify the importance of the symbols of authority, frequently at the expense of good government itself, nationalists took pride in substantive achievements when they appeared. In particular, the progressive policies of Baroda and Mysore were cited as evidence of how wise and responsible Indians in power might be. And when a chief demonstrated hostility toward or

[25] Quoted from M. G. Ranade's speech to the 1894 Social Conference, S. Natarajan, *A Century of Social Reform in India* (London, 1959), p. 101.

Integration of Indian Elites

even independence from the British, nationalists applauded. When the Gaikwar of Baroda failed to bow to the Queen at the Delhi Durbar of 1911, and then turned his back on both the King and Queen, the nationalist press (and the British) treated it as a major incident.[26]

Although early nationalists sympathized with the rulers of Indian states more than with the landholders of British India, and although nationalists posed a more immediate political challenge to those landholders, from the perspective of nationalists and other residents of British India, the major landholders were akin to Indian chiefs in many respects. The British Indian rajas' palaces, temples, maintenance of Brahmans, charitable giving, and trappings of power were scarcely distinguishable from those of the chiefs. References to chiefs and titled landholders in newspapers and Congress proceedings suggest that in many contexts chiefs, zamindars, and taluqdars were viewed as members of a single aristocracy. The same references, together with the appointment of titled notables to presidencies of cultural organizations and the relative immunity of rajas and *nawabs* from criticism by the major newspapers, indicated the high regard in which many chiefs and zamindars were held. Their life styles were similar despite the differences in their constitutional place in the imperial system.

In addition to taking pleasure in Indian accomplishment and sentimental attachments to survivals of a disappearing past, certain nationalists with administrative, educational, and legal skills had pragmatic reasons for acting deferentially toward the chiefs and zamindars. The prospect of a highly paid position with significant responsibility appealed to men in the crowded occupations of British India. The Begum of Bhopal commented on the "large number of Bengali pleaders" who flocked to her during a visit to Calcutta. They were seeking employment in the forthcoming reorganization of Bhopal's administration. In this particular instance, the Begum scorned their requests for administrative appointments.[27] But in many other cases, chiefs of states welcomed men from British India who had received superior educations and who were independent of cliques and family in-

---

[26] The Gaikwar claimed plausibly that his insult was inadvertent. Stanley Rice, *Life of Sayaji Rao III: Maharaja of Baroda* (London, 1930), II, 16ff.

[27] Nawab Sultan Jahan Begam, *An Account of My Life (Gohur-i-Ikbal)* (London, 1912), pp. 130–131.

fluences in the local durbar. Madras Province was noted for providing administrators for the Indian states. In 1882, of the 971 persons who had received B. A.s from the University of Madras, 68 were listed as in the service of native states.[28] Prominent non-Madrasi nationalists—including Dadabhai Naoroji, Pherozeshah Mehta, Romeshchandra Dutt, Aurobindo Ghose, and Shyama Krishna Varma—did accept temporary assignments in Indian states, and Raja T. Madhava Rao of Madras, who was chairman of the 1887 Reception Committee, spent most of his career in the Travancore, Indore, and Baroda administrations. Tej Bahadur Sapru's legal services were used by a number of states, including Bhopal, Hyderabad, and Patiala.[29] Many other Congressmen, as explained below, had professional relations with zamindars of British India.

The employment by chiefs and zamindars of Indian administrators, lawyers, and teachers from British India was one of several factors tending toward a limited integration of the new professional classes with the Indian aristocracy. Pre-Mutiny official policy had aimed at neutralizing the chiefs by keeping them disarmed and isolated from one another. England's treaties with the states forbade the chiefs from having official relations with each other, and the chiefs' own rivalries and concern for relative status prevented many from establishing close unofficial contacts. After the Mutiny, however, officials eased the policy of isolating the chiefs. Partly by design, partly as an unintended consequence of other policies, the British were tending to draw the chiefs and the titled landholders of British India together into a single, steeply graded hierarchy. The fifty or so Residents and political agents living in the princely states arranged for the assignment of British-trained administrators to head branches of the state governments; they introduced British and Indian tutors to teach English to the chiefs' children; they helped the chiefs set up schools with a common curriculum for aristocratic children, including the colleges for chiefs at Ajmere and Indore; when a chief was considered unfit to rule, the Residents and political agents arranged for a British-type of interim adminis-

[28] Evidence of D. Duncan, acting principal, Presidency College. *Education Commission: Report by the Madras Provincial Committee* (Calcutta, 1884), p. 36.

[29] Sapru's knowledge of Urdu and Persian was one reason his services were highly valued. Aiyar, *Biographical Vistas*, p. 206.

tration.[30] As a result, a growing number of chiefs were absorbing British-Indian culture and were increasingly conscious of their place in the all-Indian imperial scheme.

Titles and Honors

British officials hoped that their paternal intervention in the affairs of the Indian aristocracy would result in good government and loyalty to the Raj. British security had always rested on the continued acceptance of privilege and of the legitimacy of massive inequality. Officials knew that that acceptance would be threatened as popular expectations of government rose unless the aristocracy could be educated and prodded into adopting a higher conception of public responsibility. The British thus both honored inherited status in general and exceptional aristocratic behavior in particular. The honors for good government and public spirit were at once an inducement for aristocrats to behave responsibly and an effort to legitimize a social system which was increasingly difficult to justify by contemporary political ideals.

Yet because the British government had no intention of returning political power already taken from aristocrats, it was largely limited to symbolic and honorific means of enhancing the visibility and importance of the Indian aristocracy. It was not until 1921 that a chamber of princes was created in which the chiefs could meet officially to discuss their common concerns. The British confirmed inherited powers and titles, they conferred new titles for unusual loyalty, charity, or administrative excellence, and they honored aristocrats on ceremonial occasions. Many of the hereditary titles and honors served the purpose of identifying a person's place in the status hierarchy. For example, the rulers of Baroda, Hyderabad, and Mysore were entitled to 21-gun salutes, eight other chiefs were allowed 19-gun salutes, another thirteen were permitted 17-guns, and so on. Major zamindars of British India as well received salutes as a mark of personal distinction. But the British distributed nonhereditary honors also to stimulate aristocratic education, loyalty, and administrative responsibility. Officially, the Crown awarded the British honors, on the advice of the Viceroy.[31] In the late nineteenth century,

[30] Sir Kenneth Fitze, *Twilight of the Maharajas* (London, 1956), pp. 25ff., describes briefly the responsibilities of the Political Service.
[31] Cumulative lists of awards were published in *The India List and India Office List* (London, annually).

Indians in both the states and the British Indian provinces were eligible for knighthoods under two separate orders: The Most Exalted Order of the Star of India and The Most Eminent Order of the Indian Empire. Each of these orders had a subcategory known as the Companions (C.S.I. and C.I.E.) which recognized distinctive achievement or service without conferring the coveted title of "Sir." And in 1900, a new award, also without title, the Kaiser-i-Hind Medal for public service, was introduced. In addition to these British-created awards, the government distributed or confirmed Indian titles, starting with Rai (for Hindus), Sardar (for Sikhs), and Khan (for Muslims) and proceeding upward through Raja and Nawab to Nawab, Maharaja, and Maharaja-dhiraja. As in the case of British titles, Indian titles were given to citizens of both British and princely India, thereby blurring somewhat the distinction between the two hierarchies.[32] For example, the zamindar of Burdwan, Mahtabchand, who had given valuable assistance to the government during the 1857 Mutiny, was awarded the title of Maharaja-dhiraja; furthermore, he was allowed to be addressed as "His Highness" and was granted an increase to thirteen in the number of guns to be fired in his honor in 1877. In 1909, his adopted son and successor, Bijaychand Mahtab, was knighted after he placed himself between a nationalist gunman and his intended victim, Sir Andrew Fraser, the lieutenant-governor of Bengal.[33] These honors, together with the rents from the two million people living in his estates, placed him high in the merging hierarchies of British and princely India.

In addition to these largely symbolic privileges, the British gave British Indian notables certain substantive honors, such as magisterial powers, sometimes with the right to pass the death sentence, exemption from personal attendance in the civil courts, exemption from having their land attached through the civil courts, and the right to bear arms. Chiefs of states were allowed to maintain token military forces with specified numbers of cavalry and artillery pieces. These aristocratic privileges rarely drew adverse comments in the nationalist press.

Although the award system was intended to enchance the loyalty of the traditional ruling classes to British rule, the British

---

[32] C. E. Buckland, *Dictionary of Indian Biography* (London, 1906), p. 60.
[33] *Who's Who in India*, Part VIII, pp. 9–10.

could not afford to ignore other men of influence or other types of achievement. While birth remained the key criterion for honors in the late nineteenth century, an increasing number of knighthoods and other awards were being conferred on distinguished administrators in the service of princes and zamindars, on lawyers and judges, and occasionally on businessmen and bankers. Knighthoods went to "responsible" critics as well as men regarded as loyal supporters of British rule. S. Subramania Iyer, High Court judge and former Congressman, was knighted in 1900, three years after M. M. Bhownaggree, the Parsi opponent of the Congress and Conservative Member of Parliament. The award of a knighthood to the dominant personality in both the Congress and the Bombay Municipal Corporation (Pherozeshah Mehta) in 1904 was a further indication of the weakening in the division between the landed hierarchy and the more nationalist urban-professional hierarchies. Not only were urban professionals and moderate critics of British rule eligible for knighthoods, as zamindars and chiefs were, but men who had distinguished themselves as administrators and scholars, including Shiva Prasad of Benaras, Ban Bihari Kapur of Burdwan, Rajendralal Mitra of Calcutta, Dinkar Rao of Ratnagiri and Gwalior, and T. Madhava Rao of Madras, were awarded the title of Raja—a title customarily although by no means exclusively associated with landholding and political-military leadership.[34] Some of these men were known supporters of the Congress. Rajendralal Mitra and T. Madhava Rao were chairmen of the Congress Reception Committees in 1886 and 1887, respectively. Sayyid Muhammad of Madras was given the title of Nawab and appointed Sheriff of Madras after he joined the Congress and before he served as chairman of the Reception Committee.

The British were also encouraging the amalgamation of loyal Indian elites by increasing the contact between prominent Indians from different areas and occupations. They invited princes, major landholders, and successful professionals to durbars, audiences, and military displays with heads of administration and

[34] The term "raja" was used in Indian society regardless of government sanction. Many landholders and religious leaders were addressed as raja or maharaja. In one case, a "petty landholder" who led a peasant league against zamindari exactions in Yusafshahi pargana, Pabna district, in 1872 was known locally as the Bidrohir Raja or the raja of the rebels. L.S.S. O'Malley, *Bengal District Gazetteers, Pabna* (Calcutta, 1923), p. 26.

members of the English royal family. The Delhi durbars of 1877, 1901, and 1911, and the London coronations of Edward VII in 1901 and George V in 1910 attracted not only the invited guests, but also nationalist editors and observers. On each of these occasions, officials emphasized that chiefs and titled landholders were partners, although subordinate ones, with the British in a single political system. In the process, official guests and observers were brought closer together in a manner which had not been possible before the construction of railways and the increase of pan-Indian consciousness. Few people in the late nineteenth century thought it worthy of special comment that a Madras landowner, the Maharaja of Vizianagram, would donate a city hall to Benaras or money to Allahabad and Calcutta political and educational organizations. People were already accustomed to the lowering of the regional and social barriers that separated the Indian elites from each other.

None of this discussion is meant to suggest a total absence of conflict between the Indian aristocracy and the urban professionals who supported the Congress. In giving awards and bringing the aristocracy together, the British rulers were rewarding the most loyal rajas and emphasizing their interest in supporting the existing undemocratic, imperial system. They were also demonstrating to aristocrats and nonaristocrats alike the power of the British military and the majesty of the British Crown. These purposes worked against certain Congress interests. For example, Congress resolutions protested the expenditure of Indian revenues on wars beyond the frontiers of India, while the British rewarded princely and zamindari contributions to those wars. Maharaja Sir Madho Rao Scindhia of Gwalior was given the Knight Grand Cross of the Royal Victorian Order (previously an all-British order) and promoted to the rank of honorary major-general in the army after he supplied a hospital ship to accompany the British expedition to China during the Boxer Rebellion of 1900.[35] Also implicit in British relations with the Indian aristocracy was the preservation of inherited privilege and autocratic government which the Congress was trying to reduce. At durbars presided over by the Viceroy, a governor, or a political agent, continuity with Mughal ceremonial forms was main-

[35] Scindhia participated in the expedition as an orderly to General Sir A. Gaselle. *Who's Who in India*, Part I, p. 29, and Buckland, *Dictionary of Indian Biography*, p. 184.

tained through the presentation of *nazar* (gold bars or coins which the British immediately remitted) and the distribution of *itr* (scent) and *pan* (betel leaves wrapped in gold leaf). The preservation of these forms, together with the rich pageantry that accompanied durbars and investitures, was designed to reassure the aristocracy that the British respected their traditions and intended to maintain autocracy and the old-status hierarchy. However, in other ways the durbars and award system were operating in directions favored by the Congress. When they were used to recognize good government and constructive expenditure of state revenues and private fortunes, they probably pleased Congressmen. By rewarding the construction of hospitals, schools, roads, and waterworks, by praising the remission of revenue and distribution of relief during famines, the British were emphasizing a principle implicit in much of the Congress platform: namely, that political power should be exercised not as a private possession but rather as a public trust.[36]

It is unclear how conscious early Congress leaders and the rulers of Indian states were of the likelihood that eventually the Congress's goal of a self-ruling India with representative institutions might clash with interests of the princely states. Achievement of the goal was so remote that few people were inclined to speculate on whether the states would one day be integrated with the rest of India. In the meantime, British and princely India were administered under different laws, different forms of government, and, to a large extent, different personnel. The ideological and economic interests of Congress supporters differed from the chiefs' indirectly and by implication. When the rulers of Mysore, Travancore, and Cochin gave token contributions to the 1887 Congress session at Madras, before the Government of India forbade chiefly donation to political organizations within British India, they may have done so less because they agreed with Congress principles than to win popularity with educated Indians. Rarely did the occasion arise in which a chief or Congressman felt impelled to discuss in public the future of Congress-state relations. A number of English-speaking chiefs, including the

---

[36] The British also encouraged chiefs to give to imperial causes outside of India. Maharaja Sir Sawai Madho Singh of Jaipur, who contributed £550,000 to causes outside his own state, gave to the Transvaal War Fund and the Imperial Institute in London. *Who's Who in India*, Part 1, p. 65, and Lawrence, *The India We Served*, p. 210.

Maharaja of Mysore and the Gaikwar of Baroda, gave substantial help to the Congress's industrial exhibitions after the turn of the century. But probably the majority of the chiefs looked upon the Congress with distrust, if not hostility, despite Congress willingness to defend them from British interference with their privileges. The term *vakil raj* implied not only rule by lawyers but also government by men who had once been vakils (in the word's original sense of "agents"). "Vakil raj" suggested that men who were formerly subordinate were replacing traditional rulers in British India.

The Interdependence of Landlords and Urban Professionals in British India

Unlike the chiefs of the Indian states, the landed aristocracy of British India was not geographically and politically separate from the educated groups which supported the Indian National Congress. Unlike the chiefs, they could not defer defining their attitude toward the Congress and the political system of British India. Generally, when titled landlords and landholders' associations expressed opinions about the future shape of India's decision-making institutions, they revealed antipathy toward the politically egalitarian and democratic principles of the Congress. Yet these pronouncements suggest a much starker opposition of landlord interests and the interests of nationalist, urban professionals than actually existed. Analysis of the private economic and cultural relations between landlords and Congress supporters indicates significant areas of interdependence. This analysis is vital to understanding Congress treatment of landed and peasant interests which will be discussed in the next two chapters.

Analysis of the occupations recorded in the annual delegate lists does not reveal the extent or complexity of landlord influence within the Congress. Between 1892 and 1909, 2,629 delegates or 18 per cent returned landholding as an occupation.[37] However, a single delegate often listed more than one occupation. Moreover, not all Congressmen who owned rent-collecting rights listed themselves as zamindars, taluqdars, or landholders, while those urban Congress professionals who entered "zamindar" as one of their occupations often shared little with rural

[37] Ghosh, *The Indian National Congress*, p. 24.

zamindars in terms of life style, class attitudes, or ideology. Furthermore, some landless Congress lawyers represented zamindars in legal disputes involving land and were inclined to vote and argue on the side of the landed interests. Still other landless Congress delegates had received zamindari patronage for their education or for public and cultural activities and as a result had incurred a moral debt to a landlord benefactor. No doubt others hoped to be similarly indebted.

Publicists

The flow of favors and aid ran in two directions, of course. The Congress was dominated by vakils. Traditionally a vakil acted as an agent or representative of a man or men with a particular economic or political interest. Landlords often employed vakils (vakils in the original sense of "agents") to argue their interests and run their organizations and newspapers. Kristodas Pal is an example of a zamindar's political vakil. Born into a family of meager means and not himself an owner of land (at least not of any substantial amount), he became the premier defender of landlord interests as editor of the *Hindoo Patriot* and as representative of the Bengali zamindars' organization, the British Indian Association, in the Bengal Legislative Council.[38] Dakhinaranjan Mukherji performed a similar function for the Oudh taluqdars and Nihalchand of Muzaffarnagar, a wealthy moneylender who shifted a part of his fortune into land, was the leading spirit in the taluqdars' organization in the North-Western Provinces.[39]

Landlords also valued the literary skills of Western-educated publicists. Writers were engaged or patronized to write family histories, many of which read like *prasastis* or inscriptions detailing the good works of a raja in conventionalized form. These accounts of Indian notables amplified the information available in government publications such as the gazetteers and the Queen's Honors Lists. They paid particular attention to charitable activities, although usually without quantifying them, and

[38] Sambhuchandra Mukherji was another editor of the *Hindoo Patriot* who spent most of his life representing or working for zamindars, including the Nawabs of Rampur and Murshidabad, the Maharaja of Tippera, and the Oudh Taluqdars Association. Buckland, *Dictionary of Indian Biography*, p. 305.

[39] Minute by A. P. MacDonell, 22 Oct. 1901, MSS. Eur. F. 111/241.

Integration of Indian Elites

to the titles awarded by British and pre-British governments. The works published by the influential and wealthy Lucknow publisher, entrepreneur, and zamindar, Munshi Newal Kishore, and his son, Prag Narain Bhargava, were prime examples of this genre. They published an Urdu biographical dictionary of Indian notables (*Sahifa-i-Zarrin*) for the Coronation Durbar of 1903[40] and an English *Who's Who in India* in 1911, with supplements in 1912 and 1914. The 1911 *Who's Who* gives information (province by province) about more than 2,500 Indians, from the chiefs of the largest states to petty government officials and landholders who had received the title of Khan or Rai Bahadur. The one thousand pages of biographical data give the impression of a vast number of persons who, although physically scattered, linguistically and religiously disparate, and economically and occupationally varied, were linked together through a single, mutually recognizable system of British awards and titles.

Despite his expressed intention of kindling "loyalty and gratitude" to "our King-Emperor,"[41] Bhargava included biographies of prominent nationalists and urban professionals, such as Tilak, Gandhi, Madan Mohan Malaviya, and Surendranath Banerjea, in brief sections covering "Eminent Men" without titles. The inclusion of these urban professionals represented more than recognition of some of the best known figures in Indian public life. It signified both that urban professionals had achieved places in the upper strata of the all-Indian social hierarchy and that frequently they had overlapping interests with the titled landholders on whom Bhargava lavished the most praise and attention.

Estate Managers

Landlords also looked to the professional classes to provide estate management skills. Rarely did major landlords understand the accounts of their estates. Therefore, they were forced to rely upon professional managers whose behavior often determined whether an estate made large profits or fell into debt. Estate managers

---

[40] *Who's Who in India*, preface, p. 2. Munshi Prag Narain owned land in six districts in the U. P., including the family zamindari in Aligarh district obtained in 1792. He employed over a thousand people in his ironworks, ice factory, banks, and publishing enterprises in the U. P. and the Punjab. Ibid., Part IV, pp. 169–170.

[41] Ibid., preface, p. 1.

usually learned the preliminaries of arithmetic and accounting in village schools, and then they picked up a more detailed knowledge of zamindari accounts, ledgering, and rent law in either government or landlord *cutcheries* (land record and collection offices). Because estates were often geographically dispersed, it was also important to have a loyal and efficient subordinate staff of tehsildars (subordinate rent or revenue collectors) who would prevent the creation of rent-free tenures and who would collect full rents from all cultivated land. But the court of wards demonstrated often that a well trained manager or *diwan* could usually reassert effective control over an insubordinate rent-collecting staff to the economic benefit of the estate-holder. Strong management at the apex of an estate rental establishment was indispensable to the owner's continued prosperity.

There was considerable circulation of personnel between landlord and government service.[42] The pool of government servants experienced in rental matters was probably always large in temporarily settled areas, but as survey and settlement operations were expanded in permanently settled areas in the late nineteenth century, and as the courts of wards expanded everywhere, the pool of men knowledgeable about estate management grew also. The government hired men out of private estates; landlords employed ex-officials and men on loan from government service. Estate management was becoming less a matter of personal influence and control and more a professional, technical enterprise. The new tenancy laws of the second half of the nineteenth century were ostensibly for the protection of tenants while in fact the provisions requiring issuance of receipts and court procedures for nonpayment of rents armed the rent-collecting staffs of many large estates with new power. The managers of the Burdwan, Darbhanga, and Uttarpara estates, among many others, were able to raise their rents through careful accounting, the use of courts, and centralized estate management.

[42] In one year (1876) in which the background of all estate managers under the Bengal court of wards was surveyed, 41 of the 57 managers were Indian. Because some of the 41 Indians had more than one prior career, they were reported to have had 46 professions. Eighteen had been in government service, 14 had been landowners, 9 in zamindari service, and 5 in law. A. Mackenzie, Offg. Sec., Bd. of Rev., L. P., to Sec., Govt. of Bengal, 17 Feb. 1876. March 1876 Prog. No. 11–12, Bengal Rev. Prog.: Wards', Attached, and Govt. Estates, Vol. 902.

Lawyers

Legal expertise was a third need for which the major landlords looked to the urban professional classes. Large landlords maintained a legal staff for the day-to-day operation of estates. One or more *mukhtears* was stationed in each tehsil or administrative unit of the taluqdari or zamindari. Each was equipped with papers recognizing his authority to act for the estate in the local court. Most of his work was of a routine sort, such as filing certificates for nonpayment of rents, a preliminary step which could lead to ejectment of a tenant. The salaries of the zamindari mukhtears were small, and the total cost of the ordinary estate establishment was a fraction of what an estate paid barristers in major cases affecting inheritance or possession of large lots. For example, the budget of the Bettia raj estate, most of which was in the Champaran district of Bihar, contained Rs. 9,114 in 1897–1898 for its regular legal establishment which included 21 mukhtears and 6 pleaders stationed in Calcutta and 8 other towns. But its other legal expenses were expected to reach Rs. 1,67,406, largely to fight suits by some cousins who were claiming possession in an inheritance dispute.[43] Many barristers and High Court pleaders, on whom landowners depended in crucial legal disputes, were active in the Congress.

Estates were particularly vulnerable to law suits when an estate-holder died at a time his heir was a child, especially if the heir was adopted as often was the case. Not only were many successions disputed, but creditors with or without valid claims presented themselves for a share of the estate with the help of enterprising lawyers, as the Darbhanga Raj family discovered in the 1860s. Three separate suits were pressed by bankers and merchants against the Raj for alleged debts of Rs. 6.7 lakhs which were claimed to have been incurred by the deceased raja. Lawyers for the Darbhanga Raj, acting under the court of wards, eventually obtained settlements of the claims for a total of Rs. .5 lakhs as a result of court decisions in two cases and an amicable adjustment in the third.[44] The example is an extreme one, but a

[43] J. R. Lowis, Manager of Bettiah Raj Estates, to Col., Champaran, 28 Sept. 1897. Sept. 1898 Rev. Prog. No. 8–9, Bengal Rev. Prog., Vol. 5,404.

[44] Report on the administration of the Durbhunga Raj by the court of wards from Nov. 1860 to 30 Sept. 1879, pp. 29–30. Aug. 1880 Rev. Prog. No. 49–52, Bengal Rev. Prog.: Wards', Attached, and Govt. Estates, Vol. 1,488.

review of the history of almost any major estate will reveal serious legal challenges which required the services of highly paid legal experts. It was said in 1876 that it was not uncommon to pay prominent barristers Rs. 1,500 per day to conduct a case in a mofussil court.[45] With high stakes involved, the best legal counsel was worth the fees.

CONGRESS SUPPORTERS AND LANDLORD CONTACTS

There was no province in which urban professionals, including nationalists, did not have significant economic connections with titled landholders.[46] The connections were especially common in Bihar and Bengal where professional relationships, caste membership, attitudes toward social reform, and the purchase of rent-collecting rights linked urban lawyers and editors with titled zamindars. The list of prominent Bihari and Bengali politicians with zamindari connections was a long one. It included Guruprasad Sen, lawyer, zamindar, and editor of the *Behar Herald*, the mouthpiece of the Behar Landholders' Association;[47] Saligram Singh, lawyer, zamindar, and secretary of the Behar Landholders' Association;[48] Baikuntanath Sen, a lawyer who owned extensive properties, managed the Kasimbazar Raj estate, and held legal briefs for most of the important zamindars of Murshidabad district;[49] Janakinath Ghosal, a zamindar and merchant who was connected through marriage to the Maharaja of Cooch Behar and the Debendranath Tagore family;[50] and Asutosh Chaudhuri, secretary of the Bengal Landholders' Association and related by marriage to the Tagores. In addition, although not a zamin-

[45] H. A. Cockerell, Com. of Burdwan Div., to Sec., Bd. of Rev., L. P., 17 Nov. 1876. May 1877 Rev. Prog. No. 17–22, Bengal Rev. Prog.: Wards', Attached, and Govt. Estates, Vol. 902.

[46] Occasionally families divested themselves of most of their land and moved into urban professions. The Sinhas of Raipur are an example of this. Nirmal Kumar Bose, *Modern Bengal* (Calcutta, 1959), pp. 20ff.

[47] *Bengalee*, 21 Oct. 1900.

[48] See obituary in *Hindustan Review*, Vol. XII, No. 71 (July 1905), 93.

[49] *Bengalee*, 10 March 1903. Baikuntanath complained at the 1893 Congress that the Bengal zamindars had not been given a seat on the reformed legislative council. *Report of the 9th INC*, p. 51.

[50] Janakinath married Svarnakumari Debi, daughter of Debendranath Tagore, and their son, J. Ghosal of the Bombay Civil Service, married the eldest daughter of the Maharaja of Cooch Behar.

dar, Surendranath Banerjea had a "great friend" in Raja Benoyakrishna Deb,[51] and he received money on various occasions from the Maharaja of Vizianagram and Maharani Svarnamayi of Kasimbazar.[52] There were also a number of other Congress leaders from Bengal who called themselves zamindars: Anandamohan Bose, Romeshchandra Dutt, Bhupendranath Basu, Aswinikumar Dutt, Abdul Kasim, Ambicacharan Mazumdar, Jogendranath Mukherji, and Prithwischandra Roy. In other words, it was in the ordinary course of things for a Bengali politician to own land or receive rent.

Outside of Bengal and Bihar, it may have been less common for nationalist politicians to own rent-collecting rights, but it was by no means rare. B. G. Tilak, C. Sankara Nair, S. Subramania Iyer, and G. M. Chitnavis were among those who did. And among Congress leaders who were lawyers, probably few did not accept briefs at some time from zamindars and taluqdars. Pherozeshah Mehta, Tej Bahadur Sapru,[53] and Motilal Nehru,[54] for example, were said to have done so often.

Landlords in the Cities

Another factor which tempered the political rivalry between titled zamindars and urban professionals was landlord participation in city cultural and political life. Titled landholders had been coming to cities for urban pleasures, educated companionship, and access to high administrative officers long before British rule began. The jealousy over relative status and the physical separation which prevented landholders from joining together in rural areas for convivial and other collective purposes were less important in the cities. Many titled landholders maintained houses in the cities and inevitably they entered some associations to which urban professionals belonged. They were welcomed in urban organizations and were particularly active as patrons and officers in religious, educational, literary, and philanthropic societies.

Landlord participation in urban cultural and political life was prolonging the fabled zamindari role of philanthropist. In

---

[51] Banerjea, *A Nation*, pp. 144–145.   [52] Ibid., pp. 104–105.
[53] Sapru, who owned zamindari rights himself, worked in suits involving the Darbhanga estate. Aiyar, *Biographical Vistas*, p. 206.
[54] Nanda, *The Nehrus*, p. 28.

Integration of Indian Elites

continuing their customary patronage of cultural activities, landlords had contributed to colleges and other enterprises whose effect was the gradual substitution of achievement for ascription as the major criterion for gainful employment and political influence. This is not surprising in that many landlords were dependent upon professional expertise and in that many estates had been formed since the mid-eighteenth century by men employed by the East India Company—men who owed their landed fortunes to "professional" talents.[55] At the end of the nineteenth century, urban professionals still looked as a matter of course to big landholders and chiefs of Indian states for support of their political as well as their cultural activities.

Individual landlords subsidized newspapers which advocated the causes they believed in. Numerous nationalist newspapers which supported social reform and Congress efforts to obtain a more open society received money from educated landholders. Rai Jaiprakash Lal, Diwan of the Dumraon Raj, gave funds for the maintenance of the *Behar Herald* which was edited by Guruprasad Sen, for years the most active Congress worker in Bihar.[56] Dyal Singh Majithia, the wealthy Sirdar who was known to finance nationalist causes in the Punjab,[57] set up the *Tribune* Press and continued to pay for its operation for many years.[58] Raja Benoyakrishna Deb helped Surendranath Banerjea convert the *Bengalee* from a weekly into a daily in 1899.[59] Raja Rampal Singh of Kalakankar supported the *Hindustani* of Lucknow.[60] And C. Y. Chintamani, who edited newspapers in Madras Province before moving to Allahabad in 1902 where he edited the *Indian People* and the *Leader*, apparently obtained financial help from the Maharaja of Vizianagram.[61] The examples could be continued.

---

[55] Bernard S. Cohn, "Recruitment of Elites in India Under British Rule" in *Essays in Comparative Social Stratification*, ed. by Leonard Plotnicov and Arthur Tuden (Pittsburgh, 1970), pp. 136–140.

[56] *Bengalee*, 21 Oct. and 25 Dec. 1900. [57] *Statesman*, 29 Sept. 1898.

[58] Nair and Kirpal, *Dyal Singh Majithia (A Short Biographical Sketch)* (Lahore, 1935), pp. 46, 90–91.

[59] Banerjea, *A Nation*, pp. 144–145. [60] *Bengalee*, 25 Dec. 1900.

[61] A Telegu Brahman, Chintamani's father was the guru of the Maharaja of Vizianagram, who contributed to many nationalist enterprises in the U. P., Bengal, and Madras. Banerjea, *A Nation*, pp. 97–98, and *Second Supplement to Who's Who in India* (Lucknow, 1914), p. 61.

SUBSIDIES FOR FOREIGN TRAVEL

Another common form of assistance given to educated Indians by zamindars and chiefs was money for travel, study, political work, and maintenance outside India. Dadabhai Naoroji started the East India Association in London in 1866 with donations from the Gaekwar of Baroda, Holkar of Indore, Scindhia of Gwalior, and the Rao of Kutch.[62] In 1873 the Gaekwar of Baroda gave Naoroji Rs. 50,000 for various services he had performed in London.[63] The Raja of Bhinga established a scholarship for Kshatriyas to study at Oxford or Cambridge;[64] the Raja of Vizianagram was believed to have given Rs. 5,000 toward Surendranath Banerjea's expenses as a member of the Congress delegation to England in 1890;[65] the Raja of Ramnad sent Vivekananda to the Parliament of Religions in Chicago in 1893;[66] and Sir Muncherji Bhownaggree drew an annual pension from Bhownagar state while he was in the House of Commons.[67] In most of these and in many other acts of philanthropy, zamindars and chiefs gave to persons outside their own caste, religion, and region. They were contributing to all-India communication while cultivating links with men who could help mediate with the highest political authorities.

What anxieties existed about the relative positions of landholders and urban professionals were largely the landholders'. When a literary or political society was started, a landholder was often asked to be president, as well as to donate funds. At public functions, major zamindars were given the most visible seats on the speaker's platform. Newspaper accounts of public gatherings listed titled landholders ahead of prominent nation-

[62] *Famous Parsis: Biographical and Critical Sketches*, pub. by G. A. Natesan (Madras, 1930), p. 110.
[63] Masani, *Naoroji*, p. 137.
[64] Rao, *Indian Biographical Dictionary, 1915*, p. 45.
[65] Note by C. S. Bayley, 18 June 1899, enclosure to Curzon to Hamilton, 28 June 1899, MSS. Eur. D. 570/2. However, Banerjea says in a passage of his autobiography, which is seemingly intended to show his self-sacrifice, that he cashed Rs. 4,000 worth of government securities to finance his trip. This was, according to Banerjea, the larger part of his and his wife's only savings. Banerjea, *A Nation*, p. 111.
[66] L.S.S. O'Malley and Monmohan Chakravarti, *Bengal District Gazetteers, Howrah* (Calcutta, 1909), p. 48.
[67] *Bengalee*, 25 Aug. 1900.

alist politicians: Maharaja-dhirajas preceded Maharajas, Maharajas preceded Rajas, Rajas preceded Rai Bahadurs and Babus. Even in the advertisements for hair oils which appeared in nationalist newspapers such as the *Bengalee,* the testimonials of titled men were placed before those of untitled politicians. There seems to have been little hesitation in according honored treatment to major landholders. Both landholders and urban politicians appeared to recognize that in balance the forces at work in Indian society favored the latter. While the size, combined income, and education of urban professional groups were rising steeply, zamindari incomes were endangered by occasional peasant combinations such as those which resulted in the Pabna riots of 1873, new tenancy laws and jotdar ability to use the courts effectively, poor estate management, partition of inherited holdings, and inelastic rents from *patnidars* (leaseholders whose rents were permanently fixed). With important exceptions, especially among government wards, major zamindars were failing to provide their children with education sufficient for either better estate management or successful alternative careers.[68] Few zamindars' children who attended the university were returning to the land. Of the 1,701 graduates of Calcutta University from 1858 to 1881, perhaps as few as several dozen chose careers in managing land or collecting agricultural rent.[69] The major zamindars such as Jaikrishna Mukherji of Uttarpara, Maharaja Durgacharan Laha [Law], and Maharaja Lachmeshwar Singh of Darbhanga belonged to an apparently small minority who were able to expand their land holdings. The general pattern was one of fission. Accordingly, defense of landlord interests against legislative attacks was a matter of vital concern to major landholders.

Several conclusions have emerged from this discussion. The

[68] Pradip Sinha suggests that possession of large estates may have "tended to dampen the desire" for English education, although possession of small holdings helped many families finance their children's education. *Nineteenth Century Bengal,* pp. 41–42.

[69] Pradip Sinha (ibid., Appendix D) provides an alphabetical list of the 1,701 graduates with the occupations of 1,326. Six graduates are listed as zamindars, one as a tea planter, and about a dozen as diwans, managers, tutors, secretaries, or legal representatives of rajas or zamindars. These figures are somewhat misleading inasmuch as some major zamindars provided tutors for their children or sent their children abroad instead of enrolling them in Calcutta University. That there is not a single Tagore on the list warns against using the list as more than a very general index of zamindari education.

cultivating classes were not pressing their claims upon the educated groups which controlled the skills and media of public advocacy. The major landholders, by contrast, had easy access to urban publicists from whom they enjoyed deference. Second, British educational and legal efforts to arrest the decline in the influence of titled landholders met with mixed results at best. Indians tended to look upon English education as a means to employment and not as a source of the culture they most valued. Without a strong cultural motivation, and with little economic need of finding employment, the children of major landholders rarely sought formal education with the singlemindedness of high-caste, nonlanded families. Third, insofar as titled landholders received modern education, they tended to share a general intellectual orientation with urban professionals. Fourth, insofar as titled landholders lacked the professional and publicist skills of the educated classes that joined the Congress, they depended upon their talents as lawyers, educators, and political intermediaries. And consequently, urban-educated families often did not regard the landed aristocracy as an obstacle to their advancement; rather, they looked to them as potential employers, as patrons of their cultural and political activities, and as honored if sometimes effete members of their evolving traditional society. Finally, the integration of titled landholders and the more successful professionals was but a partial one. Few titled landholders joined the Congress, few viewed the Congress as committed to the protection of landed interests from legislative attack. In Bengal, titled landholders faced the prospect of losing their privileged position in consultive institutions to the professional classes. And what happened in Bengal often foreshadowed developments in other parts of India.

Chapter Seven

CONGRESS AND THE LANDLORD INTEREST

The limited integration of educated elites was tending to provide an all-Indian political consciousness, a common political idiom, and a greater awareness of the benefits of organization for the promotion of specific interests. On the other hand, the deeper men were drawn into the modern organizational life of British India, with its common forms and language, the more likely they were to differentiate between their specific interests. Educated men were gaining a sharper appreciation of the multiple or plural character of their interests. Here lies a seeming paradox in modern political development. With greater integration of economic and political systems, the more differentiation occurred within those systems. It was becoming common for educated men to belong simultaneously to several organizations, each representing a different sphere of activity, each directing appeals to the government which all Indians shared. A man, for example, might at the same time belong to an economic interest group, such as a bar or landholders' association, a religious organization such as a Muslim anjuman or Hindu sabha, and a local political society such as the Poona Sarvajanik Sabha, the Madras Mahajan Sabha, or the Lahore Indian Association. The complexity of modern life guaranteed the proliferation of limited-interest organizations and increased competition for the attention of the government and for the support of the public. And with more competition, there was more controversy and conflict. The very nature of a nationalist body such as the Indian National Congress required that it attempt to contain and moderate the conflicts between competing interest groups.

In the years immediately preceding the founding of the Congress, a serious conflict was raging in Bengal over government efforts to afford tenants greater protection from their landlords. This conflict made the leaders of Bengali and north Indian landlords particularly anxious about their position in the legislative councils which were due to be reformed. The demands by the early Congress for expanded and elective representation threatened their ability to influence the course of agrarian legislation, an ability they demonstrated effectively prior to the passage of the Bengal Tenancy Act of 1885. The leaders of the Congress wanted to achieve reform of the legislative councils without alienating major landholders. The economic ideas subscribed to by Congress leaders kept alive this possibility.

Congress Economic Ideology

As nation-builders, Congressmen needed a critique of British colonialism which would give all Indians a common interest in joining together to diminish British control over Indian affairs and a shared vision of a better society, achievable once foreign rule was terminated. As achievement-oriented individuals, though, Congressmen sought to expand their personal incomes by bringing about favorable changes in the occupational structure and in investment opportunities. In the process of increasing their earning capacity, it was important to many nationalists not to appear either to others or themselves to be trampling the economic opportunities of the poorer sections of the population. Prevention of open conflict between economic interests was an integral part of nation-building. Therefore, Indian nationalists looked for a rationale or ideology for their economic activities which would justify their high economic status on grounds of general economic progress for the country as a whole. This search was complicated by the small but growing minority of men within the Congress who recognized and deplored the gigantic gaps between the incomes of the wealthy and the poor majority. Their dilemma was to find a means of addressing the problem of inequality without jeopardizing the fragile unity among the propertied groups which supported the Congress.

After World War I, Gandhi developed a formula for bridging these two concerns, based upon his idealized view of a noncompetitive, harmonious ancient Indian model. He attacked the present gross inequalities of wealth as an unjust and regrettable departure from former conditions. In ancient India, he said, servants

> were regarded and treated as members of the family. They suffered with the employers in their misfortunes and the latter shared the servants' joys and sorrows. In those days India was

The Landlord Interest

reputed for a social order free from friction, and this order endured for thousands of years on that basis.

Gandhi hoped to restore that order through what he called "trusteeship" or a revival of the spirit of the ideal jajmani system. He imagined that propertyholders could be reeducated to believe that every form of labor was of equal value and deserving of respect. He also thought that propertyholders should be persuaded, if necessary by their employees' and tenants' "nonviolent non-cooperation," to hold their property in trust for the poor and to turn over their surplus wealth to society.[1]

Although Gandhi's trusteeship theory was not particularly threatening to the well-to-do, because it would have left them in possession of their property, it was nevertheless an advance over earlier Congress economic positions inasmuch as it attacked the existing inequalities of income distribution. Pre-Gandhian Congress leaders, by contrast, tended either to ignore or defend contemporary trends in income distribution. Despite some ambivalence about their new wealth, the successful professionals had not voluntarily denied themselves, with a few significant exceptions,[2] the high standard of living made possible by their rising incomes. Their economic ideas tended to justify their position and inequalities of wealth. When they spoke about ideology, most relied on classical English economic theory, modified by both their knowledge of recent developments in other societies and their perception of India's special characteristics. Thus, nationalists supported state aid to and protection of Indian industry. However, in general they were economic liberals. They believed in "the magic of property," as Ranade called it, or the tendency of property ownership to produce the economic man. Many men with savings invested them in land, an act which made economic sense in the absence of safer and more profitable alternatives but which few seemed to regard as patriotic. Many, though, invested in industries as part of their effort to develop and modernize the Indian economy. Among the prominent Congress leaders who invested in swadeshi manufacturing concerns in the late nineteenth century were K. T. Telang, Pherozeshah Mehta, D. E. Wacha,

[1] Nirmal Kumar Bose, *Studies in Gandhism*, 3rd ed. (Calcutta, 1962), pp. 46–50.

[2] Tilak, Gokhale, and the other members of the Deccan Education Society restricted their salaries voluntarily.

B. G. Tilak, R. N. Mudholkar, Madan Mohan Malaviya, Lajpat Rai, and J. Chaudhuri. Perhaps none was more active in the early swadeshi movement than M. G. Ranade, who was involved in a cotton and silk factory, a metal factory, a dyeing company, and a paper mill.[3]

Ranade's thoughtful writing on economic theory and policy influenced the thinking of pre-Gandhian Congressmen on both agrarian and industrial issues. Because his influence was substantial and because his ideas were reflected in nationalist arguments regarding land policy, they will be summarized.

Ranade approached agrarian issues with several assumptions about Indian society and its class structure. He believed that the number of Indians with education and capital was so small that for all practical purposes India had no middle class.[4] He thought a wise public policy should promote the growth of a middle class which would apply its savings and education to the development of agriculture and industry, as the middle class in England had. He specifically identified "the Bania and Brahmin classes" with "the saving classes."[5] In Ranade's case this identification does not reflect animus toward other castes but rather his observation of which castes in late nineteenth-century Bombay were investing and attending college. Conversely, Ranade opposed policies such as periodic revisions of land revenue settlements and prohibitions on the transfer of land to nonagriculturalists which he felt tended to "undo the legitimate influence of the saving classes." Such policies he feared "can only end in a great disaster."[6]

He was not doctrinairely opposed to all government interference. He was willing for the state to regulate the transfer of property in order to reduce hardship.[7] He also proposed that the Government of India follow the Prussian example and encourage tenants to buy land from their landlords so that they would become independent proprietors. To preserve the existing tangle of conflicting and overlapping interest would guarantee endless litigation and class conflict. However, Ranade's scheme would have left a major share of the land in the hands of landlords and it

[3] Chandra, *Economic Nationalism*, pp. 85–86.
[4] M. G. Ranade, *Essays on Indian Economics: A Collection of Essays and Speeches* (Bombay, 1898), pp. 4 and 22.
[5] Ibid., p. 326. [6] Ibid., p. 327.
[7] For example, he supported the Deccan Agriculturalist Relief Act of 1879.

would have required tenants to pay generous compensation to landlords for the land they purchased.⁸ As a result, his proposal for land redistribution neither threatened landlords nor attracted much attention or support from advocates of peasant ownership. Except for this redistribution, Ranade wanted the state to avoid major interference in conflicts and competition between classes because official paternalism could only succeed in "paralyzing private efforts," "increasing the sense of dependence on the State," and aggravating "existing helplessness."⁹ To interfere in the overall historical process would perpetuate passivity and poverty, and would even run against natural law:

> The Country is in a transition stage, passing from semi-Feudal and Patriarchal conditions of existence into a more settled and commercial order of things, from a period of disturbance and wars into one of peace and tranquility, from payments in kind to cash payments, from the laws of custom to the rule of competition, from a simple to a more complicated Social Organization. No Economical Legislation can succeed under such circumstances, which seeks to run against the current, or stem the torrent. In all countries property, whether in land or other goods, must gravitate towards that class which has more intelligence, and greater foresight, and practises abstinence, and must slip from the hands of those who are ignorant, improvident, and hopeless to stand on their own resources. This is a law of Providence, and can never be wisely or safely ignored by practical Statesmen for any fancied political or sentimental considerations. As long as the difference in the habits and education of the saving few represented by the Bania and Brahmin classes, and the spending many who count by millions among the Military and the Cultivating classes remains good, property will gravitate from the one class to the other, notwithstanding all prohibitory Legislation. The utmost that Government can safely venture to do is to regulate this inevitable transfer, to temper the change so as to avoid all immediate hardships.¹⁰

When the state went beyond this and took away vested interests without providing full compensation, as in the case of the Bengal

---

⁸ "Prussian Land Legislation and the Bengal Tenancy Bill," ibid., pp. 258ff.
⁹ Ibid., pp. 281 and 326.   ¹⁰ Ibid., pp. 325–326.

Tenancy Act of 1885, it "savours very much of a Communistic and Latter-day Saints Revolution."[11] Thus Ranade's belief in the desirability of capital accumulation and the economic differentiation this implied led him to argue against strong land alienation and tenancy legislation. Most nationalists appeared to agree with him that society was becoming more open and competitive and that if this led to a greater concentration of wealth among certain high castes, it was the necessary price of economic progress.

Nationalist acceptance of Ranade's brand of economic liberalism meant that most nationalists reacted to conflicts between capital and labor as the bourgeoisie did in other societies in the late nineteenth century. By later standards, nationalist positions on tenancy legislation, legislation restricting alienation of land to money-lenders, and industrial labor laws seemed harsh and unfeeling. For example, nationalists were almost uniformly opposed to or silent on the Indian Factory Acts of 1881 and 1891 which limited the hours children could work to nine and seven hours, respectively, and which set the minimum working age at seven and nine years of age, respectively. Nationalists were aware that these acts were passed under pressure from Lancashire textile interests which feared competition from the Indian cotton industry. Indian opposition, therefore, was in large measure motivated by the belief that England was using its political domination to choke nascent Indian industrialization.[12]

Nevertheless, some nationalists were uncomfortable in siding with Indian capital against Indian labor. Nationalists were vying rhethorically with British officials in claiming to best represent the interests of workers and peasants. Some Congressmen took special pleasure in catching the government in an act which appeared to damage the interests of the Indian poor. In the 1890 Congress, Pandit Madan Mohan Malaviya twitted the government for reimposing a cess for maintenance of *patwari* records on the ryots of the North-Western Provinces and Oudh. He ridiculed official claims to have obtained the Oudh taluqdars' agreement to the cess. "Fancy, gentlemen, the justice of adding to the burthens of the ryot on the strength of the consent of the Zamindar!" He went on to point out that "hundreds of thousands of ryots" in the North-Western Provinces and Oudh were forced to cover themselves with grass at night because they could not afford

[11] Ranade made this comment on the Tenancy Bill in 1883, ibid., p. 291.
[12] Chandra, *Economic Nationalism*, pp. 329–346.

enough cloth "to protect themselves and their children from the piercing chill and cold of our northern winter nights."[13]

Similarly, when the government compromised with the European tea planters during the passage of the Assam Labour and Emigration Act of 1901, which regulated the recruitment and employment of coolie labor, nationalists were indignant. In this case, the employers and capital were European and the nationalist position was easily reached, although it was inconsistent with positions taken when Indian factory and mine owners were involved.[14]

THE BRITISH INDIAN ASSOCIATION AND URBAN NATIONALISTS

Bengal was the province in which the largest number of educated Indians were openly critical of landlord behavior. The willingness of certain urban politicians in Bengal to attack landlord use of their wealth was closely related to the desire of urban nationalists to gain a larger share of political power from landlords. In fact, urban attacks on landlord profligacy often seemed secondary to the political goal of displacing landlords from their dominance in municipal and other representative bodies. From the 1870s onward, urban professionals were gaining at the expense of the landlords. With each expansion of the franchise and elected representation, the role of zamindars in Bengal was correspondingly weakened. In the 1870s, for example, Kristodas Pal, Rajendralal Mitra, and other associates of the zamindars of the British Indian Association were the dominant Indians in the municipal government of Calcutta. By the end of the century, the Calcutta Corporation had been captured by Surendranath Banerjea and other urban professionals who did not belong to zamindari organizations. The expansion of the legislative councils under the Councils Act of 1892 was an even more serious threat to landlord political influence, not only in Bengal but throughout India.

In the parts of British India where landlord holdings were large, zamindars and taluqdars had formed separate landholders' associations, such as the British Indian Association, in most cases before the Congress was organized. In Madras, the North-

[13] *The Hon. Pandit Madan Mohan Malaviya: His Life and Speeches*, 2nd ed. (Madras, n. d.), pp. 25–28.
[14] Chandra, *Economic Nationalism*, pp. 353 and 372.

The Landlord Interest

Western Provinces, Oudh, and Bihar, these associations functioned sporadically, depending on the presence of an issue, such as tenancy legislation, or of a committed organizer. In Bengal, by contrast, with its relatively large number of educated zamindars and its nearness to the Government of India, the principal zamindars' association operated more continuously. The British Indian Association had been founded in 1851 in circumstances similar to those in 1885 when the Congress was formed. Its start closely followed a successful agitation by the British community against proposals to reduce the racial privileges held by Europeans in the matter of the jurisdiction of law courts over criminal cases.[15] The British Indian Association made what was probably the first attempt to bring political agitation in Bengal, Bombay, and Madras under a common organization,[16] and as the Congress did in later years, it maintained a paid agency in London from 1852 to 1856 for the purpose of influencing Parliament.[17] During the indigo disturbances of the 1850s and early 1860s, the association continued in the role of protector of Indian rights against British violation. It joined nonlanded nationalists in crticizing the oppression of peasants by the European planters. But after the indigo system collapsed and most foreign managers and landholders left the low-lying, Bengali-speaking districts, the British Indian Association's attention shifted to the growing friction between Bengali zamindars and their own tenants and to what was preceived to be a threat to the Permanent Settlement. In the process, the association became identified more exclusively with the class interests of landlords. Faced in the 1870s with the imposition of special road and educational cesses, peasant combinations against rent enhancements and illegal exactions, and the prospect of new tenancy legislation, the association tended to modify its criticism of the government, except when landlord interests were threatened.[18]

[15] Majumdar, *History of Political Thought from Rammohun to Dayananda (1821–1884)*, I, 174–176.

[16] See Sujata Ghosh, "The British Indian Association (1851–1900)," in *Report of the Regional Records Survey Committee for West Bengal (1957–1958)*, p. 40. Also, Iris M. Jones, "The Origins and Development to 1892 of the Indian National Congress" (unpublished M.A. thesis, University of London, 1947), pp. 165–166.

[17] Ibid., p. 168. Also Ghosh, "The British Indian Association (1851–1900)," p. 22.

[18] In its younger days, the British Indian Association took a leading part in

The Landlord Interest

A growing number of university-educated Bengalis in Calcutta, some of whom with the zamindars had idealized the peasantry during the indigo controversy,[19] were eager to find outlets for their own more populist and democratic views. They suggested that the British Indian Association lower its membership fees to accommodate professional people with limited incomes.[20] When the association refused, members of the urban professions founded two political societies in 1876, the Indian Association and the short-lived Indian League. It is clear that even if the British Indian Association had opened its membership, many urban professionals would have felt socially and ideologically out of place with titled landholders. Despite important exceptions, Bengali zamindars had gained a reputation for profligacy and oppressive behavior toward their tenants. In an unusually candid editorial in 1871, the *Amrita Bazar Patrika* expressed the ambivalence felt by some educated Bengalis toward zamindars. It alleged that the majority of zamindars were "unenterprising, idle, weak and ignorant, oppressive and selfish." Yet the *Patrika* said that "we must support them" because in the absence of a significant middle class, only the zamindars had the resources necessary to finance public movements.[21] Newspaper editors, whose papers had circulations of less than three thousand and small advertising revenues, were especially dependent on landlords and other private benefactors.

The British Indian Association welcomed the establishment of the Indian Association in 1876 "in an openly patronising manner."[22] Within a few years, however, the two associations found themselves arguing over the Bengal Tenancy Bill. Members of the Indian Association first supported the principle of tenancy protection, and then they criticized the government for compromising with the zamindars before the bill was enacted.[23] Indian

---

the demand for more favorable working conditions and legal rights for the indigo plantation ryots, after the indigo disturbances of 1859–1860. It also gave financial assistance to Rev. James Long in the *Nil Darpan* case. See Sujata Ghosh "The British Indian Association and the Indigo Disturbances in Bengal," *Indian Historical Records Commission: Proceedings*, Vol. XXXIV, Part II (Dec. 1958), 141–142.

[19] Sinha, *Nineteenth Central Bengal*, p. 21.
[20] Bagal, *History of the Indian Association 1876–1951*, p. 9.
[21] Chandra, *Economic Nationalism*, p. 435.
[22] Ghosh, "The British Indian Association (1851–1900)," p. 41.
[23] Bagal, *History of the Indian Association*, pp. 70–72.

Association organizers went out into the villages to help form peasant unions. Not only members of the Indian Association but "a large majority of the nationalist newspapers of Bengal . . . adopted a pro-tenant attitude."[24] The British Indian Association resented urban nationalists' accusations about zamindari oppression of their tenants, and it withheld its assistance from the national conference, organized by the Indian Association in 1883.[25] Then the passing of the modified Bengal Tenancy Act in 1885 removed this source of friction, clearing the way for limited cooperation between the two associations at the Calcutta Congress in 1886.[26]

Members of the British Indian Association entered the Congress with the understanding that delegates from various local political bodies would meet once a year, formulate a general policy on issues of national importance, and then disband for twelve months, "leaving the execution of that policy" to the individual local organizations. When a constitution was drafted in 1888 which would have converted the Congress into "a separate and permanent organization," the British Indian Association informed the Congress "that while the Association had co-operated with the Congress for the past three years and would do so in the future, it definitely objected to the tentative" constitution. The delegates from the association tried without success to have a resolution adopted by the 1888 Congress embodying their view that the functions of the Congress should be limited, and in the following year the association instructed its delegates to participate only in the discussion of the expansion of the legislative councils and the extension of the Permanent Settlement.[27]

LANDLORDS IN THE CONGRESS

After the late 1880s, participation by major Bengali zamindars diminished. Disagreement over the Congress's functions was only one point of contention: in addition, the Congress campaign to have elective procedures included in the contemplated legislative council reforms and Hume's efforts to persuade peasants they were oppressed were displeasing to zamindars. It is likely that

[24] Chandra, *Economic Nationalism*, pp. 449–451.
[25] Bagal, *History of the Indian Association*, p. 64.
[26] *Report of the 2nd INC*, p. 10.
[27] Ghosh, "The British Indian Association (1851–1900)," pp. 42–43.

The Landlord Interest

zamindars were also influenced by the public attacks on the Congress by officials such as Lord Dufferin and Sir Auckland Colvin. The following respected and wealthy men from Bengal who had joined the Congress were not listed as delegates in the decade beginning in 1892, the year of Hume's controversial warning that peasants might turn on the upper classes: Sir Jatindramohan Tagore; Raja Rajendranarain Deb, president of the Indian Association; Maharaja Kumar Nilkrishna Deb; Nawab Ghulam Rubbani, a member of the Mysore Princes family residing in the 24 Parganas; Raja Rajendralal Mitra, president of the British Indian Association;[28] Raja Pearymohan Mukherji, honorary secretary of the British Indian Association; Syamacharan, Joyobind, and Durgacharan Laha, zamindars and three of Bengal's wealthiest Indian merchants; Sitanath Roy, zamindar, merchant, and secretary of the National Chamber of Commerce; Rajkumar Sarvadhikari, zamindar and editor of the *Hindu Patriot*, and Raja Shashi Sekhareswar Roy of Tahirpur. In the rest of India, where fewer men of great wealth or grand titles had joined the Congress, there were also significant defections.[29]

In addition to major zamindars who had attended early Congresses, there was a group of titled landholders who had made small contributions to the early Congress who rarely if ever gave from 1890 to 1904. They included the Raja of Venkatigiri (president of the Madras Landholders' Association from 1890 to 1916)[30] and the Raja of Bobbili in Madras,[31] the Maharajas

[28] Rajendralal, who was chairman of the Reception Committee in 1886, apparently did not attend again. He died in 1891.

[29] In Madras, they included Sir Savali Ramaswami Mudaliar, vice president of the Mahajan Sabha and sheriff of Madras; Raja Sir T. Madhava Rao who died in 1891; P. Somasundaram Chettiar, a leader of the Madras mercantile community; Hazi Mahomed Abdulla Badshaw, merchant and vice president of the Central Mahomedan Association; Raja T. Rama Rao and P. Chentsal Rao Pantulu, zamindars and members of the Madras Legislative Council. From northern India there was Sirdar Uttam Singh, landowner, banker, and political pensioner (Lahore), Nawab Reza Ali Khan, landowner (Lucknow), and Nawab Shameshad Dowla, landowner (Lucknow).

[30] Venkatigiri gave Rs. 500 to the 1887 Congress and then nothing more, it seems, until 1898 when he donated Rs. 200. (*Bengalee*, 31 Dec. 1898.) In the latter year, several Congress leaders who were members of the Madras Legislative Council sided with the zamindars in their attack on a tenancy bill.

[31] The annual incomes of the largest zamindari estates in 1904 in Madras were as follows:

The Landlord Interest

Hutwa and Dumroan in Bihar, and the Maharaja of Natore in Bengal.[32]

The withdrawal of major zamindari support after the first few years was by no means the end of assistance from this social stratum. In the years between 1890 and 1905, when many major zamindars resumed their aid temporarily, the Congress received support from members of the Debendranath Tagore family[33] and Raja Benoyakrishna Deb (before his resignation from the Congress in 1897) in Bengal proper, from the Maharaja of Darbhanga (until his death in 1898) in Bihar,[34] from Raja

Vizianagram	Rs. 16,00,000
Venkatagiri	12,14,000
Ramnad	9,25,732
Sivaganga	9,28,433
Pittapuram	9,13,919
Nazvid	7,91,354
Karvetnagar	6,26,036
Kalahasti	5,35,159
Nidadarole	5,24,002
Jeypore	4,75,000
Parlakimedi	4,67,433
Bobbili	4,60,000

J. Thompson, Gov. of Madras, to Lord Ampthill, 20 Sept. 1904. No. 370. MSS. Eur. E. 233/34/2.

[32] Zamindari contributions to the Congress in Bengal and Bihar are analyzed in C. W. Bolton's letter to C. S. Bayley, 18 July 1899, enclosure in Curzon to Hamilton, 2 Aug. 1899, MSS, Eur. D. 510/2.

[33] Including Jyotirindranath and his younger brother, Rabindranath, and Janakinath Ghosal and his daughter, Sarala Debi.

[34] The relative value of the largest holdings in Bengal, Bihar, and Orissa may be seen in the following list of "Capitalized Values." The list was quoted from *Capital* (Calcutta) by the *Moslem Chronicle*, 11 Nov. 1899.

Darbhanga Raj	Rs. 2,50,00,000
Cooch Behar Raj	2,50,00,000
Orissa Temple Endowments	1,00,00,000
Burdwan Raj	75,00,000
Nawab Abdul Guni's Estate	50,00,000
Hutwa Raj	30,00,000
Gidhur Raj	30,00,000
Dumroan Raj	25,00,000
Murshidabad Nawab's Estate	25,00,000
Mohsin Endowment	25,00,000
Tagore Family Endowment	15,00,000
Tippera Raj	15,00,000
Natore Raj	15,00,000

Rampal Singh in the North-Western Provinces and Oudh, from Dyal Singh Majithia (until his death in 1898) in the Punjab, and from the Raja of Ramnad (until his death in 1903) and Nawab Sayyid Muhammad in Madras. These were the prominent landholders who gave financial help to the Congress and who permitted themselves to be known publicly as Congressmen. They were exceptions to the general aloofness of the major zamindars. But they also held out the possibility of more widespread zamindari support, a possibility to which Congress leaders were alert. The zamindars included some of the wealthiest men in India; they exercised influence over sections of the population that were still beyond the reach of most urban politicians; and their backing was thought likely to impress English public opinion and officials. For their part, many zamindars appreciated the potential value of Congress efforts to protect zamindari economic interests. Landlord interests had come under attack at the hands of Anthony MacDonnell and other young officials who drafted tenancy legislation in the early 1880s. Therefore, in the early years of the Congress there was a mutual although unequal watchfulness and curiosity between the larger zamindars and the urban professionals who ran the Congress. The mutual interest was weakest in northern India where the new urban professions were small and where many major zamindars were Muslims and Rajputs with an openly hostile attitude toward the Congress. But in Bengal, Bihar, and Madras, it seemed that major zamindars might give at least covert support if the Congress adopted satisfactory positions on the Permanent Settlement and tenancy legislation. Nationalist leaders and English officials were sensitive to zamindari concern for their economic interests and they openly competed for the zamindars' allegiance.

Landlord economic interests presented Congressmen with a dilemma. How was the Congress to reconcile the abstract goal of representing all Indians with the concrete class interests of its supporters? Could the Congress avoid adopting partisan stands on economic issues of consequence to its members and financial backers and still retain their allegiance? Should the Congress place itself in positions in which the government would be able

---

Zamindar Congress supporters are listed in C. W. Bolton's letter to C. S. Bayley, 18 July 1899, enclosure in Curzon to Hamilton, 2 Aug. 1899, MSS. Eur. D. 510/2.

to accuse it of acting on behalf of the rich against the poorer and lower-caste sections of the population? In the case of the Permanent Settlement, the Congress did not give up its advocacy when it was charged with class bias. But under the guidance of Romeshchandra Dutt, its members did stretch the meaning of the term "permanent settlement" in a way that permitted advocates of tenant rights to support it. The treatment of the Permanent Settlement is an excellent example of how Congress leaders accommodated themselves to the movement's pluralism.

THE PERMANENT SETTLEMENT AND THE EARLY CONGRESS

Before the Permanent Settlement was first discussed in the Congress, there was little ambiguity about its meaning. Most advocates meant a permanent agreement *with zamindars* who would collect the land revenue from their cultivator-tenants without major interference from the government. The critics of the Permanent Settlement, on the other hand, generally preferred retaining for the government the right to reassess the land's value and alter the settlements periodically, as well as to legislate protection for tenants against unfair ejection and rental increases. But when the Congress took up the issue in 1886, many nationalists argued that periodic revisions of revenue settlements were impoverishing the peasantry and discouraging agricultural improvements. They wanted fixity of the government's demand to be extended to most settlements in India, whether zamindari, taluqdari, or ryotwari.

It might seem odd that nationalists attached so much weight to the absence of a permanent ceiling on land taxes as an explanation of India's poverty. In retrospect, there was little possibility that the Government of India would again deny itself tax benefits from rising prices or increased productivity. Land revenue remained the largest single source of governmental finance, and alternative revenue sources were seen as inelastic. Yet nationalists did push for an extension of the Permanent Settlement into new areas. The relative freedom of Bengal from the great nineteenth-century famines and some doubtful assumptions about Bengal's prosperity compared to temporarily settled areas made it possible for nationalists to focus on a permanent settlement as a key to rural poverty. Many men who would not personally

The Landlord Interest

gain from such a settlement were convinced that it would be economically beneficial to India as a whole.

Nevertheless, it is evident that the Congress defense of permanent settlements was closely related to zamindari economic interests as well as to the general issue of India's poverty. It seems that the most vocal Congress proponents of permanent settlements were obliquely defending zamindari interests against new tenancy laws or surveys of rights in areas which had already been permanently settled. This is indicated by the fact that those Congressmen who spoke for the extension of the Permanent Settlement were generally spokesmen for zamindars from permanently settled areas in Bengal, Bihar, and the Northern Circars of Madras.

Congressmen who spoke about class interests at the annual sessions were either very guarded in their remarks, or the compilers of the annual *Reports* edited the remarks so as to obscure their meaning. Moreover, the Subjects Committees became increasingly adept at filtering out contentious subjects and placing only consensus speakers on the agenda. The earliest discussions, however, do reveal some of the nuances of the disagreements within the Congress over the Permanent Settlement. The first discussion was at the 1886 session, less than two years after the passage of the Bengal Tenancy Act which zamindars attacked as a violation of the Permanent Settlement. Apparently, someone had suggested outside the open session that the Permanent Settlement should be extended to periodically settled areas, for D. E. Wacha observed that Bengali ryots were not materially better off than ryots in other parts of India.[35] A. O. Hume alleged that the Bengali "masses" were the poorest in India, implying that the Permanent Settlement should not be extended.[36] In reply, Motilal Ghose, who had opposed the recent tenancy legislation, gave "an unqualified denial" to Hume's estimate of the conditions of the Bengali lower classes under the Permanent Settlement.[37]

In 1888 a resolution advocating the extension of the Permanent Settlement was approved by the Subjects Committee for the first time. But an English delegate, one J. E. Howard of Allahabad, argued that a careful study ought to be made of the subject before the Congress as a whole passed such a resolution. He

[35] *Report of the 2nd INC*, p. 61. [36] Ibid., p. 68.
[37] Ibid., p. 69.

mentioned J. S. Mill's maxim that unearned increment from the land should go "to the whole people" rather than to individual proprietors. He and Telang advised the Congress to postpone discussion of the Permanent Settlement until it had been fully considered.[38] It is clear that these delegates thought either that the draft resolution was pro-zamindari or that it might be interpreted that way by enemies of the Congress. Accordingly, the issue was referred to the standing committees which were instructed to submit reports at the 1889 Congress.[39] In what was to become the usual response to such referrals, the reports were not handed in the following year. Nevertheless, the 1889 Congress passed a resolution advocating the extension of permanent limitations on the revenue demand. It was introduced by Baikunthanath Sen, who had held briefs for most of the major zamindars of Murshidabad district. During Maharani Svarnamayi's lifetime, he helped manage the Kasimbazar Raj estate of which his father had been treasurer.[40] The resolution was supported by S. Subramania Iyer who had been retained by the permanently settled Ramnad zamindari and whose father had been vakil for the Raja of Ramnad.[41] Iyer told the Congress how he had first become a landowner fifteen years earlier when he invested money saved from his legal career in Tanjore. Since that time, he complained, the revenue demand on his land had been raised.[42]

In subsequent years if there was opposition to the extension of the Permanent Settlement, it was expressed in the secrecy of the Subjects Committee. Almost every year the Congress resolved itself without debate in favor of extension. If one were to attempt to draw inferences about Congress attitudes to the Permanent Settlement from the meager information available in the first twenty Congress *Reports*, four facts would have to be considered. First, the three persons who were most insistent that championing the Permanent Settlement might be inadvisable were British.[43] Sec-

[38] *Report of the 4th INC*, pp. 115–117.

[39] Resolution XIV of 1888.

[40] Baikunthanath also helped open the extensive coal mines on the Kasimbazar Raj estate. *Bengalee*, 10 March 1903.

[41] Anon., *Heroes of the Hour*, pp. 219 and 222.

[42] *Report of the 5th INC*, p. 60.

[43] Hume, J. E. Howard, and Captain Banon. Robert Knight, editor of the *Friend of India and Statesman*, also opposed its extension. He thought the Bengal Permanent Settlement had been an "economic mistake." (Robert Knight to Ram Gopal Sanyal, 13 Sept. 1886, quoted by Ram Gopal Sanyal,

The Landlord Interest

ond, four other persons who seemed hesitant about supporting the Permanent Settlement in the early years before its meaning became ambiguous were from Bombay.[44] Third, the three persons who spoke most often in favor of the Permanent Settlement were Peter Paul Pillai, barrister, zamindar, and agent of the Madras Landholders' Association, Baikunthanath Sen, zamindar and zamindars' pleader, and R. N. Mudholkar, zamindar and pleader.[45] Finally, there were almost no Indian delegates from outside Bombay who openly suggested within the Congress sessions that there was a conflict of interests between landlords and cultivators.[46] This silence or omission may only in part be explained by the unwritten rule of the Congress that subjects likely to arouse controversy should be avoided. The more likely explanation is that the Congress was courting zamindars and trying to cultivate one of its major sources of financial help and rural influence.

That the Congress was not above tailoring its program in order to please its benefactors is clear from its treatment of the Cadastral Survey in 1893 and 1894. The Government of Bengal was preparing a record of landed rights in order to give tenants

---

Reminiscences and Anecdotes of Great Men of India, Both Official and Non-Official, for the Last One Hundred Years, p. 158.) However, the Permanent Settlement Resolutions of 1891 and 1897 were introduced by Pringle Kennedy and John Adam, respectively. (Kennedy's wife and daughter were murdered by a terrorist in the Muzaffapur bomb case in 1908.) Wedderburn wrote in 1897 that he favored the extension of the Bengal type of permanent settlement in which collection of the land revenue would be assigned "to men of good local standing, and on terms which made them interested in the improvement and prosperity of the land." He had written in 1878 that "we merely state a commonplace when we condemn government interference between Labour and Capital." (S. K. Ratcliffe, *Sir William Wedderburn and the Indian Reform Movement* [London, 1923], pp. 35, 44.)

[44] Wacha, Tyabji, R. M. Bhide, and V. R. Natu. Ranade, on the other hand, tried to add a plea for the extension of the Permanent Settlement to a resolution at the 1887 Congress. (*Report of the 3rd INC*, p. 143.)

[45] B. N. Sen spoke in 1889, 1892, 1893, and 1894; P. P. Pillai in 1892, 1893, 1894, and 1903; and R. N. Mudholkar in 1890, 1896, 1901, and 1904.

[46] An exception was Pandit Madan Mohan Malaviya whose speech in the 1890 Congress was quoted above. In that speech he both ridiculed the government for seeking the consent of the Oudh taluqdars for a patwari cess to be paid by their tenants and criticized Indian members of the Legislative Council who "betray a cruel want of sympathy" for the poor. *Speeches and Writings of Pandit Madan Mohan Malaviya*, pp. 5–6.

greater security under existing tenancy laws. The 1893 and 1894 Congresses passed resolutions expressing "the profound alarm which has been created by the action of the Government in interfering with the existing permanent settlement in Bengal and Bihar (in the matter of survey and other cesses) . . . and deeming such interference with solemn pledges a national calamity." The Congress pledged "itself to oppose in all possible legitimate ways all such reactionary attacks on permanent settlements and their holders." The survey cesses referred to in this unusually strong-worded resolution were those levied on the zamindars of Bihar for the Cadastral Survey.[47] While the Congress resolution itself objected to the cess and not the Cadastral Survey itself, the speech made by Baikunthanath Sen in introducing the resolution in 1894 revealed that more than the cess was involved. He said that the survey (as distinct from the cess for the maintenance of the survey records) was a violation of the Permanent Settlement and that tenureholders and agriculturalists "do not require it." Baikunthanath Sen also criticized the government for including the lands of the Maharaja of Darbhanga in the survey and then proceeded to praise Darbhanga for "the bold attitude he has taken, the noble and magnanimous way in which, at considerable sacrifice, and I may say even risk, he has been trying to maintain the integrity of the Permanent Settlement."[48] This is interesting because some of the villages in the Darbhanga Raj estate had been singled out as areas in need of government interference in determining fair rents. The Maharaja of Darbhanga's brother, Raja Rameshwar Singh, had also been mentioned for having "of late years very greatly and severely enhanced his rents."[49] It is likely that the Congress position on the Cadastral Survey was related to the Maharaja's extensive financial support for the Congress,[50] although the Maharaja was noted for his generosity

[47] Immediately before this resolution was unanimously adopted by the 1893 Congress, a Brahmo missionary named Pundit Lakshman Prasad intimated that he wished to move an amendment if the proposed resolution "goes against the Cadastral Survey." President Naoroji said it did not, so the Brahmo withdrew his amendment. *Report of the 9th INC*, p. 116.

[48] *Report of the 10th INC*, p. 35.

[49] P. P. No. 188 of 1892, East India (Bihar Correspondence) Copy of Correspondence . . . as to the Advisability of carrying out the proposed Cadastral Survey. Enclosure No. 7 to No. 3. H. S. Beadon, Col. of Darbhanga, to Com. of Patna Div., 20 Feb. 1889.

[50] Lord Randolph Churchill sent a paper criticizing the Cadastral Survey

The Landlord Interest

to his peasants in the form of rent remissions, famine relief, and medical services. It was calculated that during the thirty-eight years he held the estate, the estate spent the equivalent of two million Pounds on charity and public works.[51]

ROMESHCHANDRA DUTT'S REDEFINITION OF THE PERMANENT SETTLEMENT

Not long after the Congress protested the Cadastral Survey, discussion of the Permanent Settlement took a new turn when Romeshchandra Dutt retired from the I.C.S., joined the Congress, and wrote a series of open letters to Lord Curzon on the subject. It was Dutt who was largely responsible for giving the term a wider meaning. And Dutt succeeded in eliciting from the government a lengthy resolution in 1902 on the Permanent Settlement which made it clear that there was little prospect that the government would ever again permanently limit its revenue demand. Moreover, the government's resolution chided Dutt (a zamindar who became a member of the British Indian Association), and other nationalist critics for paying so much attention to zamindari interests and so little to tenant rights.[52]

---

to *The Times* of 31 July 1893. He said the paper came from "an Indian gentleman of high position. . . . I cannot vouch for every allegation in the letter, but I can endorse from knowledge its general tenour." Lord Lansdowne was "quite sure" that the paper had been written by Darbhanga or his advisers because both the actual language and the argument agree "exactly with those Memoranda which Durbhanga has, at different times, sent me." (Lansdowne to A. MacDonnell, 26 Aug. 1893, Ms. Eng. Hist. c. 236.) The paper was published while Gladstone's Home Rule Bill was before Parliament and when Conservatives were apprehensive about the future of Irish landlords under the prospective Irish Legislative. The paper seemed calculated to play on Conservative sympathies. It stated that if the Government of India's present antizamindari policy was continued, it "must lead to the same state of things in India as is now the case in Ireland. It sets one class against another." The author of the paper went on to say that Sir Anthony MacDonnell, one of the Cadastral Survey's architects, was "a Home Ruler and holds very strong Irish views on the subject. His scheme is nothing more than an attempt to be generous to the tenants at the expense of the landlord." In the author's view, the ryots were not in "need of any further protection."

[51] *Who's Who in India*, Part VIII, pp. 8-9.

[52] Resolution of 16 Jan. 1902, para. 9. [Govt. of India], *Land Revenue Policy of the Indian Government* (Calcutta, 1902).

Many Congress leaders must have been uneasy with Lord Curzon's efforts to pose as friend of the peasant while portraying the Congress as champion of the privileged classes. This was probably one of the reasons that the Congress gave less emphasis to the Permanent Settlement after the Government of India's resolution. However, it was ironic, and probably disingenuous, that Lord Curzon should have capitalized on Dutt's advocacy of the Permanent Settlement in order to claim the government was defending tenants against zamindars. For when Dutt asked for a permanent settlement to be introduced in all parts of India, he was asking for the extension of the principle of permanency and not of zamindari settlement. He wanted the government to fix its assessment permanently everywhere, in ryotwari as well as zamindari areas. And although he was no longer as fervent an advocate of tenant rights as he had been as a young civil servant, Dutt did want a permanent limitation of zamindar claims on tenants.[53] Effective tenancy laws had a definite place in his panacea for Indian agriculture.[54] The Congress asked for an extension of the Permanent Settlement almost every year, but the only time before 1910 it passed a resolution recommending tenancy legislation was in 1899, the year Dutt presided. Pandit Madan Mohan Malaviya also spoke in favor that year of a restriction of landlord demands upon their tenants. Dutt was probably responsible for the 1899 resolution because it was in line with his open letters to Lord Curzon[55] and because it was not repeated in subsequent years when Dutt was absent. In any case, Dutt had redefined the term "Permanent Settlement" in a way that allowed even advocates of tenant rights to accept it.

By the turn of the century, the Congress contained a considerable number of nationalists who for various reasons were willing

[53] Letter of 12 May 1900, *Open Letters to Lord Curzon and Speeches and Papers* (Calcutta, 1904), p. 15. In his 1874 book, *The Peasantry of Bengal*, Dutt had described the peasants as "a worthier class" than the zamindars (p. 59) whom he regarded as highly oppressive. In 1874 he wrote that the Permanent Settlement of 1793 was "calamitous" and "ill-conceived," while in his *Open Letters* (p. 15) he said the Permanent Settlement had contributed more to prosperity than any other act of government.

[54] See, for instance, his paper "Famines in India, 1770 to 1900" (*Open Letters to Lord Curzon*, p. 18) in which he wrote, "wise laws have been made to restrict the demands of landlords [in Bengal and Northern India], though a further extension of these may still be necessary."

[55] Resolution II of 1899.

The Landlord Interest

to give up the Congress efforts to woo the zamindars. These men included persons such as Romeshchandra Dutt who did not want to give the government any opportunities to pose as protector of the poor majority while accusing the Congress of class bias. They included K. Perraju, a pleader and member of the Madras Legislative Council, who argued that "zamindars have not done anything socially or politically to merit state aid and protection."[56] They also included C. Sankara Nair who, although a Malabar landlord himself, fought for tenant rights against landlords, apparently as an expression of Nair anti-Brahmanism.[57] Some Congressmen may have felt better about themselves and the Congress movement when the Congress detached itself from particular class interests. In rising above sectional interest, the Congress was conforming to both Hindu cultural ideals of selflessness and the universalism implied in the building of a nation. It is also likely that nationalists who criticized the government for its compromises with zamindars over tenancy legislation felt they had scored a moral victory in their competition with officials to establish themselves as guardians of the public interest. Yet the gains for the Congress of the actions of the pro-tenant minority were more psychological than practical. Advocacy of tenant rights undoubtedly contributed to the reluctance of zamindars to join the movement. The social composition of the Congress changed very little during its first twenty-five years.

POLITICAL REPRESENTATION OF LANDLORDS UNDER THE 1892 REFORMS

As suggested above, after the first years of the Congress, the question of landlord political representation overshadowed tenancy laws as a source of friction between landlords and Congress supporters. The passage of tenancy acts in most provinces meant that that issue receded from public controversy, while the application of the new elective system under the Councils Act of 1892 focused attention upon representation. Landlord dissatisfaction with the working of the Councils Act was most pronounced in Bengal.

---

[56] K. Perraju, "Impartible Estates in India," *Hindustan Review and Kayastha Samachar*, Vol. VII, No. 5 (May 1903), 424.

[57] *The Statesman*, 6 Jan. 1898, quotes a biographical sketch of Nair from the *Pioneer*.

The Landlord Interest

By establishing a system of elections, the 1892 reforms enabled urban professionals, most of whom were Congress supporters, to gain seats on the legislative councils previously given to landlords through official nominations. In Bengal, it is unlikely that titled zamindars would have considered any Congress support for their economic interests as adequate compensation for their relative loss of influence in the Legislative Council. Their experience with the elective system under the Councils Act of 1892 showed that the Bengali Congress leaders were opposing and usually defeating the zamindars in races for the half-dozen seats on the Bengal Council which were not reserved for officials and official nominees.

In the first Bengal Council elections, in 1893, only two of the six Indians elected were known as zamindars,[58] and one of these, Maharaja Jagadendranath Roy of Natore,[59] was nominated after the government had disallowed the election of a lawyer whose residency qualifications were held to be inadequate. Of the six, four were important Congress supporters: Surendranath Banerjea, Anandamohan Bose, W. C. Bonnerjee, and the Maharaja of Darbhanga; one was a Muslim; and only the Maharaja of Natore was an active member of the British Indian Association.

In the second elections in 1895, not a single important zamindar candidate was successful, as four lawyers and a newspaper editor (S. N. Banerjea) were returned. Anandamohan Bose defeated Rajkumar Sarvadhikari for the university seat; and Guruprasad Sen, another Congress leader, was elected after his opponent, Raja Surjakanta Acharea Chowdhury of Mymensingh, withdrew.[60] The key contest was for the Calcutta Municipal

[58] Not including Ananda Mohan Bose, who came from a family owning estates in Sylhet and Mymensingh and who himself owned a tea plantation. Hem Chandra Sarkar, *A Life of Ananda Mohan Bose* (Calcutta, 1910), p. 2. The Government of Bengal and the British Indian Association, in deprecating the successes of the professional classes in elections, invariably ignored the fact that many middle-class politicians owed zamindaris or rent-collecting rights.

[59] The Maharaja was at various times closely associated with the middle-class nationalists. He presided over the 1892 protest meeting against the Bengal Municipal Bill, and he was chairman of the Reception Committees of the 1897 Bengal Provincial Conference and the 1901 Indian National Congress. He also became secretary of the Bengal Landholders' Association. *Bengalee*, 14 Dec. 1901.

[60] *Bengalee*, 27 July 1895. Previously, a candidate from another old family

The Landlord Interest

Corporation's seat between S. N. Banerjea, secretary of the Indian Association and the favorite of the Congress press in Bengal, and Kalinath Mitter, who was supported by the British Indian Association, the *Hindoo Patriot,* the *Englishman,* and the *Pioneer.*[61] After Banerjea won, by 41 votes to 23,[62] the *Pioneer* alleged that he had received the votes of persons acting "under the terror of immediate personal pressure and the horror of being shown up in a certain native newspaper," and it stigmatized the voting system as "a scandal and a deception."[63] The *Hindoo Patriot* commented similarly, attributing Banerjea's victory, firstly, to his bullying of municipal councilors by threatening to expose them in the press and, secondly, to Kalinath Mitter's "resolute contempt for the vulgar arts of the professional canvasser."[64] The *Amrita Bazar Patrika* suggested that zamindars should not be returned to the legislative councils, because, it said, being in possession of large estates, they would not act independently of the government and the district officials.[65] In any case, the elections indicated a decisive victory for the urban, professional Congress candidates over their moderate opponents who were identified with zamindari interests.

There was talk of starting a new "moderate" party in Bengal, separate from the Congress. A meeting was held at the Calcutta town hall to discuss the possibility, and the *Hindoo Patriot* backed the prospect with an editorial entitled "The Parting of the Waters." The general superintendent of the Thagi and Dakoiti Department reported that he knew of no other "such definite change of opinion . . . among the leaders of Native Opinion and this may be the beginning of a new departure, which will probably be echoed in the [other] Provinces."[66]

—Sitanath Roy of the Bhagyakul family—had withdrawn from the contest. *Bengalee,* 27 Apr. 1895.

[61] Ibid., 8 June 1895.

[62] Later in the year, when the Bengal Legislative Council was about to select one of its members for a seat on the governor general's legislative council, Banerjea withdrew his candidacy, leaving the field clear for the election of the Maharaja of Darbhanga. Ibid., 26 Oct. 1895.

[63] Quoted by the *Bengalee,* 1 June 1895.

[64] Quoted from the *Madras Standard* by the *Bengalee,* 15 June 1895.

[65] Ibid., 8 June 1895.

[66] Lt. Col. A. S. Lethbridge to H. Babington Smith, 1 July 1895. Register No. 413B. MSS. Eur. F. 84.

The new moderate party did not materialize, but most of the larger Bengali zamindars remained outside the Congress. At the time of the 1897 council elections, when again not a single zamindari candidate was elected,[67] the *Hindoo Patriot* explained why the zamindars did not join the Congress.

> The chief cause, in our opinion, has been the attitude of the so-called leaders of the people towards the zamindars. Many of the former look upon the latter in the same light in which the followers of Tom Mann and John Burns look upon the territorial magnates' of Great Britain. . . . In the elections to the Council or to Municipalities, the zamindars have seldom received even the scantiest support from the rising village politicians. The zamindar is approached only when money is wanted.[68]

The 1892 Councils Act, besides ending the predominance of the landlords in the Bengal Legislative Council, had considerably reduced the relative strength of the landholders in the other provincial councils and in the governor general's Legislative Council. Before the 1892 Act, from 1862 to 1888, out of a total of 36 Indian members of the governor general's Legislative Council, 23 had been landholders and only 3 had been lawyers. In the same period, 17 Indians on the Bengal Council had been diwans, zamindars, or zamindari agents, and 9 had been in the legal profession. In Madras the balance between landholding and professional interests had been roughly even; in Bombay, the number of merchants had been equal to the number of zamindars, sirdars, Chiefs, Amirs, Nawabs, and ex-diwans. In the North-Western Provinces and Oudh, where a legislative council was established in 1887, 3 of the first 4 Indians to receive appointments were landholders.[69]

The situation was very different after the 1892 Councils Act was passed. The government had expected the zamindars to obtain representation through the district boards. Contrary to this

[67] One of the successful candidates, Saligram Singh, a vakil occasionally practicing in Calcutta, did own land.

[68] Quoted by the *Bengalee*, 26 June 1897.

[69] P. P. C. 5950(42) of 1890, Vol. liv. Statement of the Additional Members of the Council of the Governor General, Bengal, Bombay, Madras, and the Northern-Western Provinces and Oudh for making laws and regulations.

The Landlord Interest

expectation, from 1893 to 1907 the district boards in Bengal, Bombay, Madras, and the North-Western Provinces returned 36 barristers and pleaders and only 10 landholders out of a total of 54 councilors. In the elections by district municipalities to the four provincial councils, 40 out of 43 members chosen were barristers or pleaders. This imbalance was partially corrected through government appointments, so that, of all the 338 non-official members returned to the reformed legislative councils in the first fourteen years, 77 (22 per cent) were landowners while 123 (36 per cent) were lawyers.[70]

The success of the lawyers in elections to the legislative councils, and in politics in general, may be explained by several factors. A lawyer usually possessed a web of contacts through colleagues in the legal profession and through his clients. Important towns, including district headquarters, contained a bar library and a local court which served as foci for the district lawyer's professional activities. There the lawyer might make contacts and friends, and acquire a widespread influence and reputation which few merchants, doctors, and small landlords could match. This was even more true of the High Court advocates to whom district pleaders referred major cases and appeals. Thus, when it came to canvassing for votes, the legal profession had a distinct advantage.[71] Second, lawyers often spoke English and debated and understood administrative problems better than men of other vocations. They were elected in many cases because they were recognized by their colleagues as better qualified to serve in the legislative councils. It should be remembered that members of the legal profession did not ordinarily constitute a majority on district boards or municipalities. Finally, as the Arundel Committee lamented in 1907, "the more stable elements of the community" (the zamindars) were not always willing to run for office because canvassing for votes was regarded as derogatory and, more im-

[70] Report of the committee appointed to consider reforms in the Indian councils (Arundel Committee), para. 45. MSS. Eur. D. 575/29. Also P. P. Cd. 4435 of 1908, East India (Advisory and Legislative councils), Vol. II, Part I, Replies of the Local Governments. Sir Harold Stuart, Offg. Sec. to Govt. of India, to Ch. Secs. of Prov. Govts., 24 Aug. 1907. Home Dept. Public, Enclosure No. 1 to letter from Govt. of India, No. 21, 10 Oct. 1908.

[71] S. W. Edgerley, Sec. to Govt. of Bombay, Leg. Dept., to Sec. to Govt. of India, Home Dept., 12 Apr. 1899, para. 3. July Prog. No. 20. IHP, Pub., Vol. 5,639.

portantly, these elements would not risk defeat by persons of inferior social status.[72]

The issue of representation came to a head in 1898 when the Government of Bengal introduced and passed a minor bill to amend the Bengal Tenancy Act of 1885. This bill, which had been demanded by the Bengal zamindars, was intended to ease some of the restrictions placed on the realization and enhancement of rents by the Tenancy Act of 1885. During the debate in the Legislative Council on the Amendment Bill, three of the elected members, Surendranath Banerjea, Kalicharan Banerji, and Narendranath Sen, opposed the bill as being harmful to the interests of the ryots because it gave zamindars and their agents new opportunities to raise their tenants' rents.[73] The secretary of the Bengal Revenue Department, Michael Finucane, who had himself edited the Tenancy Act of 1885, rejected the amendments moved by the three members who, he said "represent the popular view." "There is scarcely a single alteration proposed in the law in favour of zamindars which," he complained, "one or other of those Hon'ble Members is not prepared to strike out."[74] And the amendments were defeated.

The zamindars reacted sharply to the pro-ryot stand of the Congressmen. Raja Pearymohan Mukherji denounced the Congress at the annual meeting of the British Indian Association, and he advised the government to remember that "men of wealth and station, men who have a large stake in the country, are the real pillars of State, that anything which strikes at their influence and authority reacts on the strength of the Government," whose stability depended upon the maintenance of "social gradations."[75] The *Hindoo Patriot* warned officials against mixing "with the noisy agitators, who know more of the exploits of a Garibaldi or a Mazzini" than of the peasants. "The local aristocracy" alone were familiar with peasant needs and conditions.[76] The zamindars would remember that the *Bengalee* had supported the

[72] Report of the committee appointed to consider reforms in the Indian councils.

[73] Bengal LCP, 2 Apr. 1898, pp. 66–82.

[74] Ibid., p. 68. It would be interesting to know if these Congressmen or their associates possessed rent-collecting rights as tenants of zamindars. No evidence of this was found.

[75] Quoted by the *Bengalee*, 6 Aug. 1898.

[76] Quoted by ibid., 14 Aug. 1898.

The Landlord Interest

ryots "when the hat is again sent round to them for the benefit of the microscopic minority the sole ambition of which seems to be to secure monopoly of representation in the Legislative Council."[77]

The British Indian Association and another Bengal landholders' organization, the Zamindari Panchayat, sent representations to the government in which they requested the right to return a representative of zamindari interests directly to the council.[78] The British Indian Association maintained that the regulations issued under the 1892 Councils Act had in effect withdrawn from the association the privilege of electing a member of the council, a privilege of "long established usage, sanctioned by the action of successive Lieutenant-Governors" who had appointed or recommended members of the British Indian Association to the Indian and Bengal councils 39 times between 1863 and 1892.[79] In 1893 the association had asked for the right under the new regulations to recommend members to the reformed Bengal council. Although the Viceroy, in his reply, refused to grant that right, he did say that the lieutenant-governor of Bengal "intends ordinarily to consult the British Indian Association and other bodies of land-holders, and the Governor-General in Council has no doubt that the recommendations of the Association will receive full consideration at the hands of the Government." Despite this assurance, the British Indian Association had not been consulted since the Councils Act of 1892 was passed.[80]

When it received the zamindars' 1898 representations, the Government of India agreed to reexamine the position of the landed interests in the legislative councils throughout India. The result of the government's inquiries was that only in Bengal was it possible and desirable to increase the representation of the landholding classes. This was effected by taking one of the two seats

[77] Quoted by ibid., 11 June 1898.

[78] Pransankar Roy Chaudhuri, Hon. Sec., Zamindary Panchayet, to Gov. Gen. of India, 8 Oct. 1898. Nov. Prog. No. 118., IHP, Pub., Vol. 5,414. Rai Rajkumar Sarvadhikari, Sec., British India Assn., to Ch. Sec., Govt. of Bengal, 30 Apr. 1898. Nov. Prog. No. 114. Ibid.

[79] Sarvadhikari, 30 Apr. 1898. para. 12. The names of these members are contained in Appendix B to Sarvadhikari's letter. This evidence indicates that Indians were elected in certain cases to the legislative councils even before the Councils Act of 1892.

[80] Ibid., para. 15.

previously assigned to the mofussil municipalities and giving it to the Bengal zamindars.[81]

It is interesting that no change was recommended for Madras where most of the members elected since 1893 also belonged to the legal profession. The difference may have been that in the same year that Bengali Congressmen argued on behalf of tenant interests in the Bengal Council, Madrasi Congressmen took the side of landlords in the Madras Council over a bill which provided tenants with expanded occupancy rights. P. Ratnasabhapati Pillai, C. Jambulingam Mudaliar, C. Vijayaraghava Chariar, and P. Rangia Naidu expressed resentment at the imputation that zamindars and ryots (ryots could also have tenants) oppressed their tenants and at the interference with the freedom of landlords' rights to make their own contracts with their tenants.[82] Pillai, Mudaliar, and Vijayaraghava Chariar also opposed an 1899 bill to secure tenants in the Malabar district compensation for improvements they made to their land. The bill was intended to remove one of the causes of the periodic Moplah riots against their Hindu landlords and the British,[83] but these three Congress leaders argued that the Moplahs had already received sufficient compensation for eviction and that to provide more would reward Moplahs for their violence.[84]

When the Government of Madras was asked about the representation of landlord interests on the local council, it replied that it regularly appointed a landholder. However, the landholders' seat was not an adequate measure of the influence which that class possessed in the Madras Council: "There is a most intimate connection between the professional classes and the richer Government ryots, the former being to a very large extent recruited from the latter and constantly investing their savings in the purchase of land." Although all five of the elected Indian members were lawyers, the Government of Madras thought that "no better representatives could possibly be found for the interests of the Government ryots." With the zamindars, also "the legal members are closely associated, because investment in small

---

[81] Gov. Gen. in Council to S. of S., 6 July 1899, para. 5. July Prog. No. 21, IHP, Pub., Vol. 5,639.

[82] Madras LCP, 13 June 1898, Vol. xxv, 146–153, 166–168, 186–190, and 192.

[83] Madras LCP, 24 Jan. and 14 Nov. 1899, Vol. xxv, 21–29 and 344.

[84] There were Moplah risings in 1873, 1885, 1894, and 1896. Wilfred Cantwell Smith, *Modern Islam in India: A Social Analysis* (London, 1946), p. 244.

The Landlord Interest

zamindaris coming into the market is much in favour with the professional classes."[85] In fact, since 1893, legal members had defended zamindari interests with greater ability than the zamindars themselves could have, although some of the lawyers supported the rights of the tenants.[86]

It would seem that the Bengali Congressmen lost a seat on their provincial legislative council for representing tenant interests while Madrasi Congressmen retained all their seats because most of them voiced landlord objections to tenancy bills. In neither case could Indian votes significantly affect the outcome of legislation. Rather, it was a matter of official desire to placate zamindars and to drive a wedge between the major zamindars and the Congress. Perhaps in addition some officials were affronted by what may have seemed to be a nationalist usurpation of a role traditionally belonging to the English, the role of protecting the poor.

In Bengal, English officials made no attempt to hide their delight with the verbal hostilities between the zamindars and Congressmen. H. H. Risley told the Legislative Council that the pro-tenant stand of the three Bengali members was further proof that the elective system was not suited to India. Risley argued that the elective system

> gives undue prominence to a section of the community—Young Bengal, New India—whatever you choose to call it, the *soi-disant* democratic section of a society which, from top to bottom, is essentially undemocratic. . . . It leaves the elder generation and those who follow in their steps out in the cold. . . . It does not give us, as a rule, either here or in the Mufassal, the genuine representative Hindus, the men we really want.[87]

This was a reversal of a common justification for refusing to give Indians increased representation in the legislative councils. The usual argument was that only British officials understood and

---

[85] H. Tremenheere, Sec., Govt. of Madras, Leg. Dept., to Sec., Govt. of India, Home Dept., 31 Jan. 1899. July Prog. No. 17, IHP, Pub., Vol. 5,639. The percentage of the numbers of the legal class who owned land in Madras in 1891 was stated to be 18.98 per cent. In Bombay it was 13.57 per cent and in the North-Western Provinces it was 15.16 per cent. *General Report on the Census of India, 1891*, p. 116.

[86] Tremenheere's letter of 31 Jan. 1899.

[87] Bengal LCP, 4 Apr. 1898, pp. 195–196.

sympathized with the needs of the Indian "people" as distinct from the Indian "classes."[88] It seems there was little the nationalists could do to deserve more representation. If the nationalists adopted a position based upon narrow self-interest, they were apt to be told that they were not yet ready for democracy because democratic institutions could function only in a society in which class divisions were tempered by breadth of vision and a spirit of compromise. If, on the other hand, nationalists took a radical or democratic stand, they were likely to be told, as they were by Risley, that India was by nature undemocratic and therefore more democracy could not be granted. The issue was as much a question of power as ideology or the nature of Indian society, although perhaps few British officials were conscious of this. There was enough truth in the British claim to guardianship of the poorer classes that officials could easily overlook the occasions when the nationalists sided with the underpriviledged against the government and the wealthy classes. The years 1885 and 1898 were two such occasions. Both times the government yielded to the pressure of the zamindars over the tenancy legislation despite the protests of urban nationalists.[89]

The lieutenant-governor of Bengal, Sir Alexander Mackenzie, exploited the fight between the zamindars and their Congress opponents. He boasted to Elgin that he had "not failed to accentuate" the split which he regarded as "a great gain." He talked with Sir Lachmeshwar Singh, the Maharaja of Darbhanga, who in addition to being president of various landholding associations was probably the Congress's most generous and influential benefactor. Mackenzie reported that he thought he had "brought him

[88] See Dufferin to Cross, 20 March 1887, No. 33. MSS. Eur. E. 243/22. Also Lansdowne to Cross, 12 Feb. 1889, No. 10. MSS. Eur. E. 243/26; Curzon's Farewell Address to Byculla Club, Bombay, 16 Nov. 1905, *Lord Curzon in India . . . 1898–1905*, ed. Sir Thomas Raleigh, p. 585; G. N. Curzon, *British Government in India: The Story of The Viceroys and Government Houses* (London, 1925), p. 131; and Govt. of India Despatch to S. of S., 21 March 1907, No. 7 of 1907. Govt. of India, Home Dept., Pub., MSS. Eur. D. 573/29.

[89] Rokeya Rahman, "Social and Administrative Policy of the Government of Bengal: 1877–1890" (unpublished M.A. thesis. University of London, 1959), pp. 342–343. Also, Bagal, *Indian Association*, pp. 50ff.; *Bengalee*, 2 Apr. 1898. There can be few times when the Government of India modified a bill in response to Indian opinion as radically as it did the Bengal Tenancy Bill between 1883 and 1885. In the face of zamindari opposition, sections providing protection to tenants from enhancement and ejection were altered substantially.

to see that the Congress is hostile to the zamindars and ought not to be allowed to 'blackmail' him any longer."[90] It is unlikely that the Maharaja was blackmailed into supporting the Congress, for he agreed with many of its aims. However, he had complained in 1897 that he had "been obliged to subscribe to more than one public movement simply to save myself from unpleasant abuse from newspapers of the 'Bangbashi' class."[91] Probably Darbhanga felt himself caught in the same dilemma faced by many titled landholders. They were pressured on one side by alien officials who still held almost a total monopoly of administrative power which, as in the case of the Cadastral Survey, could be turned against them, and on the other by a rapidly growing number of their own educated countrymen who would soon begin to inherit that power, as the legislative council elections indicated. Whether Mackenzie had been successful in drawing Darbhanga away from the Congress could not be tested because Darbhanga died in December 1898. He was succeeded by his brother, Rameshwar Singh, who was not a friend of the Congress.

The Government of India also increased its pressure on the zamindars in 1899 by initiating a survey of zamindari financial contributions to the Congress. Whether, in the process of making their inquiries, officials also warned zamindars that continued donations would result in sanctions against them is not known. But a zamindar need not have been very perspicacious to realize how dependent he was on official good will when revenue settlements were made, when tenancy laws were passed and enforced, and when honors and titles were awarded. The reports of both the 1898 (Madras) and 1899 (Lucknow) Congresses mentioned the decline in zamindari financial contributions.[92]

By the early years of the twentieth century, Congress relations with the major landholders had settled into an established pattern. Throughout India, titled landholders with some significant exceptions resented the electoral success of Congress politicians, who were generally urban professionals. Landholders drew closer to the government as a result, hoping that the English would insure zamindari representation in the legislative councils and

[90] Mackenzie to Elgin, 5 Apr. 1898, App. No. xx, MSS. Eur. F. 84/72.
[91] Maharaja of Darbhanga to H. Babington Smith, 16 Aug. 1897, MSS. Eur. F. 84/71.
[92] *Report of the 14th INC*, p. iii, and *Report of the 15th INC*, pp. v-vi.

district boards and that the English would help them educate their children and manage their estates. The Congress as an organization rarely adopted specifically landlord positions on economic issues after the Cadastral Survey episode. The Congress did not, for example, protest tenancy legislation, although individual Congressmen did so outside the Congress. On the other hand, the Congress continued annually until 1908 to call for the extension of a permanent settlement into periodically settled areas. Beginning in 1908, the Congress asked for "a Settlement for a period of not less than sixty years."[93] Permanency of the revenue demand, the Congress resolved again and again, was "the true remedy" and even "the only" remedy for "the growing impoverishment of the agricultural population."[94] There seems to have been little discussion within Congress circles of alternative solutions to the problem of rural poverty such as land redistribution, ceilings on holdings, or expanded cultivator-ownership. Until World War I, the Congress was still trying to consolidate its hold among educated Indians who came almost exclusively from the high-caste and property-owning sections of the population. Because educated nationalists rarely had intimate connections with the rural poor, either through caste, schools, or careers, the possibility of making the concrete interests of the poor into a major Congress cause was still remote, except when those interests could be perceived to be identical with the welfare of the propertied groups, as in the case of the Permanent Settlement. The early Congress antagonized few Indians by arguing that the economic drain and the high pitch and inelasticity of the land revenue demand, rather than flaws in the social structure or value system, were the basic causes of rural poverty. It would be ahistorical to expect other behavior from a body with the Congress's social composition. Insofar as the Congress reacted to conflicts between the low-caste poor and the property-owners, creditors, and employers of labor, it was more responsive to the latter who were usually well represented in the Congress. This happened in the case of Cadastral Survey as we have seen. It happened again with the introduction of new usury laws into the Punjab and Bombay.

[93] Resolution XV of 1908.

[94] The word "only" was dropped from the Permanent Settlement resolution in 1911 when the Congress resolved that permanency would "substantially" help alleviate poverty.

Chapter Eight

THE CONGRESS, PEASANTS, AND THE ALIENATION OF LAND

Congress supporters believed that they spoke on behalf of the cultivating classes when they advocated a permanent and lower settlement of the land revenue demand, a policy of flexible collections in years of scarcity, and a cheaper, more representative form of government, administered by Indians. As suggested earlier, nationalists generally attributed the crushing poverty of the lower classes to the misguided policies of their alien rulers rather than to defects in indigenous values and social structure. They assumed that without the kinship of race, British officials lacked the understanding and natural sympathy necessary for wise government.

British officials were particularly resentful of nationalist allegations of unfeeling treatment of the lower classes. The British perceived their own civilization as more humane and democratic than Indian civilization, and they were aware of the absence of representatives of the cultivating classes in the nationalist movement. Moreover, British control over the administration and the legislature gave the British practical responsibility for famine relief, surveys of tenant rights, tenancy legislation, and other measures intended to benefit the ryots. British officials cited their guardianship of the poor as a reason for not sharing political power with educated Indians who, they said, would either exploit the poor or would be unable to keep order between the educated and propertied classes and the remainder of the population. Officials tended to view Indian society as a cockpit of competing classes and communities which might overwhelm each other if the British were not present to regulate the conflicts. This was part of what Lord Dufferin meant when he spoke of the Raj's "august impartiality" in the face of India's "multifarious interests" and "tessellated nationalities," and it was also what Lord Curzon meant when he said the British mission was to hold "the scales even."[1]

[1] B. L. Grover, *A Documentary Study of British Policy Towards Indian*

Alienation of Land

There was an element of cant in British suggestions that officials were motivated by humanitarian values while the social vision of the urban nationalist was circumscribed by his selfish, class interests.[2] As we have seen, a section of British officialdom was highly solicitous of the welfare of landlord and aristocratic families and correspondingly indifferent to their tenants. Similarly, other officials who attempted to protect peasants from landlords and money-lenders often did so in order to protect the British Raj's security, rather than from disinterested concern for the general welfare. After accounting for the varieties and complexity of British motivation, the basic, underlying concern of the British administration—stripped of righteous rhetoric—was the security of its colonial possession. And the nationalist movement was the fastest growing danger to continued stability in the late nineteenth century.

Officials were reminded by the founding of the Congress and Hume's attempts to reach the peasants that British security depended on keeping the landlords loyal and the ryots apolitical. The government was consciously seeking to demonstrate that it, and not the Congress, was the true guardian of landlord and cultivator interests. At the same time, officials hoped to alleviate agrarian grievances which nationalist politicians would surely exploit if they had the opportunity.

If any man could be described as the architect of this strategy it was Sir Anthony MacDonnell, an unusually able and tough administrator whose Irish Catholic background was said to explain his determination to strengthen cultivators vis-à-vis landlords and money-lenders.[3] During the last two decades of the century, MacDonnell, Denzil Ibbetson, and a group of pro-peasant officials reached key positions in the Governments of India, Bengal, and the North-Western Provinces and Oudh. They succeeded in passing a series of measures, including the Bengal Tenancy Act of 1885, which promised security of tenure and free-

---

Nationalism 1885–1909 (Delhi, 1967), p. 184, and Raleigh (ed.), *Lord Curzon in India*, pp. 584–585.

[2] As, for example, in Lord Dufferin's speech on 30 Nov. 1888 in which he denounced the Congress as "a microscopic minority."

[3] Anthony MacDonnell was Home Secretary, 1886–1889; a member of the Viceroy's Council, 1893–1895; lieutenant-governor of the North-Western Provinces and Oudh, 1895–1901; and chairman of the Famine Commission, 1901. Gopal, *British Policy*, pp. 155 and 351.

dom from enhancement, security from forfeiture of mortgaged land to nonagriculturist money-lenders, and cadastral surveys of tenant rights. In most cases, there was strong opposition from within the British official community,[4] as well as from zamindars or money-lenders, to the bias of the proposed measures in favor of the cultivating classes. In most instances these critics succeeded in forcing compromises before enactment. But almost all officials were persuaded that new laws were needed in order to stabilize agrarian relations, for the benefit of the poor and propertied classes alike. Altogether, MacDonnell and his colleagues gained passage of their measures which were intended to remove a threat to the security of the British Raj. In doing so, they again tested the national representativeness of the Congress, for they forced the Congress into the uncomfortable position of seeming to choose sides between capital and labor and between high- and low-status groups.

The dimensions of official political anxieties were revealed in a lengthy Government of India memorandum prepared under Sir Anthony MacDonnell in 1895. The memorandum, which prepared the ground for the acts limiting the transfer of land in the Punjab and Bombay in 1900 and 1902, presented a summary of official views on the likely economic and political consequences of not restricting the alienation of agricultural land. Its authors concluded that indebtedness was causing land to pass out of the hands of traditional landholders to a dangerous degree in western, central, and northern India, including the North-Western Provinces.[5] As a result, "a feeling of sullen discontent is spreading [in many areas], which must open the ears of the people to those various forms of political agitation that are but now showing signs of organization."[6] From other comments, it is clear that the authors were thinking of both the Indian National Congress and the cow protection movements. They were worried about the effect of indebtedness and transfer upon several, overlapping

[4] See the attacks on MacDonnell's policies by Sir Roper Lethbridge in the *Imperial and Asiatic Quarterly Review* (New Series), Vols. VIII and X (1894 and 1895).

[5] Note on Land Transfers and Agricultural Indebtedness, 18 March 1895, prepared under the instructions of Sir A. MacDonnell. Published in Government of India, Department of Revenue and Agriculture, *Selections of Papers on Agricultural Indebtedness and the Restriction of the Power to Alienate Interests in Land* (Simla, 1898), Vol. I, para. 186.

[6] Ibid., para. 58.

categories of the rural population. They were concerned about the masses in general, whose contentment would leave "the professional agitator powerless." More particularly, they were concerned about "the sturdy yeomanry from whose ranks we draw our native soldiers, the safe foundation upon which our rule can rest secure."[7] They were worried about the discontents of those tenants who had once been independent owners or secure tenants but who were now rack-rented by ruthless new owners and intermediaries.[8] They also feared the displacement of the "great landlords" who were "generally at the disposal of the authorities" and who "served as handles by which to move or control" the masses.[9] Neither the authors of the memorandum nor the officials whom they quoted seemed to believe that rural discontent was an immediate danger to British rule. But the Mutiny, the Deccan riots of 1875, and other disturbances suggested that "tropical storms break suddenly" and that it would be unwise to wait for eruptions of violence before acting to stem the alienation of land.[10]

THE PUNJAB

Discussion of this memorandum by provincial governments revealed that official support for legislation limiting land transfers was strong only in the Punjab,[11] although some officials in Bombay favored strengthening the law which restricted transfers in the Deccan also. The Punjab was the province where groups supporting the Congress stood to lose the most from such protective legislation. The stage was set for casting the government and Congress into the roles which officials often projected, with the government protecting the poor and the Congress the privileged.

The extent and danger of land transfers in the Punjab had been dramatized by S. S. Thorburn, a member of the Indian Civil Service whose book, *Musalmans and Money-Lenders in the Punjab*, was published in 1886. Thorburn had warned that the land of the Western Punjab was passing out of the hands of the Muslim peasantry into the hands of the Hindu money-lenders at an

[7] Ibid., para. 57.   [8] Ibid., paras. 50 and 178–181.
[9] Ibid., para. 50.   [10] Ibid., para. 59.
[11] One official commented that the cultivators and the government were left with the oyster and the shell while the Punjabi money-lenders took the pearl.

alarming rate. He believed that unless there was "some Act of Bunniah spoliation," "half of our magnificent peasantry" might rise up against the hated money-lenders. Or there might be a serious rebellion if the agrarian unrest came into contact with an Islamic religious fanatic, a famine, or a land reform agitator.[12] These and other warnings of the likely consequences of unchecked borrowing and alienation had attracted the attention of the Punjab administration. As a result, Thorburn had been appointed to inquire into the problem in the area between Rawalpindi and Lahore. His conclusions, which bore out his earlier estimates of the extent of land alienation, were set out in his "Report on Peasant Indebtedness" in 1896.

The amount of land changing legal ownership in the Punjab had increased rapidly, if official statistics have validity. Sales averaged about 88,000 acres a year from 1866 to 1874. From 1875 to 1879, sales averaged about 93,000 acres annually; from 1880 to 1884, 160,000 acres; from 1885 to 1889, 310,000 acres; and from 1890 to 1894, 338,000 acres a year. Mortgages were registered at the annual rate of 143,000 acres from 1866 to 1874, and then at "212,000, 296,000, 590,000, and 554,000 acres a year in the succeeding quinquennial periods."[13] These figures may give an exaggerated picture of the actual displacement of cultivators from their holdings, because many former owners remained in physical possession of the land, either as tenants of the new owners or as litigants challenging the validity of the transfer transaction. But even after taking these qualifications into account, the Government of India shared the concern of Thorburn and the Punjab administration about the alienation and transfer of land to nonagricultural castes. As a matter of social justice, officials felt that the British legal system, which had enabled the cultivator to offer his land as security for loans, had worked to the cultivator's disadvantage. The laws were contrary to village customs which had generally prevented the transfer of land outside the community; the laws were too complicated for unsophisticated peasants to understand; and the laws gave a decisive advantage to money-lenders and their lawyer friends with superior educa-

[12] S. S. Thorburn, *Musalmans and Money-Lenders in the Punjab* (London, 1886), pp. 39–41.

[13] H. Calvert, *The Wealth and Welfare of the Punjab*, 2nd ed. (Lahore, 1936), p. 263.

tion and economic resources, or with traditions "of minute parsimony and accurate ledgering."[14]

The rapid transfer of land also presented a security danger. The Punjab castes which were losing land provided many recruits for the army. To permit disaffection to grow in the army or among the people who lived near the strategic northwest frontier could be disastrous. As members of the Punjab administration repeatedly warned the Government of India, the Punjab's loyalty was essential for any war the British might fight in Afghanistan and for resisting any invasion that might come from the northwest. In an age of rapidly changing military technology and intense big power rivalry in central Asia, this was a persuasive argument. Finally, land alienation in the Punjab had a communal aspect, with implications for domestic politics and relations with Muslim peoples on and beyond the frontier. In many areas land was passing from Muslim cultivators to Hindu money-lenders so that class tensions were compounded by communal antagonisms.[15] And communalism was a more serious problem in the Punjab in the late nineteenth century than in any other province.

Although the government and Thorburn agreed on the nature of the problem, Thorburn's instincts were for a more radical solution. In a novel published in 1897, he showed that he favored a return to the Lawrence school of administration in the Punjab. The novel, *His Majesty's Greatest Subject*, was a fantasy about a future viceroy of India who had all of Thorburn's distaste for educated and political India and a hankering for the good old days of swift, decisive action without elaborate debate and constitutional procedure. Thorburn's ideas were held by other civil servants who felt a sense of frustration with the working of British legal, political, and educational institutions in India.

One of the first things Thorburn's viceroy did after assuming office was to consider "measures to elasticise the Land Revenue collections, disable money-lenders from holding agricultural land, and substitute village courts of equity for the detested technical law-courts and system of the Government."[16] However, in 1907,

[14] Note on Land Transfers, 18 March 1895, para. 178.

[15] Govt. of India, Dept. of Rev. and Agric., Land Rev., Confid. Circ. No. 24/75–1, 26 Oct. 1895, to all local governments and administrations. Enclosures to Govt. of India, Dept. of Rev. and Agric., Land Rev. No. 58 of 1895, to S. of S., 30 Oct. 1895, Rev. Letters from India, 1895. Also, S. S. Thorburn, *The Punjab in Peace and War* (London, 1904), pp. 229ff.

[16] S. S. Thorburn, *His Majesty's Greatest Subject* (London, 1897), p. 151.

Alienation of Land

before this viceroy could carry out his reforms, the Muslims formed a no-rent league in the Punjab, refused to pay the Hindu money-lenders until their accounts were "examined, principal separated from interest, compound interest cut out, and all payments already made duly credited." The district collector, Mattra Das, a member of a Lahore banking family, informed the no-rent league that under the Contract Act and the Civil Procedure Code, they had to pay the money-lenders their demands. The Hindu servants of the courts were sent to attach the property of the cultivators, a Hindu-Muslim riot ensued, and soon communal explosions flared up throughout India.[17] The British were taught a much-needed lesson—like that of 1857[18]—and the viceroy was able to get rid of "a great part of the existing laws and institutions" and substitute "simple protective and restrictive laws adapted to the mental darkness of the needy peasant millions."[19] From 1908 onward, the peasants "were no longer harassed and fleeced by usurers and usurers' allies, the law-courts and the pleaders. They were no longer required to pay land revenue when their crops had failed." They were able to borrow from the government at 4 per cent interest rather than from the money-lender at 36 per cent. Hereafter India was to "be governed on Indian lines, the form of rule being a benevolent and conservative despotism."[20] One of the viceroy's more despotic actions was to lock up 300 Indian politicians and to deport a half-dozen visiting British M. P.s. The results were beneficial: "treason-mongering ceased to be attractive."[21] Thorburn's viceroy was unusual in another way: he threw over his English fiancee and married an Indian princess with very light skin.[22]

The remedies prescribed by Lord Curzon's government for the Punjab's problems were more prosaic. It restricted the transfer of land by means of a new law, the Punjab Land Alienation Act of 1900. This act applied restrictions only to the section of population categorized as agricultural tribes. A member of an agricultural tribe was permitted to sell land to other members of his

[17] Ibid., pp. 155–159.
[18] Ibid., p. 304.
[19] Ibid., p. 277.
[20] Ibid., pp. 303–304.
[21] Ibid., pp. 97–99.
[22] Ibid., p. 279. Marriages between Indian Civil Service officers and indigenous women were discouraged. In 1903, government officers in Burma, where intermarriage was becoming increasingly frequent, were warned that such marriages would damage their opportunities for future promotion. *Summary of the Administration of Lord Curzon in the Home Department*, p. 324.

Alienation of Land

own tribe or group as he wished, but if he chose to mortgage his land to someone not belonging to his own tribe or group of tribes, the mortgage had to be "in one of three prescribed forms, which secure that either the mortgagor shall remain in cultivating possession at a reasonable rent, or that the mortgagee shall hold possession for a reasonable time not exceeding 20 years, at the expiry of which the mortgage debt and interest thereon will be considered cancelled."[23]

It was realized that the money-lenders of nonagricultural castes would be reluctant to lend money to peasants who were unable to offer their land as security. However, members of the agricultural tribes could be expected to be less improvident and when they did need capital, they would be able to borrow from their own caste members or from agricultural banks and cooperative societies.[24] There would be far less political danger in the alienation of land by, for instance, a Jat peasant to a Jat money-lender than by a Jat to a Khatri.

Before the act was passed, it encountered strong criticism from many Punjabi Congress supporters. The common argument against the act was that it ignored the basic causes of indebtedness which were said to be the exorbitant level of the government's land revenue demand and the inflexibility with which it was collected in years of distress. However, the majority of the Punjabi Hindus who attended the Congresses more than once belonged to the money-lending and commercial castes. Those most active in the Congress in the Punjab, excepting the domiciled Bengalis, were nearly all Khatris, Aroras, or Agarwals. Lala Lajpat Rai and Lala Murli Dhar were Agarwals, Bakshi Jaishi Ram was a Khatri, and Lala Harkishen Lal was an Arora. Although none of these persons seems to have been a money-lender, and although there is no necessary identity of interests between rural money-lenders and urban commercial classes, Lala Lajpat Rai, Dyal Singh Majithia,[25] Lala Harkishen Lal, and at least ten

---

[23] *Summary of the Administration of Lord Curzon in the Department of Revenue and Agriculture*, p. 25. Norman G. Barrier, *The Punjab Alienation of Land Bill of 1900* (Durham, 1966), has a thorough discussion of the bill and its preparation.

[24] The number of cooperative societies in the Punjab rose from 300 in 1901 to 1,000 in 1911. A. Latifi, *The Industrial Punjab: A Survey of Facts, Conditions and Possibilities* (Bombay, 1911), p. xviii.

[25] Dyal Singh died in September 1898 and therefore was not a party to the Alienation Bill controversy.

Alienation of Land

other persons who attended the Congress were officials of two of the earliest swadeshi or nationalist economic enterprises in the Punjab—the Punjab National Bank and the Bharat Insurance Company.[26] It seems reasonable to assume that more than a few Punjabi Congressmen had family and business ties to village money-lending interests.

The Indian Association of Lahore and the Congress press in the Punjab were united in opposition to the Alienation Bill. The Indian Association addressed an open letter to all the *sahukars* (money-lenders) of the Punjab, asking them for their opinions and commenting that the bill would lower the value of the land, destroy the credit of the agricultural classes, and injure the livelihood of the classes who, "unable to compete with Europeans in commerce and manufacture," invested their money in land.[27] The *Tribune* also estimated that the Punjabi sahukars would lose about twelve crores as a result of the bill.[28] It is interesting to note that no other major Congress newspaper was so definitely identified with a single class as the *Tribune* was with the money-lenders.[29] In 1891 the *Tribune* had published a series of articles and a pamphlet complaining about "the illegal and outrageous oppression of money-lenders by executive authorities."[30] One of the examples of oppression it gave was of the district magistrate of Amballa district who ordered the panchayats to settle disputes between debtors and money-lenders. The panchayats then coerced

---

[26] Harkishen Lal as honorary secretary, Dyal Singh Majithia as chairman, Jaishi Ram, Lala Lal Chand, and Bhagwat Ishar Das—all Congress members—had started the Punjab National Bank in Lahore in 1897, with capital of almost two and a half lakhs. By 1901 it had opened a branch in Rawalpindi and had a working capital of fifteen lakhs. The Bharat Insurance Co., Ltd., was said to be the first exclusively Indian life insurance company. Delegates to the Congress were often elected on the grounds of the Bharat Insurance Co. The Bharat Insurance Co. was floated in 1896 with the help of Seth Jassawala, a Parsi merchant of Lahore, and others. Its constitution required all its shareholders to be Indian. *Bengalee*, 19 Jan. 1901. See also Nair and Kirpal, *Dyal Singh Majithia*, p. 36, and K. L. Gauba, *The Rebel Minister: The Story of the Rise and Fall of Lala Harkishen Lal* (Lahore, 1938), p. 20.

[27] The letter was published in the *Rafiq-i-Hind* (Lahore), 25 Nov. 1899, T. and D. Selections, 1 Jan. 1900, para. 21, PSLI, Vol. 119.

[28] *Tribune*, 9 Dec. 1899, T. and D. Selections, 18 Dec. 1899, para. 953(ii), PSLI, Vol. 118.

[29] See *Tribune*, 21 Nov. 1899, T. and D. Selections, 4 Dec. 1899, para. 914(iii), PSLI, Vol. 118.

[30] [*Tribune*], *Philanthropy Run Mad* (Lahore, 1892), p. 22.

Alienation of Land

the money-lenders into surrendering part of their claims on the debtors.[31]

Not all the Muslim newspapers favored the bill, although it was the Muslim peasantry who stood to benefit most from the restriction on alienation. Lord Curzon and the Punjab government were prepared to abandon the bill in the event of Muslim opposition. Curzon thought there would be "no loss of dignity in withdrawing a Bill which has been designed in the interests of parties who are unwilling to accept it."[32] But this was not necessary because spokesmen for the Muslim community, including in the end the *Paisa Akhbar*, the newspaper with the largest circulation in the Punjab, backed the government.[33]

The educated Muslims of the Punjab had with a few exceptions remained aloof from the Congress prior to the Alienation Bill. At the 1899 Congress—the second consecutive session at which no Punjabi Muslims appeared—a resolution was adopted which would not have been accepted by Punjabi Muslims. It expressed regret at the introduction of the bill which would reduce the credit of the agriculturists and landholders and "make them more resourceless."[34] The Congress opposition to the Punjab Land Alienation Bill had been foreshadowed by an 1895 resolution criticizing proposals to restrict the right of private land alienation. The 1895 Congress endorsed the view that agricultural indebtedness was due not to the abusive use of the right of alienation, but to the ignorance of the agricultural classes and the "application of a too rigid system of fixed revenue assessment which takes little account of the fluctuating conditions of agriculture in many parts of India."[35]

The 1899 resolution was introduced by Lala Murli Dhar, a

[31] Ibid., pp. 63–66.

[32] Curzon to Hamilton, 10 May 1899, and its enclosure, Rivaz to Curzon, 3 May 1899, MSS. Eur. D. 510/1.

[33] *Paisa Akhbar* (Lahore), 17 Feb. 1900, T. and D. Selections, 12 March 1900, para. 247, PSLI, Vol. 121. Maulvi Muharram Ali Chisti, editor of the *Rafiq-i-Hind*, law student, and staunch Congress supporter, organized the Muslim zamindari support for the Alienation Bill. The Legislative Department of India printed 87 pages on translations from Muharram Ali's *Rafiq-i-Hind* articles on the bill. The views of no other person, official or nonofficial, were given so much space. Translations from *Rafiq-i-Hind*, enclosure to Sec., Rev. and Fin. Dept., Punjab, to Sec., Govt. of India, Leg. Dept., 7 July 1900, Appendix A-37, India Leg. Dept. Prog., Vol. 5,938.

[34] Resolution II of 1899. [35] Resolution X of 1895.

Alienation of Land

pleader from Amballa who owned no land himself and who was anxious not to appear to be an advocate of the sahukars. He admitted that the agricultural classes had suffered at the hands of the money-lender, whom he called "a money-grabber, a contemptible leech, . . . a man who sucks the blood of the poor agriculturist." His concern, he said, was with the zamindar who would not be able to transfer his land or to borrow in order to pay the government's revenue demand.[36] On the other hand, Lala Kanhaiya Lal, a pleader in the Lahore High Court, complained that the object of the legislation was "to crush down the money-lender."[37] The anonymous author of the introduction to the *Report* of the Lucknow Congress of 1899 also left no doubt about his sympathies. "Why," he asked, "in your zeal to protect the agriculturist from the consequences of his extravagance or improvidence . . . punish the money-lender for his shrewdness in making the best investment of his money? Surely he, too, in equity is entitled to some protection."[38]

In the months following the 1899 Congress, Muslims in the Punjab began organizing meetings in the towns and villages in support of the legislation. It was increasingly clear that public opinion was dividing along communal lines.[39] When the bill was debated at Simla in the summer of 1900, none of the Congress members of the Indian Legislative Council attended. The only Muslim member, Nawab Muhammad Hayat Khan, a retired Punjabi judge, supported the government, while Sir Harnam Singh of Kapurthala, a Congress sympathizer,[40] argued against the bill in speeches which Lord Curzon believed to have been written by "some interested pleader at Lahore."[41] Sir Harnam maintained that the bill would cause a decline in the market value of agricultural land and in "its availability for the investment of capital" which in turn would hamper "the accumulation of capital itself in the hands of the commercial classes."[42]

Muslim backing for the bill placed the Congress in the awkward position of having sided with a group of Hindus against a

[36] *Report of the 15th INC*, pp. 44–45. It is possible but unlikely that Murli Dhar's references to the character of a money-lender were ironic.
[37] Ibid., pp. 46–47.   [38] Ibid., p. xviii.
[39] Barrier, *The Punjab . . . Bill*, p. 67.   [40] Ibid., p. 71.
[41] Curzon to Hamilton, 15 Aug. 1900, MSS. Eur. D. 510/5. However, Harnum Singh was "highly educated." Barrier, *The Punjab . . . Bill*, p. 77.
[42] India LCP, 22 June 1900, XXXIX, 211–212.

Alienation of Land

cause widely supported by Muslims. When the 1900 Congress met at Lahore, the Muslim delegates from the Punjab objected to the repetition of the resolution condemning the Punjab Land Alienation Bill. In the Subjects Committee, Muharram Ali Chisti, the only Punjabi Muslim member of the committee, succeeded in persuading the delegates to omit this resolution from the list of resolutions to be presented to the open session of the 1900 Congress.[43] This was one of the few occasions on which the delegates from one religious community tried to block a resolution favored by the majority community.[44] The decision of the Subjects Committee, which was composed of 6 Muslims and 116 non-Muslims,[45] to give in to Muslim opinion was an indication of the leaders' determination to keep communal problems out of the Congress. However, the leaders' compromise was not popular with Punjabi Hindus, and it failed to win over many Punjabi Muslims to the Congress. In 1901 Sheik Umar Baksh, a Lahore pleader, Muharram Ali Chisti, and four other Punjabi Muslims went to the Congress in Calcutta. But in 1902, 1903, and 1904 no Punjabi Muslims attended, and in 1905 only Sheik Umar Baksh made the trip to Benaras.[46]

The forebearance of the 1900 Congress in dropping the Punjab Alienation Act resolution was notable when one considers that besides the money-lenders, many members of the legal profession stood to lose some of their practice under the working of the act.[47] Most of the leaders of the Congress in the Punjabi were

---

[43] *Bengalee*, 30 Dec. 1900. President Chandavarkar announced to the Congress that the matter had been dropped at the request of the Muslim members of the Subjects Committee, at least until the working of the act had been studied. (*Report of the 16th INC*, p. 70.) The decision was reached in deference to the Muslims, and not out of general sympathy with peasants as as Azim Husain has suggested in *Fazl-i-Husain: A Political Biography* (Bombay, 1946), p. 77.

[44] Resolution XIII of 1888 provided that when the Hindu or Muslim delegates as a body objected to the discussion of a subject, then it would not be discussed.

[45] *Report of the 16th INC*, pp. 24–25.

[46] See the lists of delegates for those years.

[47] The act confined jurisdiction over cases under the act to revenue officers and thus kept them out of the law courts. There was a certain amount of animus toward the legal profession in the writings of British observers who said that lawyers took unfair advantage of the poor. See Thorburn, *Musalmans and Money-Lenders* (pp. 133–134) and *His Majesty's Greatest Subject* (p. 65). Also Monier Williams, *Modern India and the Indians: Being a Series*

Alienation of Land

lawyers, including Lala Harkishen Lal, Lajpat Rai, Lala Murli Dhar, Kali Prasanna Roy, and Bakshi Jaishi Ram. At the Lahore Congress of 1900, 203 out of the 420 Punjabi delegates were in the legal profession. The only specific mention of lawyers in the 1900 Congress session was made by Surendranath Banerjea who asked with regard to the Alienation Act, "who has ever heard of a law which places the whole of the legal profession under a ban?"[48] The number of students in the Punjab Law School declined from 433 in 1896–1897 to 248 in 1900–1901, and to 159 in 1901–1902. Sir Charles Rivaz, lieutenant-governor of the Punjab, attributed the drop in part to the Alienation Act.[49]

Despite earlier signs of stiff opposition to the Alienation Act, it came into effect in June 1901 without much excitement or difficulty. But official figures on net sales and mortgages indicate its effects were significant. Whereas before 1901 the agricultural tribes were losing land, after the enactment of the Alienation Act the process was first slowed, and then after 1906–1907, as the table shows, the tribes experienced a net gain in acres sold, according to official statistics.

ANNUAL AVERAGE AREA SOLD, IN ACRES[50]

	By Agricultural Tribes	To Agricultural Tribes	Gain or Loss
1902–1903 to 1905–1906	150,000	149,000	− 1,000
1906–1907 to 1910–1911	170,000	178,000	+ 8,000
1911–1912 to 1915–1916	188,000	217,000	+39,000 (sic)*

* This should read +29,000; the error is in the original table.

Similarly, the amount of land mortgaged to and reclaimed by the agricultural tribes exceeded the amount of land mortgaged by the agricultural tribes by an annual average of 150,000 acres from 1902–1903 to 1905–1906, by an average of 275,000 acres

---

of *Impressions, Notes, and Essays* (London, 1878), p. 145. Sir Michael O'Dwyer (*India As I Knew It: 1885–1925* [London, 1925], pp. 254-255) wrote in 1925 that the Punjab Land Alienation Act "was and still is strongly opposed by the urban middle classes, who regard the peasantry as theirs to exploit."

[48] *Report of the 16th INC*, p. 71.   [49] *Bengalee*, 10 Feb. 1903.
[50] The table is from Calvert, *The Wealth and Welfare of the Punjab*, p. 266.

Alienation of Land

from 1906–1907 to 1910–1911, and by an average of 244,000 acres from 1911–1912 to 1915–1916.[51]

The Punjab Land Alienation Act did not in the long run reduce either peasant indebtedness or the transfer of land. Rather, it forced peasants in need of credit to turn to a new class of money-lenders made up of wealthier members of their own agricultural communities.[52] Its effects, therefore, were more political than economic. Although officials had hoped the act would benefit cultivators economically, "the primary purpose" had been the political one of restricting the opportunities of Khatris, Aroras, and other urban trading castes from acquiring the land of Muslim and low-caste cultivators.[53] In this negative and political sense, the act was a successful measure of social engineering.

The act both angered and embarrassed Hindu Congressmen. It was perceived as an attempt to drive a wedge between Hindus and Muslims and between rural and urban economic interests.[54] It also showed that when forced to choose between, on the one hand, a protective measure which was apparently welcomed by spokesmen for the peasants it was intended to help and, on the other, opportunities for money-lenders and urban professionals to obtain interest and land, Punjabi Hindu Congress members choose the latter with few exceptions.[55] This was not due to any moral failing peculiar to Congressmen in the Punjab. They did not pursue their economic self-interest in ways noticeably different from economic interest groups in other colonial and noncolonial societies. Nationalists movements everywhere are subject to strains imposed by the spread of the institutions associated with capitalism, including a cash economy, a legal system based upon European rather than indigenous traditions, and competitive examinations. When these strains appear in colonial societies, they present colonial governments with welcome chances to weaken and embarrass nationalist movements at the same time they pose difficult choices for nationalists with divided alle-

[51] Ibid., p. 267.
[52] Barrier, *The Punjab . . . Bill*, pp. 82–83.
[53] Ibid., p. 89.   [54] Ibid., pp. 90–92.
[55] This interpretation differs from Bipan Chandra's. Bipan Chandra attributes nationalist opposition to land alienation legislation almost wholly to intellectual judgments about the fundamental causes of indebtedness, and he ignores, for the most part, the connections between nationalists, money-lenders, and the money-lenders' lawyers. See *Economic Nationalism*, pp. 473, 476, 478, 481, and 483.

giances. The Punjab case was an extreme example, for in no other province of India was Congress membership so closely identified with such a narrow range of economic interests. And yet in the end, the Lahore Congress of 1900, with its large delegation of Punjabi Hindus, upheld the principle that the interests of national unity should prevail over those of particular class or religious groups. Upholding this principle was costly because as a result the Congress "lost considerable Punjabi Hindu support."[56] This loss was not compensated by any immediate increase in Punjabi Muslim membership in the Congress. As we have seen, Punjabi Muslims avoided the Congress almost to a man during the succeeding years. However, the Congress's decision to drop the Land Alienation Act issue did set an important precedent and it did leave open the possibility of a future rapprochment with Punjabi Muslims.

Bombay

The politics surrounding the land alienation legislation in Bombay in 1901 resembled those of the Punjab in certain respects. The Government of Bombay was trying to limit the transfer of land from cultivating castes (Marathas and Kunbis) to the money-lending and professional castes (Marwaris, Gujars, and Brahmans). When the nationalists in Bombay, most of whom were Brahmans, lined up solidly against the bill, government officials accused them of class partisanship. Beyond this, the resemblances diminish. Indian opinion in Bombay did not divide clearly along class, communal, or caste lines. The Muslim population of the Deccan was small and it was scarcely affected by the legislation. There did not appear to be widespread Maratha and Kunbi support for the legislation. If officials hoped to rally Maharashtrian cultivating castes behind the government in opposition to the Brahmans, they had to wait for other issues. The latent anti-Brahmanism did not emerge much more clearly in 1901 than it had during the Deccan riots of 1875 when cultivators attacked money-lenders in Poona and Ahmednagar districts but, in the process, generally spared the Marathi-speaking Brahman sahukars and singled out the alien-seeming Marwaris and Gujars instead.[57]

[56] Barrier, *The Punjab . . . Bill*, p. 89.
[57] *Deccan Riots Commission Report*, paras. 12 and 39. Altogether, the rioters

The 1875 riots had led to the Deccan Agriculturalists Relief Act of 1879 which curtailed the legal advantages enjoyed by money-lenders belonging to noncultivating castes in realizing their debts. The Relief Act covered the four districts of Ahmednagar, Poona, Satara, and Sholapur.

Although the act stimulated an increase in money-lending by members of cultivating castes, especially Marathas, who were not limited under the act,[58] it failed to halt the alienation of land. By 1899 the percentage of land alienated in the four districts was reported to be 35.02, 24.42, 12.53, and 21.72, respectively.[59] Sir Anthony MacDonnell, whose 1895 recommendation of new legislation had not originally been accepted by the Government of Bombay, used his Famine Commission Report of 1901 to call attention again to the extent of indebtedness in Bombay. The Famine Commission estimated that probably "one-fourth of the cultivators in the Bombay Presidency have lost possession of their lands; that less than a fifth are free from debt; and that the remainder are indebted to a greater or lesser extent."[60]

Although the Bombay government's own statistics did not yield as grim an estimate, the provincial administration had been converted to the position that remedial legislation was needed. Fear of the nationalist movement seems to have been a decisive element in official discussions. In justifying amendments to the Deccan Agriculturalists Relief Act, the Bombay government explained that the rapid transfer of land was "fraught with alarm" because the dispossessed would be fertile ground for political agitators. Brahman agitators had organized the no-tax campaign in 1896–1897 and, according to the Bombay government, they directed from Poona an organization "for calling public meetings

---

were selective and discriminating. Not only did they distinguish between castes, they also avoided major violence to persons, generally, concentrating on money-lenders' records instead. There were 951 arrests and 501 convictions for assault, arson, and other offences in the two districts. Ibid., para. 10.

[58] I. J. Catanach, *Rural Credit in Western India 1875–1930: Rural Credit and the Co-operative Movement in the Bombay Presidency* (Berkeley, 1970), p. 26.

[59] J.W.P. Muir-Mackenzie, Sec., Govt. of Bombay, to Sec., Govt. of India, Dept. of Rev. and Agric., 7 Oct. 1899, Rev. No. 7100/168 of 1899, para. 8. Bombay Rev. Prog., Land, Vol. 5,777.

[60] *Report of the Indian Famine Commission, 1901*, para. 355.

to protest against the acts of Government whenever they appear distasteful to certain classes."[61]

However, the separation of cultivator class interests from those of Brahmans was by no means as complete as officials might have wished. The fact that in the 1875 riots Brahman lenders usually had not been molested and that "in some cases the rioters had the support and countenance of persons of influence in their neighborhood"[62] indicated that Brahman sahukars, who were often landholders themselves, exercised a hold on their debtors that was not entirely coercive. During the 1899–1900 famine, money-lenders were thought to be withholding the cultivators' revenue payments to the government with the object of getting the cultivators' obligations for the year suspended or canceled. This meant that some Brahman money-lenders and some Brahman politicians were ostensibly acting on behalf of non-Brahman cultivators.[63] This complicated official efforts to place the government between peasants and nationalists in the role of protectors of the former.

Nevertheless, the Government of Bombay introduced the Bombay Land Revenue Code Amendment Bill in May 1901 to check the extensive transfer of agricultural land. The bill gave revenue officials the authority to cause lands for which the revenue was in arrears to be forfeited, and to grant the former cultivator a new short-term lease for the land on the condition that the right of occupancy would lapse if the leasee alienated his land without official permission. The government expected that under the bill a new class of occupants would appear alongside the older type of occupants. The older type were the men with means and credit who would retain their transferable and hereditable right to the land. The new class would consist of the cultivators without means who could not pay the land revenue and who would have neither the power of transfer nor the traditional thirty-year settle-

[61] J.W.P. Muir-Mackenzie, 7 Oct. 1899, para. 12.
[62] *Deccan Riots Commission Report*, para. 119.
[63] Although money-lenders would not necessarily have shared the amount remitted with the cultivators. Catanach, *Rural Credit in Western India*, p. 40. It should be remembered that Brahmans not only rented and owned agricultural but also, in some cases, worked the land themselves. Anandibai Karve, a Chitpavan, makes it clear, without suggesting that it was unusual, that her parents burned over their field, ploughed, sowed, transplanted, milked cows, etc. D. D. Karve (ed.), *The New Brahmans*, pp. 59 and 63.

ment.⁶⁴ Under the new law it was theoretically possible for as much as one-fifth of the land in Bombay Presidency and up to one-half in certain districts, to come under the new form of tenancy.⁶⁵ It therefore could significantly alter the economic status of many thousands of peasants, leaving them dependent upon official policy to an unprecedented degree.

The bill was "unanimously" condemned by the Indian newspapers of Bombay Presidency,⁶⁶ and it was severely criticized in numerous public meetings. The new governor, Lord Northcote, and the secretary of state believed that the money-lenders were responsible for the opposition.⁶⁷ Money-lenders were aroused, of course, for not only was the bill designed to prevent them from acquiring land, it would place obstacles in the way of recovering their debts. A number of nationalist critics were motivated by concern for the money-lenders' welfare. Tilak, for instance, predicted that the bill would ruin the sahukar and destroy the mutual relationship between money-lender and ryot.⁶⁸ Tilak's newspaper, the *Mahratta*, whose editor, N. C. Kelkar, was the son of a money-leader,⁶⁹ complained of the government's "zeal to kill money-lenders." The government, it said, feared the social and political influence of the money-lender over the ryot, and "it was evidently to the interest of the Government that the money-lender be crushed and his influence undermined."⁷⁰ N. C. Kelkar wrote an article in which he protested that the bill would interfere with the realization by the money-lenders of their "legal

⁶⁴ Speech of James Monteath, Sec., Bombay Rev. and Fin. Depts., Bombay LCP, 30 May 1901, XXXIX, 178–186.

⁶⁵ Catanach, *Rural Credit in Western India*, p. 40.

⁶⁶ Summary of newspaper comment on the bill. T. and D. Selections, 24 June 1901, para. 432, PSLI, Vol. 135. Actually, there was at least one newspaper which supported the bill. It was *Dnyanodaya*, a Bombay Anglo-Marathi weekly which was edited by an Indian Christian. Its circulation was 625.

⁶⁷ Hamilton to Curzon, 2 Oct. 1901, MSS. Eur. C. 126/3.

⁶⁸ Pradhan and Bhagwat, *Tilak*, pp. 132–133.

⁶⁹ Statement of English Newspapers and Periodicals Published in the Bombay Presidency during 1905, May Jud. Dept. (Confid.) Prog. No. 2, Jud. Dept. Prog., Confid., Vol. 7,476. The editors of the *Gujarati* (Bombay) and the *Shri Sayaji Vijaya* (Baroda) were Banias, and the editor of the *Dnyan Prakash* and the *Karmanuk* (Poona) was a money-lender. These newspapers were among the most widely circulated in the presidency. Statement of Anglo-Vernacular and Vernacular Newspapers and Periodicals Published in Bombay Presidency during 1905.

⁷⁰ *Mahratta*, 7 July 1901, Bom. NNR, 13 July 1901, para. 30.

Alienation of Land

dues" from the cultivators.[71] Daji Abaji Khare, another prominent Congressman, defended the money-lenders in the Legislative Council and alleged that the bill was aimed "at the extinction of the saving classes."[72] Two well-known extremists, S. M. Paranjpe, editor of the *Kal*, landowner, and the son of a money-lender,[73] and Bala Sahib Natu, a landowner and a major money-lender, were active in the agitation against the bill.[74] There is no doubt, then, that part of the opposition to the bill came from nationalists with money-lending interests and associates.

The official in charge of the bill in the Bombay Legislative Council tried to capitalize on that fact by implying that the opposition arose out of misrepresentations and concern for the money-lender by organizations such as the Sarvajanik Sabha rather than out of broader economic or practical objections.[75] Five of the elected members of the council claimed this was "a breach of decorum" and an insult to their integrity, and they walked out of the Legislative Council in protest.[76] This seems to have been the first walk-out in the history of the nationalist movement.

Officials miscalculated when they attributed the deep resentment against the bill so exclusively to the money-lenders and their friends. Despite the close ties between individual Maharashtrian nationalists and money-lenders, there is little reason to believe that intimate family, caste, or professional links with sahukars were general among Chitpavan Congress supporters. Most of the arguments marshaled against the bill seem not to have been inspired by concern for the welfare of money-lenders. G. K. Gokhale, for example, saw two possible consequences, neither of which, he said, would help the large class of ryots who were "practically serfs in the hands" of the sahukars. Either the sahukars would pay the revenue themselves in order to prevent land mortgaged to them from being forfeited to the government and at

[71] N. C. Kelkar, "The Recent Land Legislation in Bombay," *Kayastha Samachar*, Vol. IV, Nos. 3 and 4 (Sept.–Oct. 1901), 237.

[72] Bombay LCP, 23 Aug. 1901, XXXIX, 327.

[73] Statement of the Anglo-Vernacular and Vernacular Newspapers and Periodicals Published in the Bombay Presidency during 1905.

[74] See *Kesari*, 3 Sept. 1901, Bom. NNR, 7 Sept. 1901, para. 50.

[75] Speech of James Monteath, Bombay LCP, 23 Aug. 1901, XXXIX, 272.

[76] Ibid., pp. 367–368. The five were P. M. Mehta, Sir Balchandra Krishna, G. K. Parekh, D. A. Khare, and G. K. Gokhale.

Alienation of Land

the same time keep the cultivators in a state of debt bondage; or, if a large portion of the land was forfeited into government hands, then the bill would constitute "a scheme for the nationalization" of agrarian holdings. In neither case would the professed beneficiaries of the bill be better off.[77]

From editorial comments, it was clear that many educated Indians feared the bill would lead to nationalization of the land or state landlordism.[78] Effective nationalization would occur in the following way. Because a landed proprietor could no longer offer his land as security, he would be unable to borrow from the money-lender. In consequence, the cultivator in many cases would not be in a position to pay the revenue demand and the government would cause the land to be forfeited. The landed proprietor would become a tenant-at-will of the government or perhaps even a field laborer. The general view was that to come under the new short-term lease would be far more objectionable than whatever hardships were involved in the alienation of land to the money-lenders under the standard thirty-year settlement.[79]

The Bombay government made a tactical mistake by not making a convincing effort to persuade its opponents that it had no intention of bringing large areas of land under direct state control. James Monteath, the member of the Bombay Legislative Council in charge of the bill, actually gave the impression that state landlordism was the aim of the government when he said that unless arrears of revenue were paid up more fully than in the past, "there will be an opportunity of creating the special [nontransferable] tenure in some districts on a very extensive scale."[80] Instead of emphasizing how the bill might free cultivators from bondage to the money-lenders, Monteath's statement encouraged people to believe that the government was planning to use the famine-induced borrowing of peasants as an excuse to interfere in the thirty-year revenue settlement and, in the process, threaten their occupancy rights.[81]

[77] Bombay LCP, 24 Aug. 1901, XXXIX, 336–344.

[78] State landlordism was distinguished from the ryotwari system in that, under the latter, the cultivator was secure from enhancement for thirty-year periods.

[79] There is a general summary of newspaper comment on the Bombay Revenue Code Amendment Bill in Bom. NNR, 22 June 1901, para. 43.

[80] Bombay LCP, 30 May 1901, XXXIX, 186.

[81] Hamilton to Curzon, 2 Oct. 1901, MSS. Eur. C. 126/3.

Alienation of Land

Critics of the bill had reason to assume on the basis of recent experience that the government would be far less flexible than private creditors in times of scarcity. Popular confidence in the government's intentions and responsiveness to human suffering had been undermined in the preceding five years. Two famines had levied a major toll upon the health, savings, and livestock, as well as on human spirits, in rural areas. Bubonic plague was still bringing violent death periodically to the towns and villages of Maharashtra. The Bombay administration had reacted to these natural disasters with harsh measures. When educated nationalists complained of the forcible searches for and detention of plague patients, the high food prices, and the failure to grant extensive revenue remissions, they were undoubtedly speaking for many uneducated Maharashtrians. The government was aware that distrust was widespread, but officials considered that the government's authority had been challenged by the resistance to its plague measures, the Rand-Ayerst murders, and the no-rent campaign. It was determined to demonstrate its power and to leave no doubt in people's mind about its political strength. In the towns it did this by using the military for plague work and by detaining the Natus and prosecuting newspaper editors. In the villages it was actually engaged in a trial of strength with cultivators over the payment of the revenue. Reference has been made to the stringency employed in collecting the revenue during the 1896–1897 famine in consequence of the no-rent campaign. In the two years intervening between that famine and the next, the government experienced further difficulty in collecting the revenue and resorted to coercive measures on an exceptional scale, especially in the Central Division where Poona is located, as the figures given in the table on the following page show.[82]

The determination not to pay the revenue increased in both Marathi- and Gujarati-speaking areas with the famine of 1899–1900. The collectors of Surat, Nasik, Kaira, and Ahmedabad Districts reported organized combinations against the payment of the revenue demand. In all four districts, the principal offenders, they said, were the money-lenders and the more prosperous agriculturists who were in a position to meet the demand. Members

[82] Reports of the Revenue Settlements of the Northern, Central, and Southern Divisions and of the Department of Land Records and Agriculture for the Year 1898–99. Bombay Rev. Dept. No. 6,680, 25 Oct. 1900. Bombay Rev. Prog., Land, Vol. 5,967.

Alienation of Land

	Average from 1892–1893 to 1896–1897	1897–1898	1898–1899
Number of notices served annually for nonpayment of revenue demand			
Northern Division	32,605	44,713	53,651
Central Division	35,284	126,665	109,216
Southern Division	13,933	28,987	32,973
Cases of distraint and sale of moveable property			
Northern Division	189	475	375
Central Division	26	194	2,269
Southern Division	226	352	667
Number of forfeitures and sales of occupancy			
Northern Division	573	942	565
Central Division	92	287	703
Southern Division	90	136	413

of the Sarvajanik Sabha were not implicated in this as they had been during the earlier famine. Revenue officials succeeded in breaking the resistance to payment by serving notices on, and causing the forfeiture of, lands belonging to defaulters, and by singling out the leaders of the no-rent campaign for the more extreme forms of compulsion such as attachment of moveable property.[83] But the impression remained among nationalists and even many officials that the revenue assessment in Bombay was too high and that in years of drought it was collected with too much rigidity.[84]

Officials in the Government of India were aware of popular

[83] Extracts from Reports by Collectors of Kaira, Ahmedabad, Broach, Surat, Khandesh, and Nasik. Bombay LCP, 24 Aug. 1900, Appendix H, XXXVIII, 189–192.

[84] See *Report of the Indian Famine Commission, 1901*, paras. 241 and 265–268; Gerald F. Keatinge, *Rural Economy in the Bombay Deccan* (London, 1912), p. 25; Vaughan Nash, *The Great Famine and Its Causes* (London, 1900); and Evan Maconochie, *Life in the Indian Civil Service* (London, 1926), pp. 125–127.

Alienation of Land

dissatisfactions with recent Bombay administrative performance, and they were impressed by the opposition to the Land Revenue Code Amendment Bill as expressed in the Legislative Council, editorials, and more than five hundred vernacular petitions. The secretary of state considered rejecting the bill but decided against it, "for such a slap in the face to a Presidential Government would be an encouragement to the money-lending class all throughout India."[85] Instead, the Government of India scolded the Bombay administration for its haste in enacting the legislation.[86] And when the Government of India sanctioned the act, it imposed administratively some limits on its scope. The operation of the act was restricted by insisting that the new form of tenure should not be "forced upon cultivators whose revenue had been remitted or suspended."[87]

There was one other piece of land legislation, the reception to which gives additional clues to how nationalists in Bombay regarded class legislation. It was a bill to amend the Khoti Settlement Act of 1880. The bill, which was introduced in 1899, applied only to Ratnagiri district and in comparison to the land alienation bill, it aroused little controversy. The section to which a number of nationalists objected required tenants to pay their rents to the khots, the hereditary revenue collectors, in a fixed cash payment instead of as a share of the crop. The Bombay government hoped that tenants would thereby sell their own crop and gain the profits of a cash sale, instead of surrendering all the profits to the khots.[88]

Many khots were Chitpavan Brahmans. The ancestors of several key nationalists (for example, Ranade,[89] Gokhale, and Tilak)[90] had been khots in Ratnagiri district on the Bombay Konkan. Tilak's family, at least, still owned khoti rights. Possibly the connections between nationalist Chitpavans and Ratnagiri khots explain why the five Indians on the Bombay Legislative

[85] Hamilton to Curzon, 22 Aug. 1901, MSS. Eur. C. 126/3.

[86] The Bombay government had prepared a draft bill in 1899, but it had decided not to introduce it at that time. Then in May 1901, without advance notice, it submitted a revised bill to the Legislative Council for rapid action. Catanach, *Rural Credit in Western India*, p. 41.

[87] *Summary of the Administration of Lord Curzon in the Department of Revenue and Agriculture*, p. 27.

[88] Bombay LCP, 25 Jan. 1899, XXXVII, 13-14.

[89] *Ranade: His Wife's Reminiscences*, p. 17.

[90] Wolpert, *Tilak and Gokhale*, p. 14.

Council who were connected with the Congress voted against the first reading of the bill.[91] Daji Abaji Khare, who acted as spokesman for landlord and money-landing interests, argued that the khots had converted Ratnagiri from a sterile to a fertile district, that the bill would excite "false hopes in the breasts of ignorant ryots," and that "above all it entirely supersedes vested interests."[92] In the Congress itself, M. R. Bodas, a Brahman High Court pleader, had complained of the "retrograde" policy of the government in introducing the khoti and "other tenancy Bills."[93] Tilak wrote a series of articles deploring government usurpation of khoti rights. "Just as the Government has no right to rob the Sowcar and distribute his wealth among the poor, in the same way Government have no right to deprive the Khot of his rightful income and distribute the money to the peasant."[94] The Khot Amendment Bill was finally passed as Act III of 1904.

This review of nationalist reactions to the Bombay legislation restricting land transfer and protecting the khots' tenants yields few determinate conclusions about the class bases or social ideas of the nationalist movement. The land alienation legislation imposed a constraint on the opportunities of Brahmans to lend money and obtain land. That reason alone explains the opposition of some individuals. But it also offered the government potential control over the landed resources of non-Brahman cultivators which no other provincial administration possessed. This was worrying to people who distrusted either the wisdom or the intentions of the government. The legislation also ignored the inflexibility and the pitch of the land revenue demand which nationalists considered to be the major causes of rural poverty and debt. It is important to recognize the plausibility of nationalist arguments about the land revenue demand. Nationalists tended not to see elements of class self-interest in their reasoning when they could reach the same conclusion through an alternative line of argument, through an argument which ignored their particular vested interests and emphasized instead how all Indians would benefit from a change in policy. By attributing rural in-

[91] D. A. Khare, G. K. Parekh, G. B. Garud, Balchandra Krishna, and N. Chandravarkar.
[92] Bombay LCP, 25 Jan. 1899, XXXVII, 21–28.
[93] *Report of the 14th INC*, p. 65.
[94] Pradhan and Bhagwat, *Tilak*, p. 134.

debtedness to revenue administration and the economic drain rather than to weaknesses in tenancy and usury laws, they were protecting their self-respect as disinterested nation-builders. Most nationalists were also guarded in their comments about relations between classes. Little immediate advantage was to be gained by discussing the Indian social structure because it would surely divide educated Indians and divert attention from the drain, the excessiveness of the land revenue demand, and political reform.

Peasants remained an abstraction for most nationalists just after the turn of the century as the controversies about property rights subsided. Although Congressmen had an improved intellectual awareness of the tangle of rural property rights and of the depth of disagreement about these rights within Indian society, before 1905 only Tilak, Lajpat Rai, and a handful of others had made serious organizational efforts to reach cultivators. Peasants were still pressed into rhetorical service at political meetings as a group which would benefit from representative government. Yet few politicians felt it necessary to explain in what sense they represented the specific interests of landless laborers or cultivating tenants. Particular peasants may have appeared in memories of a rural childhood, and they may have been casually greeted on visits to an ancestral village or family holding, but few Congressmen had kinship or sustained face-to-face relations with cultivators. Most cultivators were still "non-citizens," as Nirad C. Chaudhuri put it in his autobiography, even for Congressmen who lived in rural towns. Nationalists in metropolitan areas lived in a separate world altogether, in a world whose language and activities would have seemed alien to most peasants, if they had had an opportunity to observe them. This separation, though, had its own limited, positive consequence for the development of nationalism. It meant an absence of conflict between urban professionals and cultivators, except in the Punjab. The major political tensions were within the elites in most parts of India prior to 1905, and thus, Congress leaders were far more concerned with competition and cooperation between themselves and zamindars than with an apolitical peasantry.

PART IV

Chapter Nine

COW PROTECTION AND NATIONAL POLITICS

The last two decades of the nineteenth century witnessed a growing reaction against religious reform movements among Hindu and Muslim groups. Organizations for the defense of traditional religions were founded in every province in India. In addition, reformist groups split as moderate factions charged that radical reformers had become denationalized or too extreme in their rejection of community customs. Hindus who had previously been unorganized now openly defended idol worship, caste, the sanctity of the Puranas and cows, and the legitimacy of customary marriage practices. Muslims stressed Pan-Islamic identification with the interests of non-Indian Muslims, a revived role for the ulama, and resistance to the study of modern science. And although defenders of religious tradition often accepted part of the reformers' programs and although the process of debate often led to new syntheses and religious reconstruction, arguments over what constituted proper religious behavior in the 1880s and 1890s divided Hindus from Hindus and Muslims from Muslims to a degree that was unprecedented in the nineteenth century. Brahmo Samajists, Arya Samajists, and Sudharaks clashed with Sanatanists, as orthodox Hindus were coming to be known. And the Wahabhis and Deobandi scholars differed fundamentally with the Aligarh school. In terms of the numbers of people involved and the intensity of passions aroused, intracommunal conflict would seem to have been much greater in late nineteenth-century India than Hindu-Muslim conflict.

However, controversies about religious obligations did affect Hindu-Muslim relations as well. The revived interest in one's own cultural identity led to a sharper consciousness of the cultures of the other religious groups which inhabited the Indian subcontinent. Certain Hindus and Muslims who were seeking a clearer identity asserted the superiority of their own community's traditions and attacked religious and linguistic syncretism within their communities. As Indians developed new pride in their Indianness, often they did so through a heightened appreciation of their particular religious traditions, with the result that they mistook a specifically Hindu or Islamic identity for an Indian identity. Hindus reacted to British overlordship by discovering ethical and spiritual qualities in Hinduism that enabled them to regard their own culture as equal or superior to Christianity. This was true of reformers and nonreformers alike. Whether they supported the Arya Samaj, the Theosophical Society, the Hindu Tract Society of Madras, a Hindu Sabha, a kirtan singing group, or a Shivaji festival, Hindus tended to define their Indian identity in a Hindu manner. Muslims were at least as likely to find the pride necessary to face the British exclusively within Islamic history and religion. Muslim revival movements were stimulated by the double consciousness of their former imperial dominance and their minority status. The developing appreciation of the worthiness of Indian culture was therefore producing not a single cultural revival but separate revivals with potential for rivalry.

The anxieties arising out of controversies about religious obligations and out of the tensions associated with accelerating social change led certain Hindus and Muslims to seek scapegoats outside their own religious groups. The unsettling developments of the late nineteenth century triggered religious antagonisms between Hindus and Muslims where they had not existed. The new competition between elites for access to education, bureaucratic employment, and decision-making bodies often gave religious differences a political significance. The founding of the Indian National Congress in particular encouraged Muslims to define the elite rivalry for secular power in terms of religious community. The competition between Hindu and Muslim elites in turn merged with disagreements over popular religious practices on occasion. Most notably, elite conflict became intertwined with the controversy over the right to slaughter cows. The Hindu cow protection movement of the late 1880s and early 1890s challenged the Muslim practice of cow slaughter and provoked a series of serious riots in 1893.

The year 1893 was one of the worst years for Hindu-Muslim relations in the nineteenth century. More than one hundred people were killed in communal riots related to cow slaughter in such widely separated places as Bombay city, Junagadh state, the

North-Western Provinces and Oudh, Bihar, and Rangoon. Over eight hundred persons were arrested in the North-Western Provinces district of Azamgarh alone. Although each incident of communal violence was contained within a relatively small area, the unusual spread of the riots from one side of the Indian empire to the other was interpreted as a sign of a general deterioration in Hindu-Muslim relations. The riots gave credence to Muslim and British arguments that a third party was needed to arbitrate disputes and maintain a balance between Hindus and Muslims. Some British officials concluded from the riots that nationalists were starting to mobilize the lower classes for political purposes. The Viceroy, Lord Lansdowne, said that the cow protection movement was transforming the Indian National Congress from "a foolish debating society into a real political power, backed by the most dangerous elements in native society."[1] Actually, Lansdowne misunderstood the Congress attitude toward the movement, for the Congress leaders deeply regretted the movement's effect on Hindu-Muslim relations. But he was correct in perceiving that the Congress organization and program had aroused concern among social strata which never attended Congress meetings.

Both the timing of the riots and the newspaper comments indicated that the disturbances were connected with Congress-Muslim disagreements over the legislative council reforms that were passed in 1892. Cow protectors hoped to achieve a legislative restriction on the slaughter of kine. This stiffened Muslim resistance to the idea of majority rule and the Indian National Congress. The refusal of Congress leaders to allow the Congress to support cow protection did not lead Muslims to differentiate clearly between the Congress and the protection movement. Rather, the Congress demand for representative government and the cow protectors' call for legal measures against slaughter appeared to Muslims to be closely related threats to the Muslim minority. The protection movement and the 1893 riots therefore dimmed what still remained of Congress hopes of attracting significant Muslim support for their goals. They accentuated the very cultural differences the Congress sought to overcome, and they threw into relief a seemingly irreconcilable conflict over religious obligations and rights.

[1] Lansdowne to Kimberley, 22 Aug. 1893, quoted in Ghose, *The Indian National Congress*, p. 63.

Cow Protection

The 1893 riots were the climax of a cow protection (*gaurakshini*) movement which had spread in the previous five years through western Bihar, eastern North-Western Provinces and Oudh, and the Central Provinces. Prior to the late 1880s, concerted efforts to stop cow killing had been mainly limited to the Punjab. The new cow protection movement was supported by groups of Hindus with varied social backgrounds, as well as different (although often overlapping) motives. For some, it was an expression of the belief that the cultural values of the original inhabitants and the majority should prevail. Although many of these persons regarded Muslims as alien offenders of Hindu custom, many considered the British, as the rulers and major consumers of beef, to be the chief culprits. A second group first joined the movement for reasons which were primarily economic. They saw improvement in the quantity and quality of India's cattle as a means of increasing the health and prosperity of all Indians. A third group, active in the events which precipitated the riots, seemed to be defending the cow in order to strike back at the attacks on orthodox Hinduism by Hindu social reformers and British legislators. Anxious about their status in the emerging social order, they approached the cow protection issue as an opportunity to reassert their role as upholders of eroding Hindu values. Thus within each of these three categories of cow protectors, there were substantial numbers of persons who were not motivated primarily by antagonism toward Muslims or Islam. The fact that the movement culminated in communal violence in 1893 and that it provoked counterassertions of community identification among Muslims was regretted, and not anticipated, by many original supporters of the movement.

The development of an organized cow protection movement, beginning with the Sikh Kuka (or Namdhari) sect in the Punjab around 1870 and dissipating in the aftermath of the 1893 riots, is revealing of the dynamics of Indian communalism. The original spread of the movement from the Kukas to the Arya Samaj in the Punjab and then to landholders, shopkeepers, lawyers, and sadhus in central and north-central India was the result of strains within Hindu and Sikh society more than of Hindu-Muslim rivalry. The history of the nineteenth-century gaurakshini movement indicates that reformist attacks on traditional religious practices stimulated counterorganization by conservatives who, in competing with reformers, appropriated major elements of the reformers' program. It was only after the Kukas and Arya Samaj reformers had adopted cow protection that large numbers of conservative Hindus joined the movement. And it was only after conservative Hindus took over leadership of the gaurakshini movement that serious communal violence occurred.

The gaurakshini movement was a species of subnationalism. When cow protectors filed suits in the law courts challenging the right to kill kine, or when they tried to intercept cattle on the way to commissariats, butcher shops, cattle fairs, and Muslim sacrifices, they affirmed the supremacy of Hindu customs and openly challenged the right of Muslims and the British to violate religious traditions of the majority. They were shaping and defining the Hindu community by affirming what was and was not right Hindu behavior. In the process, they were excluding Muslims from the primary community or nation.

Cow slaughter subsided soon after the 1893 riots as a major political problem. But it has reemerged on several occasions since 1893 as a troublesome issue. As recently as November 1966, eight persons were killed and 47 injured in front of parliament in New Delhi during a demonstration by 200,000 people in favor of an all-India ban on cow slaughter.[2] The cow issue has not otherwise been a major source of controversy since 1947, presumably because Congress majorities in a number of state legislative assemblies have fulfilled the goal of nineteenth-century gaurakshini agitators by passing laws prohibiting the slaughter of cows and because Indian Muslims are too weak to block such legislation now that the British are gone and India is partitioned. The passage of state cow protection laws since 1947 and the inclusion of Article 48 in the Directive Principles of State Policy in the Indian Constitution, which says "The state shall . . . take steps for preserving and improving the breeds, and prohibiting the slaughter, of cows and calves and other milch and draught cattle," are measures of the persistence of Hindu sentiment regarding cow protection.[3] It is also significant that after independence, Indira Gandhi's Congress Party used as its electoral symbol a representation of a cow suckling her calf and maternally licking the calf's back.

[2] *New York Times*, 21 Nov. 1966.
[3] Individual Muslims have supported the laws in some cases. Donald Eugene Smith, *India as a Secular State* (Princeton, 1963), pp. 484-487.

THE BACKGROUND

Ancient Hindu religious attitudes toward the cow probably stemmed from the animal's economic significance. The practical value of the *Gau Mata*—the mother cow—is suggested in an ironic rhyme from Mysore:

> Living, I yield milk, butter and curd, to sustain mankind
> My dung is as fuel used,
> Also to wash the floor and wall;
> Or burnt, becomes the sacred ash on forehead.
> When dead, of my skin are sandals made,
> Or the bellows at the blacksmith's furnace;
> Of my bones are buttons made . . .
> But of what use are you, O Man?[4]

If the special feeling for the cow originated in a need to protect a valuable resource in an early period of Indian history, religious practices and texts, beginning with the Veda, magnified its significance. In the Vedic period, Brahman priests were paid for their sacrifices with cows; goddesses were flattered by comparing them with cows; the cow and the bull became common Vedic symbols for maternity, fertility, and virility; and the products of the cow occupied a central place in Vedic sacrifices. And yet, for all the importance assigned the cow in the Vedic literature, it was not treated as "sacred and inviolable."[5]

By the start of the Gupta period (fourth century), literary sources were referring to the cow's inviolability, although there is no reason to believe that it was generally accepted by non-Brahmans. Both the *Mahabharata* and the *Ramayana* contain episodes illustrating the divine qualities of the Kamdhenu, or the cow who grants wishes, which belonged to the great sage Vasishtha. In

[4] *New York Times*, 8 Nov. 1966. Gandhi also compared the cow's value with the value of humans. He once said that "Mother cow is in many ways better than the mother who gave us birth. Our mother gives us milk for a couple of years and then expects us to serve her when we grow up. Mother cow expects from us nothing but grass and grain. Our mother often falls ill and expects service from us. Mother cow rarely falls ill. Our mother when she dies means expenses of burial or cremation. Mother cow is as useful dead as when alive." Quoted from *Harijan*, 15 Sept. 1940 in M. K. Gandhi, *Hindu Dharma* (Ahmedabad, 1950), p. 309.

[5] W. Norman Brown, "The Sanctity of the Cow in Hinduism," *Journal of the Madras University*, XXVIII, 2 (Jan. 1957), 30–31.

the *Mahabharata*, the milk of Vasishtha's cow, Nandini, is said to make man immortal.[6] In the *Ramayana*, Vasishtha's cow is called Sabala and is a "fountain of unfailing plenty" who gives the rishi enormous wealth.[7]

Veneration for the cow increased in medieval times. Although "the stages by which the doctrine of the cow's sanctity spread throughout the Hindu community are not clearly discernible," it "comes conspicuously into view during the period of Muslim invasions, when Hindus were shocked by the constantly recurring examples of cow slaughter."[8] Early Muslim invaders killed cattle in the same iconoclastic spirit with which they smashed idols. This slaughter probably intensified Hindu veneration for the cow. The manner and extent of permitted slaughter became both a gauge of the status of Hindu and Muslim communities and a means of conciliating potential opposition. For example, Akbar prohibited cow slaughter as part of his effort to consolidate Hindu support, and he made violations of his order punishable with death.[9] It is likely that the issue caused the greatest friction in times of political transition, when people anticipated an expansion or limitation on opportunities to kill cattle. When Marathas, Sikhs, Rajputs, and Dogras replaced Muslim rulers in the late Mughal period, they often forbade the killing of cows. Occasionally the English did also. The East India Company agreed to the continuation of bans on cow slaughter in some of its treaties with Indian rulers.[10] In 1802 Scindhia offered to cede the British additional territory if they would agree to a ban on slaughter within the areas he had already given up to them.[11] In this case, the British refused. But when they annexed the Punjab, they did feel it necessary to conciliate Sikhs and Hindus by temporarily continuing prohibitions on cattle slaughter. Under the Sikh Raj, as under Scindhia in Gwalior, cow slaughter had been a capital offense for which people were actually ex-

[6] C. Rajagopalachari, *Mahabharata* (Bombay, 1962), pp. 20–21.

[7] C. Rajagopalachari, *Ramayana* (Bombay, 1965), p. 20.

[8] Brown, "The Sanctity of the Cow," pp. 38–49.

[9] Vincent A. Smith, *Akbar The Great Mogul: 1542–1605*, 2nd ed. (Oxford, 1919), p. 220.

[10] W. Crooke, "The Veneration of the Cow in India," *Folk-lore*, Vol. XXIII, No. 3 (Sept. 1912), 279.

[11] Sir John Malcolm, *A Memoir of Central India Including Malwa and Adjoining Provinces* (London, 1932), pp. 328–329.

ecuted.[12] Following the annexation of the Punjab, Henry Lawrence ordered a ban on the killing of kine at Amritsar in 1847 in order to placate the Sikhs.[13] And during the Mutiny at Delhi, Emperor Bahadur Shah forbade cow slaughter, impounded cattle owned by Muslims,[14] and even threatened to blow from guns any Muslims caught sacrificing cattle during the Bakr Id. Elsewhere during the Mutiny, Muslims prohibited cow killing or promised to prohibit it "from the day the Hindus came forward to kill the Europeans."[15]

Communal riots occurred before, during, and after the Mutiny, as in the Ajudhia riot in 1855, when 86 persons were killed.[16] But most communal riots in the earlier decades of British rule were the result of local causes. Moreover, they seem often not to have disturbed relations between upper-class Hindus and Muslims. C. F. Andrews' Hindu and Muslim informants at Delhi in the early twentieth century told him that in the mid-nineteenth century, "even if at times there were outbreaks of mob violence among the ignorant and illiterate masses over some insult to religion, these quarrels never reached beyond that substratum of society, and the animosity was easily allayed."[17] This was no longer true at the end of the nineteenth century when high-status Indians had begun to identify more closely with lower-status members of their own religion and when communal relations between Hindu and Muslim elites were affected by "the bitterness of modern times."[18]

After the Mutiny, Hindus and Muslims in British India were reminded occasionally of the problems inherent in one community's political dominance by cow killing controversies in the princely states. Policies followed by the rulers of the states were contrasted, in some cases favorably and in other cases unfavorably, with British policy toward cow slaughter. A Kashmiri

[12] Gov. Gen. to S. of S., 27 Dec. 1893. Dec. 1893 Prog. No. 210, IHP, Pub.

[13] Fauja Singh Bajwa, *Kuka Movement: An Important Phase in Punjab's Role in India's Struggle for Freedom* (Delhi, 1965), p. 69.

[14] Percival Spear, *Twilight of the Mughals: Studies in Late Mughal Delhi* (Cambridge, 1951), p. 207.

[15] Sashi Bhusan Chandhuri, *Civil Rebellion in The Indian Mutinies (1857–1859)* (Calcutta, 1957), pp. 70, 208–209, and 281.

[16] W. Crooke, *The North-Western Provinces of India: Their History, Ethnology, and Administration* (London, 1897), p. 186.

[17] C. F. Andrews, *Zaka Ullah of Delhi* (Cambridge, 1929), p. 11.

[18] Ibid., p. 15.

Maulvi complained in Delhi in 1882 that eight hundred Muslims had been imprisoned in the previous two years in Kashmir where the punishment for cow slaughter was life imprisonment.[19] It is unlikely that Indian Muslims were reassured about their position under a possible future Hindu majority regime when the Maharaja of Kashmir arbitrarily released Muslims serving life sentences for cow slaughter in 1889 to celebrate one of his anniversaries.[20] Muslims occasionally cited prohibition of or interference with cow slaughter by Hindu rulers as an indication of what Muslims might experience under Hindu majority rule in British India.

Attitudes toward cow killing were hardening in the years preceding the 1893 riots among Muslim and Hindu revivalists. A growing number of Indian Muslims considered cattle as "particularly appropriate" for sacrificing.[21] Some argued that Islamic law offered a choice *between* one camel, cow, bullock, or buffalo *and* seven sheep or goats. In India, however, cows were plentiful and one cow was cheaper than seven sheep or goats. Moreover, the term *bakr*, which appeared in Islamic legal texts, was believed to mean cattle in Arabic,[22] and more and more Muslims thought the sacrifice of cattle was obligatory on the Bakr Id festival. As a result, the incidence of Muslim cattle sacrifice was increasing in the late nineteenth century, in the opinion of some British officials. In certain areas, the sacrifice had political meaning as politics became more communal. Some Punjabi Muslims felt it symbolized their "freedom from Hindu [and Sikh] supremacy."[23] They tended to kill cattle in a more open and provocative manner in times of communal controversy, thereby exacerbating the original trouble. Some officials attributed the spread of violence

[19] Note on the agitation against cow killing by D. F. McCracken, Offg. Gen. Supt., T. and D. Dept., 9 Aug. 1893. Dec. 1893 Prog. No. 210, IHP, Pub.

[20] Note on the agitation regarding the cow question in the Punjab, compiled in the office of the Asst. to the Insp.-Gen. of Police, Punjab, Special Branch, n. d. Pub. Letters from India and Gen. Letters from Bengal, 1894, Vol. 19. Also, Charles Lewis Tupper, *Our Indian Protectorate: An Introduction to the Study of the Relations Between the British Government and the Indian Feudatories* (London, 1893), p. 294.

[21] Gov. Gen. to S. of S., 27 Dec. 1893.

[22] This was a subject of debate. Some persons argued that *bakr* was exotic Arabic for kine and that the term really meant *bakri* (goat) and not *baqrat* (cow). G. W. Leitner, "Cow-Killing Riots, Seditious Pamphlets, and the Indian Police," *The Imperial and Asiatic Quarterly Review*, New Series, VII, 13 (Jan. 1894), 87–88.

[23] Note on the agitation by D. F. McCracken, 9 Aug. 1893.

over cow killing in the Punjab in the 1880s to Muslim retaliation against persecution by Hindu bureaucrats.[24]

The more significant change in attitude toward the cow occurred among non-Muslims. Cow protection was an early and central concern of modern Sikh and Hindu revival movements, from the Kukas in the 1860s and the Arya Samaj in the 1870s to the Jan Sangh in the second half of the twentieth century. It seems that Hindus and Sikhs searching for symbols of identity found the cow among the more universal and less divisive ones within their own communities. Hindus as a community shared few other values as obviously Hindu as veneration of the cow. That is why Gandhi once said that the sanctity of the cow was "the central fact of Hinduism," and "the one concrete belief common to all Hindus."[25] In a religious group lacking institutional integration or linguistic unity, the cow became a basis for sentimental community for orthodox and reformist Hindus alike.

The Punjab and the western districts of the North-Western Provinces and Oudh, especially Rohilkhand, had been the scene of the sharpest conflicts over cow slaughter before the late 1880s. Many Punjabis remembered that before annexation in 1849, the Sikh Raj had prohibited cow slaughter. During the early 1870s, the Sikh reform sect, the Kukas, had tried to prevent Muslims and the British from killing cattle. Cow protection had been but a minor part of the Kukas' program before the 1870s, and most of their efforts had been directed toward the internal reform of Sikh society. They preached a return to a purer Sikhism, to a Sikhism in which there would be no reliance upon Brahman priests, no infanticide, adultery, dowries, dishonesty, stealing, and caste. Their main acts of lawlessness before 1870 involved the destruction of graves and images. In most instances, the objects

---

[24] N. Gerald Barrier, "The Punjab Government and Communal Politics, 1870–1908," *JAS*, XXVII, 3 (May 1968), 534.

[25] L.S.S. O'Malley, *Indian Caste Customs* (Cambridge, 1932), p. 14. It is important, though, to realize the context in which Gandhi wrote this. He was giving rhetorical support to the principle of the cow's sanctity in order to persuade cow protectors to drop the issue at least temporarily. He wrote it during the Khilafat agitation in 1920 as part of an appeal to Hindus to abandon efforts to legislate a ban on slaughter. "Let us recognize frankly," he said, "that complete protection of the cow depends purely upon Mussalman goodwill. It is impossible to bend the Mussalmans to our will. . . ." Mahatma Gandhi, *Young India, 1919–1922* (New York, 1924), pp. 410–411.

damaged belonged to Hindus and Sikhs.[26] Sikh *mahants* and *nihangs*, whose privileges and religious practices were challenged by the Kukas, were apparently far more anxious about the Kukas than Muslims were. The evidence printed in official documents relating to the Kukas also indicates that insofar as Kuka Sikhs were hostile to other religious communities, they particularly detested Christians. Apart from the destruction of a few Muslim graves and places of worship and the conversion of several Muslims to the sect, Muslims and Islam are seldom mentioned in published government documents about the early years of the movement. Then, at a time when the Kuka movement was reportedly losing momentum, a dispute arose at Amritsar over the slaughter of cattle by Muslim butchers. Perhaps Kuka leaders realized their movement had become *thanda* (cold), as some Indian observers remarked,[27] and chose cow protection as a means of gaining new converts. In any case, in 1871 in an effort to halt Muslim cattle slaughter, Kukas murdered four Muslim butchers at Amritsar and two at Raikot in Ludhiana district. In 1872, a small band of Kukas was captured after they attacked two towns in an effort to secure arms, horses, and money for a large-scale rebellion. Sixty-five Kukas suspected of participation in the raids were blown from guns, Kuka leaders were deported from the Punjab, and the sect, which according to some estimates had had over 300,000 members,[28] never recovered from the government's repression.

The Kukas had derived most of their support from Jat (cultivator caste) and other nonelite groups,[29] and many of their religious reforms and their alleged goal of reviving a Sikh state had been opposed by the mahants of *gurdwaras*, *sardars* (ex-military leaders), and the chiefs of Punjabi states.[30] But non-Muslims in general were said to appreciate their efforts to prevent cow slaughter, however much they disapproved of other Kuka activi-

[26] Nahar Singh (compiler), *Gooroo Ram Singh and the Kuka Sikhs* (*Rebels Against the British Power in India: Documents 1863–1871*) (New Delhi, 1965), pp. 32–36 and 70–73.
[27] Ibid., p. 112.
[28] Bajwa, *Kuka Movement*, p. 63, and M. N. Ahluwalia, *Kukas: The Freedom Fighters of the Punjab* (Bombay, 1965), p. 71.
[29] Of the fifty Kuka "chiefs" listed in an 1871 police report, twenty-seven were Jats. Singh, *Gooroo Ram Singh*, pp. 156ff.
[30] Bajwa, *Kuka Movement*, pp. 187–188.

ties. It may have been the Kuka example which members of the Arya Samaj had in mind when they took up the defense of the cow in the 1880s. In any case, some Aryas did become the most active cow protectionists in the Punjab in the late nineteenth century. Perhaps it is significant that most Arya leaders belonged to Khatri and other commercial castes, many members of which, like the Jats, were displeased with the low ritual status accorded them. Like the Jat Kukas, Aryas attacked caste practices, ritual, superstition, and priestly functions. Again like the Jat Kukas, Arya Samajists at the same time championed one cause popular with nonreformist Hindus—the sacredness of the cow. The cow protection activities of both Kukas and Aryas won them a limited respect among some of the very orthodox people their other reforms threatened.

The Arya Samaj not only assumed leadership of cow protection activities in the Punjab, its founder, more than any other individual, was responsible for the conversion of cow protection sentiment into an organized, all-Indian campaign. The official government report describing the spread of the movement, while failing to explain convincingly the connections between the regional manifestations in different parts of India, does attribute the movement's transformation to Swami Dayananda Saraswati and the Arya Samaj. It cites an 1882 report from Ludhiana "that a committee consisting chiefly of Bengalis" under Dayananda's presidency had begun collecting signatures on a petition asking the British to ban the slaughter of cows in India. Six or seven lakhs of rupees were said to have been subscribed in Calcutta.[31] Whether such a committee was in fact formed—Dayananda was in Bombay and Rajputana from March 1881 until his death in 1883—there is no doubt that he was instrumental in spreading the movement and popularizing the idea of legislative action to limit cow slaughter. For thirty years, Dayananda had traveled through northern India, to Calcutta, Benaras, Hardwar, Poona, Bombay, and hundreds of other places. Although idol worship and Puranic Hinduism were the chief targets of his energetic iconoclasm, he repeatedly criticized the killing of cows. In February 1881, he published his pamphlet, *Gaukarunanidhi* or "Ocean of Mercy," which condemned meat-eating and suggested bylaws for gaurakshini sabhas (cow protection societies).[32] His biogra-

[31] Note on the agitation in the Punjab.
[32] Harbilas Sarda, *Life of Dayananda Saraswati* (Ajmer, 1968), p. 414.

pher, Harbilas Sarda, who apparently had not seen government accounts of the movement, also believed that Dayananda was "the first to start establishing Gaurakshini Sabhas."[33] Moreover, branches of the Arya Samaj organized by Dayananda were leading agencies of the movement in the Punjab. Harbilas Sarda wrote that his supporters collected millions of signatures on petitions requesting a British ban on cow slaughter.[34] A police report said that one Bengali claimed to have collected 300,000 signatures, while another man claimed 350,000 signatures from Jaipur, Jodhpur, and Bikaner.[35]

Dayananda's efforts to obtain a ban on cow slaughter, his championing of Hindi to replace Urdu as an official language, and his criticisms of Islam for intolerance and for killing animals and nonbelievers aroused Muslim ire. Yet it would be a mistake to regard Hindu-Muslim friction as the chief consequence of Dayananda's tours. Dayananda seemed to consider Hindu superstitions, sectarianism, and caste, as well as Christian missionaries, as more serious problems than Islam for Hinduism's revitalization. He devoted a relatively small portion of his unusual energies to Islam, Hindi, or cow protection and instead generally concentrated on the degeneracy of priestly and Puranic Hinduism. In fact, in his only extended tour of the Punjab, on at least three occasions he stayed on property belonging to Muslims,[36] apparently because orthodox Hindu feeling prevented him from finding Hindu accommodations. And the first Arya Samaj in the Punjab was founded at Rahimkhan's kothi in Lahore.[37] In his severe criticism of Christianity and Islam in the final chapters of *Satyarth Prakash*, it is significant that when accusing Muslims of exploiting the poor by taking alms, he said "Prophet Mohamed, you have successfully vied with the Gosains" (ascetics or sadhus) in taking "the substance of the lay people."[38] Orthodox Hinduism provided a standard by which Islam's depravity could be gauged. Repeatedly, Hindus tried to poison Dayananda, they threw stones and bricks at him, and they plotted to have him beaten up. When Dayananda finally did die from a severe stomach disorder, some of his followers accused the Muslim

---

[33] Ibid., p. 462.   [34] Ibid., p. 278.
[35] Note on the agitation in the Punjab.
[36] Sarda, *Life*, pp. 182, 184, and 194.   [37] Ibid., pp. 182–183.
[38] Durga Prasad, *An English Translation of the Satyarth Prakash* (Lahore, 1908), p. 514.

doctor who treated him of poisoning him, but if Dayananda was poisoned at all, it is far more likely that the culprit was a Hindu.[39] Almost all the attempts to kill him prior to 1883 had been made by Hindus.

What emerges clearly from a study of Dayananda's career is that religious disputes among Hindus were stormy, vituperative, and carried on in an ethos of rowdyism and petty violence. Dayananda contributed to that ethos by making abusive, scathing remarks about his Hindu, Christian, and Muslim enemies. But Dayananda himself seems not to have advocated Hindu violence against Muslims. Far from encouraging Hindus unilaterally to prevent Muslims from killing cows, he urged them to stay within the law and to petition the government, Parliament, and the Queen to pass cow protection legislation.

In his campaign to persuade people to return to Vedic Hinduism and to convince Hindus that meat-eating was not necessary for physical strength, he sought support from Western-educated, urban professionals, major zamindars, and chiefs of princely states, as well as from common people. Among the influential people he met and talked with were M. G. Ranade, Keshabchandra Sen, Debendranath Tagore, the Maharana of Udaipur, and the Maharajas of Jodhpur and Benaras. Some of the most prominent men in India gave a sympathetic hearing to Dayananda's attacks on Puranic Hinduism and the caste system. In reaching the titled landholders and princes, Dayananda was making deeper inroads on the highest social strata than the Brahmo and Prarthana Samajes had been able to. He also carried his attacks to the temple and pilgrimage towns where orthodox Hindus congregated, such as Benaras, Hardwar, Brindaban, and Allahabad. Orthodox Hindus at Benaras, Hardwar, and many other places were alarmed by Dayananda's impact, and they argued with him in *shastrarths* (debates on Shastras) and they wrote against his teachings. In an unusual meeting at Calcutta University, four hundred pandits met in the Senate House to condemn his views.[40]

[39] Dayananda was treated by several doctors during the month of his fatal illness. The Muslim was Dr. Alimardankhan who had been sent to Dayananda by Maharaja Pratapsingh of Jodhpur. Sarda, *Life*, pp. 324ff.

[40] Rev. John Morrison, *New Ideas in India During the Nineteenth Century: A Study of Social, Political, and Religious Developments* (London, 1907), p. 134.

Dayananda's biographer does not say what individual notables thought of the cow protection issue, but it is apparent that many were sympathetic to Dayananda's plea that cows be protected. Even a broad-minded reformer such as Ranade had criticized Muslims in a college essay on Shivaji for having driven "before our sight the humble, the useful (and still more the sacred) cow to the slaughter-house."[41] The Maharaja of Benaras, although initially hostile to Dayananda, reportedly supported his efforts to collect signatures on petitions throughout northern India asking for restrictions on cow slaughter.[42] Many notables were willing to support the movement prior to the 1893 riots because it was directed toward educating Hindus and the British about the dangers of unrestricted slaughter, and not at taking extralegal action to stop that slaughter.

Economic arguments were a key factor in the spread of cow protection sentiment to the better educated and high-caste Hindus and to provinces beyond the Punjab. Possession of cattle had been an indication of prosperity for centuries, both in mythology and actual life. But in the late nineteenth century, journal articles and agricultural fairs had publicized the fact that compared to cattle in other countries, Indian cows were sickly and gave little milk. Moreover, it seems that the spread of charitable institutions and "humane" standards of behavior extended quite naturally to the care of old, nonproductive cattle. As a consequence, the nineteenth-century cow protection movement was supported by many well-educated Hindus who may have been indifferent to the question of cows' sacredness but who wanted to improve the feeding, breeding, and general care of cattle. This aspect must be kept in mind because otherwise it may seem that prominent cow protectors were motivated by anti-Muslim or anti-British sentiments when many probably were not. A good example of how kine killing was associated with India's poverty is the Urdu Tract called *Sada-i-Hind* (Voice of India) by Lala Nand Gopal, editor of *Inquilab*. Although it was not published until 1909, as Lala Nand himself said, "there is nothing new" in it. He argued that the closing of government forests to grazing, the rising cost of fodder, and the slaughter of cattle for food were threatening the existence of cattle in India. Without cattle,

[41] Richard P. Tucker, "M. G. Ranade: The Historian as Liberal Nationalist" (mimeographed paper, May 1970), p. 4.
[42] Sarda, *Life*, p. 75.

neither Hindus nor Muslims would be able to till their fields. Mothers would not be able to suckle their children. He urged all his countrymen, regardless of religion, to realize that unless cattle were protected, it "means the end of the Indian people within a very short time." Already the average income had declined to a dangerous level, he wrote, and thousands of Indians were starving.[43]

Similarly, Dayananda had argued in his speeches and in the *Gaukarunanidhi* that "the race" was degenerating physically because of the shortage of dairy products. He claimed that a dead cow would feed twenty persons while a living cow and her six female offspring could during their lives produce food sufficient to feed over one hundred thousand people for one day.[44] These economic arguments against cattle slaughter applied, and were directed to, Indians of all religions.

An example of an educated Hindu reformer who was active in the cow protection movement for economic reasons was Gopalrao Hari Bhide, a prominent Brahman lawyer and Congressman in Nagpur. Born of poor parents, he worked at one time as a railway signaler. He was convinced that India's economic plight was more pressing than political or social problems. He set up a fruit farm and he was mainly responsible for starting and supervising the Swadeshi Cotton Mills at Nagpur. He also organized the Nagpur Gaurakshini Sabha which had its own press and newspaper. He traveled through the villages, urging peasants to take better care of their cattle and to use manure for agriculture. In addition, he was noted for his advocacy of social reform and better treatment of the poor.[45] He was assisted by C. Narayanswami Naidu, a Madrasi lawyer and zamindar who served as chairman of the 1891 Congress Reception Committee, president of the Nagpur Municipal Board, secretary of the Nagpur District Board, and president of the local Theosophical Society.[46] The Nagpur Sabha was said to have been responsible for reducing the number of cows slaughtered annually in Nagpur from 16,000 in

[43] Translation of *Sada-i-Hind*, Appendix B, in N. Gerald Barrier, *The Punjab in Nineteenth Century Tracts: An Introduction to the Pamphlet Collections in the British Museum and India Office* (East Lansing, 1969), pp. 53–59.

[44] Morrison, *New Ideas*, p. 136; also Sarda, *Life*, pp. 232 and 461.

[45] Pillai, *Representative Indians*, p. 309.

[46] Ibid., and *Report of the 7th INC*, delegate list.

1887 to less than 500 five years later.⁴⁷ The second anniversary of the founding of the Nagpur Sabha was celebrated in 1889 with pomp. Sriman Swami of the Allahabad Central Cow Protection Society was the featured guest and was showered with flowers en route from the Nagpur railroad station. The Sabha staged a procession through the streets which was led by elephants, camels, and horses and included an estimated 20,000 people and 452 cattle purchased from local butchers. Sriman Swami then spoke in English for more than two hours to a crowd of 4,000 people.⁴⁸ The Nagpur Sabha also was said to have sent a marble statue of a cow to the King-Emperor in 1902 in the hopes of inducing him to proclaim a ban on slaughter at the Delhi Coronation Durbar.⁴⁹ Undoubtedly it was the economic emphasis of the Nagpur Sabha's activities which accounted for the widespread support given to the movement in the Central Provinces by Maratha Brahmin pleaders and other prominent persons.⁵⁰ Similarly, it was agricultural efficiency, malnutrition, high infant mortality, and comparable issues which drew educated men such as Lajpat Rai,⁵¹ the Maharaja of Darbhanga, and Sir Dinshaw Manackjee Petit to the cause. The notion was spreading that milk and grain supplies were dwindling and "the time is looming in the distance when natives will have to live on grass, dust, and the leaves of trees."⁵²

Of course, educated men who used economic arguments to justify limits on kine killing may often have had more complex motivation. They may have been embarrassed to admit less secular or rational motives or they may not have recognized within themselves an emotional abhorrence of beef-eating or animal slaughter which, after all, clashed with one of traditional Hinduism's core values. Moreover, the economic justification for restricting cow slaughter was the one rationale which was acceptable to all advocates of cow protection.⁵³ Other justifications

⁴⁷ *Subodh Sindhu* (Khandwa), 24 May 1893, NWP and O, CP, and R NNR No. 22 of 1893.
⁴⁸ *Nyaya Sudha* (Harda), 6 Nov. 1889, ibid. (1889), p. 705.
⁴⁹ *Curzon Gazette* (Delhi), 1 June 1902, P NNR No. 23 of 1902, para. 7.
⁵⁰ "Marwaris of sorts" were also supportive. Note on the agitation by D. F. McCracken, 9 Aug. 1893.
⁵¹ *Lala Lajpat Rai: Writings and Speeches*, pp. 160–161.
⁵² *Godharm Prakash* (Cawnpore), Oct. 1888, NWP and O NNR (1888), pp. 662–663.
⁵³ William Crooke said in 1911 that "at present all Hindus accept this

depended upon religious sanctions, superstition and a belief in the magical qualities of the cow's products, or some value which conflicted with the rational, secular, and noncommunal norms encouraged both by university education and the universalism of modernist Hindu reform movements.

Economic motives won the cow protection cause respectability, but both Hindu-Muslim competition for participation in education, administration, and consultive bodies and Hindu orthodoxy's fear of Hindu reformism helped elevate the issue to a new level of controversy. As nationalism and communal competition stimulated the search for categories of mutual identity and for definitions of nationality, the cow took on symbolic meaning. Gradually, the old familiar determinants of power were dissolving. The local raja, with his known ways of doing things, was losing ground to an impersonal, remote, and novel bureaucratic order and to a class of urban-based Indians unbeholden to local custom. The cultivator, shopkeeper, or priest may not have controlled his environment in the traditional system in the sense of directing the forces which shaped his life. But he had controlled them in another sense. He had been surrounded by predictable behavior and familiar reference points. Mentally he could control by anticipating and comprehending the processes of human interaction about him. That his landlord or patron, his clients or his tenants might have belonged to a different religious community or have behaved erratically made less difference than that the personnel and the parameters of behavior were familiar and that the rules of authority were known. But during the last two decades of the nineteenth century, signs of impending change multiplied. In rapid order, education, civil service recruitment, official languages, tenancy laws, legislative councils, caste precedence, and the age of marriage were discussed in terms that suggested major alterations were likely over a wide range of Indian institutions. A sense of the approach of a new competitive system with unpredictable consequences seemed to be spreading. Already the new system had caused ill-will between the government and the Indian National Congress, between the Congress and Aligarh educators, between the Aligarh educators and more traditionalist Muslims, and between Hindu reformers and non-

---

[economic rationale] as the explanation of their devotion to the animal." "The Veneration of the Cow in India," p. 300.

reformers. The new competitive order undoubtedly created unease among those who traditionally held positions of authority but who were not gaining the education necessary for ultimate success in the new professional and administrative hierarchies. For certain Hindus faced with social conflicts and uncertain futures, the cow may have represented a benign figure, symbolic of the harmony which ideally had existed but which was now threatened. The cow, as the gentle provider as well as the unquestioning dependent, incorporated reassuring aspects of good Hindu behavior. Again and again the cow was referred to as humble. Humility was being lost in the aggressiveness and competitiveness of modern institutions. The cow may also have reminded people of the idyllic, pastoral youth of Krishna and of the agrarian life now being undermined by overpopulation, the working of debt laws, and the impersonality of bureaucracy. The competitive institutions of the late nineteenth century seemed the antithesis of the idealized past, for they were urban-based, foreign in origin, dependent upon self-seeking, and conducive to social friction.

In different contexts, the cow provided solace, reassurance, and purification. Many Hindus still regarded the cow as a guard against evil. Some men kept a cow present so that when they awoke in the morning the cow would be the first object they saw. To dream about a cow was considered a good omen. Some Hindus also believed that if they died holding on to a cow's tail, their passage "across the dread river of death" would be assured. William Crooke reported in 1896 that a major Brahman at Hardwar waved a cow's tail over the bathers in the Brahma Kund (sacred pool) to keep away evil spirits.[54] And when a person or place was defiled, the cow's dung and other products were used to clean away the impurities. Similarly, food cooked in ghi was thought to be purer than *kaccha* food (cooked without ghi). In numerous ways, the cow and its products were associated with health, prosperity, order, merit, purity.[55] Conversely, the absence or the misuse of the cow and its products were linked to ill-health, bad luck, and defilement. In a society whose main source of protein was dairy products, the nutritional value of the cow was assumed

[54] W. Crooke, *The Popular Religion and Folklore of Northern India* (London, 1896), II, 232–233.

[55] See E.A.H. Blunt, *The Caste System of North India* (London, 1931), pp. 295–297, and R. E. Enthoven, *The Folklore of Bombay* (Oxford, 1924), p. 213.

if not understood. And at least in the not-too-distant past, misfortunes such as crop blight, poor harvests, and epidemics were blamed upon the gods' anger at the failure to prevent kine killing.[56] The affective importance of the cow, reinforced as it was at so many different points, must have penetrated to the deepest recesses of many Hindus' instinctual beings.

The British, as administrators and as controllers of the legislative process, were the focus of complaints about cow killing. It seems that cow protectors initially were quicker to blame their rulers than their fellow Indians, the Muslims, for failing to protect cows. When Hindu cow protectors tried to stop Muslim sacrifices or sales, and even when Muslims killed cattle provocatively, the responsibility for interfering and keeping the peace fell upon the British. British officials were extremely wary of the cow killing issue because of this tendency to blame alien Christians as often as Muslims and because of their memories of the religious motivation in the 1857 Mutiny. The lieutenant-governor of the Punjab, in looking back over the decades preceding the 1893 riots, wrote

> The cow-killing question is the question of all others, which, at least for the last 20 years, has been regarded by us all as the gravest danger that threatens us in India. If it spread, as it might, to our Native Army and Police, it is not too much to say that over large tracts of country British rule would be for a time wiped out, and that in many districts our two or three British officers would be like so many black ants that by some accident had got between the upper and the nether millstone.[57]

The various provincial administrations tried to keep cow killing disputes from reaching unmanageable proportions by ordering subordinate officials to follow a policy of strict neutrality. It is doubtful, however, that most British officials *felt* neutral. As

---

[56] Sleeman gave examples of how cholera, wheat blight, and poor harvests were associated with cow slaughter. Sir W. H. Sleeman, *Rambles and Recollections of an Indian Official*, ed. by Vincent A. Smith (London, 1915), pp. 163, 194, and 202–203.

[57] Extract from a note on the proposal for an examination in India for admission to the Civil Service by Sir Dennis Fitzpatrick, Lt. Gov. of the Punjab, n. d. Pub. Letters from India and Gen. Letters from Bengal, 1894, Vol. 19.

regular beef-eaters and as officials responsible for feeding the army, the British purchased larger orders of beef than any other community. Moreover, there was a widespread British assumption that health, manliness, and meat-eating were interrelated. In addition, many nineteenth-century Englishmen looked down upon Hindu veneration of the cow as a pagan superstition. As Claude Lévi-Strauss has argued with regard to Westerners' analyses of totemism, Christian observers have often failed to understand the place of animals in non-Western cultures. Instead many have caricaturized "mental attitudes incompatible with the exigency of a discontinuity between man and nature which Christian thought has held to be essential."[58] As with many Indian values and institutions, British officials may have used Hindu attitudes toward the cow to reassure themselves about their own value system, and in the process shut themselves off from the sympathy necessary for a policy of genuine neutrality. But even with sympathy and a determination to be even-handed, neutrality in practice was an elusive goal.

In both the Punjab and the North-Western Provinces and Oudh, a ban on cow slaughter was an anathema to Muslims, while permission to kill cows antagonized many Hindus. A series of *ad hoc* arrangements had been worked out between British officials and local leaders which were based upon local custom and which were designed to accommodate both Hindu and Muslim feelings at the same time. Slaughter was permitted in certain customary and inconspicuous places. Transportation and display of beef for sale were also regulated. Trouble arose when Hindus claimed that more than the usual number of animals were being sacrificed or butchered or that the slaughter and sale of beef were more ostentatious than usual. At one time there had been a clause in the Punjab penal code which made "wrongful innovation" a punishable offense. An innovation had been "wrongful" if it was likely to lead to a quarrel. And in the closing decades of the century there was an increasing willingness to innovate. In 1893, a high-ranking Sikh official from a native state was asked why there were so many more Hindu-Muslim disturbances, and he replied that it was due to the *azadi* (freedom or, in this context, license) which the British had granted. Formerly, a feeling had prevailed that when members of a sect had habitually done something, they

---

[58] *Totemism* (Boston, 1963), pp. 3 and 103.

should be permitted to continue and if they were not in the custom of performing an act, they should not begin.[59]

Dastur (custom) was being challenged by something similar to consciousness of a group's civil rights. Increasingly, Hindus and Muslims were learning and insisting upon the rights and privileges provided by formal law. One community adjusted or expanded its behavior toward the limit permitted by the law or the limit the community thought should be permitted, while the other community held that local custom and precedent should prevail. When local custom, municipal regulations, and civil law were in conflict with popular notions of fairness, the potential for trouble was considerable. As elected Indian majorities gained control of more municipal councils in the late nineteenth century, the greater was the opportunity to alter municipal regulations governing cow slaughter, sometimes under the pretense of improving urban sanitary conditions. Thus, in 1886, for example, Hindus in Allahabad, many of whom were members of the Allahabad People's Association, the local Congress organization, passed a temporary "by-law forbidding kine-slaughter within the municipal limits."[60] The following year the conflict over the circumstances in which cows might be legally slaughtered reached the Allahabad High Court and attracted attention throughout India.

In 1887 the High Court at Allahabad twice overturned lower court decisions which had seemed to offer expanded protection to cows. In the first and less controversial decision, the court set aside the conviction of two Muslims who had been convicted of committing a public nuisance for slaughtering two cows in a private compound whose broken wall allegedly enabled a Hindu to witness the act.[61] In the second decision, which seemed to act as a major stimulus for the organization of cow protection societies, all five High Court justices agreed to reverse the conviction of two Muslims of Shahjahanpur district. The lower court had found the two Muslims guilty on the grounds that by killing a cow on the Bakr Id, they had violated Section 295 of the Indian

[59] Extract from a note on the proposal for an examination in India by Sir Dennis Fitzpatrick.
[60] Bayly, "Patrons and Politics in Northern India," p. 55.
[61] *Indian Law Reports*: x Allahabad 44. Queen Empress v. Zakiuddin and Another (22 June 1887).

penal code which makes it an offense to destroy "an object held sacred by any class of persons" with the knowledge that it would be regarded as an insult to the religion of that class. The High Court rejected the argument of Hindus that a cow was "an object" within the meaning of Section 295.[62] Some disappointed Hindus believed that the decision was the responsibility of Justice Mahmud, Sayyid Ahmad Khan's son and the only Indian justice on the Allahabad High Court.[63]

The Allahabad High Court's decisions seemed to end the possibility that cow slaughter would be prohibited through judicial review of existing laws. A number of Hindu newspapers in the North-Western Provinces and Oudh, Bihar, and Bengal announced their support for a petition initiated by a Bombay Parsi asking the Government of India to legislate an anti-cow killing law.[64] The leading Congressmen in the North-Western Provinces, Pandit Ajudhia Nath, introduced a bill into the local legislative council in January 1888 to regulate the killing of animals in sport. Although the bill applied to cock-fighting, pigeon-shooting, and pig-sticking and did not mention cows, its purpose was to expand protection of animals,[65] and its timing seemed to be a reaction to the failure to win the High Court cases.

The fact that Hindus were challenging the legal right of Muslims to kill cows and the fact that Indian judges were now disposing of appeals involving religious rights highlighted the political changes which were taking place.[66] Few Muslims were ready to concede the possibility that the rights of Hindus included the ability to stop cow slaughter. Muharram Ali Chisti, editor of *Rafiq-i-Hind* (Lahore) and subsequently a Congressman, argued in 1888 that "if Muslims were prevented from kine slaughter merely because the practice was prohibited by Hinduism, the Hindu idols and temples would have to be razed to the ground

---

[62] *Indian Law Reports*: x Allahabad 150. Queen Empress v. Imam Ali and Another (20 Dec. 1887).

[63] Note on the agitation by D. F. McCracken, 9 Aug. 1893. Also *Rahbar* (Moradabad), 20 Feb. 1888, NWP and O NNR, p. 168.

[64] NWP and O NNR (1888), p. 93, and B NNR, Nos. 44, 45, 46, and 47 of 1887.

[65] *Hami-i-Hind* (Allahabad), 15 Jan. 1888, NWP and O NNR (1888), p. 75.

[66] In 1895, one of the six High Court judges was Indian, as were 7 of the 31 district and sessions judges. W. Crooke, *The North-Western Provinces of India*, p. 189.

and many other religious matters not allowed by Islam would have to be interfered with."[67]

It was a sign of advancing political development that the cow killing question was debated in the courts, newspapers, and pamphlets in terms of legal rights and legislative enactments. Administrative politics merged with the new, mass-based politics in the controversy leading to the 1893 riots. Traditionally, a durbar between community leaders, followed by an administrative edict, would often have determined in what circumstances cattle would be killed. Now, however, the avenues for settling disputes had been expanded, and people looked to the courts, Parliament, and the legislative councils, and even the Indian National Congress as arenas for dispute and solutions. The cow killing issue demonstrated to Muslims in particular the importance of India's constitution and safeguards for minorities. Because Indian and British politicians were debating the reform of India's legislative councils in the late 1880s, the cow gained a political importance it might otherwise not have had.

THE CONGRESS AND COW PROTECTION

In 1892, Parliament passed the India Councils Act, expanding the size of the legislative councils and giving Indians the opportunity for the first time to elect members to the councils. As an installment of self-rule, it was a small one. But it conceded the principle of representative government for which the Congress had been agitating. The first elections in the North-Western Provinces and Oudh under the new act were being carried out in the weeks immediately preceding the 1893 riots. The powers of the reformed councils were too slight for the elections to have aroused much passion, although they did stimulate some communal feeling. For example, the delegates from district boards in Oudh met at Lucknow on June 19, a week before the Azamgarh riots, and elected a member to the provincial legislative council. The six Muslim delegates and the English deputy commissioner voted for Kunwar Muhammad Faiyaz Ali Khan, while the sixteen Hindus voted for Seth Lachman Das, a former president of the Bharata Dharma Mahamandal. This was further proof to the *Aligarh Institute Gazette* that the Muslim minority would always

[67] Quoted from *Civil and Military Gazette* (Lahore), 25 July 1888, in Note on the agitation in the Punjab.

be defeated and that India was not ready for representative government.[68] In another case, Haji Muhammad Ismail Khan of Aligarh stood for election by the Lucknow group of municipalities. After he lost, he said he had run in order to test the Hindus' claim that they were not prejudiced. He claimed his defeat had convinced him that the Indian National Congress was "strongly opposed and hostile" to Muslim political rights.[69] Allegations of communal voting were more common and received more publicity than evidence of political alliances which cut across religious boundaries. Yet some electoral results were determined by noncommunal factors. For example, when the representatives of municipal boards chose a Hindu government pleader over a Lucknow Muslim lawyer who was active in the Congress (Hamid Ali Khan), the two Congress Lucknow newspapers, the *Hindustani* and the *Advocate*, objected and claimed that the deputy commissioner had pressured the electors to vote for the pro-government Hindu candidate.[70]

Another issue which was a central item in the Congress platform from its inception was the expansion of Indian participation in the Indian Civil Service. The Congress repeatedly asked that I.C.S. examinations be given simultaneously in India and England so that Indians would be able to sit for the examinations in India. Muslims associated with Aligarh College, on the other hand, feared changes in the rules for civil service recruitment which would result in an increased proportion of Hindus by virtue of their superior education in most parts of India. On June 2, three weeks before the cow protection riots in the North-Western Provinces and Oudh, members of Parliament who were friendly toward Congress aspirations succeeded in passing a resolution in a sparsely attended House of Commons session asking for simultaneous examinations. This resolution was nonbinding and was not acted upon, but like the Councils Act, it was seen by both Congressmen and their opponents as a Congress victory.

There seems to be no conclusive evidence of a connection between these two partial Congress victories and the change in the character of the cow protection movement which touched off the 1893 riots. A connection, though, is a distinct possibility. It is

[68] *Aligarh Institute Gazette*, 27 June 1893, para. 6, NWP and O, CP and Rajputana NNR No. 27 of 1893.
[69] *Aligarh Institute Gazette*, n. d., para. 24, ibid., No. 42 of 1893.
[70] Para. 8 and 9, ibid., No. 27 of 1893.

suggested both by the timing of the movement's escalation and by the assumption of Muslims and British officials that the Congress was linked to the cow protectors.

This assumption grew out of the encouragement individual Congress supporters gave the cow protection cause. It was inevitable that the Congress, standing as it did for majority rule and parliamentary government, should have attracted advocates of restrictions upon cow slaughter. Sentiment for limiting the killing of cows was so widespread among high-caste Hindus that the Congress would have been unrepresentative of a major section of the population if it had not included at least some such advocates. And cow protectors had long before recognized legislative prohibition as an obvious fulfillment of their objectives. Three decades earlier, in 1862, the Sikh Maharaja of Patiala had tried unsuccessfully to introduce a bill into the Indian Legislative Council to stop the sale of beef.[71] Since that time, the signature-gathering campaigns had had the same aim.

The tendency of both Muslims and the British to view the Indian National Congress in the North-Western Provinces and Oudh as a Hindu organization was heightened by the direct clash between the Congress and the Aligarh Muslim leaders in 1888. In that year, Congress preparations to hold the Congress session in Allahabad for the first time and to attract Muslim leaders had been countered by Sayyid Ahmad Khan, the patriotic society consisting of titled north Indian notables, and the lieutenant-governor, Sir Auckland Colvin. The Congress had drawn little significant Muslim support in any province before 1893, but it was only in the North-Western Provinces and Oudh that opposition to the Congress had been given such a communal character. An important stimulus to the communalization of politics in the North-Western Provinces and Oudh in the 1880s had been the growth of Hindu power in municipal government in the western districts of the province. Trade had grown much more rapidly in the western than in the eastern districts, and Hindu merchants, bankers, and money-lenders used their new wealth and independence from Muslim landowners to reduce Muslim influence in municipal affairs. From the vantage point of Aligarh, Muslim leaders were therefore threatened by elective institutions. Muslims of the western districts were more likely than those of the east to have witnessed Hindus using their municipal votes to limit the sale and

---

[71] Note on the agitation in the Punjab, para. 210.

slaughter of beef "under the guise of hygienic management of slaughter house and kebab shops."[72]

In contrast, communal politics in the towns of the eastern half of the North-Western Provinces and Oudh, where most of the leading Congressmen lived, were relatively harmonious. Trade had developed at a slower rate and had not disturbed many of the interdependencies between Hindu and Muslim elites. Many Hindu professionals spoke Urdu and maintained professional ties with Muslim associates and landowners. Moreover, Hindus were not displacing Muslims from municipal boards in the eastern districts where, as late as 1908, Muslims held 38.4 per cent of the seats which equaled the Muslims proportion in the urban population and was more than double the proportion of Muslims (15 per cent) in the provincial population as a whole.[73] Therefore, the communal polarization apparent in Congress politics was to some extent a regional split and to some extent a division between the pro-British taluqdars and the urban commercial and professional groups which supported the Congress. But the overall impression left by the Congress efforts to draw in Muslims in 1888 was that those efforts had been rebuffed. Muslim rejection of Congress overtures is a possible explanation for the subsequent spread of the cow protection movement and for the movement's growing hostility to Muslims. However, the movement spread in the eastern districts where communal friction had been less severe, and within the eastern districts it showed its greatest strength in rural areas where knowledge of and concern for the Congress was low.

The spread of the cow protection movement in the North-Western Provinces and Oudh, Bihar, and the Central Provinces was also linked to the Age of Consent Bill controversy. First, the Indian supporters of the bill, who were few but who had access to influential newspapers, argued that postponement of marriage was necessary to strengthen the physique of Hindus. The consent controversy helped to popularize the concern about the physical deterioration of Hindus which was a major rationale for reducing cow slaughter.[74] Second, the British and reformist attack upon an

[72] Frances Robinson, "Municipal Government and Muslim Separatism in the United Provinces, 1883 to 1916," in Gallagher, Johnson, and Seal (eds.), *Locality, Province and Nation*, p. 73.

[73] Ibid., pp. 74–93.

[74] *Godharm Prakash* (Cawnpore), Dec. 1889, argued that early marriages and the scarcity of milk and grain had "rendered Hindus physically weak as a

institution as central to Hinduism as mariage customs may have led Hindus to counterattack by rallying around the cow as a symbol of the integrity and independence of Hinduism. The debate over the bill to raise the legal age of marriage to twelve "reached fierce proportions" in 1890, and it was finally passed in March 1891.[75] Much more than the proper age of marriage was involved. For some nationalists, nothing less than the nation's pride and self-respect were at stake. The public discussion of exceptional, grueome aspects of Indian family life had been humiliating, and the issue of the reasonable marriageable age was overshadowed by the question of the colonial power's right to probe and legislate in such extremely private and religious spheres of behavior. Defenders of Hinduism's right to regulate its affairs popularized the notion that Hinduism was in danger and "aroused great public support for orthodoxy."[76]

The cow protection movement lost some of its momentum in 1890 and 1891 while people's attention was diverted by the Age of Consent Bill controversy and other concerns. But the new strength of the gaurakshini agitation in 1892–1893 was in part a reaction to the Consent Bill. It seems that many Hindus who supported the movement were asserting the inviolability of the cow in order to demonstrate their determination to protect their values and customs from foreign interference.

Soon after the Age of Consent Act was passed, cow protection meetings were held in two towns which were particularly active in disseminating cow protection propaganda. The first was at Nagpur, the home of Gopalrao Hari Bhide's Gaurakshini Sabha which was mentioned above as emphasizing the economic reasons for improving the treatment of cattle. The 1891 session of the Indian National Congress was held at Nagpur, and immediately after its conclusion, the Nagpur Gauraksha Sabha sponsored a meeting which was held in the Congress pavilion and which was attended by between 1,000 and 1,500 persons. Some Congress delegates attended and "two prominent Congress delegates" gave speeches, according to a government report.[77]

The second meeting was at the 1892 Kumbh Mela at Hardwar, a pilgrimage town which attracted hundreds of thousands of

---

nation" and that British rule had saved Hindus from being "annihilated" by Muslims. NWP and O NNR (1889), p. 777.

[75] Heimsath, *Indian Nationalism*, p. 168.   [76] Ibid., p. 173.
[77] Note on the agitation by D. F. McCracken, 9 Aug. 1893.

Cow Protection

devout Hindus. Among the many institutions at Hardwar which were associated with popular Hinduism, at least two contributed to the cow protection movement. One was a Gaurakshini Sabha which published its own journal;[78] the other was the Bharata Dharma Mahamandala which had been founded in 1887 to work for the revival of Hinduism and the protection of cows.[79] After the Age of Consent Bill was passed, a new committee was formed at a meeting at Hardwar which "decided to attack with increased vigor the Muhammadan practice of kine-killing as a mark of displeasure at the new [Consent] Act and also to prevent further interference in Hindu religious matters."[80] The government's dispersal of the Hardwar pilgrims in 1892 because of a cholera epidemic increased orthodox dissatisfaction.[81] Whether the Hardwar or Nagpur meetings led to practical steps for spreading the movement is not known, but unquestionably they helped popularize it in the two years between the Age of Consent Bill and the riots. One cow protectionist journal in Farukhabad claimed that it was mainly because of the Hardwar Gaurakshini Sabha "that cow-protection societies sprang into existence in every part of the country."[82] It is highly likely that wandering ascetics who became

[78] According to the *Din Bandhu* (Farukhabad), Aug. 1895 (NWP and O, CP and R NNR No. 39 of 1895, para. 19), the Hardwar Gaurakshini Sabha was largely responsible for the spread of cow protection sabhas.

[79] Note on the agitation by D. F. McCracken, 9 Aug. 1893. In announcing the second meeting of the Bharata Dharma Mahamandal for Brindaban in March 1889, the *Bharat Bhandu* (Aligarh) stated there were over two hundred Dharma Sabhas whose aims included refutation of reformist teachings, promotion of Sanskrit, and preservation of Hindu manuscripts. (28 Dec. 1888, NWP and O NNR [1889], p. 11.) The 1892 meeting of the Mahamandal at Benaras was reported to have attracted ten thousand people. Delegates performed a puja to the four Vedas which lay on a silver throne and they gave three cheers for Sanatan Dharma and Her Majesty, Queen Victoria. (*Bharat Jiwan* of Benaras, 21 March 1892, NWP and O, CP, and Rajputana NNR [1892], p. 101.) Charles Heimsath wrote that by 1900, when the Mahamandala had its "first comprehensive conference" at Delhi, the organization had seven hundred Hindu sabhas associated with it. (*Indian Nationalism*, p. 318.)

[80] This information was given to the commissioner of Calcutta police in late 1895 by a Bengali sadhu from Chandernagore called Paramananda whose real name was Hiralal Mukherji. "Political Activities of the Sadhus (up to 1909)," Paper 49, State Committee for the Compilation of the History of the Freedom Movement in India, Bengal Region.

[81] The dispersal was frequently commented upon in the press in the NWP and O during 1892.

[82] *Din Bandhu*, August 1895, NWP and O, CP, and R NNR No. 23 of 1895, para. 19.

active in the movement had visited Hardwar and had come into contact with protectionist advocates.

The other pilgrimage town which was a major center for the spread of the movement was Gya in Bihar, a region of exceptional cow protection activity and large-scale cattle trade. A domiciled Bengali zamindar founded a gaurakshini sabha in the Gya district in 1887 which began to take a compulsory religious tax for the movement in 1889. The sabha was implicated in a serious riot in Gya town during the Bakr Id of 1891 when Hindus tried to prevent the "ostentatious parading" of a sacrificial cow by Muslims. The district magistrate reported that after the riot, the *gyawals* or priests sent word to their pilgrimage agents, who were numerous in Rajputana and Benaras, to agitate against cow killing.[83] Large bands of agitators and ascetics, many from Benaras, tried to interfere with the sale of kine at the cattle fairs in Patna division in which Gya was located, leading to fifteen riots in 1893.[84]

Government reports suggest that cow protection riots often followed visits by sadhus or *sannyasis*, many of whom traveled in large bands of "a hundred or more." Unfortunately, little is known about who these sadhus were or why they took up the cause of the cow. There was an ancient oral tradition current among "all sannyasis in North India" in 1925, according to J. N. Farquhar, that provided a precedent for non-Brahman ascetics being enlisted to protect Brahmans from Muslim violence, and it is conceivable that the wandering bands of ascetics in the 1890s were acting upon the residual role represented by this tradition. The tradition was that during Akbar's reign in the sixteenth century, armed Muslim faqirs were killing Brahman sannyasis, that Raja Birbal persuaded Akbar to permit a Benaras pandit named Madhusudana Saraswati to recruit and arm non-Brahmans to protect the pacific Brahmans. Certainly many sannyasis in the eighteenth and early nineteenth centuries were trained to fight, although it seems that the most frequent sannyasi violence was directed against rival sannyasi orders over bathing and processional places at Hardwar and other pilgrim towns.[85]

[83] Note on the agitation by D. F. McCracken, 9 Aug. 1893.

[84] A. Forbes, Com., Patna Div., to Ch. Sec., Bengal, 27 Oct. 1893. Dec. 1893 Prog. No. 213, IHP, Pub.

[85] It would be interesting to know if the bands of ascetics who joined the gaurakshini movement were *naga sannyasis* or members of other former

Cow Protection

Although many individuals, organizations, and newspapers were responsible for the spurt of cow protection activity in the late 1880s across central and north-central India, one sadhu stands out for his efforts to carry the movement across regional boundaries. He called himself Sriman Swami and he was associated at times with the Indian National Congress. In 1888 and 1889, Sriman Swami toured extensively through the North-Western Provinces and Oudh, Bihar, Bengal, Madras, and Bombay, much of the time on behalf of the Allahabad Cow Protection Society. He lectured on cow protection, collected contributions for a cow memorial fund, set up new gaurakshini sabhas, and urged that the Legislative Council overturn the Allahabad High Court's decision with new legislation. Among the landed notables who were said to have given him funds were the Maharajas of Darbhanga, Hatwa, and Bettia. He adopted "a tone of satire and derisiveness towards the English, which elicited much applause from his Hindu audiences." Sriman Swami also went to Nepal in late 1888 and reportedly sought funds from the Nepali durbar to be used in overthrowing the British Raj.[86] In late 1889, he was exposed first while he was in Madras and later by the *Pioneer* of Allahabad as an ex-convict named Desika Chari. Until this identification, Sriman Swami had been an effective agitator. He was credited by a Thagi and Dakoiti Department report with reviving the cow protection movement in "Bengal" (presumably meaning the Bihari-speaking districts). And he had been able to attract money and influential supporters in various parts of India, including the English lawyer and Congressman, Eardley Norton, who allegedly suggested at one of the Swami's meetings that the Congress should make the cow issue part of its program. Sriman Swami reappeared in the Punjab in 1891 and agitated against the Age of Consent Bill and again in 1892 when he presided over a Lahore meeting to protest the dispersion of Hardwar pilgrims. He avoided other provinces while official inquiries were being

---

fighting orders of Hindu mendicants. J. N. Farquhar reported seeing large numbers of men who belonged to these orders in the second decade of the twentieth century at Allahabad and elsewhere but few by this time had the opportunity to fight any more. J. N. Farquhar, "The Fighting Ascetics of India," *Bulletin of the John Rylands Library*, Vol. 9, No. 2 (July 1925), pp. 442–443 and 450–452.

[86] He was temporarily confined in Katmandu after making his request. Note on the agitation by D. F. McCracken, 9 Aug. 1893.

made about his handling of cow protection funds but then attended the 1892 Congress at Allahabad.[87]

Sriman Swami was exceptional in the geographical range of his movements and the breadth of his social contacts. He was, however, only one of many sadhus who entered the cow protection movement and whose teachings had implicit or explicit anti-British content. Whether the sadhus traveled alone or moved in bands, generally they were on their own and not affiliated with local gaurakshini sabhas, although in a few cases sabhas or zamindars hired sadhus to preach for the movement. Most of them had been sadhus before the rise of the cow protection movement but a few, like Sriman Swami, seem to have donned the guise of a sadhu for political purposes. A man calling himself Swami Bhaskaranand was another political sadhu. He impersonated a swami of Jodhpur of that name and traveled about giving lectures. He opened his lectures with sleight-of-hand tricks and then spoke about the Congress, swadeshi industry (especially arms factories), the Arya Samaj, as well as cow protection and vegetarianism. He frequently lied to his audiences, claiming to have been a playmate of Nana Sahib's before the Mutiny. He said that during the Mutiny he served in the 5th Bombay Cavalry but afterward became a sannyasi "from compunction at having fought against his own countrymen." A Thagi and Dakoiti Department memorandum suggested his lectures were not popular.[88]

A third itinerant *gaurakshak* (protector of cows) was Swami Brahmanand Saraswati. A well-educated man who spoke English and several vernaculars, he emphasized the economic reasons for protecting cows in his lectures. However, while speaking to an audience in Bahraich in Oudh in 1893, he displayed a picture which, in addition to showing the distribution of milk to Hindus, Muslims, Parsis, and Christians, contained a scene of a creature with a human body and animal head attempting to kill a cow composed of Hindu deities. The government prosecuted him successfully for violating Muslim religious feelings on the ground that the figure, which it claimed had a pig's head, was intended to represent a Muslim in an offensive manner. Swami Brahmanand was fined Rs. 200 and was prevented from speaking elsewhere by

[87] Ibid.
[88] Memo on Swami Bhaskaranand Saraswati, imposter, 26 July 1895. C.S.B. Memoranda, T. and D. Dept. 1894–1913.

the detectives who followed him and by nervous local officials.[89]

In ordinary times, villagers tended to be skeptical of the honesty and sexual morality of unknown sadhus. Whether protectionist sadhus were able to overcome the usual wariness of villagers and popularize the movement in the early 1890s is not clear. What may be said is that Hardwar, Benaras, and Gya attracted pilgrims and sadhus from all over India, that Hardwar, Benaras, and Gya each appears prominently in government reports on the movement, that large bands of sadhus were present in some districts shortly before cow protection riots occurred. It is obvious that among tens of thousands of sadhus, in addition to orthodox devotees who supported cow protection as a matter of religious or political conviction, there was no shortage of men who were economically destitute, socially maladjusted, or otherwise potential recruits for a movement some of whose supporters eventually committed violence in the name of religion.

When, in 1893, the gaurakshini movement in Bihar turned violent, not only did bands of ascetics play a key role but people native to the western districts of Bihar (Patna division) were involved in the riots there and across the border in the eastern districts of the North-Western Provinces and Oudh. While it is not evident why cow killing became an issue of such importance in western Bihar, it may have been related to the presence there of some of the largest cattle markets in Asia and to social tensions arising from the extreme poverty and overpopulation in the area. It may only be a coincidence that the movement gathered momentum in Bihar in 1888, the year which saw a struggle across the border between the Allahabad Congress and its Muslim and government opponents. Congress leaders faced both counterorganization in the form of the Patriotic Association and repeated obstacles to their efforts to find a meeting place in Allahabad in 1888. After officials used reasons of sanitation and military regulations to force the Congress to change its venue, the largest landholder in Bihar, the Maharaja of Darbhanga, and others secured Lowther Castle in Allahabad for the session just seven weeks before it was due to begin.[90] The Government of India's report on the

[89] Pandit Bishan Narayan Dar, *An Appeal to the English Public on Behalf of the Hindus of the N.-W. P. and Oudh* (Lucknow, 1893), pp. 46–51.

[90] Besant, *How India Wrought*, pp. 54–56, and Mazumdar, *Indian National Evolution*, p. 73.

cow protection movement said that it was also in the autumn of 1888 that the Maharaja of Darbhanga became "actively" interested in the movement. The government received a report that the Darbhanga Gaurakshini Sabha was started at this time under the Maharaja's "auspices" in revenge for Muslim refusal to join the Congress and for Justice Mahmud's part in the High Court decision regarding the inclusion of cattle as sacred objects under the Indian penal code. The Maharaja of Darbhanga was president of the Darbhanga Gaurakshini Sabha and he contributed money to it annually, as he did to the Congress. In recognition of his services to the protection cause, the Nagpur Gaurakshini Sabha invited him, apparently in 1893, to be president of all the sabhas of the Central Provinces, the North-Western Provinces and Oudh, and Bihar.[91]

The other important Congress patron in Bihar who was identified with the movement was the Maharaja of Dumraon. Dumraon gave funds to both the Indian Association of Calcutta and the Congress,[92] and his diwan subsidized the *Behar Herald*, a pro-Congress newspaper.[93] Amla (estate agents) of the Dumraon Raj were active in spreading the movement from Shahabad district, where the Maharaja had his headquarters, northward across the Ganges into Ballia district in the Benaras Division of the North-Western Provinces and Oudh where the Maharaja also owned estates.[94]

When persons associated with the Congress involved themselves publicly with cow protection activities, they embarrassed the Congress leaders who insisted they represented the interests of all Indians. The effort to pass a resolution at the 1887 Congress calling for cow killing to be made a penal offense had caused consternation. The leaders, recognizing that it would mean disaster for their efforts to bring Muslims into the Congress, rejected the proposed resolution and passed instead a resolution which prohibited discussion of any new subject to which either Hindu or Muslim delegates "unanimously or nearly unanimously" were opposed.[95]

[91] Note on the agitation by D. F. McCracken, 9 Aug. 1893.
[92] Seal, *The Emergence*, p. 219.
[93] *Bengalee*, 21 Oct. and 25 Dec. 1900.
[94] H. B. Finlay, Offg. Com., Benaras Div., to Ch. Sec., NWP and O, 29 Sept. 1893. Nov. 1893 Prog. No. 183, IHP, Pub.
[95] A. O. Hume to Sec., Congress Standing Com., 5 Jan. 1888. Govt. of Bombay, *Source Material*, II, 66–67.

Congress leaders could not, however, prevent individual delegates from engaging in communal activities between sessions. The involvement of a small number of prominent Congressmen in the gaurakshini movement led British officials and Muslims hostile to the Congress to assume a much more extensive connection between the Congress and the cow protectionists than actually existed. In most provinces there were enough individuals involved in both movements to encourage suspicions of a general connection.

In the Punjab in particular, support for cow protection and the Congress overlapped among a number of individuals, most often in members of the Arya Samaj. As a group, Aryas were cool toward the Congress until 1893, when they finally joined the Congress in large numbers. Gerald Barrier has suggested that Arya Samaj preoccupation "with cow protection, internal politics, and defense of Hindu interests" was a reason why Aryas did not work for the early Congress.[96] But individual Aryas did actively support both cow protection and the Congress before 1893. One of the Punjab financial commissioners believed that the cow protection agitators were "very generally" Congressmen,[97] while the lieutenant-governor reported in 1894 that cow protection was discussed at meetings of the Congress, Kukas, Singh Sabhas, and, "above all," the Arya Samaj. On the other hand, feeling about the cow issue in the Punjab was less intense in the early 1890s than in the 1880s and than in the provinces to the east, and the protection movement was less well organized in the Punjab than elsewhere.[98] The most important Punjabi Congressmen active in the movement was Lala Murli Dhar, a vakil from Amballa. He was convicted on charges arising from Hindu-Muslim riots in 1886 but his conviction was later overturned by the High Court.[99] In 1893 he was reported to be the only "openly active" cow protectionist in Amballa district.[100] Swami Ala Ram of the Amritsar Arya Samaj was another active protectionist who was associated with the Congress. He spoke in Hindi at the 1888, 1890, 1891,

[96] Barrier, "The Arya Samaj," p. 366.
[97] Note by G. M. Ogilvie, Offg. 2nd Fin. Com., Punjab, n. d. Pub. Letters from India and Gen. Letters from Bengal, 1894, Vol. 19.
[98] Note by Sir Dennis Fitzpatrick, 10 Jan. 1894, ibid.
[99] Note on the agitation in the Punjab, para. 166.
[100] Capt. C. G. Parsons, Depty. Com., Umballa, to Col. L.J.H. Gray, Com. and Supt. of Police, Delhi Div., 12 Dec. 1893. Pub. Letters from India and Gen. Letters from Bengal, 1894, Vol. 19.

and 1892 Congress sessions. Between sessions he spoke on behalf of both the Congress and cow protection. Once he spoke at the *Tribune* Press; another time he "preached at Majithia under the patronage" of Sardar Dyal Singh, the wealthy benefactor of the Congress.[101] While circulating Congress petitions in 1890, he reportedly told people that the reformed legislative councils could be used to stop cow slaughter and abolish the income tax.[102]

In the Central Provinces, according to the head of Thagi and Dakoiti Department, the main backers of the cow protection movement were "the Mahratta Brahmin pleaders, the same men who are the chief supporters of the Congress." It has already been mentioned that the Nagpur Gauraksha Sabha was permitted to use the Congress pavilion in 1891, a privilege which was denied the Social Reform Conference at Poona in 1895. The leader of the Congress in Berar, M. V. Joshi, suggested upon his return from England as a member of the Congress mission pressing for council reform that the Congress make common cause with the cow protection movement and share the funds collected.[103] Altogether the protection movement was strong in the Central Provinces and Berar, but perhaps because of its economic emphasis and because Muslims constituted less than 3 per cent of the population, the movement led to much less communal friction than in the provinces to the north.

Congressmen were involved in the protection societies started in both Poona and Bombay city in 1887. Bal Gangadhar Tilak belonged to the Poona society although he seems never to have been very active. The movement was much weaker in the Marathi-speaking districts of Bombay Province than in the Central Provinces. In Bombay city, on the other hand, the movement had surprising strength. Sir Dinshaw M. Petit, the Parsi businessman, former president of the Bombay Presidency Association, and sometime Congress supporter, was president of the Gau Rakshaha Mandali in 1893.[104] This cow protection society had a major portion of the Bombay political establishment on its managing com-

---

[101] Note on the agitation in the Punjab, paras. 279, 282–283, 286, 290–291, and 324.

[102] Note on the agitation by D. F. McCracken, 9 Aug. 1893.

[103] Ibid.

[104] S. Krishnaswamy, "A Riot in Bombay, August 11, 1893: A Study in Hindu-Muslim Relations in Western India During the Late Nineteenth Century" (Ph.D. dissertation, University of Chicago, 1966), p. 29.

mittee, including 35 justices of the peace. Even K. T. Telang, a founder of the Presidency Association and the Indian National Congress, publicly supported the movement before his elevation to the Bombay High Court.[105] The reason such prominent Indians, including Parsis and even some wealthy Khoja Muslims, supported the Bombay Mandali was because the society's basic thrust was economic, not religious.

In the North-Western Provinces and Oudh, several prominent Congressmen were connected to the movement. In Allahabad, Pandit Madan Mohan Malaviya was known to be sympathetic to the peaceful objectives of the sabhas.[106] Malaviya's close associate, Lala Ram Charan Das, the wealthy Allahabad banker and trader who served on three Congress Reception Committees, was "the major local donor to Swami Ala Ram's cow-shed fund" in or before 1888.[107] Munshi Roshan Lal, an Allahabad barrister and Congressman, belonged to the local cow protection society and attended the 1889 meeting of the Nagpur Sabha.[108] Raja Rampal Singh's *Hindustan* of Kalakankar published articles advocating protection of cows,[109] and the Raja presided over at least one protection meeting.[110] After the 1893 riots, the two Congress leaders from Lucknow, Ganga Prasad Varma and Pandit Bishan Narayan Dar, investigated the Azamgarh disturbances and then concluded in an article that Muslims killed more kine than usual because of government administrative bungling.[111] Insofar as they absolved the cow protection societies of all guilt, they identified themselves with the cow protection cause, although their case against officials in Azamgarh was highly plausible. Previously, Ganga Prasad Varma's newspaper, *Hindustani*, had tried to allay Sayyid Ahmad Khan's fear that a Hindu majority in the Legislative Council might ban cow slaughter.[112] What is striking about

[105] Note on the agitation by D. F. McCracken, 9 Aug. 1893.
[106] Malaviya spoke at both the Bharata Dharma Mahamandal and the Prayag Hindu Sabha in 1889. Both organizations advocated protection. *Hindustan* (Kalakankar), 6 and 18 Apr. 1889, NWP and O NNR (1889), pp. 219 and 251.
[107] Bayly, "Patrons and Politics in Northern India," pp. 48–50.
[108] *Nyaya Sudha* (Harda), 6 Nov. 1889, NWP and O NNR (1889), p. 705.
[109] *Hindustan*, 19 Apr. and 16 May 1889, ibid., pp. 252 and 316.
[110] *Hindustan*, 15 May 1889, ibid., pp. 318–319.
[111] *Hindustani* (Lucknow), 2 Aug. 1893, NWP and O, CP, and R NNR No. 32 of 1893, para. 3.
[112] *Hindustani*, 30 March 1890, NWP and O, CP, and R NNR No. 14 of 1890.

Ganga Prasad Varma is that while he was one of the few Congress publicists sensitive enough to Muslim apprehensions to have tried to ease them before the 1893 riots, Varma seemed unwilling after the riots to concede that gaurakshini sabhas bore the major responsibility for the violence. Apparently the pressures within Hindu society overcame even the least communal of Congress leaders who generally failed to speak out against the protection movement.

In those areas of India where the movement was weak or nonexistent, as in south India and the Bengali- and Gujarati-speaking districts, almost no Congressmen were associated with cow protection. However, it was a Bengali zamindar, the Raja of Tahirpore, who tried to introduce a protection resolution in the Congress in 1887.[113]

On the eve of the 1893 cow protection riots, the protection movement was geographically and socially diverse. It was almost universally motivated by a concern to improve agriculture and the health of Indians. Protection was seen as a logical response to Indian poverty. It also represented an effort to protect one primary religious symbol as compensation for the loss of face and autonomy suffered in the passing of the Age of Consent Bill. Further, it was an attempt by orthodox Hindus, especially among mendicant orders, to recover their role as protectors of Hinduism's central values. And it was a testing of the new, fluid competitive arrangements governing administrative and legislative decision-making. As far as the Congress was concerned, the movement damaged its goal of uniting Hindus and Muslims in a single nationalist party because the cow protectors agitated for a legislative ban on the slaughter of kine at the same time the Congress pressed for legislative council reform, thereby leading Muslims to perceive the Congress and cow protectors as part of a single challenge to Muslim interests.

[113] Lalmohan Ghose represented Hindu defendants in court following a communal riot at Dhumri in 1888, but there is no reason to assume communal motivation in his acceptance of that case. Note on the agitation in the Punjab, para. 230.

Chapter Ten

COW PROTECTION RIOTS AND THEIR AFTERMATH

Gaurakshini Sabhas

The heart of the protection movement in the Gangetic districts which experienced rioting in 1893 was neither the occasional Congress lawyer or zamindar nor the wandering sadhus but rather the local gaurakshini sabhas. The sabhas were an expression of Hindu revival and anxiety. By focusing people's attention on the status of the cow, they communicated a concern for the preservation of one of Hinduism's oldest, commonest, and most reassuring symbols. At the same time, by giving Hindus concrete economic goals to fulfill in protecting cattle, the sabhas were appealing to sentiments in favor of modern material improvements and philanthropy. The sabhas were strongest in the heavily Hindu area of western Bihar [Patna division], Benaras division, Oudh, and Eastern Allahabad division.[1] There seem to be no accurate figures about the number of sabhas or about the geographic range of any single sabha. One official report says there were 44 sabhas in the Central Provinces in 1890;[2] another cites the existence of 23 sabhas in Patna division in 1893.[3] The great majority of sabhas had been started with the noncoercive objectives of improving the breed of cattle, of caring for aged and sick animals, and of teaching people the economic and religious reasons for protecting cattle. The nonoffensive character of these original goals explains the membership of men such as the Maharaja of Darbhanga, prominent lawyers and Marwaris, Hindu officials, honorary magistrates, members of municipal and district boards, and, in the case of Bombay city, wealthy Khoja Muslims.[4] It also explains why the Government of the North-Western Provinces and Oudh described the goals of the societies as "innocent, and even laudable" until

---

[1] Note by C. J. L[yall], 6 Oct. 1893. Nov. 1893 Prog. No. 169, IHP, Pub.
[2] Note on the agitation by D. F. McCracken, 9 Aug. 1893.
[3] A. Forbes letter of 27 Oct. 1893.   [4] Krishnaswamy, *A Riot*, p. 151.

a short time before the 1893 riots.⁵ After a period of growth in the late 1880s, the movement receded in many areas during the Age of Consent Bill controversy. But in 1892 and 1893, for reasons which have been suggested, the sabhas grew more aggressive and began to interfere more frequently in the sale and slaughter of cattle. Some also began to take compulsory contributions from Hindus and to denounce meat-eaters in terms which suggested they were subhuman. It is difficult to document or explain this change because official descriptions of the sabhas were mostly composite. An individual sabha, as in the Gya district of Bihar, took compulsory contributions as early as 1889, while in the North-Western Provinces and Oudh (and probably in most of Bihar also) the sabhas "passed out of the form of voluntary associations and assumed the organization of leagues," rescuing cattle and compelling contributions, only at the start of 1893.⁶

The funds collected were used to build *gaushalas* (cattle pounds), to buy cows from butchers and markets in order to prevent them from being killed, and to pay the cow protection agents and lecturers. Methods of collection varied, but tin donation boxes decorated with the figure of a cow were placed in public places such as post offices, bazaars, money-lenders' stalls, and food and liquor shops. Merchants were asked to give a percentage of each sale, litigants to contribute a share of a successful settlement, cultivators to pay a tax on each plough. The agents, called *sabhasads*, also collected grain from individual families. Each family was expected, and in some places forced, to save one *chutki* of grain (an amount worth one paisa) from each person for each meal. The sabhasads then sold the grain and used the proceeds for the sabhas' activities. Individual families were also asked or forced to give donations upon the occasion of marriage and other feasts.⁷

The organization for collecting funds was complex. One or more sabhasads were assigned to each village. A group of villages was placed under a *sabhapati*. And a whole district was under a *sadar sabhapati*. The same hierarchy, assisted by other agents, enforced the sabhas' injunctions upon the Hindu population.

⁵ Ch. Sec., NWP and O, to Sec., Gov. of India, Home Dept., 28 Aug. 1893. Nov. 1893 Prog. No. 169, IHP, Pub.

⁶ Ch. Sec., NWP and O, letter of 28 Aug. 1893.

⁷ Ibid. Also, A. Forbes letter of 27 Oct. 1893 and Note on the agitation by D. F. McCracken, 9 Aug. 1893.

Offenders were boycotted, outcasted, and fined. Special courts were set up to try persons who sold cattle to Muslims, the Commissariat, or to Nats, Banjaras, Dosadhs, and Chamars who traditionally supplied cattle to butchers. The following is a report of two decisions made by gaurakshini sabha courts:

Gao Maharani (Cow Empress) versus Sita Ram Ahir of Haldi
Charge—Impounding a cow in the Government pound.

The cow was sold by auction (from the pound) to one Gangu, a butcher, for Rs. 10. The fact was brought to the notice of the Sabhapati, who sending for Sita Ram, ordered him to buy back the cow, which he did for Rs. 14, and then sent him up for trial before the Sabha. The court was formally held in ----'s house in ----. Sita Ram pleaded guilty, and was sentenced to Rs. 4-8-0 fine. He refused to pay the fine, and was brought before the Sadar Sabha, and sentenced to 24 days' outcasting and various religious penalties.

Gao Maharani versus Sheo Lochan
Charge—Impounding a cow in the Government pound.

Tried by the head Sabhapati. Sentenced to 12 days' outcasting with the accompanying religious penalties, and to pay a fine of 8 cows. On default to four times the above punishment. Any one abetting his default to pay half the above fine.[8]

The general accounts of the cow killing riots did not specify the extent of the courts' functioning. The report on the riots in Ballia district, though, suggests they were not widespread: "Courts, original and appellate, were established in several villages in the district, the proceedings in which were a somewhat flattering imitation of the proceedings in the Magistrates' Courts."[9] In both Ballia and Azamgarh, zamindars acted as judges[10] and thereby resumed one of the traditional functions they were gradually losing. In some instances, courts and panchayats exerted social pressure for offenses not directly involving cows. In Ballia, a Hindu cloth broker named Jit Singh was excommunicated and

[8] From C. J. Lyall, Case for the Consideration of the Advocate General (n. d.), reprinted in John R. McLane (ed), *The Political Awakening in India* (Englewood Cliffs, N. J., 1970), p. 112.

[9] H. B. Finlay, Offg. Com., Benaras Div., to Ch. Sec., NWP and O, 29 Sept. 1893. Nov. 1893 Prog. No. 183, IHP, Pub.

[10] H.E.L.P. Dupernex, Offg. Mag., Azamgarh, to Com., Gorakhpur Div., 7 July 1893. Nov. 1893 Prog. Nos. 170–178, IHP, Pub.

boycotted for having, as was his custom, participated with his gymnastic students in the 1893 Muharram procession.[11] One district magistrate, in describing the sabhas' efforts to establish "an *imperium in imperio*," wrote that the cow protection "League watches over the private life of individuals with the tyranny of the inquisition."[12]

Both the sabhas and the itinerant cow protectors made efficient use of the printing press. They distributed thousands of pamphlets and drawings. One illustration called "The Present State" showed a cow about to be slaughtered by three Muslim butchers. Another entitled "The Kali Yug" showed a cow whose body was composed of Hindu gods confronted by a *raksha* or demon with a drawn sword.[13] Still another portrayed the former Dharmraj (rule of right conduct) with a cow drinking from a stream to the sound of music and then the contrasting present Kaliyug in which a cow was about to be butchered. A Hindu explained the scene:

> As every man drinks cow's milk, just as he, as an infant, has drawn milk from his mother, the cow must be regarded as the universal mother, and so is called "Gau Mata." It is therefore matricide to kill a cow. Nay more, as all the gods dwell in the cow, to kill a cow is to insult every Hindu.[14]

Plays about cow killing were also circulated. A Hindu drama called *Bharat-dimdima Natuk* was sold in railway bookstalls. It linked India's grim economic conditions to kine slaughter.[15] Parts of another Hindi play were published in the *Gosewak*, a Benaras weekly. It concerned a Brahman in Rajputana and the cow given to him by a generous landowner. Three Muslims entered his house and seized the beloved cow for an Id sacrifice. While the Brahman helplessly protested, the Muslims carried away the cow, singing a song about the Hindu kafirs and their intention to kill them.[16]

The distribution of the cartoons, plays, and pamphlets, together with the other activities of the sadhus and the sabhas,

---

[11] *Tohfa-i-Qadiri* (Ballia), 6 Aug. 1893, para. 6, NWP and O, CP, and R NNR No. 33 of 1893.

[12] H.E.L.P. Dupernex letter of 7 July 1893.

[13] Gov. Gen. to S. of S., 27 Dec. 1893.

[14] Note on the agitation by D. F. McCracken, 9 Aug. 1893.

[15] Gov. Gen. to S. of S., 27 Dec. 1893.

[16] *Gosewak* (Benaras), 22 and 29 Dec. 1892 and 5 Jan. 1893. NWP and O, CP, and R NNR No. 2 of 1893, para. 28.

created an atmosphere which was increasingly hostile to Muslims. The danger of communal violence grew as the sabhas escalated their demands and activities from pleas of kindness to cows to calls for punishment of offenders, from purchase of animals to forcible seizure, from complaints to officials of illegal Muslim sacrifices to direct interference. Some local officials tried to diminish the possibility of bloodshed by accommodating the changed Hindu mood. These officials asked Muslims to surrender cows upon payment and insisted that Muslims hold their prices down to a fair level.[17] Officials also mediated disputes and, when serious friction occurred, set up conciliation committees composed of leading Hindus and Muslims. However, by June 1893 the cycle of provocation and counterprovocation had gone beyond the point at which administrators could be confident that trouble could be predicted at specific places. Muslims were countering gaurakshini activities with demonstrative slaughter, perhaps to spite Hindu communalists, perhaps to establish their right to exercise a religious and civil liberty.[18] And when violence did erupt in 1893, it did so in places where special, local ambiguity existed concerning the right to kill cows. It seems that in Azamgarh district, where the first riots occurred which triggered disturbances in other parts of India, cow protectors interfered in Muslim kine killing in the belief that the government was not enforcing local laws and administrative regulations.

The Azamgarh Riots

Three points of law and administrative practice were in dispute in Azamgarh district in the eastern end of the North-Western Provinces and Oudh. The first concerned the number of cows which were normally sacrificed in the district on Bakr Id. Muslims were required to give notice to the government of their intention to make sacrifices in order that the government could prevent sacrifices in numbers and in places which were not customary. Hindus claimed that the 426 notices received in Azam-

[17] The much criticized Mr. Dupernex, district magistrate of Azamgarh, did both of these things according to a letter from an Azamgarh Muslim pleader. *Hindustani* (Lucknow), 19 July 1893, NWP and O, CP, and R NNR No. 30 of 1893, para. 17.

[18] The Government of India dispatch on the riots commented: "We fear" some Muslims had demonstrated "an increasingly ostentatious exercise of their right to slaughter kine." Gov. Gen. to S. of S., 27 Dec. 1893.

garh district in 1893 were more than usual; the government replied after the riots that "there are no means of ascertaining whether the number . . . is more or less than the number which is customarily sacrificed."[19] In the absence of such means, government efforts to prevent violence were obviously handicapped. The second dispute involved sacrifices in the town of Azamgarh. Hindus pointed out that the Azamgarh municipal bylaws forbade animal sacrifice "in private houses," but H. Dupernex, the thirty-one-year-old district magistrate, ruled that the bylaw did not apply to Id sacrifices.[20] Here again, there seemed to be an honest disagreement over the exact meaning of administrative regulations.

Finally, there was an old dispute, dating back to 1806, in the town of Mau where the worst riots took place. In 1808, following a serious 1806 riot, the governor general in council had issued an order, based upon a decision by the Sadar Nizamat Adawlat, "sanctioning the prohibition as a special measure of all cow sacrifices" in the town of Mau. Local Hindus believed that the order applied not merely to cattle *sacrifices* but to all cattle slaughter. In the early nineteenth century, local officials often enforced the order in the way it was interpreted by Hindus. But in other periods, local officials agreed with Muslims that the order pertained only to "sacrifices." In the 1860s the latter interpretation prevailed, and Muslims were permitted to build a slaughter house in Mau, to the intense dissatisfaction of some local Hindus.[21] The 1893 dispute was the culmination of the old argument over the meaning of the 1808 order, and it was apparently stimulated by an 1886 government decision to permit Muslims to move the site of the slaughter house which had fallen into disuse. The failure of British officials to enforce prior legal and administrative decisions in a consistent manner had encouraged people in Mau and its neighborhood to believe that public pressure and changes in administrative personnel might lead to alteration of the rules governing the killing of cows. These local disputes seem to be the main reason why Mau, rather than some other place, erupted in violence in response to the growing coerciveness of the protection movement.

[19] Ch. Sec., NWP and O, letter of 28 Aug. 1893.

[20] Dar, *An Appeal*, Appendix, p. 15.

[21] Order by John J. F. Lumsdon, Com. of Benaras Div., on petition regarding slaughter of kine in Mow, 9 Dec. 1886. Published in Dar, *An Appeal*, Appendix, pp. 26ff.

Mau was a town with 15,000 inhabitants, almost half of whom were Muslim. Azamgarh district as a whole was only 15 per cent Muslim. Perhaps it was the relatively high proportion of Muslims in Mau which gave them the courage to resist the Hindu demands that no cows be sacrificed. In any case, when a local Muslim zamindar insisted upon sacrificing an animal for his daughter's wedding, a crowd of local Hindus gathered to object. They were joined by two thousand men from Ghazipur district on the south and then by four thousand men from Ballia district on the east. The cow protectors attacked Muslims and looted a bazaar in Mau. The entry into Mau of Hindus from neighboring areas was apparently motivated by a righteousness born of a rumor that cows had not been killed in Mau since Akbar's time and of a belief that British authorities were allowing Muslims to sacrifice in new places. A Muslim claimed the riots reminded people "of the dark days of the Mutiny. The Hindu rioters had with them horses, elephants and tents."[22] Another said that "for three days it looked as if British rule had ceased in the district."[23] Officials estimated that seven Muslims were killed in the Mau riots; local persons put the death toll at two hundred.

The divisional commissioner said he had never seen anything like the Mau riots in his long career. They "were not so much riots . . . as an actual invasion of enemies bound on intimidating and robbing and killing." He thought the cow protection society of Azamgarh was aiming "at the annihilation" of Islam.[24] The district magistrate of Azamgarh commented that "the Hindus appear to have suddenly woke up to the fact that the Muhammadans are no longer their masters, and the insolent aggressiveness of their attitude towards them is a natural re-action from their former enforced submissiveness."[25]

The Spread of Violence

The Mau riot was the most spectacular disturbance in either the North-Western Provinces and Oudh or Bihar in 1893 because

[22] *Nur-ul-Anwar* (Cawnpore), 22 July 1893, NWP and O, CP, and R NNR No. 30 of 1893, para. 18.
[23] Letter from Munshi Abdul Gafar, *Hindustani*, 19 July 1893, ibid., para. 17.
[24] M. L. Ferrar, Com., Gorakhpur Div., to Ch. Sec., NWP and O, 18 July 1893. Nov. 1893 Prog. No. 170, IHP, Pub.
[25] H.E.L.P. Dupernex letter of 7 July 1893.

of the convergence there of organized crowds from outside the district. No other riot represented such an audacious challenge to Muslims and to the government's responsibility for maintaining law and order. Most of the cow protectors who entered Azamgarh district came from the east, from Ballia district. The Ballia district was the home of a particularly aggressive gaurakshini sabha led by the Bishen Rajput zamindar of Nagra, Jagdeo Bahadur. Jagdeo Bahadur and his followers had extended their activities into several districts in the eastern North-Western Provinces. He had also taken two or three hundred followers into Saran district in Bihar in May 1893 and held meetings at which Hindus were urged to rescue cows from butchers. There seems to be no obvious explanation of the strength of the movement in Ballia district. However, it may be relevant that it was the most densely populated district in the North-Western Provinces and Oudh and probably one of the poorest. Moreover, in recent years, many zamindars, a high proportion of whom were Rajputs, had been struggling over rights to land. An 1888 report said:

> There is everywhere [in Ballia district] a movement of impatience against subjection to a common obligation, and of assertion of individual right. The proprietary bodies or zamindars envy the comparative freedom of the fixed-rate tenant. A universal partition is going on, very feebly represented by the number of cases for partition which come before the Courts. By division of the land or of the rents and separation of *sir* holdings the zamindars are making a partition in their own way, and each man endeavours to exercise the privilege of paying his own revenue direct, and resents the obligation to advance that of another man.[26]

Possibly this new competitive spirit in agrarian relations affected attitudes toward the Muslims and the government. In any case, Jagdeo Bahadur and his sabha were among the most active and coercive cow protectors in 1893, and they were blamed by officials for some of the violence in Azamgarh, Ballia, and Saran districts.

If Azamgarh was the scene of the most spectacular rioting and Ballia of the most comprehensive organization, the Bihar districts of Saran, Gya, and Patna had the largest number of riots

[26] Memorandum by F. B. Mulock, Offg. Col. and Mag. of Ballia, in *An Inquiry into the Economic Condition of the Agricultural and Labouring Classes in the North-Western Provinces and Oudh* (Naini Tal, 1888), pp. 143–145.

in 1893. Bihar experienced 22 riots that year, compared to the North-Western Provinces and Oudh's 9.[27] Bihar, like the eastern North-Western Provinces, contained some of the most densely populated districts in India and a high percentage of destitute peasants. Also, Bihari Muslims were so few (about 15 per cent of the population) that they may have been less effective in deterring cow protectors than Muslims in the Punjab and the western districts of the North-Western Provinces. Most of the western Bihari districts had cow protection societies organized in 1887 and 1888. Agents of major zamindars, including the Rajas of Darbhanga, Dumraon, Hatwa, and Bettia, were reported to have helped the movement to spread. And so did the priests of Gya. After a Bakr Id riot at Gya in 1891, which was provoked by "the ostentatious parading" of a "sacrificial cow,"[28] the gyawals were reported to have "issued instructions" to their pilgrim touts and other agents throughout India to press for the protection of cows. But the large cattle fairs in Bihar, more than any other factor, seemed to have served as the goad or the opportunity for the cow protectors in Bihar. The movement of herds of cattle to and from the Dinapur commissariat and the cattle markets at Berhampur, Patna, and other towns were targets of the protectors.[29] The protectors often carried lathis and in some cases shouted "Kali ki jai" and "Pawari Baba [the drinker of milk] ki jai."[30] The cattle markets also attracted substantial numbers of agitators from the North-Western Provinces in 1893. The agitators, who were reported in every district of Patna division, came "chiefly from Benares and its neighborhood." In addition there were "hordes of wandering Sadhus, sometimes in gangs of a hundred or more, . . . who do not appear to be directly under the orders of the local Gaurakshini Sabhas."[31]

The 31 communal riots in Bihar and the North-Western Provinces in 1893 may seem unimpressive in comparison to the large number of riots in the 1920s. But they were impressive at the

[27] Statement of Hindu-Muhammadan riots in the past 5 years (1889–1893). Enclosure to Gov. Gen. to S. of S., 26 Sept. 1894. Sept. 1894 Prog. Nos. 363–364, IHP, Pub.

[28] A. Forbes letter of 27 Oct. 1893.

[29] Note on the agitation by D. F. McCracken, 9 Aug. 1893.

[30] See The Empress versus Ram Nath Sahu and 6 others, Judgment by H. W. Gordon, Sessions Judge, Saran, 28 Dec. 1893. Nov. 1894 Police Prog. Nos. 47–49. Bengal Jud. Prog., Vol. 4,547.

[31] A. Forbes letter of 27 Oct. 1893.

time, both because communal riots were relatively rare in the nineteenth century and because the 1893 riots were, unlike earlier disturbances, the product of an all-Indian agitation. The notion that Hindu-Muslim riots were common in the nineteenth century seems to be a myth. The riot statistics for British India exclusive of the Punjab (where few riots occurred)[32] for the four year period between 1889 and 1892 bear this out. The period is too brief to permit broad conclusions. However, it was a period in which government officials believed there was an exceptionally high degree of communal friction. What official figures show is that from 1889 through 1892, seven people were killed in roughly 45 Hindu-Muslim riots in British India exclusive of the Punjab.[33] In view of the fact that in most years the Government of India recorded more than 10,000 riots and "other offences against the public peace,"[34] communal friction was not ordinarily a major source of civil disturbance in the 1880s and 1890s.

The year 1893 was an exception. In that year alone, 107 people died in approximately 45 communal disturbances. The bulk of the 107 deaths occurred in Bombay city in riots which were part of the chain reaction to the Azamgarh disturbances. The spread of violence from Azamgarh to Bombay indicates both the all-Indian spread of the cow protection movement and the growing sensitivity of local communal politics to violent developments in remote areas of the country.[35] Many pre-1893 interprovincial connections have been mentioned: Swami Dayananda's preambulations, the trips of Arya Samaj missionaries to places as distant as Madras, Sriman Swami's tours of almost every province in India,

[32] The Punjab had only nine communal riots from 1881 to 1893. Five of those were in 1885–1886 and were attributed to the overlapping of Hindu and Muslim religious festivals. "After that, there was a prolonged period of practical immunity from disturbance." Memorandum submitted by the Government of the Punjab, n. d., *Indian Statutory Commission* (London, 1930), x, 105.

[33] Statement of Hindu-Muhammadan riots in the past 5 years (1889–1893).

[34] "Rioting and other offences against the public peace" were reported at the following rate: 7,825 (1880); 10,286 (1884); 10,8–7 (1886); 11,195 (1888); 10,845 (1890); 11,086 (1891). East India Parliamentary Paper, *Statement Exhibiting The Moral and Material Progress and Condition of India During the Year 1891–92, and the Nine Preceding Years* (London, 1894), p. 144.

[35] The Rangoon riot occurred on the same day as the Mau disturbance and was also over Muslim sacrifice. Fifteen persons were killed and 107 military police were said to have been injured. Statement of Hindu-Muhammadan riots in the past 5 years (1889–1893).

the wandering bands of sadhus that entered Bihar, and the cow protection meeting at Nagpur attended by delegates from Bombay, Poona, Allahabad, Benaras, Calcutta, and other places. Just as railways and the printing press helped popularize the issue before 1893, the telegraph and newspapers disseminated news of the 1893 riots in Azamgarh and western Bihar to every corner of India, sometimes with sad consequences.

The violence reached Bombay city via the princely state of Junagadh. The riot in Junagadh on 25 July 1893 was in the ancient Hindu pilgrimage town of Prabhas Patan, better known as Somnath Patan. Somnath occupies a special place in the history of Islamic expansion and iconoclasm. Mahmud of Ghazni's destruction of the Shiva temple and massacre of Brahmans at Somnath in 1026 had been glorified by Muslims as a major victory over idolatry. And it had been deprecated by Hindu historians. It is unclear if this was a contributing factor to the 1893 riot. What is certain is that Prabhas Patan had grown in popularity with devout Hindus after it had been linked to other towns by railway in the late nineteenth century. Gujarati banias and Chitpavan Brahmans, among others, had come from British India and donated funds for the restoration of local temples. Shortly before the 1893 riots, two issues had caused friction between Muslims and Hindus in Junagadh. Junagadh Muslims had been agitating to persuade the Nawab of Junagadh to stop favoring Hindus in the state's administrative services, while Hindu pilgrims were complaining of maltreatment at the hands of the Nawab's Muslim officials. According to S. Krishnaswami's careful analysis, the news of the June riots in the North-Western Provinces and Oudh exacerbated the local friction by angering some Junagadh Muslims.[36] When Junagadh Muslims attacked Hindus on 25 July during Muharram, they were in part taking revenge for the attacks on Muslims in Azamgarh.[37]

Soon after the Prabhas Patan riot, Junagadh Muslims traveled to Bombay city to seek support for those Muslims who had been arrested in the disturbance. The arrest of Muslims in Junagadh and the attacks on Muslims in Azamgarh and Bihar contributed to a feeling among Bombay Muslims that they "generally were suffering at the hands of the Hindus."[38] Public feeling in Bombay

---

[36] Krishnaswami, *A Riot*, pp. 74–89.   [37] Ibid., pp. 148–149.
[38] Govt. of Bom. to S. of S., 26 Oct. 1893, para. 16. Nov. 1893 Prog. No. 185, IHP, Pub.

had already been aroused by the anniversary celebration of the founding of the Gau Rakshaha Mandali which was attended by "delegates from all parts of India." The organizers had wanted to parade thousands of cows through the streets but were prevented from doing so by officials who feared violence. After the Junagadh disturbances, Hindus from Junagadh also came to Bombay to enlist support for the riot victims and to seek British interference in Junagadh affairs. "Lavannas, Banias, and Bhatias" held meetings, and one of the meetings was attended by "all the Maharajas" (priests) of those castes.[39] An unusual aspect of the public meetings was the attendance of "lower class Hindus, particularly... the Maratha mill-hands."[40] The person credited with initiating the meetings of Maratha workers was Lakhmidas Khimji, a wealthy Bhatia cotton mill owner. Khimji also organized the Gau Palana Upadeshak Sabha (Society for the Propagation of Cow Protection) earlier in 1893. The new sabha conducted an inflamatory campaign against cow slaughter in the days preceding the Bombay riot.[41] In assessing the causes of the Bombay riot, the commissioner of police placed the major blame on the cow protection movement and the Hindu agitation over Prabhas Patan.[42] The Government of Bombay specifically questioned this interpretation and offered the possibility that the news of riots elsewhere had exacerbated a "predisposing cause" —a Muslim impression that Muslims were losing influence and position to Hindus.[43]

Muslims did in fact commit the first violence. Armed with staves, Muslims emptied out of the Jama Masjid and attacked a nearby Hanuman temple whose bells and music were allegedly disturbing their prayers. After this the rioting spread to many areas of the city and included much looting, arson, and fighting between groups of Hindus and Muslims. Officials reported that in the three days of rioting, 80 persons were killed, 1,500 were arrested, and 300 temples, mosques, and shops were damaged or destroyed. Many of the Muslims who participated in the rioting were not originally from the Bombay region. The Pathans were

[39] R. H. Vincent, Actg. Com. of Police, Bom., to G. C. Whitworth, Actg. Sec., Govt. of Bom., Judic. Dept., 9 Sept. 1893, ibid.

[40] Of the 100,000 workers employed in Bombay's 67 cotton mills in 1893, almost 70,000 were Marathas. Krishnaswami, *A Riot*, p. 212.

[41] Ibid., pp. 103–104 and 155–157.

[42] R. H. Vincent letter of 9 Sept. 1893.

[43] Govt. of Bom. letter of 26 Oct. 1893.

from the northwest frontier; the Chili Chors, many of whom were bullock cart drivers, had come from Kathiawar; while the Julahas, some of whom were Wahabhis, had migrated from the Gangetic districts.[44] Julahas were also centrally involved in the Mau and Rangoon riots, and while officials seem not to have suggested it, it is possible the Bombay Julahas were hoping to avenge the death of fellow Muslim Julahas in those two towns.[45] Official reports did not indicate whether there was rivalry in the textile mills between Julaha weavers and Maratha workers.

It seems that a higher proportion of Hindu rioters, who outnumbered the Muslims by roughly two to one, came from the neighboring region, although Komatis from south India joined in the attacks on Muslims. A disproportionate number of Muslims were killed in the riots because, as the Government of Bombay explained, Hindu mill-hands "not only retaliated upon their Muhammadan aggressors, but did so in large and apparently organized gangs." The government believed that the mill-hands "capacity for organization" was a new element in the city's life.[46] Altogether, an estimated 25,000 persons participated in the rioting.[47]

The Effect of the Riots on Indian Politics

Each of these riots from Azmagarh to Bihar to Bombay had special local causes which explain why those disturbances occurred when most of India experienced no violence. But the links between one riot and the next stand out. It was the broad movement to stop the killing of cows in upper India that led to the riots in Bihar and North-Western Provinces and Oudh. Those riots, in turn, seemed to have been a crucial factor in the Prabhas Patan disturbances, and so on. Violence in a rural area was reported and commented on throughout India. When people of one community in a particular locality were perceived to have suffered communal injustice, elements in the larger religious

---

[44] Enclosures to Govt. of Bom. letter of 26 Oct. 1893.

[45] According to Herbert Risley (*The People of India,* 2nd ed. [Calcutta, 1915], p. 136), throughout India "the stupidity of the weaver, especially of Muhammad weaver (Jolaha), is a staple subject of proverbial philosophy." It is also possible that urban disturbances enabled the Julaha migrants to express resentments against Hindus which they normally kept bottled up.

[46] Govt. of Bom. letter of 26 Oct. 1893.

[47] R. H. Vincent letter of 9 Sept. 1893.

group were responding as if the whole group were threatened. The expanded sense of community membership was bridging class and geographical barriers, and in that sense it was part of the nation-building process. But in times of communal conflict such as the summer of 1893, it was also contributing to a sense of separate communal identification. In 1893, it seemed momentarily as if two nations were emerging in many parts of India.

The cow protection movement and the riots drew the attention of some educated Muslims to India's future constitution once again. Perhaps no issue dramatized so well the problem of minority rights under a future Hindu majority rule as the cow killing problem did. The issue evoked dissimilar responses from people claiming to speak for Muslim and Hindu interests. Muslims were unable to draw Hindus into a dialogue about majority rule and constitutional safeguards. Perhaps because eventual independence and majority rule seemed, at the same time, both inevitable and remote, Hindus showed little inclination to examine in a searching way the awkward questions involved. For many educated Muslims, the issues of what privileges, protections, and powers would be given to minorities was at the heart of constitutional politics. These Muslims felt discussion of guarantees of minority rights should come sooner rather than later because the British still controlled India and because the British alone could be trusted to provide adequate constitutional protections.

Not all educated Muslim commentators drew similar conclusions from the 1893 riots, but one view is of special interest because it seemed to represent an attitude common in the North-Western Provinces and Oudh. It was expressed in two letters to the *Aligarh Institute Gazette* by Haji Muhammad Ismail Khan, a landowner from Aligarh district who was appointed to the provincial legislative council in November 1893. He also was a member of the Simla deputation and the Provisional Committee of the All-India Muslim League in 1906. Muhammad Ismail Khan blamed the riots upon Parliament's interference in Indian affairs. He wrote: "Ignoring the fact that India is inhabited by two nations which differ in race and religion, Parliament has introduced into the Indian administration the principle of government by the majority" by passing the Councils Act of 1892.[48] "India is like a balance whose two pans are of unequal weight,

---

[48] *Aligarh Institute Gazette*, 5 Sept. 1893, NWP and O, CP, and R NNR No. 37 of 1893, para. 7.

and to equalize them a compensating weight is required to make the lighter pan equal to the heavier." In one of his letters he said, "this compensating weight will always be a foreign nation; and it is an occasion of congratulation that God has entrusted the British nation with this duty, who are a generous and free people."[49] But in his other letter, he threatened a different kind of compensation. "If the common people come to know that the Government has passed into the hands of Hindus a terrible conflagration will at once spread from Peshawar to Calcutta, and from the Himalayas to Cap Comorin."[50] This was an unmistakable echo of Sayyid Ahmad Khan's 1888 warning that if the British ever relinquished control of the administration, it would be necessary for one of the "two nations" to "conquer the other and thrust it down." And if the Indian Muslims were not strong enough, Sayyid Ahmad had said, "our Musalman brothers, the Pathans, would come out as a swarm of locusts from their mountain valleys" and "make rivers of blood to flow from their frontier on the north to the extreme end of Bengal."[51] How representative this "two nation" view was of educated Muslim opinion as a whole is not known, but it expressed the sentiment of that important group of Muslims connected with Aligarh College who took a leading role in starting the Muslim League in 1906.

It also seems that educated Muslims, at least in the North-Western Provinces and Oudh, associated the cow protection movement with the activities of the Indian National Congress. The limited sampling of opinion about the riots made possible by the government selections from the vernacular press indicates that many Muslims identified the Congress, directly or indirectly, with the communal disturbances. The *Nizam-ul-Mulk of* Moradabad said the cow protection movement was "but one offshoot" of the Congress.[52] The *Agra Punch* blamed the riots upon the Congress and the gaurakshini sabhas and joined the *Aftab-i-Islam* of Agra in recommending the suppression of the Congress.[53] The *Tohfa-i-Hind* of Bijnor, the *Najm-ul-Akhbar* of Etawah, and the *Riyaz-ul-Akhbar* of Gorakhpur also linked the riots to the Congress although less directly.[54] All these newspaper reports had

[49] Ibid. (n. d.), ibid., No. 42 of 1893, para. 24.
[50] Ibid., 5 Sept. 1893.
[51] *Sir Syed Ahmed on the Present State of Indian Politics*, pp. 37–38.
[52] NWP and O, CP, and R NNR No. 38 of 1893, para. 11.
[53] Ibid., and No. 40 of 1893, para. 19.
[54] Ibid., No. 34 of 1893, para. 4, and No. 35 of 1893, paras. 18 and 21.

been anticipated by Sayyid Ahmad Khan who had associated the cow protectors with the Congress in one of his 1888 speeches, saying some Hindus were joining the Congress in the belief that "by increasing the power of the Hindus they will perhaps be able to suppress those Mohomedan religious rites which are opposed to their own, and, by all uniting, annihilate them."[55]

Few Hindu newspapers, on the other hand, were willing to attribute the riots chiefly to the cow protection movement. Instead, they tended to lay the blame upon the British, either accusing the British of partiality or inconsistency in administering regulations governing slaughter or accusing Muslims of a new aggressiveness which had developed from the belief that the government was pleased with Muslims for opposing the Congress and angry with Hindus for joining it. Prominent officials conceded that this last belief had an important role in the riots.[56] The lieutenant-governor of the Punjab, Sir Dennis Fitzpatrick, thought the "worst feature" of the riots was the belief that the British instigated the riots to keep the Muslims out of the Congress.[57] One reason Hindus had gained the impression of differential treatment was that officials had sometimes granted new rights of slaughter to Muslims while almost never forbidding slaughter where it had previously been allowed. Chastened by a widespread Hindu assumption of British complicity, officials showed a new determination after the riots not to appear to favor Muslims. The Government of India issued a fresh order that official policy was and should continue to maintain the existing limits on slaughter in public and private places if there was any likelihood of trouble.[58] But even this policy was in effect a rejection of one of the cow protectors' goals. It meant that officials would not roll back slaughter, as the gaurakshini sabhas had demanded. If change came, it would be an expansion of the right of slaughter.

The communal antagonism accompanying the cow protection movement naturally pleased some officials. The secretary of state, Lord Kimberley, thought the movement made "impossible" a Hindu-Muslim "combination." It "cuts at the root of the Con-

[55] *Sir Syed Ahmed on the Present State of Indian Politics*, p. 35.

[56] Note by C. J. L[yall], 6 Oct. 1893.

[57] Extract from a note on the proposal for an examination in India by Sir Dennis Fitzpatrick.

[58] C. J. Lyall, Sec., Govt. of India, to Local Govts., 4 Oct. 1893. Pub. Letters from India and Gen. Letters from Bengal, 1894, Vol. 19.

gress agitation for the formation of a united Indian people, who are to force us to surrender power into their hands."[59] As long as Hindus and Muslims sought separate political goals, British officials tended to feel secure about the Raj's future.

The inability of Badruddin Tyabji and A. O. Hume to draw Muslims to the Congress had become apparent long before the 1893 riots. The cow protection movement in the late 1880s unquestionably had been a factor in their failure. The riots perhaps did less to diminish the Congress's appeal for Muslims, which was already low, than to cause some Congressmen to abandon their efforts to make the Congress congenial to Muslims and to give up the practice of bringing large numbers of Muslim delegates into the annual sessions in an effort to give the appearance of Muslim support. As much as the Congress leadership wished to disassociate themselves from the protection movement, the riots weakened the noncommunal image of the Congress and diminished Muslim attendance, as the table giving delegate statistics indicates.

MUSLIM DELEGATES TO THE INC BEFORE AND AFTER 1893 RIOTS[60]

	1885–1892	1893–1905
Muslim delegates	868	761[62]
Total number of delegates	6,413	10,677
Muslim percentage	13.5	7.1
Annual average number of Muslims	108.5	58.5
Average number of Muslims from outside host province	51.1[61]	7.3

The rapid collapse of the organizational apparatus of the cow protection movement after 1893 makes a final estimate of its importance difficult. Not only did sabhas disappear and itinerant cow protectors cease working, but over the next decade communal

[59] Gopal, *British Policy*, p. 363.
[60] Compiled from Majumdar and Mazumdar, *Congress and Congressmen*, p. 98, and from Wasti, *Lord Minto*, p. 221.
[61] This is a seven-year average which excludes 1891.
[62] Of these, 313 attended the Lucknow session of 1899.

clashes were rare and the product of local issues. Stricter official adherence to the policy of neutrality and administrative consistency may have removed some of the local sources of friction which sparked the 1893 riots. And stiff punishments and the operation of joint Hindu-Muslim conciliation committees may have deterred both spiteful cow slaughter by Muslims and Hindu coercion in the post-1893 years. Moreover, many original supporters of the movement had fallen away as it had become openly aggressive, and in places violent, toward Muslims. Yet the failure to sustain even the lawful activities of the movement raises doubts about the depth of feeling on the issue. If substantial numbers of Hindus wanted legislative or administrative limitations on cow slaughter, there were legal ways they might have campaigned for them. That the campaign evaporated suggests that popular sentiment was not broad or adamant and that Hindu leaders regarded the alienation of Muslims and the government as too heavy a price to pay for any possible benefits. Probably the issue of cow slaughter was more symbolic than substantive, although the symbolic value varied from group to group. Undoubtedly, the questions raised by the Congress and the Aligarh leaders concerning the distribution of political power had contributed to the climate of communal rivalry. The cow was not central to that rivalry in the way that India's constitution was. It was not surprising that when educated Muslims finally established a permanent political party for Muslims in 1906, they did so in connection with impending constitutional changes, not over cow slaughter, language, or other cultural concerns. For many other Hindus and Muslims who found themselves aligned on opposite sides of the cow killing issue, they were defending religious customs that were being discounted by the forces of modern education and secularism. The cow issue enabled groups who were threatened with displacement to occupy the center stage again, however briefly. But once Hindu and Muslim communalists realized that no major changes in the rules governing the killing of animals were imminent, the issue lost its symbolic importance. Both cow protectors and cow slaughterers had conveyed their determination not to accept an unfavorable revision of the rules. The protectors had obtained reaffirmation of the principle that if cows were killed, it must be discrete and limited. And Muslims had removed doubt about their right to continue their sacrifices. The controversy was a time of testing. All sides emerged with a clearer understanding of what could and could not be altered. The founding of the Congress, the Age of Consent Bill, and the council reforms of 1892 had awakened both hopes and apprehensions. The results of the cow protection agitation demonstrated that communal extremists had the power to poison Hindu-Muslim relations in limited areas without altering the structure of privilege, at least as long as the British kept a firm hold on the reigns of power.

SEQUELS TO THE RIOTS

There was a curious sequel to the cow protection agitation. In 1894 and 1895 government officers over a large area found trees smeared with a mixture of mud and animal hair. The phenomenon began in districts along the Nepal border and eventually spread "throughout Bihar" and parts of the North-Western Provinces and Oudh and the Punjab.[63] The fact that no satisfactory explanation of the smears was found and that tree smearing occurred in areas in which the cow protection movement had been strong led officials to suspect an orthodox Hindu political campaign of some kind. At the end of 1895, a sadhu gave the commissioner of police in Calcutta a plausible explanation. He attributed the tree smearing to a decision made by a committee of sadhus meeting at the Magh Mela at Allahabad. The same committee had decided at the previous Kumbh Mela at Hardwar to express their determination to prevent further interference with Hindu religion of the sort involved in the Age of Consent Bill by agitating against cow killing. At Allahabad the sadhus discussed ways to frighten the government and protect Hindu orthodoxy. They decided to borrow from the Mutiny example of chapatti passing.[64] They thought that by daubing trees with mud and animal hair, they could arouse public anxiety about the future and convince the government of popular disaffection.[65] This explanation seems possibly too clever and calculating, and

[63] Political Activities of the Sadhus (up to 1909).

[64] The circulation of objects such as chapattis or lotas happened in local areas occasionally, often without explanation. In 1894 some chapattis were passed. Gopal, *British Policy*, p. 195. In 1890, the political agent of Kotah reported the passing of chapattis together with an injunction against selling cattle. Note on the agitation by D. F. McCracken, 9 Aug. 1893.

[65] The sadhu was Paramananda. Political Activities of the Sadhus (up to 1909).

it may be that the tree daubing was merely an attempt to attract pilgrims to the Janakpur shrine in Nepal.[66] But whatever the cause, the phenomenon was never cleared up and it did make many officials anxious.

The 1893 riots were also followed by the founding of new communal organizations. The first was the Mahomedan Anglo-Oriental Defence Association of Upper India. Theodore Beck, the secretary of Aligarh College, was the moving force behind the Defence Association. He apparently shared the view of many officials that the cow protection movement was "part of the Hindu revival of which the National Congress is another manifestation, the aspiration at the root of both being directed to the formation of an Indian nation and the displacement from power, place and emolument of the ruling race." In his opening speech at the association's first session, he stressed the common interest of the Muslims and the British in resisting the twin threat posed by the Indian National Congress and cow protectors. He claimed that the Congress's object was to have political power "transferred to some groups amongst the Hindus." And he appealed for cooperation between Muslims and Englishmen in resisting "democratic political institutions" and attempts to prevent the slaughter of cows. It is interesting that the Defence Association had little vitality and that it soon disappeared.[67] While the association's failure may have been due to Beck's sponsorship, it may also have been a result of Muslim perceptions regarding the links between the cow protection movement and the Congress. Despite the involvement of individual Congressmen with the protection issue, the two movements were largely separate in personnel and purpose. As Sir Dennis Fitzpatrick put it, "nothing could be more opposed to the views of the principal leaders in it [the Congress] than any idea of stirring up strife" between Hindus and Muslims.[68] Many Muslims may have reached the same conclusion.

Less than two years after the Mahomedan Defence Association was started, a group committed to the preservation of orthodox

[66] The Government of India was inclined to accept this latter explanation, while the heads of the Bombay, Bengal, and North-Western Provinces and Oudh administrations were more alarmed. Gopal, *British Policy*, p. 195.

[67] Prasad, *India Divided*, pp. 104–105.

[68] Extract from a note on the proposal for an examination in India by Sir Dennis Fitzpatrick.

Hinduism founded the Sanatana Dharma Sabha[69] at Delhi and Hardwar, aimed possibly as much at defending Hinduism from the Arya Samaj and other reform groups as from Islam. This Sabha was the precursor of the much larger organization formed at Delhi in August 1900. Representatives of seven hundred Hindu sabhas convened at Delhi that year as the Bharata Dharma Mahamandal under the presidency of Maharaja Rameshwar Singh of Darbhanga.[70] But by 1900, little was heard of cow protection. The elevation of Hindi to the status of an official language had become the main issue of Hindu-Muslim rivalry. In 1900, the Government of the North-Western Provinces and Oudh did grant Hindi official status, alongside Urdu, to the chagrin of many Muslims.

Although the founding of separate religious organizations and the agitation for the equalization of Hindi suggest a growing communalization of culture and politics, few communal leaders behaved in a provocative manner in the aftermath of the 1893 disturbances. The decade following the riots was largely free of communal violence. Apart from the Punjab, officials rarely commented upon the existence of communal tension. Perhaps communal leaders were sobered by the violence of 1893. Perhaps people were relieved that the controversies surrounding the legislative council reforms, the cow protection movement, and the Age of Consent Bill had subsided and had not altered their lives. Possibly communal leaders felt that they had given proof of their determination to protect the status quo and that their British rulers were contemplating no major changes which might affect the communal balance of privilege and influence.

But behind the lull, the major problems of Hindu-Muslim relations remained. Each time the Government of India carried out reforms, it was bound to have communal implications for the areas where communal rivalry was strong. When the British altered agrarian laws, rearranged administrative boundaries, or granted Indians new legislative power, they awakened old anxieties and created new ones. Moreover, many university-educated Indians were seeking ways to overcome the cultural alienation

---

[69] This was also the name of a sabha established at Hardwar in 1887 "to foster the Hindu revival and the protection of cows," according to Note on the agitation by D. F. McCracken, 9 Aug. 1893.

[70] Heimsath, *Indian Nationalism*, p. 318.

that so often accompanied university education and urban professional life. To do so, they looked for integrative issues and symbols. This search left them trapped between "affectivity and intellectuality."[71] On a series of issues, substantial numbers of Hindu graduates joined the side of Hindu orthodoxy in arguing against particular British policies. But in order to reconcile their Hindu goals with their ideals of secular rationalism and anti-communalism, they relied on nonreligious arguments. Thus, in the Age of Consent Bill controversy, many Hindu graduates based their opposition on the question of the right of foreigners to interfere with and dictate changes in family life, rather than on the sacredness of the Shastras or the alleged harmlessness of early marriage. In the cow protection issue, the need to husband scarce resources provided a rationale sufficiently nonsectarian and scientific to allow educated Hindus to support or, more frequently, to remain silent about the gaurakshini sabhas. For the Congress in particular, it was silence as much as individual Congressmen's involvement in communal activities which hurt the chances of attracting Muslims. If the Congress were to allay Muslim fears about kine slaughter, language policy, or representative institutions, the Congress would have to make positive and imaginative gestures toward Muslims. During the cow protection movement and in the decade after the riots, the Congress did nothing, thereby demonstrating that it was at least as concerned with the opinion of Hindu communalists as with the anxieties of Muslims.

During the Khilafat movement, Gandhi did what earlier Congress leaders had not dared to do. He appealed to Hindus neither to interfere directly with Muslim cow slaughter nor to attempt to pass laws in their municipalities limiting slaughter. He said that Muslims must be persuaded to abandon slaughter voluntarily. He wrote that while the question of cow protection was "the greatest" facing Hindus, "the only chance Hindus have of saving the cow from the butcher's knife, is by trying to save Islam from the impending peril [in the Middle East] and trusting their Mussalman countrymen to return nobility, i.e., voluntarily to protect the cow out of regard for their Hindu countrymen. . . . The best and only way to save the cow is to save the Khilafat."[72] Gandhi's efforts at Hindu-Muslim reconciliation

[71] The phrase is from C. Lévi-Strauss' *Totemism*, p. 101.
[72] Gandhi, *Young India, 1919–1922*, pp. 410–413.

were reciprocated by the Muslim League which passed a resolution supporting cow protection[73] and by Muslim Khilafat agitators who gave up eating beef and sacrificing cows and who urged fellow Muslims to follow their example.[74] Yet when the Khilafat movement collapsed following Ataturk's revolution, so did Congress and League efforts to compromise on the cow issue. The Khilafat movement was an external matter which did not directly affect the distribution of power and influence within India. Once the Khilafat question disappeared, Hindus and Muslims were left once again divided over that distribution, with treatment of the cow a symbol and a barometer of communal feeling within both communities.

[73] Ibid.   [74] Prasad, *India Divided*, p. 122.

Chapter Eleven

THE HINDU MARTIAL REVIVAL AND THE CHAPEKAR TERRORIST SOCIETY

In the decade following the 1893 riots, evidence of ferment among Hindu revivalists continued to accumulate. Generally, Hindu revitalization movements were more interested in the comparisons and relations between Hinduism and the West than between Hinduism and Islam. Nevertheless, the 1893 communal disturbances were one of the factors which encouraged the critical self-examination occurring in the Indian National Congress, in orthodox Hindu groups, and in Hindu reformist societies. This chapter is concerned with one aspect of that self-examination: Hindu attitudes toward physical courage and violence. It attempts to show how nationalists with diverse backgrounds came to share an interest in muscle-building and the development of courage. These nationalists lived in a society whose martial opportunities had atrophied since British pacification and the decision to restrict military recruitment to a small fraction of the population. Alternative forms of physically demanding activity were scarce because nationalists belonged to elites which avoided manual labor and contact sports. The latter part of the chapter concentrates on a single member of these elites: Damodar Chapekar, the Chitpavan Brahman who founded a tiny terrorist sabha in Poona and participated in the murder of two British officials in 1897. Chapekar's sabha was organizationally isolated from the Congress and other nationalist groups; socially, Chapekar was on the outer fringes of the circles which supported the Congress. Yet the preoccupations and resentments revealed in Damodar's autobiography, written in jail after his arrest, were shared by other politically conscious Hindus on the margins of the Congress. An understanding of those preoccupations helps to delimit the social boundaries of the Congress, to clarify the impediments to Indian nation-building, and to define the complex dynamics of the nationalist movement.

Courage and the Hindu Revival

Communal disturbances had led many persons who did not ordinarily dwell upon religious differences to reflect upon the character of their own particular religious group. There was a pronounced tendency to identify deficiencies within Hindu society and to seek means of overcoming them. Many educated Hindus who had been sympathetic to the cause of social reform seemed to feel that the polarization between reformers and Sanatanists had been harmful to the cause of national unity and unproductive of important social change. The organized social reform movement was less visible, less aggressive in the decade following the Age of Consent Bill and the cow protection movement's rapid expansion. Reformers instead emphasized the value of gradual change and increasingly looked to the Shastras for legitimation of the reforms they advocated. There was an implicit understanding that orthodoxy might be aroused by proposals for even moderate reform. Hindu unity had emerged as a major goal in its own right.

The controversies of the early 1890s awakened some nationalists to another alleged deficiency within Hindu society. This deficiency was the supposed lack of courage. The need to revive Hindu martial traditions and to restore physical vitality to Hindus was by no means new. As we have seen, fear of physical degeneracy contributed to the development of the cow protection movement. But it is clear from some explicit comments and Hindu revivalist activities that a growing number of Hindus were concerned about the stereotyped view which held that Hindus, as compared with Muslims or Englishmen, were deficient in manly qualities. Even some nationalists who regretted the Hindu-Muslim violence took a certain pride in the behavior of Hindu rioters which seemed to challenge the image of Hindu pacificity and Hindu disunity.

The reaction of Pandit Bishan Narayan Dar to the Hindu-Muslim riots of 1893 exemplifies this ambiguous attitude toward Hindu violence. Dar was a prominent Brahman moderate from Lucknow who was elected president of the Congress in 1911. Like other early Congress leaders, Dar had received his legal training in England and he had a lucrative practice. He was also typical in that his ancestors had been in government service. His grandfather had come from Kashmir to work for the Nawab of Oudh, his father was a civil servant under the British, and his uncle, Pandit Shambhu Nath, was the first Indian appointed to a judgeship on the Calcutta High Court. Bishan Narayan Dar himself was a social reformer with a liberal-minded approach to religious and communal problems. Upon his return from his studies in England, he had refused to undergo the compromises and purification ceremonies that would have won him acceptance back into his caste, with the result that his jati split into two groups, the Dharam Sabha and the Bishan Sabha. He was an accomplished Urdu poet and he wanted Muslims to join the Indian National Congress.[1] He did not approve of the gaurakshini movement because of its effects on communal relations.[2]

However, following the Azamgarh disturbances, Pandit Dar and Ganga Prasad Varma, the other leading Congressman of Lucknow who edited the *Advocate* and the *Hindustani* and who later became chairman of the U. P. Hindu Sabha, conducted a private investigation of the riots. They interviewed close to one hundred persons and gave wide publicity to their conclusions. Pandit Dar concluded that the government and its officers were "wholly and solely" to blame for the riots, while the gaurakshini sabhas were "harmless and even humane." He went out of his way to avoid attacking Muslims or Islamic civilization, saying that Muslims "are bone of our bone and flesh of our flesh" and that the trouble between Hindus and Muslims was the result of British failure to treat Hindus and Muslims equally, as Muslim governments had.[3] But having made generous comments about Muslims, he then undercut the effect of these remarks by discussing the beneficial results of the riots. The riots, he said, were good inasmuch as they had demonstrated "that the Hindus are not quite such a meek, unmanly, and contemptible race as they have been imagined." More than that, the riots and subsequent trials of Hindus

> will go far to bind the Hindu community together more firmly than ever. It has always been the tendency of persecution to create a spirit of fierce resistance and unity in the persecuted. Intense heat is necessary for the fusing of metals; and by pass-

[1] *Who's Who in India*, Part IV, pp. 221–222.
[2] Dar, *An Appeal*, Appendix, p. 6.   [3] Ibid., pp. 22–23.

ing through the burning ordeals of political persecution, the diverse sections of Hindus, the hetrogenous (*sic*) elements of east and west and north and south will be fused together into one homogenous (*sic*) whole, strong enough to take care of itself. . . .

Thus, while accusing the British of tearing "the great fabric of Hindu and Mahomedan union," Pandit Dar was finding important positive consequences of that very process of divide and rule.[4]

Pandit Bishan Narayan Dar was not alone among nationalists in finding advantages in Hindu-Muslim conflict. Lajpat Rai's specific reaction to the 1893 riots is not known, but in general he did welcome communal friction as a means by which the fragmented Hindu community would realize their common identity. For Lajpat, Muslims would be the Hindus' foil for overcoming what he called "our national malady of disunity." A Hindi-Urdu dispute had first drawn Lajpat into politics.[5] He later attempted to discard Urdu in favor of Hindi. He developed "hatred" of Islam through reading about Muslim rule.[6] He wrote in 1901 that Muslims still regarded themselves as rulers and that "there is still lurking in the minds of at least one community, that they can crush out the other or others." It is evident that Lajpat's perception of Hindu deficiencies was colored by being a Punjabi and living near India's border with Muslim countries. He had what has been called "a frontier mentality," an appreciation that to the northwest lived a vast number of persons united, as Hindus were not, by Islam, capable of invading India again under the stimulus of their imperial legacy and tradition of warfare. He was afraid that because Hindus lacked

[4] Ibid., pp. 28–31.

[5] Two prominent nationalists whose interest in politics had been stimulated by Hindu-Muslim violence were Vinayak Damodar Savarkar and Dr. Keshav Baliram Hedgewar. Savarkar, who later organized terrorist activities from London and Paris, "resolved to avenge the woes and deaths" of fellow Hindus after the 1893 Azamgarh riots when he was ten years old. He led a stone-throwing attack on a village mosque and fought with Muslim boys near Nasik. Hedgewar founded the Rashtriya Swayam Sevak after Hindu-Muslim riots in Nagpur in 1924 and 1925 in which "the Hindu community generally made a weak and disorganized showing." Dhananjay Keer, *Veer Savarkar*, 2nd ed. (Bombay, 1966), pp. 4–5, and J. A. Curran, *Militant Hinduism in Indian Politics: A Study of the R.S.S.* (New York, 1951), p. 12.

[6] *Lajpat Rai: Autobiographical Writings*, ed. Joshi, p. 74.

self-respect and unity, any early attempt to combine with Muslims against the British might be interpreted by Muslims "as the outcome of fear."[7] Therefore, Lajpat favored strengthening the Hindu community before seeking a united front between Hindus and Muslims for the recovery of India's independence. Lajpat agreed with the Congress policy of avoiding issues likely to cause friction between Hindus and Muslims. However, he advocated in 1901 that an all-India Hindu congress or sabha be established to work for Hindu "unity and strength as a religious nationality." The program Lajpat outlined for this Hindu congress was mainly cultural: the championship of Hindi and the Nagri script, the adoption of textbooks which would emphasize what Hindus shared, "the teaching of Sanskrit language and literature all over India," *shuddhi* (reconversion), and protest against government favoritism toward non-Hindus.[8] In Lajpat's mind, the primary task of nation-building was to overcome the deep cleavages within Hindu society. He realized this would mean postponing efforts to unite Hindus and Muslims and to bring about major social reform. Like it or not, Hindu orthodox opinion was the majority opinion, and Lajpat asked his fellow social reformers to recognize that.[9]

Lajpat's emphasis upon Hindu revival and the consolidation of Hindu society won him respect from other Hindu nationalists throughout India and made him a natural ally of Tilak within the Congress. In looking for explanations for the affinity between Lajpat and Maharashtrian extremist nationalists, it is interesting to note how different Lajpat's family background was from those of the Maharashtrians discussed below. Lajpat was not trying to restore a family reputation or return a regional elite to a position of former dominance. He had to go outside his family and caste, to the Arya Samaj, to find a new religious identity. Lajpat's grandfather had been a Jain shopkeeper, his father had been a Muslim "by conviction" as a young man and had been under the influence of Sayyid Ahmad Khan. Lajpat himself had joined the Brahmo Samaj before turning to the Arya Samaj.[10] For a person with such a diffused cultural heritage,

[7] See ibid., pp. 87–88.

[8] This and the following recommendations and observations were made in Lajpat's "The Coming Indian National Congress—Some Suggestions," *Kayastha Samachar*, Vol. IV, No. 5 (Nov. 1901), 377ff.

[9] Ibid., pp. 383–384.

[10] *Lajpat Rai: Autobiographical Writings*, pp. 11–12.

the relative discipline and doctrinal clarity of the Arya Samaj must have offered a more certain personal identity as well as a vehicle for integrating a fragmented society, for becoming a part of a larger society. The Arya Samaj, with its deemphasis of caste and its universalism, represented an effort to combat the narrow-mindedness and selfishness which many Hindu revivalists felt stood in the way of Indian nation-building. Lajpat Rai was much better known as a champion of moral courage than of physical courage. Yet his interest in Mazinni and secret societies, his concern that Muslims might misinterpret friendly Hindu overtures as evidence of Hindu fear, and his admiration for Lekh Ram's courage in attacking Islam prior to the latter's assassination by a Muslim in 1897, indicate that he was by no means indifferent to the problem of physical courage. The Arya Samaj, in fact, devoted considerable energy to Hindu physical regeneration. But Lajpat was more concerned with moral integrity, with raising the standard of personal conduct in Hindu society. Possibly Lajpat's concern with honesty in public life was related to his own experience of having paid a bribe to pass his law exam after failing the exam several times.[11] Whatever the reason, Lajpat, like most Hindu revivalists, tended to look upon the development of physical and moral courage as connected goals.

Nationalists in Bengal were more persistent than any other regional group in the attempt to develop a culture of courage. Bengalis had often been singled out by north Indians and the British as peculiarly lacking in courage. Bengalis fought the stigma of cowardice in novels, on the stage, in historical research, in *akhara*s (gymnasia), and, beginning in the early twentieth century, through the student *samitis*. The best known example of the Bengali interest in Hindu martial traditions was the popularity enjoyed by Bankimchandra Chatterji's *Ananda Math*. In its first edition, *Ananda Math* described a sannyasi rebellion against the British, but in its later editions it was rewritten to avoid prosecution for sedition by substituting Muslim rulers for the British as the object of the revolt.[12] In all editions, Bankimchandra showed Bengalis overcoming their fear and attachments to worldly possessions as they devoted them-

---

[11] Ibid., p. 34.
[12] Bimanbehari Majumbar, "The Ananda Math and Phadke," *Journal of Indian History*, Vol. XLIV, Part 1 (Apr. 1966), 97ff.

selves to the mother goddess Kali in order to fight for their freedom. *Ananda Math* served as a model for the Bengali terrorist societies after 1905.

Before Bankimchandra's death in 1894, Swami Vivekananda had taken up the cause of Hindu physical regeneration. Vivekananda was not always consistent and at times he applauded Hinduism's tolerance and gentleness. For example, a short time after the 1893 riots in Bombay, he said, "I have heard the creed of the Moslem applauded when today the Moslem sword is carrying destruction into India. Blood and sword are not for the Hindoo, whose religion is based on the laws of love."[13] At other times, though, he rebuked Hindus for weakness and passivity. "We have become real earthworms, crawling at the feet of everyone who dares to put his foot on us." He called upon Hindus to become strong. "Religion will come afterwards," he said. "You will be nearer to Heaven through football than through the study of the Gita."[14] Neither Bankimchandra Chatterji nor Swami Vivekananda were Congressmen, but their concerns were echoed in the writings of Surendranath Banerjea, Romeshchandra Dutt, Rabindranath Tagore, among others, and in the activities of Sarala Debi Ghosal in the pre-1905 period.

The most immediate and best publicized Hindu martial activities, following the 1893 communal violence, were in and around Poona. There are several explanations for the strength of the Hindu heroic revival among Marathi-speaking Brahmans. First, the tradition of a Hindu Raj was a living one, Maharashtrian independence having ended only in 1818. Second, Brahmans in Maharashtra seem to have been more anxious about their status than Brahmans elsewhere because of attacks on Maharashtrian Brahman privileges by British officials, European missionaries, the Maharaja of Kolhapur, and Jyotirao Phule's non-Brahman movement. Third, Maharashtra, including Bombay city, was the center of the most vigorous social reform movement in India. Ranade's advocacy of widow-remarriage and other changes in Hindu custom and Malabari's assault on child-marriage aroused orthodox forces in Poona to defend traditional customs with energy and occasional violence. The defenders of orthodoxy

---

[13] R. C. Majumdar, *Swami Vivekananda: A Historical Review* (Calcutta, 1965), p. 42.

[14] *The Complete Works of Swami Vivekananda*, 9th ed. (Calcutta, 1964), III, 237–238 and 241–242.

viewed reformist activities as a sign of weakness, division, and cultural surrender. Tilak and his followers tended to associate the reformers' cultural compromises with a lack of both moral and physical courage. Fourth and ironically, the relative paucity of Muslims in the Marathi-speaking districts may account for the willingness of Hindu communalists to risk antagonizing Muslims. Where communities were more evenly balanced, Hindu and Muslim elites had a greater stake in maintaining communal peace. In Poona, if nationalists could use Muslims to help arouse anti-British feeling, the local communal consequences would be less severe than in northern India.

The timing of Tilak's decision to convert the festival in honor of the god Ganapati into a political celebration of populist Hinduism stemmed directly from the 1893 riots.[15] Tilak was outspoken in his denunciation of the government and Muslims for their role in the riots, despite the efforts of Telang, Ranade, and other nationalists to persuade him to moderate his criticisms. He argued that if Hindus were to make themselves heard by officials, they should use the same tactics as Muslims. According to a government report, "he advocated that all Hindus, educated and uneducated, should go in for gymnastics and acquire a familiarity with weapons."[16] His newspaper, *Kesari*, urged Hindus not to "purchase peace with Mohammedans with dishonour to their own religion or with loss of self-respect."[17] Tilak and other Chitpavan Brahmans called for a Hindu boycott of the Muslim Muharram festival. In explaining his appeal, Tilak referred to the communal trouble at Prabhas Patan, saying that Muslims had forgotten "our long-standing friendship" and had "begun a

---

[15] Tilak's motivation, on the other hand, was primarily to arrest the upper-class tendency to abandon popular Hinduism and to unite upper- and lower-class Hindus. He wrote in 1896, "No man can deny that our country is badly in want of a religious revival. Well, such a revival is taking place; only it is observable in different phases. Swami Vivekanand and the high philosophy of the Upanishads have appealed to the B. A.'s and M. A.'s of our Universities. The God Ganapati and the vigorous preachings of Ramdas have appealed to the common people. Religion is the main stay, the only prop for a falling nation and some of our friends are committing a national suicide in withholding themselves from a movement which is making us hopeful for the future." Gordon Johnson, *Provincial Politics and Indian Nationalism: Bombay and the Indian National Congress, 1880–1915* (Cambridge, 1973), p. 89.

[16] "Life of Bal Gangadhar Tilak" (n. d. 1899?), C.S.B. Memoranda, T. and D. Dept., 1894–1913.

[17] N. C. Kelkar, *Life and Times of Lokamanya Tilak* (Madras, 1928), p. 233.

regular campaign of harassing Hindu mendicants that inevitably led to estrangement."[18] In view of Muslim attacks on Hindus in Junagadh and Bombay,[19] Tilak not only appealed for Hindu withdrawal from the Muharram festival, he also incorporated features of the Muharram into a militant, exclusively Hindu, public celebration of the Ganapati festival. On 13 September 1894, one of the Ganapati *melas* or parties of young men marched past a mosque. Despite police orders and with the apparent intention of annoying Muslims in the mosque, the processionists played music and shouted, Muslims rushed out to fight and, in the ensuing melee, one Muslim was killed.[20]

Tilak himself was not a participant in the Poona disturbance. But Tilak's name was linked with the riot in many minds because he had been an organizer of the melas which accompanied the images of Ganapati. Furthermore, he had convened a meeting to raise funds for the Hindus accused in the death of the Muslim, and he had agitated after the riot for a revision of the music rules so that in certain circumstances Hindus would be able to play music in front of mosques. For a period following the riot, Tilak was protected by a band of young Hindu bodyguards against possible Muslim retaliatory attacks.[21]

The use of disciplined bands of men in the politico-religious processions of the Ganapati festival was an innovation in the nationalist movement. Many Hindu and Muslim religious processions had traditionally been accompanied by lathi-bearing men who were expected to discourage interference with the processions' progress. In some cases, these bands had fought with rival bands, especially in places of Hindu pilgrimage. Thus, lathi fights between sectarian groups were not new to Hinduism. Nor were akharas new. Hindus had patronized akharas long before the 1890s. What was new was that between 1890 and 1910, English-educated students began to attend akharas, especially in Maharashtra and Bengal, and to march in political processions in paramilitary formation. Tilak's association with the young

[18] Parvate, *Bal Gangadar Tilak*, p. 116.
[19] Pradhan and Bhagwat, *Tilak*, p. 84.
[20] T.R.M. MacPherson, Dist. Supt. of Police, Poona, to Dist. Mag., Poona, 21 Sept. 1894. Feb. 1895 Prog. No. 143, IHP, Pub. Thirteen other persons were killed in communal riots in 1894 and 1895 in Nasik and Khandesh districts.
[21] Govt. of Bombay, *Source Material*, II, 205.

men of the Ganapati melas was another sign of the growing links between a minority of Congress leaders and Hindu revivalism.

One of Tilak's closest associates, Tatia Sahib Natu, led the mela which provoked the Hindu-Muslim fight in Poona. It was through men such as Tatia Sahib Natu that Tilak was reaching high-caste Hindus beyond the relatively small group of educated men who attended the Congress. The Natus belonged to the urban commercial class which was the backbone of the Hindu revival in the inland cities of northern and central India and which represented a large reservoir of potential anti-British feeling. The Natus were members of a well-known and very prosperous Brahman family whose most prominent ancestor held a state appointment under the last independent Peshwa, Baji Rao. The ancestor, Balaji Narayan Natu, had switched sides and had helped the British overthrow the Peshwa, for which the British granted him nine *inam* (grant of revenue-free land) villages. Those villages provided him and his descendants with Rs. 30,000 each year. In the 1890s, some Maharashtrians still considered the Natus as traitors. The fact that Tatia Sahib and his elder brother, Bala Sahib, were active in the Age of Consent Bill controversy, the cow protection movement, and the Ganapati festival perhaps represented an effort to diminish the stigma attached to their ancestor's assistance to the British. Bala Sahib was orthodox in his religious observances, and when he became president in 1894 of the panchayat which managed the temple on Parbati Hill in Poona, he excluded Europeans from the temple for the first time. In 1895, Bala Sahib was appointed to the Poona Standing Committee of the Congress, the Managing Committee of the Sarvajanik Sabha, and the treasurership of the committee to repair Shivaji's tomb at Raigarh.[22] For each of these appointments, it is likely that Tilak's support was crucial.

In addition to Bala Sahib's prominent role in Poona religious and political life, both he and Tatia Sahib Natu had a wide range of economic activities and investments. They owned shares in the Poona Reay paper mill, the Gokuldas spinning and weaving mills at Bombay and Sholapur, the Poona metal factory,

---

[22] This and other biographical information about the Natu family comes from "Life of Balwant Ramchandra Natu" (n. d. 1899?), C.S.B. Memoranda, T. and D. Dept., 1894–1913. The details of the Natu family's financial interests may be found in the same volume and was an accompaniment to Bombay Government Resolution, Police Department, No. 6,551, 23 Oct. 1897.

and the Agra leather factory. They owned considerable rental property (a *chawl* and houses) in Bombay and Poona. But their largest source of income was "alienated land." In 1899 they had outstanding loans worth Rs. 103,725. Altogether the Natus seem to have used the income from their inam villages to exploit successfully the growing entrepreneurial opportunities available in British India. Their new wealth may have heightened their desire to win favor with Hindu orthodox forces in and around Poona. It seems evident that resentment against the material successes of the English-educated professional classes, to which most reformers belonged, was an element in the orthodox reaction against the social reform movement. Thus, the Natus, with their new wealth and family reputation for collaboration, may have had a double stigma to overcome, and this may account for their enthusiasm for the orthodox revival and for Tilak's politics.

The Natu brothers were major participants in the Maharashtrian martial revival. Tatia Sahib started an akhara in one of his houses, apparently about the time of the 1893 riots, and as mentioned, he personally led the band of gymnasts in his Ganapati mela which became embroiled in the 1894 Hindu-Muslim riot. Bala Sahib helped Tilak raise funds for the restoration of Shivaji's *samadhi* (mausoleum) which Tilak incorporated into the Shivaji festival he started in 1896. The Shivaji festival honored the seventeenth-century hero for fighting for Maratha independence. Although both the Ganapati and Shivaji festivals created bad feeling between Hindus and Muslims, it seems that the Natus, like Tilak, were motivated primarily by anti-British sentiment. The acting commissioner of the Central division shared the view of Poona notables following the 1894 riot that probably "the agitation fomented by the Deccani Brahmans is directed in reality not against the Muhammadans but against the Government."[23] There is little doubt about that.

If the Natu brothers hoped to win respect by making patriotic sacrifices, they received the opportunity during the plague epidemic in 1896–1897. The Natus were highly critical of British treatment of Hindus during the plague. Bala Sahib's only daughter died of plague, and Tatia Sahib was removed from his home by the authorities and placed in a segregation camp.

[23] Wolpert, *Tilak and Gokhale*, p. 70.

Hindu Martial Revival

Many persons of the Natus' status were spared this treatment, and Tatia Sahib was heard to say that he would get even with Mr. Rand, the plague commissioner, for his detention.[24]

When Rand and Lt. Ayerst were assassinated on 22 June, 1897, during the celebration of Queen Victoria's Jubilee, officials suspected that both the Natus and Tilak might be responsible. Tilak was arrested and charged with sedition for his newspaper articles justifying assassination, but the government had no solid legal grounds for prosecuting the Natus. Therefore, the government arrested the Natus and attached their property under Regulation XXV of 1827. They were detained for over two years without being charged with a crime. Their incarceration became a *cause célèbre* in both the Congress and the House of Commons, and it was frequently compared to the Dreyfus affair. The arrest of Damodar Chapekar, who confessed to the killing, did not lead the Bombay government to release the Natus.

Damodar Chapekar's Terrorist Society

No evidence has yet been produced to prove that either Tilak or the Natus had any part in the planning of Rand's murder. It is reasonable to assume, nevertheless, an identity of views between Tilak, the Natus, and Damodar Chapekar. Tilak publicly had justified Shivaji's killing of Afzal Khan on the grounds that it was done for the public good, not for personal gain. Damodar Chapekar used the same justification. Tilak, the Natus, and Damodar were all outraged by the forcible detention of plague patients and by the use of British troops to search Hindu houses and destroy contaminated property. Damodar had visited the Natus' akhara and house, and he had sought Tilak's aid in finding military employment. Damodar's secret society drilled in paramilitary fashion similar to Tatia Sahib's Ganapati mela. The day after the shooting, Damodar was believed to have sent Tilak a message, saying "by the grace of God Ganapati, the mission has succeeded." Damodar had ample reason to believe that Tilak would approve of his shooting of Rand and Ayerst.[25]

The police tracked down Damodar Chapekar several months

[24] "Life of Balwant Ramchandra Natu."
[25] Wolpert, *Tilak and Gokhale*, p. 91.

after the assassination. He admitted that he and his brother had committed the murders, but he seemed to have taken care not to implicate, even indirectly, Tilak or anyone else outside his immediate circle in his decision to kill Rand. His confession was made "in no penitential spirit, but rather in the spirit of one who had done and dared for the cause of his countrymen."[26] While he waited in jail for his trial, he received favored treatment from his British interrogators, and he was persuaded to write his autobiography. He hoped that by putting his life on paper he might receive the recognition for his patriotism and bravery he had previously been denied. The autobiography reveals with remarkable honesty the emotions of an unfortunate and ill-educated Brahman who felt that all that was good in society was threatened with destruction. He blamed his misfortunes on the non-Indian institutions and influences which he thought were corrupting the Aryan way of life. He wanted to destroy these influences.

A striking feature of Damodar's confession and autobiography was the degree to which he saw Indian social reformers, including Congress leaders, as partners with the British government and missionaries in undermining proper Hindu values. Damodar seemed to feel that in the absence of a Hindu government, he should act to uphold the Hindu moral order. He seemed to rely upon the ancient concept of *danda* (force, or literally, stick) to sanction his violence against Hindu reformers, Christians, and the government. Because force was such an important part of the militant Hindu revival, in the cow protection and terrorist movements as well as in Damodar's own life, a definition of danda drawn from widely read Hindu sources may help explain the righteous feelings behind the use of coercion.

> Among the precepts of the *Mahabharata* there is one which states, "Right leans on might (danda) as a creeper on a tree. As smoke follows the wind, so right follows might." The *Puranas* declare, "As the reins check the steed, as the yoke controls the bull, as the iron hook restrains the elephant, so danda controls the world." . . . It is danda and danda alone, irresistible and terror-striking, that makes the earth prosper, that brings about morality and makes virtue possible.

[26] *Poona Observer and Civil and Military Journal*, 13 Oct. 1897.

Hindu Martial Revival

Danda restrains the ungovernable and punishes the wicked. It creates a fierce dread, makes men tremble for their fields, their possessions, their cattle, their families and themselves, and through this fear renders them docile and subservient and thus maintains peace and order in the state. Without danda men will never obey the law or tread the path of righteousness. Without danda no maiden would marry the man selected for her by her parents but would give herself to any plausible rogue. Without danda no one would milk the cows, no warrior would go forth to battle, no brahmin study the Vedas, no sudra remain servile.[27]

Damodar's anger at the violators of Hindu custom and his determination to use danda were fueled by the contrast between his Brahman status and his poverty. His family lived without affluence on the edge of Maharashtrian Brahman society. Damodar described his grandfather as having been "a whimsical person" who had tried his hand without success at gardening, a dispensary, "a grocer's shop, a printing press, a sweetmeat stall, and a loom." Damodar thought that the poverty which fell upon his family when he was a boy might have been the result of the pilgrimage on which his grandfather had taken the family. Twenty-five of them with two servants and three carts had walked to Benaras and back, taking nine or ten months. In any case, the goddess of wealth withdrew her favor from the family and Damodar's grandfather was reduced to begging in the town of Indore while his uncles, after the disintegration of the joint family, followed marginal callings. One joined a dramatic troupe, a second became a singer, a third played the tambora, and the fourth was a vagrant.[28]

Damodar's father had become an itinerant *kirtan* singer after studying English at Poona High School. A kirtan is a recitation

[27] Benjamin Walker, *Hindu World: An Encyclopedic Survey of Hinduism* (London, 1968), I, 267.

[28] "Autobiography of Damodar Hari Chapekar," pp. 959-962. The "Autobiography" has been published as an appendix to Govt. of Bombay, *Source Material*, II. All references are to that source. The "Autobiography" may also be found in the IOL, where it is an enclosure to S. W. Edgerley, Sec., Govt. of Bombay, to Sec., Govt. of India, Home Dept., 25 Aug. 1899, Sept. Prog. No. 6, IHP, Pub., Vol. 5,640. This latter copy contains comments by the police which confirm the accuracy of many details.

of the gods' virtues with devotional songs and music. As a boy, Damodar traveled with his father's troupe, performing kirtans at shrines and at the durbars of native states.[29] However, the Chapekar family had traditionally been restricted to lay occupations. Furthermore, while kirtan performing had once been a respected profession, Haridasis (kirtan performers) had gained a reputation for promiscuous sexual behavior.[30] In consequence, local Chitpavan Brahmans, including their own relatives, disapproved of Damodar's family's calling and would not help his father in the early, difficult years of kirtan singing.[31] One year Damodar was forced to beg for his food.[32]

Damodar's formal education was neglected while he traveled about western India with his father. He learned to compose kirtans and religious verses called *shloks*, and his father taught him about five hundred shloks from Hindu medical books in the hope that he would become a medical practitioner. His father encouraged this occupation, he wrote, because it would enable him to be independent and free him from the necessity of taking service under anyone. During their travels, Damodar and his brother tended to neglect their studies and "thus suffered in the estimation of our father."[33] Damodar studied for two years at the New English School in Poona, which also failed to engage his interest. He claimed that he found the influence of English pernicious. It not only destroyed a man's respect for his elders and his religion, it was apt to turn a man into "an Englishman from top to toe and an earnest votary of the bottle." A truly educated man, in Damodar's opinion, was one who knew and obeyed the Shastras.[34]

Damodar did not know precisely how he came to despise the English. Undoubtedly his own educational deficiency was one cause. As a young man, he was poor and often unemployed and his knowledge of English was too slight to help him find work. He claimed that his first thoughts of terrorism came to him almost by chance when he was about fifteen years old. He and his brother, Balkrishna, were riding on a train when they passed through some wild and densely wooded mountains. It struck them that this would be an ideal place to hide after committing "terrible deeds." With this romantic thought as a beginning,

[29] "Autobiography," pp. 963–964.　[30] Ibid., p. 966.
[31] Ibid., p. 960.　[32] Ibid., p. 962.
[33] Ibid., pp. 965–966.　[34] Ibid., p. 964.

they became fascinated with warfare and terrorism.[35] The brothers set themselves an arduous regime of physical training to prepare for a military career. Damodar learned to prostrate himself twelve hundred times in succession and to run eleven miles in an hour. They wanted to receive a proper military training, but after some unsuccessful attempts to enter the armies of two native states, Damodar and Balkrishna decided to form their own military club. They tried to recruit their friends but found they would not follow orders. They turned to younger boys who were more pliable and who could be expected to obey their commands. Damodar and Balkrishna taught the boys how to shoot and to fight mock battles with sling shots. At one point, one hundred and fifty boys belonged to the club.[36]

Damodar chose the monkey-god, Hanuman, as the patron deity of the club. This was an appropriate choice because Hanuman was the military leader whose strength and courage helped Rama to rescue Sita from the clutches of Ravanna and whose portrait may still be seen in wrestling and weight-lifting establishments. At first the boys worshipped Hanuman in the form of a stone daubed with vermilion. Later, Damodar and Balkrishna told the boys they had dreamed that Hanuman had come to them in their sleep and had told them where to look for his image. The boys went to the place specified in the dream and dug until they found Hanuman's idol.[37]

The boys deserted the club, however, when the police questioned Damodar about a complaint that one of the boys had hit a stranger with a rock. Damodar and Balkrishna started a new club, this time with fifteen selected members. They hung pictures of Shivaji, Baji Rao, and other famous warriors on the walls of the club's gymnasium; they discussed historical events "in a way suited to impress upon the minds of the boys a sense of self-respect and love for one's religion, and to show how easy a matter it was to lay down one's life for these"; and they practiced boxing, wrestling, sword fighting, and other traditional sports. The boys tried to discourage others from playing foreign games by breaking up cricket matches and stealing the equipment. In addition, they collected disguises and small arms for future use. This club disintegrated because of a quarrel between Chapekar and another member.[38] From this time (about 1894)

[35] Ibid., pp. 965–966. [36] Ibid., pp. 968–970.
[37] Ibid., p. 970. [38] Ibid., pp. 975–977.

until 1897, Damodar and Balkrishna seem to have had but one close associate, Dattatraya Bhuskute. It was during these years that they committed most of their terrorist acts.

A turning point in the Chapekars' lives came in 1895 when the Indian National Congress met in Poona. Damodar scoffed at the Congress. He called it a mere "sham" invented by Hume, Bradlaugh, and other British agents. He was contemptuous of its Westernized leaders and especially of someone he thought was Manmohan Ghosh who, "though a Hindu by religion, . . . dresses like a European from tip to toe, . . . shaves his mustache like a eunuch," and travels about in a carriage with a European driver. In general, Damodar thought the Congress was a waste of time and money because demands not backed with violence were futile.[39]

Among Congress leaders, Damodar had a special hatred for Daji Abaji Khare, that "vilest of Brahmans" who had eaten beef with the prominent Muslim Congressman, Badruddin Tyabji. One shlok which Damodar recited asked people to treat Khare as a Chandal (untouchable) and to hit him with shoes.[40] An attempt to recite a similar shlok at a Shivaji meeting resulted in one of the severest humiliations of his life. Tilak was in the chair and Khare rose to speak. Damodar "flew into a rage. I consider[ed] it a disgrace that a vile cow-eater, who ate beef in company with Muhammedans, should deliver a speech about Shivaji the cow protector." Damodar pushed his way to the front of the audience to give his shlok, but Tilak had him ejected by a Brahman wrestler. Damodar vowed that after this dishonor, he would never attend another public meeting. Although Damodar resented Tilak's treatment of him on this occasion and although he despised some of Tilak's associates, Damodar considered him "a far better man than a reformer," especially as he had recently been conforming more closely to the customs of the Brahman community.[41]

Damodar also had an unsuccessful meeting with Mahadev Govind Ranade. Damodar wanted to attend the National Social Conference in 1895 to listen to the social reformers speak, but could not gain admission without tickets. He appeared before Ranade, the secretary of the conference, pretending to be an officer of a young men's reform club which wanted tickets.

[39] Ibid., pp. 983–985.   [40] Ibid., p. 981.
[41] Ibid., pp. 994–995.

Hindu Martial Revival

Ranade refused to give the tickets unless Damodar could produce a recommendation from "some respectable gentlemen." Damodar could not, but he managed to enter the Congress itself by using a ticket he snatched from the hands of a Madrasi delegate.[42]

Damodar wrote with as much passion about social reformers as he did about the British. He was particularly incensed by the controversy about the use of the Congress pandal by the National Social Conference in 1895. Damodar, Balkrishna, and their friend, Bhuskute, made a series of attacks with iron pipes on noted social reformers, including Wasude Balwant Patwardhan, an editor of the *Sudharak* (The Reformer).[43] Damodar believed that he was working for the good of society by attacking reformers such as Patwardhan. He sent a letter to the *Sudharak* which was published a month before the 1895 Congress met. It was warning to the reformers and its substance was that:

> Like your association for removing the obstacles in the way of widow re-marriage, (we also) have formed a society for removing the obstacles in the way of the Aryan religion, that is to say, a league prepared to lay down their lives as well as to take the lives of others for the sake of that religion. . . . There is no necessity of any innovation whatever in our religious observances or our customs of the present day. Both the reformers and the non-reformers are therefore hereby warned that . . . they should conduct themselves with great caution hereafter . . . (or we will) put them to the sword.[44]

Damodar was pleased that the reformers dared not go out without bodyguards and that the Social Reform Conference was not permitted to use the Congress pandal.[45] He claimed and deserved some of the credit for this victory over the reformers.[46]

---

[42] Ibid., pp. 981–982.

[43] That the Chapekars attacked Patwardhan suggests they were more concerned about fighting social reform than the British. Patwardhan was one of the more vehement newspaper critics of the British. In 1897, the Government of Bombay suspended him from his teaching post and considered prosecuting him for sedition. Director of Public Instruction to Chairman of Deccan Education Society, 3 Sept. 1897. Appendix L to Prog. in Educ. Dept., Dec. 1897. Bombay Educ., Eccles., Mar., and Leg. Prog., Vol. 5,321. Also, Govt. of Bombay, *Source Material*, II, 341–342.

[44] "Autobiography," pp. 979–980.   [45] Ibid., p. 981.

[46] Ibid., p. 985.

After 1895 most of the Chapekars' activities were directed against the British. They thought the British were blocking their way to a military career. Damodar petitioned the commander-in-chief at Simla four times about the possibility of enlisting in the army,[47] and when he learned that the army was organized into caste regiments and there was no Brahman regiment, he offered to raise a regiment of four hundred Brahmans for the British.[48] He made similar applications to a number of native states. Tilak tried to help him obtain employment in the Nawab of Junagadh's guard. But Damodar had no success.

Damodar stated explictly that the failure to find military service led him and his brother to despise the British.[49] He was convinced that this failure was the result of anti-Brahman prejudices the British were encouraging. When the brothers went to the bazaar in Poona to pick up military information, soldiers of the Maratha caste jeered at them and a Subhedar major taunted Damodar by saying a Brahman would be unable to observe his caste rules in the army.[50] And when Balkrishna offered his services to the Kolhapur army, he was told Poona Brahmans were not wanted.[51]

Damodar also saw anti-Brahmanism in the large following of the Satya Shodhak Sabha, the society founded by Jotirao Phule in the 1870s to educate and raise the status of backward castes and to persuade non-Brahmans not to use Brahman priests. Damodar believed that "the sole aim of this association is to stir up hatred against the Brahmans" and that the British were helping it to fulfill that goal.[52]

In 1896 and 1897, the Chapekars increased their terrorist acts. They assaulted an Indian professor who had been converted to Christianity.[53] They attacked a school teacher whom they believed was denouncing Hinduism and perverting little boys.[54] They set fire to a *mandap* (pavilion) in which the matriculation

---

[47] Ibid., p. 990.

[48] Confession of Damodar Chapekar, Govt. of Bombay, *Source Material*, II, 347.

[49] "Autobiography," pp. 992 and 998. [50] Ibid., pp. 989–990.

[51] Ibid., p. 968.

[52] Ibid., p. 987. Phule had died in 1890, but his successor, Narayan Maghaji Lokhandi, continued to send sabha workers around the countryside. Lokhandi edited the reformist *Din Bandhu*, a Bombay weekly, and was president of the Bombay Mill-Hands Association.

[53] Ibid., pp. 996–997. [54] Ibid., pp. 1,004–1,005.

examinations were scheduled to be held and then watched it burn "like an offering."⁵⁵ They tried to burn a Christian mission building⁵⁶ and a European merry-go-round.⁵⁷ They stoned missionaries preaching in Bombay,⁵⁸ and they disfigured a statue of Queen Victoria with a tarlike substance.⁵⁹

It was British interference with Hindu customs during the plague operations which moved the Chapekars to their greatest act of terrorism. Damodar wrote frankly about his motives. He alleged that under Rand's direction, British soldiers were raping women, desecrating temples, breaking idols, smashing in the walls of houses, and dragging people away to hospitals.⁶⁰ Moreover, Rand had committed a "notorius [in-] justice" by sentencing Brahmans to prison in Wai for playing music in front of a mosque.⁶¹ At the time that Rand was enforcing his unpopular plague measures in Poona, the plague claimed the life of Bhuskute. The death of their close friend suggested to the Chapekars that they too might die at any moment and that they had little to lose by attempting a daring, patriotic act.⁶² They followed Rand for days, studying his movements and looking for the opportunity to strike. They found it, Damodar wrote, when the Queen was forcing the peasants to celebrate her anniversary at great expense, instead of relieving them from the horrors of plague and famine.⁶³

Damodar's autobiography is a moving and pathetic document. His life was an almost unrelieved series of failures and frustrations. One experience after another marred the dignity he felt a Brahman ought to have. Each failure added bitterness, each strengthened his determination to destroy the corrupting influence of British and non-Brahmanical ideas. He had wanted to be admired for his patriotic sacrifices but their nature required utmost secrecy. He had hoped to command a small army but instead worked with a mere handful of poorly armed youths. He had dreamed of glory but led a life of furtive and unrewarded adventure. Even in writing his autobiography, he was torn between his desire to receive recognition for his patriotic, self-sacrificing act and his sense that writing about his own and his

⁵⁵ Ibid., p. 1,003.
⁵⁷ Ibid., p. 1,005.
⁵⁹ Ibid., pp. 999–1,001.
⁶¹ Ibid., p. 1,006.
⁶³ Ibid., p. 1,012.

⁵⁶ Ibid., p. 986.
⁵⁸ Ibid., p. 985.
⁶⁰ Ibid., pp. 1,007–1,008.
⁶² Ibid., p. 1,010.

family's virtues violated the Hindu ideal of self-effacement. He lamented that because there were few persons able to describe his family's considerable merits, "I am compelled to indulge in self-glorification, for which I beg my Aryan brethren to excuse me." He wanted his readers to know that although his father was a Haridasi and poor, his parents were "high-born, possessed of greatness of mind, generous and virtuous." He seemed to be saying that society was paying too much attention to exterior appearances and signs of material success, while ignoring the fundamental inner qualities. "Success or failure depends upon chance and has no connection with greatness."[64]

Although Damodar identified himself with all Maharashtrians at times in his autobiography, the more vital identification was with his family. And his efforts to clear his family's reputation and to avenge his personal humiliations and failures were justified on the grounds that he and his family were Brahmans, not that they were Hindus or Indians or human beings. This parochial character of Damodar's "patriotism" should be emphasized for two reasons. First, the narrowness of Damodar's affective community severely restricted the organizational potential of his club. Damodar explicitly excluded Brahman social reformers and implicitly rejected non-Brahmans from those he counted in his own community. But, second, Damodar's *activity* was directed against the British, the enemy of those whose national community theoretically included all Indians. An act might be called patriotic or nationalist, therefore, even if it was motivated by relatively parochial considerations as long as, as in the case of the Chapekars, the actors sought or received approval from people with a more inclusive or nationalist community identification and objective. English observers who referred to the Chapekars' club as "a Mahratta Brahman conspiracy" were correct about its organizational limits. But the groups who would welcome the diminution of British power and economic exploitation and who would therefore sympathize with their terrorism were numerous.

After shooting Rand and Ayerst, the Chapekars fled from Poona. Their sudden departure aroused the suspicions of the police. With the help of a tip received from two Brahmans named Dravid and Apte who were serving jail sentences for forgery, the police traced Damodar through a Bombay gymnasium. He was

[64] Ibid., p. 989.

arrested after being lured back to Poona by the police.[65] Damodar stood trial for the murder of Rand and Ayerst while the police searched for his brother and other members of his club. He pleaded not guilty and claimed he had made the confession under the promise of Rs. 20,000 from a police inspector.[66] On 3 February 1898 a jury of four Indians and one European found him guilty and he was sentenced to death.[67]

Damodar Chapekar's confession, autobiography, and trial failed to show that there was any definite connection between his deeds and the newspapers, Tilak, or the Natus. The Chapekars had visited the gymnasium of Bala Sahib Natu and they had attended a Shivaji celebration in the Natus' garden.[68] But apart from this the police had little information at that time to support the suggestion that the Natus or Tilak had had any direct communication with the Chapekars and their club. The inspector general of the Poona police, writing in July 1899, tried to explain away this lack of evidence and to justify the continued detention of the Natus who, after two years, had not been told why they were being held. The inspector general believed that despite Damodar Chapekar's claim that the Rand murder was the inspiration of his own mind, Chapekar's motives and ideas "were but the echoes" of the teaching of the Natus and their friends, and that the members of the Chapekar club were probably, "unknown to themselves, being shaped to a course of action . . . by the men who for political purposes of their own worked on the religious fervor of men like the Chapekars and incited them to deeds of violence."[69]

When the inspector general wrote about the Natus and their friends, he was almost certainly thinking of Tilak. Interesting evidence about Tilak's relations with the Chapekars has been gathered by Stanley Wolpert. Tilak, it is now known, had recommended Damodar for service in the guard of the Nawab of Junagadh in 1896. Moreover, Tilak learned almost immediately after the shooting that the Chapekars had done it, although he did not inform the police. As we have seen, Damodar was said

[65] *Poona Observer and Civil and Military Journal*, 6 and 13 Oct. 1897.
[66] Ibid., 3 Feb. 1898.   [67] Ibid., 4 Feb. 1898.
[68] J. Down, Inspector General of Police, Poona, to Under Sec., Govt. of Bombay, Jud. Dept., 15 July 1899. Enclosure to S. W. Edgerley, Sec., Govt. of Bombay, to Sec., Govt. of India, Home Dept., 25 Aug. 1899, Sept. Prog. No. 5, IHP, Pub., Vol. 5,640.
[69] Ibid.

to have sent a message to Tilak the day after the shooting to the effect that "the mission has succeeded." This suggests that at least Damodar wanted Tilak to know he had shot Rand and that he expected Tilak would approve. Finally, Tilak helped Balkrishna to avoid arrest by asking an acquaintance in Hyderabad to "sustain Balkrishna while he was in hiding."[70] Therefore, it can be stated that Tilak sympathized with the Chapekars' activities, although it might be too much to say on the basis of existing evidence that he definitely approved of them. The feelings of even moderate nationalists about terrorism were often ambivalent. A nationalist who philosophically rejected violent methods might nevertheless be gratified when violence was used by others. It might seem to the British that the terrorist had turned to violence in desperation in the face of an unbending and unfeeling government. This would lend weight to the nationalist insistence upon the necessity of reform. Moderate nationalists could point to their peaceful activities and demands and say that if their advice had been heeded, violence could have been avoided. In this sense, terrorists were the allies of the constitutional agitators.

The Poona murder case came to a spectacular close in the winter of 1898–1899 with two more killings and a series of arrests. First, Balkrishna Chapekar was arrested in December in Hyderabad state where he had been hiding in the Satpura hills with a gang of *dakoits*. A British detective had searched for him for weeks, traveling at night across fields and through low jungle to avoid detection.[71]

Soon after Balkrishna was caught and brought to Poona, his younger brother, Wasudeo, and a friend tried to kill one of the police officers investigating the case. Next, they ambushed and killed the Dravid brothers in a Poona street. The Dravid brothers had been the two principal witnesses in Damodar's trial and they were expected to testify against Balkrishna also. The day after the Dravids were shot, the police caught Wasudeo Chapekar. He was taken to police headquarters in Poona for questioning where he drew a pistol and fired once again at the investigating officer. He missed this time also, but he "proudly"

[70] Wolpert, *Tilak and Gokhale*, pp. 89–91.
[71] Report of the Detective Assistant to Inspector General of Police, Mr. Stephenson, attached to the service of the Hyderabad State, Govt. of Bombay, *Source Material*, II, 362–363.

admitted that he and one Mahadeo Ranade, another member of the Chapekar club, had murdered the Dravid brothers.[72] Wasudeo Chapekar and Ranade were tried for the Dravid murder and were found guilty and sentenced to hang. Another member of the club, Sathe, was sentenced to ten years' imprisonment for abetting the murder of the Dravids. In a separate trial, Balkrishna and Wasudeo Chapekar and Ranade were sentenced to hang for the murder of Rand and Ayerst. Wasudeo Chapekar and Ranade, who had behaved defiantly in the court room,[73] faced death calmly.[74] It was reported that when Wasudeo was being led past Balkrishna's cell to the gallows, he called, "Brother, I am going." Wasudeo died clutching a copy of the *Bhagavad Gita*.[75]

With these three executions, the Poona murder case came to an end. The police knew the names of the fifteen living members of the Chapekar club and regarded five of them as dangerous. However, there was little chance of convicting them. The only evidence against these men came from convicted persons and, in any case, after the Dravid murders, few persons were likely to be willing to testify.[76]

The Chapekars' club was the first "modern" terrorist organization the British encountered. It appeared in the town most likely, in British eyes, to produce such a phenomenon. Its membership had been only twenty or so and of these less than ten men had been active. Moreover, its goals of preserving the Aryan religion and driving the British from India were so far removed from the means in their hands that the whole affair had an air of absurdity and unreality. Despite the gravity of the assassinations, the discovery that the club was so local and so limited in character was a relief to those officials who had feared a widespread conspiracy. The club did resemble the terrorist societies which sprang up a few years later in Bombay, Bengal, and the Punjab in the reckless, courageous, and conspiratorial behavior of its members. But before 1905, officials regarded the club as a development peculiar to Poona.

[72] *Poona Observer and Civil and Military Journal*, 11 Feb. 1899.
[73] Ibid., 6 March 1899.   [74] *The Times of India*, 13 May 1899.
[75] *Bombay Gazette*, 8 May 1899, quoted in Govt. of Bombay, *Source Material*, II, 381.
[76] W. D. Sheppard, Dist. Mag., Poona, to Com., Central Div., 2 May 1899, enclosure to S. W. Edgerley to Govt. of India, 25 Aug. 1899.

If there was a lesson to be drawn from the events of 1897 and their sequel in Poona, it was that the political danger to the security of British rule came from two directions. On one side there were the traditional religious forces which, in the case of both Hindus and Muslims, were showing signs of increasing vitality. In normal times these forces were not threatening, but in the extraordinary circumstances of a famine or plague or a war in the Middle East, religion was potentially the most disruptive element of all. On the other side, there was the political alienation of educated groups which was a steadier corrosive; but it was not yet dangerous in most parts of India because the number of educated Indians was small and because their influence over the rest of the population was slight. However, events in Poona during the 1890s suggested that their influence was not only growing, but also combining with religious sentiment in opposition to British rule.

The effect of the union between Western-educated groups and orthodox Hindus could be seen in the similarity of Damodar's and Tilak's ideas. Damodar criticized many of the same things Tilak did, including the drain of wealth, anti-Brahmanism, the failure of the government to prevent cow slaughter, and the general degradation of Maharashtra since Maratha independence was extinguished. It would be wrong to suggest that Tilak was somehow responsible for putting grievances into Damodar's mind. The memories and tales of Maratha independence were part of Maharashtra's cultural heritage and they were shared by Brahmans of such divergent inclinations and background as M. G. Ranade, B. G. Tilak, and Damodar Chapekar. What Tilak did do was to keep this heritage before the elites of Maharashtra. He and his fellow patriots used the newspapers, the Shivaji festivals, and the Ganapati melas to remind people of the earlier achievements of Maharashtra and to unite them for a regeneration of Maharashtrian life. In this way, Tilak, S. M. Paranjpe, the Natus, and other educated leaders identified themselves with the aspirations and grievances of men who had not shared in the benefits of British rule. Urban areas throughout India had subcultures resembling Poona's, consisting of upper-caste men who found their traditional values and talents irrelevant to new political and economic conditions. Their values and training left them unequipped to achieve the wealth and responsibility which they coveted and which had formerly been their community's right. At the same time, they saw many members of their community gradually abandoning customs and values sanctified by centuries of use in favor of the culture of their conquerors. They were both close enough to observe the widening cultural and economic gulf between themselves and some of the more successful members of their community and too far removed to benefit from the new conditions. Furthermore, they were exposed to the steady stream of news in the vernacular press about Indian poverty and British racial prejudice.

Damodar belonged to one of these subcultures. It is clear from his autobiography that he believed he was acting as a watchdog and guardian for his community. The Chapekars kept a register of men "who are very vile and whose conduct is disgusting."[77] When Damodar tried to injure a bride and groom in a reformist wedding procession, he was fulfilling his social obligation to punish anyone who contravened the Dharma Shastras.[78] The underlying assumption of his autobiography was that at least one elite segment of society both required and approved of his activities. He sensed the community feeling against social reformers and the British which Tilak had helped to create. Damodar belonged to that section of the population which included underemployed and semieducated men with some political consciousness who were usually beyond the ordinary administrative and educational reach of the government. These men would have far less to lose than the Congress leaders from a collapse of law and order. In the past, British security had depended upon Indian leaders to exercise a restraining influence among such people. But if men like Tilak and Lajpat Rai fanned the discontent and political daring among these groups on the fringes of British Indian society, then the British would need new agents and methods of political control.

[77] "Autobiography," p. 1,004. [78] Ibid., p. 977.

―――――――――――― Conclusion ――――――――――――

The Indian National Congress in its first two decades had distinguished itself by bringing together nationalists from all regions of India and by concentrating solely on those demands for reform about which the vast majority of English-speaking nationalists could agree. The very survival of the Congress in a society of loose, shifting political alliances had been a substantial achievement. However, the Congress's rational intellectual analyses of India's relationship with its British rulers had not spoken to the more emotional sides of Indian patriotism. The careful, measured speeches and resolutions sounded as if they were intended to persuade an English jurist that India deserved representative institutions rather than to arouse fellow Indians to political action or love of country. Congress leaders measured British rule against liberal principles of individual liberty, equality under the law, and self-determination. Congress leaders may have been predisposed to their universalistic principles by the universalism of Hindu philosophy. But they cited British jurisprudence and constitutional history rather than Indian tradition as the source of their ideas. Their speeches and other Congress activities inspired little pride in their own culture.

Most Congress leaders had attained prominence through educational and professional institutions designed and dominated by Englishmen. Most were social reformers who tended to look upon popular Hinduism and Islam with the critical eyes of their Christian rulers. They were more likely than not to place distance between themselves and orthodox religious leaders and practices. In their role as Congress leaders, they avoided the potential patriotic resources provided by India's literary traditions, with their abundant supply of poetic imagery, historical analogy, and appreciation of nature. Outside the Congress, many leaders drew upon these resources. But within the Congress, the leaders ignored them because they were determined not to give the Congress a communal appearance and because in some cases they had an ambiguous attitude toward Indian culture. The result was a party that held little appeal for the majority of politically conscious Indians.

Conclusion

Effective nationalist leadership requires inspiring examples of how the interests of the nation may be placed above those of self. The Congress did not provide that kind of leadership. Only an occasional Congress leader subordinated his career and income to national purposes in ways which involved sacrifice or suffering. Politics was a secondary and part-time activity. Congress leaders suffered from a disjunction between their individual economic situations and their intellectual understanding of the causes of India's poverty. They knew that Britain was siphoning capital out of India, and they believed that British policies kept India from industrializing. But in their own careers, they earned comfortable or large incomes and experienced the self-fulfillment of high achievement. This undermined their willingness to take risks for the cause of increasing Indian autonomy. It dulled their sensitivity to the plight of the majority of students who were denied degrees after being admitted to college. It left most of them with little empathy for or feeling of common interest with the many millions of peasants who lived on the verge of starvation. And it gave Congress leaders an interest in preserving the hierarchial pattern of property and income distribution modified but slightly by the gradual spread of education and competitive institutions. Despite disagreements with hereditary landowners over the expansion of economic and political competition, Congress leaders and the most loyal supporters of the Raj shared an economically privileged position which they owed to British rule. Therefore, few early Congress leaders were inclined to alienate the British or their loyalist supporters. The Congress was in a poor position to convince people without British education or property that implementation of Congress goals would bring them a better life.

By the early twentieth century, this critique of the Congress was gaining acceptance among a wide spectrum of Indians, moderate and extremist, reformist and orthodox, anglicized and nonanglicized. Parts of the critique were appearing in the speeches and writings of Lajpat Rai, Bal Gangadhar Tilak, G. Subramania Iyer, and Aurobindo Ghose, and in the columns of the *Bangavasi, Sandhya, Kesari, Punjabee,* and *Swadesamitran*—all newspapers which were among the most widely read in their respective provinces.[1] In the twenty years in which the same

[1] Govt. of India, *Statements of English, Foreign. Anglo-Vernacular and*

Conclusion

group of men ran the Congress, Congress goals and tactics had changed insignificantly. Outside the Congress, though, there had been important developments among the politically conscious classes. Orthodox defenders of Hindu culture had risen to the challenge of the social reformers, and they had resisted efforts to permit widow-remarriage, to raise the legal age of marriage, to change dietary habits, and to discredit Puranic Hinduism. Hindus had also organized to prevent cow slaughter and to revive Sanskrit and vernacular languages and literatures. Perhaps the most important indication of the strength of the Hindu revival was the aggressive affirmation of Hindu culture, Vedic or Puranic, within university-educated circles where the tendency to denigrate popular Hinduism had been strongest. Well-educated men were joining the Hindu sabhas, the Arya Samaj, and the Ramakrishna Mission in large numbers in the late nineteenth century. Socially orthodox Hindus and social reformers found Hindu values that compared favorably with Western culture. In many cases these men had gained a new appreciation of selected aspects of Hinduism through the sympathetic analyses of Western scholars such as Max Müller, through Western organizations such as the Theosophical Society, and through English translations of Hindu classical texts. But whatever the source of the "rediscovery," both social reformers and orthodox Hindus were developing a confidence that Hindu values were not inferior to Western culture.

If movements for Hindu revitalization were laying the basis for Hindu integration, what effect were those movements having upon the Congress goal of uniting Hindus and Muslims behind nationalist political demands? Existing knowledge of Indian Muslim history does not provide a clear answer to that question. Muslims in India were not an integrated community. Many Muslims realized that pride in Hindu culture did not necessarily involve any antagonism toward Islamic culture. But a higher percentage of Muslims did attend the Congress before the 1893 cow protection riots than subsequently. In addition, university-educated and landholding Muslims seemed to fear that implementation of Congress demands for representative government and Indianization of administrative services would place Mus-

---

Vernacular Newspapers Published in India and Burma During the Year 1905 (Simla, 1907).

lims in danger from an unsympathetic Hindu majority. Muslim anxieties about how the Hindu majority would act if it gained political power probably were increased by the agitations for the Hindi language and cow protection. Muslim apprehensions had been great enough to keep most Muslims out of the Congress but not so strong that Muslims formed any anti-Congress organization of consequence during the first twenty years of the Congress.

The event which led Muslims to organize against the Congress was the partition of Bengal in 1905. The partition also served to bring into the open many other conflicts and trends which had been developing within the nationalist movement. The partition, therefore, represents a major divide in modern Indian history. Not only did the partition indirectly stimulate the formation of the Muslim League, it also led to the politicization of thousands of previously uninvolved Indians, to the rupture between the moderates and the extremists at the Surat Congress of 1907, to the beginning of a sustained terrorist movement of which the Chapekars had been the precursor, to the spread of movements to Indianize industry, commerce, and education, and to the passage of legislative council reforms with the important provision that Muslims would vote in special, separate Muslim electorates.

The momentous decision to divide Bengal in 1905 was publicly justified on administrative grounds. The undivided province of Bengal, Bihar, and Orissa, with its eighty million inhabitants, was too large for efficient government, officials said. Bengali nationalists, though, suspected the British were separating the eastern Muslim-majority districts from the predominantly Hindu districts of west Bengal in order to create a Muslim counterpoise to Bengali-speaking nationalists.[2] This belief, coupled with the many practical inconveniences caused by the partition, produced an anti-British mood of unusual intensity among Bengali Hindus. The anti-partition agitators adopted the boycott of British goods as the major tactic to force the reversal of the partition. In the autumn of 1905, student patrols in the towns and bazaars and landlord pressure in the villages sub-

[2] Nationalist suspicions were justified in that one of the professed "main objects" of the government was "to split up and thereby weaken a solid body of opponents to our rule." Herbert Risley's Note of 6 Dec. 1904. Feb. 1905 Prog. Nos. 155–167, IHP, Pub.

stantially lowered the sale of British goods for several months in eastern India. The boycott was one of several new features introduced into nationalist politics which spread to other parts of India. Large numbers of college and high school students and exstudents joined societies promoting the boycott, self-reliance, and paramilitary training. Members of these samitis took risks which almost no Congress leaders had faced, including arrest and the loss of the right to attend government-aided schools and to apply for government employment. Second, nationalists founded new companies to compete with foreign-owned commercial, manufacturing, and transportation concerns. Third, the anti-partition movement sought to Indianize dress, political vocabulary, educational institutions, and, in fact, the whole culture. Finally, educated nationalists contacted industrial workers and peasants and helped them to press economic demands with demonstrations, nationalist slogans, and strikes. In sum, the political climate had been abruptly transformed. Nationalists in Bengal and in scattered parts of other regions experienced a loathing of British rule which liberated them from their political passivity. Suddenly and briefly, the means to end India's colonial subjection seemed clear: boycott everything British, promote swadeshi industry and culture, and reach out to the less educated members of their own castes and, in a few cases, even to factory workers, cultivators, and other low-status groups.

There was, however, a serious weakness in the cause of the anti-partition movement in Bengal. Bengali Muslims had been hopelessly underrepresented in secondary and higher education, government services, and consultive bodies. As the British had anticipated, they did support the partition. Increasingly, Muslims resented efforts to reverse the partition and to stop them from buying foreign goods which were generally cheaper than swadeshi goods. Muslims in Bengal and elsewhere began to organize to protect Muslim interests from the revived, predominantly Hindu, nationalist movement. In a move which disappointed Congress leaders, a delegation of influential Muslims met with the Viceroy at Simla in October 1906 to ask for separate and weighted representation of Muslims in the legislative councils. The Government of India agreed to this request, and it thereby committed itself to the institutionalization of communal separation—then so evident in political life—in India's constitution. Then many Muslims from the original Simla dele-

Conclusion

gation met in December 1906 and founded the all-India Muslim League which developed into the major opposition to the Congress and, eventually, the vehicle for the creation of Pakistan.

In Bengal, after the Simla delegation and the founding of the Muslim League, Muslims grew more aggressive in demonstrating their support for the partition. Some Muslims believed that British officials wanted them to punish the Hindu boycott agitators. A Muslim League procession clashed with Hindus at Comilla in eastern Bengal in March 1907 and a Muslim was shot to death. Subsequently, there were widespread Muslim attacks on Hindus in Mymensingh district. Some of the student samitis, which had been organized to promote swadeshi and the boycott, now were preparing to protect Hindus from Muslim violence.[3] The brief Hindu-Muslim violence, the general Muslim support for the partition, the samitis' violation of laws, and repressive government regulations led moderate nationalists, including most of the Congress leadership, to abandon the anti-partition agitation, isolating the student samitis and extremists. Finding themselves alone, some samitis began assassinating British officials and their allies during 1908.

Other provinces experienced similar developments on a more limited scale and without Hindu-Muslim violence. The partition of Bengal and the suppression of the anti-partition agitation impressed nationalists throughout India as particularly autocratic and Machiavellian. The Japanese victories over Russia in 1905 had contributed to the impression that European supremacy in Asia had passed its peak and was approaching its end. And the adoption of the boycott and swadeshi movements seemed to fit the new interest in self-help, scientific and industrial development, and cultural regeneration. Nationalists in many towns outside Bengal heaped British goods on bonfires, set up swadeshi companies, started national schools, and attempted to mobilize uneducated groups previously ignored by the Congress.

Several examples of incidents outside Bengal, each involving Congress leaders, illustrate the new directions of the nationalist movement. The first centered on the Swadeshi Steam Navigation Company which was started at Tuticorin, Madras, in November

[3] See John R. McLane, "The Partition of Bengal and the New Communalism," in Alexander Lipski (ed.), *Bengal: East and West* (Michigan State University South Asia Series Occasional Paper No. 13, 1970).

Conclusion

1906 to compete with the British-owned company that enjoyed a near monopoly of Tuticorin's passenger and cotton and rice export business. The main organizer was Chidambaran Pillai, a local lawyer, swadeshi enthusiast, and associate of G. Subramania Iyer. The founding of the Swadeshi Steam Navigation Company followed the incorporation of two swadeshi shipping companies in Bengal. The British-owned company operating out of Tuticorin cut its rates in an effort to preserve its business. As the new swadeshi company struggled to survive and complained that the South Indian Railway denied it the same facilities enjoyed by the British company, anti-British feeling spread in Tuticorin and other towns in Tinnevelly district. In February and March 1908, textile workers, who were encouraged and represented by Chidambaran Pillai, struck a British-owned mill and attended meetings at which violence was allegedly advocated. When notices for the arrest of Pillai and two other nationalists were issued, *hartals* were held in Tuticorin and Tinnevelly. In both towns the police fired on angry crowds. In Tinnevelly demonstrators stoned the office of Messrs. Parry and Company, attacked public buildings, including the post office and the police station, and burned down the municipal office.[4]

In the Punjab, the *nai haoa* (new air) was more widespread than in Madras. In late 1906 and early 1907, the public learned that the Government of the Punjab intended to modify the terms of tenure in the Chanab Canal Colony (Lyallpur district) and to raise the rates for canal water along the Bari Doab Canal (Southern Lahore district). Educated nationalists took up the cause of the peasants who would be affected, and they made a special effort to persuade Muslims and Sikhs of their common interest with Hindus in resisting these changes by withholding rents and water rates. The Punjab government was especially concerned by the effort to unite Hindus, Muslims, and Sikhs, by the strength of discontent among peasants in the central Punjab districts, and by the preaching of civil disobedience and the need to shed blood. The government succeeded in breaking the back of the movement by deporting Lajpat Rai and Ajit Singh (a

---

[4] Note on the Riots in Tinnevelly and Tuticorin in March 1908, enclosure to J. N. Atkinson, Actg. Ch. Sec., Govt. of Madras, to Govt. of India, Home Dept., 16 May 1908. June 1908 Prog. No. 95, IHP, Pol. Also, *The Life-Sketch of Sjt. V. O. Chidambaran Pillai with a Prefatory Essay on India as a Maritime Power* (Madras, 1909), pp. 12-38.

Jat Sikh who was a member of the Arya Samaj) and by modifying the proposed changes.[5]

The third and final example is from Bombay city, and it concerns the reaction of textile workers to the arrest of Bal Gangadhar Tilak for sedition. Tilak had gained popularity among Maratha workers from Bombay's 85 mills after he started in late 1907 to lecture to them about nationalism, temperance, and the need to start labor unions. After Tilak and S. M. Paranjpe were arrested for seditious writing in June 1908, sympathetic workers shut down 28 mills by striking. When 35,000 mill hands gathered to try to close other mills, the military was called to keep order. When Tilak was convicted in July and sentenced to six years in prison, 76 mills were closed, the workers rioted, and at least four persons were killed in police firings. Again, officials were alarmed by the new alliances which crossed caste and class lines. In this case, Tilak was mobilizing workers of the Maratha caste who had been assumed to have had little common interest with Brahman Congress supporters.[6]

In each of these three examples, the connections with the anit-partition movement in Bengal had been manifest. As in Bengal, educated nationalists had successfully reached workers and peasants, in each case the Bengali slogan, *Bande Mataram*, had been used, and in each case the agitation subsided soon after the arrest of Congress extremists. The extremists involved were few in number and they were acting without any formal Congress sanction. They were nevertheless watched with great interest by their Congress colleagues because they revealed the existence of a potential for mass civil disobedience which Gandhi developed after World War I.

As the movements for swadeshi, boycott, and national education had spread throughout India in 1905, 1906, and 1907, and as extremists experimented with new forms of political activity, the simmering conflict between moderates and extremists for control of the Congress came to a head. The deadening apathy that had settled on the Congress in its second decade had lifted in 1904 and 1905 as the final plans for the partition of Bengal were pre-

---

[5] Minute by Sir Denzil Ibbetson, Lt. Gov. of Punjab on the political situation in that province, 30 Apr. 1907. Aug. 1907 Prog. No. 148, IHP, Pol.

[6] H. G. Gell, Com. of Police, Bombay, to Sec., Govt. of Bombay, Judic. Dept., 27 Aug. 1908. Govt. of Bombay, *Source Material*, II, 257ff. Also Cashman, *The Myth of the Lokamanya*, pp. 172–185.

Conclusion

pared and implemented. Delegates to the 1905 Congress were buoyed by the revived spirit evident at the session at Benaras and Gokhale's presidential speech which gave qualified support to the Bengali boycott and an uncharacteristically harsh analysis of British economic policy.

The 1906 Congress was held at Calcutta. Extremists, knowing that they would be supported by hundreds of Bengali delegates, sought to have Tilak or Lajpat Rai selected as president. But the moderate leaders frustrated this move by offering the presidency to Dadabhai Naoroji, "the Grand Old Man" of Indian nationalism. The extremists next concentrated their efforts on persuading the Subjects Committee to draft resolutions in support of swadeshi, the boycott of foreign goods, national education, and the granting to India of self-government.

The Subjects Committee meeting, held in the Maharaja of Darbhanga's Calcutta palace, was attended by over six hundred delegates, more than had attended some full Congress sessions in the past. The moderates, under Sir Pherozeshah Mehta's guidance, were able to postpone a total rupture by agreeing reluctantly to modified versions of the resolutions sought by the extremists. The moderates also acceded to the demands for a constitution for the Congress.[7]

The Congress split came in December 1907, at the twenty-third session. The 1907 session was originally scheduled for Nagpur. The 1906 Constiution required that 75 per cent of the members of the Reception Committee agree on the selection of the president. But neither the moderates nor the extremists on the Nagpur Committee had enough votes to break the deadlock which emerged. The old guard leadership realized that they would have to shift the session. They met in Bombay at Sir Pherozeshah's house and decided on Surat. Surat had two distinct advantages for the moderates. Perhaps the most important was that it was in Bombay Presidency, which meant that Tilak would not be eligible to serve as president. Congress operating procedures forbade the selection of a president from the host province. Second, Sir Pherozeshah had many followers in Surat through whom the moderates hoped to control the preparations and proceedings.[8] The implications of the choice of Surat were clear to the extremists. The Bombay Congress Provincial Con-

[7] Johnson, *Provincial Politics*, pp. 134–153.
[8] Ibid., pp. 153–173.

ference had been held at Surat in April 1907 and Sir Pherozeshah had succeeded in excluding resolutions on the boycott and national education from the proceedings. Shortly before the Surat Congress in December, extremist suspicions of moderate intentions grew when an initial list of proposed resolutions was published which omitted the boycott, national education, and self-government resolutions. Apparently, the moderates intended to retreat from the compromise positions adopted at the Calcutta Congress of 1906.[9] The moderate resolve to disassociate the Congress from extremist tactics may have been stiffened by the news that terrorists had tried to blow up the lieutenant-governor of Bengal's train and that someone had shot the collector of Dacca district.[10]

Unfortunately for extremist claims to legitimacy, the extremists were a minority at the Surat Congress.[11] The opening day's proceedings had to be suspended when extremist hecklers prevented Surendranath Banerjea from finishing his speech seconding the presidential nomination of Rashbehari Ghosh. The next day, shortly after the proceedings were resumed, Tilak, who was not on the agenda, tried to speak against the election of Rashbehari Ghosh. When Tilak was ruled out of order and refused to sit down, someone in the audience threw a shoe toward the speakers' platform and hit Surendranath Banerjea on the head. At this point, according to a British journalist, extremists

> surged up the escarpment of the platform. Leaping, climbing, hissing the breath of fury, brandishing long sticks, they came, striking at any head that looked to them Moderate, and in another moment, between brown legs, standing upon the green-baize table, I caught glimpses of the Indian National Congress dissolving in chaos.[12]

The fragile unity of the Congress had been broken. Many extremists seceded from the Congress, but they were rendered almost leaderless by the arrest of their principal spokesmen: Tilak,

[9] Ibid., and Govt. of Bombay, *Source Material*, II, 163–176.
[10] Nevinson, *The New Spirit in India*, pp. 237–238.
[11] The Congress published no official report or delegate list for 1907 and estimates of the number and affiliation of delegates varied widely. However, even Aurobindo admitted that moderates outnumbered "Nationalists." Majumdar, *Indian Political Associations*, p. 211.
[12] Nevinson, *The New Spirit in India*, pp. 257–258.

Conclusion

Lajpat Rai, Aurobindo, and Bipinchandra Pal. The Government of India moved to strengthen the moderates by reforming the legislative councils in 1909 in a manner which would enhance their visibility and influence. The extremists had challenged the moderates and lost. The Congress lost its most creative politicians. It would require World War I, the Khilafat movement, and Gandhi to bring extremists and Muslims close to the moderate leadership of the Congress again.

---- Bibliography ----

I. MANUSCRIPT COLLECTIONS

A. India Office Library, London

Ampthill Collection. Arthur Oliver Villiers Russell, 2nd Baron Ampthill, Acting Viceroy of India, 1904. MSS. Eur. E. 233.

Cross Collection. Richard Assheton Cross, 1st Viscount Cross, Secretary of State for India, 1886–1892. MSS. Eur. E. 243.

Curzon Collection. George Nathaniel Curzon, Lord Curzon of Kedleston, Viceroy of India, 1899–1905. MSS. Eur. F. 111.

Elgin Collection. Victor Alexander Bruce, 9th Earl of Elgin and 13th Earl of Kincardine, Viceroy of India, 1894–1899.

Hamilton Collection. Lord George Francis Hamilton, Secretary of State for India, 1895–1903. MSS. Eur. C. 125–26. MSS. Eur. D. 508–10.

Lamington Collection. Charles Wallace Alexander Napier Cochrane Baillie, 2nd Baron Lamington, Governor of Bombay, 1903–1907. MSS. Eur. B. 159.

Lee-Warner Collection. Sir William Lee-Warner, Secretary to Political and Secret Department, India Office, 1895–1902. MSS. Eur. F. 92.

Morley Collection. John Morley, 1st Viscount Morley of Blackburn, Secretary of State for India, 1905–1910. MSS. Eur. D. 573.

B. British Museum, London

Curzon Collection. George Nathaniel Curzon, Lord Curzon of Kedleston, Viceroy of India, 1899–1905.

C. Bodleian Library, Oxford

MacDonnell Collection. Anthony Patrick MacDonnell, Lord MacDonnell of Swinford, Lieutenant-Governor of the North-Western Provinces and Oudh, 1895–1901. Ms. Eng. Hist. c. 206, 215, 235–36, 350–54, 366, and 368.

D. West Bengal State Archives, Calcutta

Papers prepared by the State Committee for the Compilation of the History of the Freedom Movement in India, Bengal Region.

Bibliography

II. GOVERNMENT RECORDS

A. India

C. S. B. Memoranda, etc., Thagi and Dakoiti Department
India Home Proceedings:
    Education
    Judicial
    Municipal
    Political
    Public
India Judicial and Public Papers
India Legislative Council Proceedings
India Legislative Proceedings
India Revenue and Agricultural Proceedings
Judicial and Public Despatches to India, Madras, and Bombay
Political and Secret Department, Demi-Official Correspondence
Political and Secret Letters and Enclosures Received from India
Public Letters from India
Public Letters from India and General Letters from Bengal
Revenue Despatches to India, Madras, and Bombay
Revenue Letters from India

B. Bengal

Bengal General Proceedings
Bengal Judicial Proceedings
Bengal Legislative Council Proceedings
Bengal Municipal, Local Self-Government, Sanitation and Medical Proceedings
Bengal Native Newspaper Reports
Bengal Political Proceedings
Bengal Revenue Proceedings
Bengal Revenue Proceedings: Wards', Attached, and Government Estates
Eastern Bengal and Assam Judicial and General Proceedings

C. Bombay

Bombay Education, Ecclesiastical, Marine, and Legislative Proceedings
Bombay Judicial Proceedings
Bombay Judicial and Home Proceedings
Bombay Legislative Council Proceedings

Bibliography

Bombay Native Newspaper Reports
Bombay Political Proceedings
Bombay Revenue Proceedings, Famine
Bombay Revenue Proceedings, Land

D. Madras

Madras Legislative Council Proceedings
Madras Native Newspaper Reports

E. North-Western Provinces and Oudh

North-Western Provinces and Oudh Legislative Council Proceedings
North-Western Provinces and Oudh Native Newspaper Reports
North-Western Provinces and Oudh, Central Provinces, and Rajputana Native Newspaper Reports
United Provinces Political and Police Proceedings

F. Punjab

Punjab Native Newspaper Reports

III. OFFICIAL PUBLICATIONS

Report of the Committee on the Riots in Poona and Ahmednagar, 1875. 2 vols. Bombay, 1876.
Report on Wards' and Attached Estates in the Lower Provinces. Calcutta annual.
Report on the Land Revenue Administration of the Lower Provinces. Calcutta annual.
Review of the Management of Estates in the Court of Wards or Under the Taluqdars Relief Act in Oudh. Allahabad annual.
Report of the Court of Wards, North-Western Provinces and Oudh. Allahabad annual.
Report of the Indian Education Commission. Calcutta, 1883.
Education Commission: Report by the Bengal Provincial Committee. Calcutta, 1884.
Education Commission: Report by the Madras Provincial Committee. Calcutta, 1884.
Education Commission: Report by the North-Western Provinces and Oudh Provincial Committee. Calcutta, 1884.
Indian Law Reports. Allahabad, 1887.

Bibliography

F. B. Mulock, *An Inquiry into the Economic Condition of the Agricultural and Labouring Classes in the North-Western Provinces and Oudh.* Naini Tal, 1888.

Selections from the Records of the Government of India, Home Department, No. CCLXV. Papers Relating to Discipline and Moral Training in Schools and Colleges in India. Calcutta, 1890.

General Report on the Census of India, 1891.

Report of the Commission to Inquire into the Working of the Deccan Agriculturalists' Relief Act, 1891–92. Bombay, 1892.

Selections of Papers on Agricultural Indebtedness and the Restriction of the Power to Alienate Interests in Land. Simla, 1898.

The Plague in India, 1896, 1897. Simla, 1898.

Report of the Indian Famine Commission, 1898. Calcutta, 1898.

Report of the Indian Famine Commission, 1901. Calcutta, 1901.

Land Revenue Policy of the Indian Government. Calcutta, 1902.

Statements of English, Foreign, Anglo-Vernacular, and Vernacular Newspapers Published in India and Burma During the Year 1905. Simla, 1907.

Summary of the Administration of Lord Curzon of Kedleston, Viceroy and Governor General of India, in the Home Department. Calcutta, 1907.

Summary of the Administration of Lord Curzon of Kedleston, Viceroy and Governor General of India, in the Military Department. Calcutta, 1907.

Summary of the Administration of Lord Curzon of Kedleston, Viceroy and Governor General of India, in the Revenue and Agricultural Department. Calcutta, 1907.

Royal Commission on the Public Services in India, *Report of the Commissioners.* London, 1917.

Sedition Committee, 1918. Report. Calcutta, 1918.

G. A. Grierson, *Linguistic Survey of India.* Calcutta, 1926.

Indian Statutory Commission: Report. London, 1930.

IV. PARLIAMENTARY PAPERS, REPORTS, AND DEBATES

1878 C. 2071. Deccan Riots in 1875 and their connection with the revision of the assessment, and the indebtedness of the agricultural and land-

Bibliography

owning classes: Report of the Commissioners of Inquiry.

1890 C. 5926. Public Service Commission: Correspondence relating to the Report, including the question as to the limits of age for the Indian Civil Service Examination.

1890 C. 5950. Numbers and Functions of the Several Councils in India: Correspondence.

1890 C. 6072. Kashmir: Papers relating to.

1892 188. Behar Cadastral Survey: Correspondence as to the advisability of carrying out the proposed Cadastral Survey.

1892 192. Salaries: Return of the number of persons who received from the Revenues of India, during the year 1889–90, annual allowances of not less than 1,000 rupees each; distinguishing number, amount, nationality, etc.

1893 C. 7181. Census: General Report of the Census of India, 1891.

1893–1894 538. Reports Relating to the Recent Religious Conflicts between Hindus and Muhammedans in India.

1894 43. Statement Exhibiting the Moral and Material Progress and Condition of India During the Year 1891–92, and the Nine Preceding Years.

1895 202. Cotton Import Duties: Representations made to the Government of India, in March 1894, against the exclusion of Cotton Manufactures from Import Duties, by Chambers of Commerce and other public bodies in India.

1895 C. 7602. Indian Tariff Act and the Cotton Duties, 1894: Correspondence.

1896 C. 8131. Suakin Expedition: Correspondence between the Government of India and the Secretary of State regarding the incidence of the cost of the Indian troops when employed out of India.

1896	C.	8258.	Expenditure of India: First Report of Royal Commission, with Minutes of Evidence. Vol. I.
1898	C.	8871.	Penal Code and Criminal Procedure Code Amendment Acts: Papers relating to amendments in the Law relating to Sedition and Defamation.
1899	C.	9178.	Famine Commission, 1898 (Sir J. Lyall, President): Report.
1899	C.	9254.	Famine Commission, 1898. Minutes of Evidence, etc. Vol. III. Bombay Presidency.
1900	Cd.	131.	Expenditure of India: Final Report of Royal Commission. Vol. IV.
1902	Cd.	876.	Famine Commission, 1901 (Sir A. P. Macdonnell, President): Report, with the Resolution of the Government of India, etc.
1905	Cd.	2658.	Eastern Bengal and Assam: Papers relating to the Reconstitution of the Provinces of Bengal and Assam.
1908	Cd.	4435.	Advisory and Legislative Councils, Vol. II, Replies of the Local Governments.
1918	Cd.	9109.	Report on the Indian Constitutional Reforms.

Parliamentary Debates

V. Dissertations

Ghosh, Pansy Chaya. "The Development of the Indian National Congress, 1892–1909." Ph.D., University of London, 1958.

Jones, Iris M. "The Origins and Development to 1892 of the Indian National Congress." M. A., University of London, 1947.

Krishnaswamy, S. "A Riot in Bombay, August 11, 1893: A Study in Hindu-Muslim Relations in Western India During the Late Nineteenth Century." Ph.D., University of Chicago, 1966.

Rahman, Rokeya. "Social and Administrative Policy of the Government of Bengal, 1877–1890." M. A., University of London, 1959.

Bibliography

Rizvi, Janet Mary. "Muslim Politics and Government Policy: Studies in the Development of Muslim Organization and its Social Background in North India and Bengal, 1885–1917." Ph.D., Cambridge University, 1969.

VI. NEWSPAPERS

The Bengalee
Bombay Gazette
The Englishman
The Friend of India and Statesman
Moslem Chronicle
The New York Times
The Pioneer
Poona Observer and Civil and Military Journal
The Times (London)
The Times of India

VII. PERIODICALS

Asiatic Quarterly Review
Bengal Past and Present
Calcutta Review
The Contemporary Review
East and West
Hindustan Review and Kayastha Samachar
India
Indian Historical Records Commission: Proceedings
Indian Review
Kayastha Samachar
The Nineteenth Century
Report of the Regional Records Survey Committee for West Bengal

VIII. BOOKS AND ARTICLES

Ahluwalia, M. N. *Kukas: The Freedom Fighters of the Punjab.* Bombay, 1965.

Aiyar, C. P. Ramaswami. *Biographical Vistas: Sketches of Some Eminent Indians.* Madras, 1966.

Andrews, C. F. *Zaka Ullah of Delhi.* Cambridge, 1929.

Anon. *Audi Alteram Partem: Being Two Letters on Certain Aspects of the Indian National Congress.* London, 1888.

Anon. *Famous Parsis: Biographical and Critical Sketches.* Madras, 1930.

Anon. *Heroes of the Hour: Mahatma Gandhi, Tilak Maharaj, Sir Subramanya Iyer.* Madras, n.d. (1918).

Argov, Daniel. *Moderates and Extremists in the Indian National Movement, 1883–1920.* Bombay, 1967.

Bagal, J. C. *History of the Indian Association, 1876–1951.* Calcutta, 1953.
Bailey, F. G. *Politics and Social Change: Orissa in 1959.* Berkeley, 1963.
Bajwa, Fauja Singh. *Kuka Movement: An Important Phase in Punjab's Role in India's Struggle for Freedom.* Delhi, 1965.
Banerjea, Surendranath. *A Nation in Making: Being the Reminiscences of Fifty Years of Public Life.* Oxford, 1927.
Barrier, Norman Gerald. *The Punjab Alienation of Land Bill of 1900.* Durham, 1966.
———. "The Punjab Government and Communal Politics," *JAS*, xxviii, 3 (May 1968).
———. *The Punjab in Nineteenth Century Tracts: An Introduction to the Pamphlet Collections in the British Museum and India Office.* East Lansing, 1969.
Bayly, C. A. *The Local Roots of Indian Politics: Allahabad, 1880–1920.* Oxford, 1975.
Beames, John. *Memoirs of a Bengal Civilian.* London, 1961.
Besant, Annie. *How India Wrought for Freedom: The Story of the Indian National Congress Told from Official Records.* Madras, 1915.
Beveridge, Lord. *India Called Them.* London, 1917.
(Bhargava, Prag Narain). *Who's Who in India.* Lucknow, 1911.
———. *First Supplement to Who's Who in India.* Lucknow, 1912.
———. *Second Supplement to Who's Who in India.* Lucknow, 1914.
(Bhopal), Nawab Sultan Jahan Begum. *An Account of My Life (Gohur-i-Ikbal).* London, 1912.
Blunt, Sir Edward Arthur Henry. *The Caste System of Northern India.* New Delhi, 1969, reprint of the 1931 edition.
———. *The I.C.S.: The India Civil Service.* London, 1965.
Bobbili, Maharaja of. *A Revised and Enlarged Account of the Bobbili Zemindari.* Madras, 1900.
Bombay, Government of. *Source Material for a History of the Freedom Movement in India,* 2 vols. Bombay, 1958.
Bonnerji, Sadhana. *Life of W. C. Bonnerji: First President of the Indian National Congress.* Calcutta, 1944.
Bose, Nirmal Kumar. *Modern Bengal.* Calcutta, 1959.
———. *Studies in Gandhism.* Calcutta, 1962.

Bibliography

Bose, Radha Krishna. *The Present Situation of the Domiciled Bengalees of Orissa and the Way Out of It.* Cuttack, 1917.

Brass, Paul. *Language, Religion and Politics in North India.* Cambridge, 1974.

Broomfield, J. H. *Elite Conflict in a Plural Society: Twentieth-Century Bengal.* Berkeley, 1968.

Brown, W. Norman. "The Sanctity of the Cow in Hinduism," *Journal of the Madras University*, XXVIII, 2 (Jan. 1957).

Buckland, C. E. *Bengal Under the Lieutenant-Governors*, 2 vols. Calcutta, 1901.

Buckland, C. E. (ed.). *Dictionary of Indian Biography.* London, 1906.

Calvert, H. *The Wealth and Welfare of the Punjab.* Lahore, 1936.

Carstairs, Robert. *British Work in India.* Edinburgh, 1891.

Cashman, Richard I. *The Myth of the Lokamanya: Tilak and Mass Politics in Maharashtra.* Berkeley, 1975.

Catanach, I. J. *Rural Credit in Western India 1875–1930: Rural Credit and the Co-operative Movement in the Bombay Presidency.* Berkeley, 1970.

Chandra, Bipan. *The Rise and Growth of Economic Nationalism in India: Economic Policies of Indian National Leadership, 1880–1905.* New Delhi, 1966.

Chaudhuri, Nirad C. *The Autobiography of an Unknown Indian.* London, 1951.

Chaudhuri, Sashi Bhusan. *Civil Rebellion in the Indian Mutinies (1857–1859).* Calcutta, 1957.

Chirol, Valentine. *Indian Unrest.* London, 1910.

Cotton, H.J.S. *New India or India in Transition.* London, 1886.

———. *New India or India in Transition.* London, 1904.

Crane, Robert (ed.) *Regions and Regionalism in South Asian Studies: An Exploratory Study.* Durham, 1967.

Crooke, William. *The North-Western Provinces of India: Their History, Ethnology and Administration.* London, 1897.

———. *The Popular Religion and Folklore of Northern India.* London, 1896.

———. "The Veneration of the Cow in India," *Folk-lore*, XXIII, 3 (Sept. 1912).

Cumpston, Mary. "Some early Indian Nationalists and their allies in the British Parliament, 1851–1906," *English Historical Review*, LXXVI, 299 (Apr. 1961).

Bibliography

Curran, J. A. *Militant Hinduism in India Politics: A Study of the R.S.S.* New York, 1951.

Curzon, G. N. *British Government in India: The Story of the Viceroys and Government Houses.* London, 1925.

———. *Speeches by Lord Curzon of Kedleston, Viceroy and Governor General of India.* 4 vols. Calcutta, 1900–1906.

Dar, Pandit Bishan Narayan. *An Appeal to the English Public on Behalf of the Hindus of the N.-W. P. and Oudh.* Lucknow, 1893.

Das, M. N. *India Under Morley and Minto: Politics Behind Revolution, Repression and Reforms.* London, 1964.

Das Gupta, Hemendranath. *Deshbandhu Chittaranjan Das.* Delhi, 1960.

Dodwell, H. H. (ed.). *The Cambridge History of India*, Vol. VI. Cambridge, 1932.

Durand, Sir Mortimer. *Life of the Right Hon. Alfred Comyn Lyall.* Edinburgh, 1913.

Dutt, Paramananda. *Memoirs of Moti Lal Ghose.* Calcutta, 1935.

Dutt, Romesh Chunder. *Open Letters to Lord Curzon and Speeches and Papers.* Calcutta, 1904.

———. *The Peasantry of Bengal: Being a view of their condition under the Hindu, the Mahomedan, and the English rule, and a consideration of the means calculated to improve their future prospects.* Calcutta, 1874.

Edwardes, Michael. *High Noon of Empire: India Under Curzon.* London, 1965.

Embree, Ainslie Thomas. *India's Search for National Identity.* New York, 1972.

Enthoven, Reginald Edward. *The Folklore of Bombay.* Oxford, 1924.

Erikson, Erik H. *Gandhi's Truth: On the Origins of Militant Nonviolence.* New York, 1969.

Farquhar, J. N. "The Fighting Ascetics of India," *Bulletin of the John Rylands Library*, IX, 2 (July 1925).

———. *Modern Religious Movements in India.* London, 1924.

Faruqi, Zia-ul-Hasan. *The Deoband School and the Demand for Pakistan.* Bombay, 1963.

Fischer, Louis. *The Life of Mahatma Gandhi.* New York, 1962.

Fitze, Sir Kenneth. *Twilight of the Maharajas.* London, 1956.

Bibliography

Forrest, George W. *The Administration of the Marquis of Lansdowne as Viceroy and Governor-General of India, 1888–1894.* Calcutta, 1894.

Fraser, Sir Andrew H. L. *Among Indian Rajahs and Ryots: A Civil Servant's Recollections and Impressions of Thirty-Seven Years of Work and Sport in the Central Provinces and Bengal.* London, 1912.

Frykenberg, R. E. (ed.). *Land Control and Social Structure in Indian History.* Madison, 1969.

Fuller, Sir Bamfylde. *The Empire of India.* London, 1913.

Gallagher, John, Johnson, Gordon, and Seal, Anil (eds.). *Locality, Province and Nation: Essays on Indian Politics 1870–1940.* Cambridge, 1973.

Gandhi, M. K. *An Autobiography: or the Story of My Experiments With Truth.* Ahmedabad, 1959.

———. *Hindu Dharma.* Ahmedabad, 1950.

———. *Young India, 1919–1922.* New York, 1924.

Gauba, K. L. *The Rebel Minister: The Story of the Rise and Fall of Lala Harkishen Lal.* Lahore, 1938.

Ghosh, P. C. *The Development of the Indian National Congress 1892–1909.* Calcutta, 1960.

Gilbert, Martin. *Servant of India: A Study of Imperial Rule from 1905 to 1910 as Told Through the Correspondence and Diaries of Sir James Dunlop Smith.* London, 1966.

Gokhale, L. R. *The First Twenty Years of the Indian National Congress.* Bombay, 1906.

Gopal, Ram. *How India Struggled for Freedom: A Political History.* Bombay, 1967.

———. *Lokmanya Tilak: A Biography.* Bombay, 1956.

Gopal, Sarvepalli. *British Policy in India, 1858–1905.* Cambridge, 1965.

———. *The Viceroyalty of Lord Ripon, 1880–1884.* London, 1953.

Gordon, Leonard A. *Bengal: The Nationalist Movement 1876–1940.* New York, 1974.

Grover, B. L. *A Documentary Study of British Policy Towards Indian Nationalism 1885–1909.* Delhi, 1967.

Gupta, J. N. *Life and Work of Romesh Chandra Dutt.* London, 1911.

Gupta, Nagendranath. *Reflections and Reminiscences.* Bombay, 1947.

Hardy, P. *The Muslims of British India.* Cambridge, 1972.
Harris, F. R. *Jamsetji Nusserwanji Tata: A Chronicle of His Life.* Bombay, 1958.
Heimsath, Charles H. *Indian Nationalism and Hindu Social Reform.* Princeton, 1964.
Hunter, Sir William Wilson. *Annals of Rural Bengal.* London, 1868.
Husain, Azim. *Fazl-i-Husain: A Political Biography.* Bombay, 1946.
Hutchins, Francis G. *The Illusion of Permanence: British Imperialism in India.* Princeton, 1967.
Irschick, Eugene F. *Politics and Social Conflict in South India: The Non-Brahman Movement and Tamil Separatism, 1916–1929.* Berkeley, 1969.
Jeejeebhoy, J.R.B. (ed.). *Some Unpublished and Later Speeches and Writings of the Hon. Sir Pherozeshah Mehta.* Bombay, 1918.
Johnson, Gordon. *Provincial Politics and Indian Nationalism: Bombay and the Indian National Congress, 1880–1915.* Cambridge, 1973.
Karandikar, S. L. *Lokmanya Bal Gangadhar Tilak; the Hercules and Prometheus of Modern India.* Poona, 1957.
Karve, D. D. (ed.). *The New Brahmans: Five Maharashtrian Families.* Berkeley, 1963.
Karve, D. G. and Ambekar, D. V. (eds.). *Speeches and Writings of Gopal Krishna Gokhale,* Vol. II. Poona, 1966.
Keatinge, Gerald Francis. *Rural Economy in the Bombay Deccan.* London, 1912.
Keer, Dhananjay. *Veer Savarkar.* Bombay, 1966.
Kelkar, N. C. *Life and Times of Lokmanya Tilak.* Madras, 1928.
Kellock, James. *Mahadev Govind Ranade: Patriot and Social Servant.* Calcutta, 1926.
(Khan, Sir Sayyid Ahmad). *Sir Syed Ahmed on the Present State of Indian Politics, Consisting of Speeches and Letters Reprinted from the 'Pioneer.'* Allahabad, 1888.
Kidron, Michael. *Foreign Investments in India.* London, 1965.
Kumar, Dharma. *Land and Caste in South India.* Cambridge, 1965.
Kumar, Ravindra. *Western India in the Nineteenth Century: A Study in the Social History of Maharashtra.* London, 1968.

Bibliography

(Lajpat Rai). *Lajpat Rai: Autobiographical Writings*, ed. Vijaya Chandra Joshi. Delhi, 1965.

———. *Lala Lajpat Rai: Writings and Speeches*, ed. Vijaya Chandra Joshi. Delhi, 1966.

Lajpat Rai. *Young India: An Interpretation and a History of the Nationalist Movement from Within*. New York, 1916.

Latifi, A. *The Industrial Punjab: A Survey of Facts, Conditions and Possibilities*. Bombay, 1911.

Lawrence, Sir Walter Roper. *The India We Served*. London, 1929.

Leitner, G. W. "Cow-Killing Riots, Seditious Pamphlets, and the Indian Police," *The Imperial and Asiatic Quarterly Review*, New Series, VII, 13 (Jan. 1894).

Lévi-Strauss, Claude. *Totemism*. Boston, 1963.

Lyall, Sir Alfred C. *Asiatic Studies: Religious and Social*. London, 1884.

Maconochie, Evan. *Life in the Indian Civil Service*. London, 1926.

Majumdar, Bimanbehari. "The Ananda Math and Phadke," *Journal of Indian History*, XLIV, 1 (April 1966).

———. *History of Political Thought from Rammohun to Dayananda (1821–84)*, Vol. I. Calcutta, 1934.

———. *Indian Political Associations and Reform of Legislature 1818–1917*. Calcutta, 1965.

———, and Mazumdar, Bhakat Prasad. *Congress and Congressmen in The Pre-Gandhian Era, 1885–1917*. Calcutta, 1967.

Majumdar, R. C. *History of the Freedom Movement in India*. 3 vols. Calcutta, 1962.

———. *Swami Vivekananda: A Historical Review*. Calcutta, 1965.

(Malaviya, Pandit Madan Mohan). *The Hon. Pandit Madan Mohan Malaviya: His Life and Speeches*. Madras, n. d.

Malcolm, Sir John. *A Memoir of Central India Including Malwa and Adjoining Provinces*. London, 1932.

Martin, Briton. *New India, 1885*. Berkeley, 1970.

Masani, R. P. *Dadbhai Naoroji*. Delhi, 1960.

Mazumdar, A. C. *Indian National Evolution*. Madras, 1917.

McLane, John R. "The Decision to Partition Bengal in 1905," *The Economic and Social History Review*, II, 3 (July 1965).

Bibliography

McLane, John R. "The Drain of Wealth and Indian Nationalism at the Turn of the Century," *Contributions to Indian Economic History II*, ed. Tapan Raychaudhuri. Calcutta, 1963.

———. "The Partition of Bengal and the New Communalism," *Bengal: East and West*, ed. Alexander Lipski. East Lansing, 1970.

———. (ed.). *The Political Awakening in India*. Englewood Cliffs, N. J., 1970.

McMinn, C. W. *Famine Truths—Half Truths—Untruths*. Calcutta, 1902.

Mehrotra, S. R. *The Emergency of the Indian National Congress*. Delhi, 1971.

Menon, K.P.S. *C. Sankaran Nair*. Delhi, 1967.

Metcalf, Thomas R. *The Aftermath of Revolt: India, 1857–1870*. Princeton, 1965.

Mody, H. P. *Sir Pherozeshah Mehta: A Political Biography*. 2 vols. Bombay, 1921.

Morrison, Rev. John. *New Ideas During the Nineteenth Century: A Study of Social, Political, and Religious Developments*. London, 1907.

Mukherjee, Haridas and Uma. *Sri Aurobindo's Political Thought (1893–1908)*. Calcutta, 1958.

Musgrave, P. J. "Landlords and Lords of the Land: Estate Management and Social Control in Uttar Pradesh, 1860–1920," *Modern Asian Studies*, 6, 3 (July 1972).

Nair, Lajpat Rai, and Kirpal, Prem Nath. *Dyal Singh Majithia (A Short Biographical Sketch)*. Lahore, 1935.

Nanda, B. R. "Gokhale's Year of Decision," *Journal of Indian History*, XLIII, 2 (Aug. 1965).

———. *The Nehrus: Motilal and Jawaharlal*. London, 1962.

Narasimhan, V. K. *Kasturi Ranga Iyengar*. Delhi, 1963.

Nash, Vaughan. *The Great Famine and its Causes*. London, 1900.

Natarajan, S. *A Century of Social Reform in India*. London, 1959.

Neale, Walter C. *Economic Change in Rural India: Land Tenure and Reform in Uttar Pradesh, 1800–1955*. New Haven, 1962.

Nevinson, Henry W. *The New Spirit in India*. London, 1908.

O'Dwyer, Sir Michael. *India As I Knew It: 1885–1925*. London, 1925.

Bibliography

O'Malley, L.S.S. *Bengal District Gazetteers, Jessore.* Calcutta, 1912.
———. *Bengal District Gazetteers, Pabna.* Calcutta, 1923.
———. *Indian Caste Customs.* Cambridge, 1932.
———, and Chakravarti, Monmohan. *Bengal District Gazetteers, Howrah.* Calcutta, 1909.
Orwell, George. *Burmese Days.* New York, 1934.
Pal, Bipin Chandra. *Memories of My Life and Times 1886–1900.* Calcutta, 1951.
Parvate, T. V. *Bal Gangadhar Tilak: A Narrative and Interpretative Review of His Life, Career and Contemporary Events.* Ahmedabad, 1958.
———. *Gopal Krishna Gokhale: A Narrative and Interpretative Review of His Life, Career and Contemporary Events.* Ahmedabad, 1959.
Pennell, T. L. *Among the Wild Tribes of the Afghan Frontier.* London, 1909.
Perelman, S. J. *The Road to Miltown or, Under the Spreading Atrophy.* New York, 1957.
Philips, C. H. (ed.). *The Evolution of India and Pakistan, 1858 to 1947: Select Documents.* London, 1962.
Pillai, G. Paramaswaran. *Representative Indians.* London, 1902.
(Pillai, V. O. Chidambaran). *The Life-Sketch of Sjt. V. O. Chidambaran Pillai with a Prefatory Essay on India as a Maritime Power.* Madras, 1909.
Plotnicov, Leonard, and Tuden, Arthur (eds.). *Essays in Comparative Social Stratification.* Pittsburgh, 1970.
Pradhan, G. P., and Bhagwat, A. K. *Lokmanya Tilak: A Biography.* Bombay, 1959.
Prasad, Bisheshwar. *Changing Modes of Indian National Movement.* New Delhi, 1966.
Prasad, Durga. *An English Translation of the Satyarth Prakash.* Lahore, 1908.
Prasad, Rajendra. *India Divided.* Bombay, 1946.
Pyarelal. *Mahatma Gandhi*, Vol. I, *The Early Phase.* Ahmedabad, 1965.
Rahman, Matiur. *From Consultation to Confrontation: A Study of the Muslim League in British Indian Politics, 1906–1912.* London, 1970.
Rajagopalachari, C. *Mahabharata.* Bombay, 1962.
———. *Ramayana.* Bombay, 1965.

Bibliography

Raleigh, Thomas (ed.). *Lord Curzon in India: Being a Selection of His Speeches as Viceroy and Governor-General of India, 1898–1905.* London, 1906.

Ranade, M. G. *Essays on Indian Economics: A Collection of Essays and Speeches.* Bombay, 1898.

Ranade, Ramabai. *Ranade: His Wife's Reminiscences.* Delhi, 1963.

Rao, C. H. *Indian Biographical Dictionary, 1915.* Madras, 1915.

Rao, C. Hayavadana (ed.). *Mysore Gazetteer*, Vol. I. Bangalore, 1927.

Rao, P. Kodanda. *V. S. Srinivasa Sastri: A Political Biography.* Bombay, 1963.

Ratcliffe, S. K. *Sir William Wedderburn and the Indian Reform Movement.* London, 1923.

Ray, Prithwis Chandra. *Life and Times of C. R. Das: The Story of Bengal's Self-Expression.* London, 1925.

Rees, J. D. *The Real India.* London, 1909.

Reid, Sir Robert. *Years of Change in Bengal and Assam.* London, 1966.

Rice, Stanley. *Life of Sayaji Rao III: Maharaja of Baroda.* London, 1930.

Risley, Sir Herbert. *The People of India.* Calcutta, 1915.

———. *The Tribes and Castes of Bengal*, Vol. I. Calcutta, 1891.

———. *Widow and Infant Marriage.* Calcutta, 1894.

Roach, John. "Liberalism and the Victorian Intelligentsia," *The Cambridge Historical Journal*, XIII, 1 (1957).

Roberts, Lord. *Forty-One Years in India: From Subaltern to Commander-in-Chief.* London, 1897.

Robinson, Francis. *Separatism Among Indian Muslims: The Politics of the United Provinces' Muslims, 1860–1923.* Cambridge, 1974.

Robinson, Ronald, and Gallagher, John, with Alice Denny. *Africa and the Victorians: The Climax of Imperialism in the Dark Continent.* New York, 1961.

Ronaldshay, The Earl of. *An Eastern Miscellany.* Edinburgh, 1911.

———. *Life of Lord Curzon.* 3 vols. London, 1928.

Rudolph, Lloyd I., and Rudolph, Susanne Hoeber. *The Modernity of Tradition: Political Development in India.* Chicago, 1967.

Saiyed, Matlubul Hasan. *Mohammad Ali Jinnah (A Political Study).* Lahore, 1953.

Bibliography

Sanyal, Ram Gopal. *Reminiscences and Anecdotes of Great Men of India, Both Official and Non-Official, for the Last One Hundred Years*. Calcutta, 1894–1895.

Sarda, Harbilas. *Life of Dayananda Saraswati*. Ajmer, 1968.

Sarkar, Hem Chandra. *A Life of Ananda Mohan Bose*. Calcutta, 1910.

Sarkar, Sumit. *The Swadeshi Movement in Bengal, 1903–1908*. New Delhi, 1973.

Sastri, K. A. Nilakanta (ed.). *A Great Liberal: Speeches and Writings of Sir P. S. Sivaswami Aiyar*. Madras, 1965.

Sastri, V. S. Srinivasa. *Life of Gopal Krishna Gokhale*. Bangalore, 1937.

Schmitthener, Samuel. "A Sketch of the Development of the Legal Profession in India," *Law and Society Review*, Vol. III, Nos. 2 and 3 (Nov. 1968-Feb. 1969).

Seal, Anil. *The Emergence of Indian Nationalism: Competition and Collaboration in the Late Nineteenth Century*. Cambridge, 1968.

Setalvad, M. C. *Bhulabhai Desai*. New Delhi, 1968.

Shay, Theodore. *The Legacy of the Lokmanya: The Political Philosophy of Bal Gangadhar Tilak*. Bombay, 1956.

Singer, Milton, and Cohn, Bernard S. (eds.). *Structure and Change in Indian Society*. Chicago, 1968.

Singh, Hira Lal. *Problems and Policies of the British in India, 1885–1898*. Bombay, 1963.

Singh, Nahar (compiler). *Gooroo Ram Singh and the Kuka Sikhs (Rebels Against the British Power in India: Documents 1863–1871)*. New Delhi, 1965.

Sinha, Nirmal (comp. and ed.). *Freedom Movement in Bengal, 1818–1904, Who's Who*. Calcutta, 1968.

Sinha, Pradip. *Nineteenth Century Bengal: Aspects of Social History*. Calcutta, 1965.

Smith, Donald. *India as a Secular State*. Princeton, 1963.

Smith, Vincent A. *Akbar, The Great Moghul: 1542–1605*. Oxford, 1919.

Smith, Vincent A. (ed.). *Rambles and Recollections of an Indian Official*. London, 1915.

Smith, Wilfred Cantwell. *Modern Islam in India: A Social Analysis*. London, 1946.

Spear, Percival. *Twilight of the Mughals: Studies in Late Mughal Delhi*. Cambridge, 1951.

Strachey, Sir John. *India: Its Administration and Progress.* London, 1903.
Suntharalingam, R. *Politics and Nationalist Awakening in South India, 1852–1891.* Tucson, 1974.
Thorburn, S. S. *His Majesty's Greatest Subject.* London, 1897.
———. *Musalmans and Money-Lenders in the Punjab.* London, 1886.
———. *The Punjab in Peace and War.* London, 1904.
Thurston, Edgar. *Castes and Tribes of Southern India,* Vol. I. Madras, 1909.
Tilak, Lakshmibai. *I Follow After: An Autobiography.* London, 1950.
Tinker, Hugh. *The Foundations of Local Self-Government in India, Pakistan and Burma.* London, 1954.
Tripathi, A. *The Extremist Challenge: India Between 1890 and 1910.* Bombay, 1967.
Tucker, Richard P. "M. G. Ranade: The Historian as Liberal Nationalist." Mimeographed, May 1970.
Tupper, Charles Lewis. *Our Indian Protectorate: An Introduction to the Study of the Relations Between the British Government and its Indian Feudatories.* London, 1893.
Tyabji, Hussain B. *Badruddin Tyabji: A Biography.* Bombay, 1952.
(Vivekananda). *The Complete Works of Swami Vivekananda,* Vol. III. Calcutta, 1964.
Walker, Benjamin. *Hindu World: An Encyclopedic Survey of Hinduism.* London, 1968.
Walsh, Sir Cecil. *Indian Village Crimes.* London, 1929.
Wasti, Syed Razi. *Lord Minto and the Indian Nationalist Movement, 1905 to 1910.* London, 1964.
Wedderburn, Sir William. *Allan Octavian Hume, C. B.: 'Father of the Indian National Congress.'* London, 1913.
Weiner, Myron. *Party Building in a New Nation: The Indian National Congress.* Chicago, 1967.
———. *Party-Politics in India: The Development of a Multi-Party System.* Princeton, 1957.
Whitcombe, Elizabeth. *Agrarian Conditions in Northern India,* Vol. I, *The United Provinces Under British Rule, 1860–1900.* Berkeley, 1972.
Wiebe, Robert H. *The Search for Order, 1877–1920.* New York, 1967.

Bibliography

Williams, Monier. *Modern India and the Indians: Being a Series of Impressions, Notes, and Essays.* London, 1878.
Wolpert, Stanley A. *Morley and India, 1906–1910.* Berkeley, 1967.
———. *Tilak and Gokhale: Revolution and Reform in the Making of Modern India.* Berkeley, 1962.
Woodruff, Philip. *Call the Next Witness.* London, 1945.
———. *The Men Who Ruled India,* Vol. II, *The Guardians.* London, 1953.

Index

Adam, John, 43, 124, 166, 227n
administrative elite, 11, 63, 77, 81–82
Advocate, 295
Afghanistan, 23, 31, 43, 47–48, 248
Agarkar, Gopal Ganesh, 120
Age of Consent Bill, 308, 310, 327, 329–30, 333, 341. *See also* marriage
agricultural fairs, 285
Ahmedabad, 144
Akbar, 277, 300, 315
akharas, 337, 340, 342–43, 347
Ali, Amir, 106, 110
alienation of land, 214–16, 245ff
Aligarh, 271, 288, 295–96, 326
Aligarh College, 106–109, 112–13, 323, 328
Aligarh Institute Gazette, 294–95
Allahabad, 8–9, 62, 76, 100, 107, 109–10, 117–18, 121, 207, 284, 301–303, 307, 327
Allahabad Cow Protection Society, 287, 301
Allahabad People's Association, 11, 292
Amballa, 147, 251, 305
Amrita Bazar Patrika, 125–27, 154, 219, 233
Amritsar, 147, 278, 281
Ananda Math, 337–38
Andrews, C. F., 278
anglicization, 5, 51ff, 74–75, 348. *See also* leaders
anjumans, 13–14
anti-Brahmanism, 231, 257, 350, 356
anti-landlord combinations, 181–82
aristocracy, 107–108; charity, 198–99; counterpoise to Congress, 26; education, 27, 180, 194–95; government policy toward, 179–80, 236; honors and titles, 195–99; Indian attitudes toward, 188–90, 193; privileges, 194–99. *See also* landlords and native states
Arms Act of 1878, 167

army, 23, 29–32, 39, 42, 46–48, 69, 150, 246, 290, 302, 332, 343, 350-51
Arundel Committee, 235
Arya Samaj, 12, 17, 30, 75, 147, 271, 274, 280, 282–86, 305, 318, 329, 336–37, 361
Aryan civilization, 46, 349
Assam, 147
Assam Labour and Emigration Act of 1901, 217
assassinations, 29, 152–54, 283, 332, 337, 351–55, 364
Ataturk, Kemal, 331
Ayerst, Lt., 152–53, 343, 352–53, 355
Azamgarh, 273, 294, 307, 311, 313–16, 318–19, 334

Badshaw, Hazi Mahomed Abdulla, 221
Bahadur, Jagdeo, 316
Bahadur Shah, Emperor, 278
Bakr Id, 278–79, 292, 300, 312–13, 317
Baksh, Sheik Umar, 254
Ballia, 304, 311, 315–16
Balrampur, 184, 189
Bande Mataram, 366
Banerjea, S. N., 52, 53, 54, 55n, 56, 68–70, 73–74, 83, 95, 99, 101, 103–105, 112, 118, 128, 131, 137–38, 149, 156, 159–60, 165–66, 171, 202, 206–208, 217, 232–33, 236, 255, 338, 368
Banerji, Kalicharan, 128, 166, 236
Banga Mahila Vidyalaya, 80
Bangavasi, 93, 98, 360
Banias, 214–15, 319–20
Banon, Captain, 124
bar associations, 59–61
Baroda, 142–44, 145n, 192–95, 200, 208
Barr, Sir David, 41
Barrier, Gerald, 305
Basu, Bhupendranath, 57, 84, 206
Basu, Dwijendraneth, 149
Bayly, C. A., 7–9
Beames, John, 34

Index

Beck, Theodore, 108, 328
Behar Herald, 205, 207, 304
Behar Landholders' Association, 205
Benaras, 96, 108, 185, 282, 284–85, 300, 303–304, 317, 345, 367
Bengal, 69–71, 76, 80, 105, 147–49, 182–87, 190, 205–206, 211ff, 337, 355; partition, 5, 18, 33, 92, 114, 172, 174, 362–64, 366
Bengal Landholders' Association, 205, 323n
Bengal Tenancy Act of 1885, 95, 183, 212, 215–16, 219–20, 225, 236, 240n, 244–45
Bengalee, 53, 126, 207, 209, 236
Bengalis, 72–73, 89, 104, 106–107, 148, 150, 164, 183, 193, 250, 282, 300, 308, 337
Benthune School, 80
Berar, 306
Bettia, 204, 301, 317
Beveridge, Henry, 41, 43
bhadralok, 71
Bhagavad Gita, 355
Bharat Insurance Company, 251
Bharata Dharma Mahamandal, 294, 299, 307n, 329
Bhargava, Prag Narain, 202
Bhaskaranand, Swami, 302
Bhide, Gopalrao Hari, 286, 298
Bhimji, Ali Muhammad, 113
Bhinga, Raja of, 109, 208
Bhopal, 193–94
Bhownagar, 143, 208
Bhownuggree, Muncherji, 67, 169, 197, 208
Bhuskute, Dattatraya, 348–49, 351
Biddulph, John, 143
Bihar, 13, 148, 183–84, 205, 207, 218, 222–23, 227–29, 273–74, 300–301, 303, 309, 316–17, 319, 321, 327
Bikaner, 283
Bilgrami, Sayyid Husain, 108
Birbal, Raja, 300
Bishan Sabha, 334
Bittleson, Judge, 59
Blavatsky, Madame, 45–46
Bobbili, Raja of, 145, 221–22
Bodas, M. R., 266

Bombay, 58–59, 69, 70–72, 77–79, 97, 121, 141–44, 150–54, 156, 160–61, 163, 182–83, 214, 234–35, 272, 282, 306, 309, 318–19, 336, 338ff, 366–68; land alienation, 257–66
Bombay Corporation, 166, 197
Bombay Land Revenue Code Amendment Act, 259
Bombay Presidency Association, 11, 48, 150, 306–307
Bonnerjee, W. C., 52–53, 54, 57, 66, 68, 74–76, 89, 93–94, 95, 112, 122, 125, 128, 131, 135–37, 148, 164, 165n, 168, 173, 232
Bose, Anandamohan, 52–53, 54, 55n, 74, 122, 148, 166, 206, 232
Bose, Pasupatinath, 84–85
boycott, 172, 362–64, 366–68; by Indian lawyers, 60; tax, 29–30, 153, 258
Bradlaugh, Charles, 98, 111, 125, 348
Brahmans, *see* caste
Brahmo Samaj, 73, 75–76, 83, 228n, 271, 284, 333
Branson, J.A.H., 38, 60
Bright, John, 115, 133
Brindaban, 284, 299
British Committee of Congress, 125, 127, 133–40, 155, 164. *See also* Congress, in England
British Indian Association, 95, 201, 217–21, 229, 232–33, 236–37
Burdwan, 184, 189–90, 196–97, 203, 222n
Burma, 23, 39, 48, 249n

Cadastral Survey, 227–29, 241–43, 245
Cadet Corps, 192
Caine, William, 161
Calcutta, 30, 40, 71, 83–85, 127, 154, 163, 185–87, 218–22, 232–33, 282, 284, 367
Calcutta Corporation, 217, 232–33
Calcutta University, 122, 209
Calcutta Wards' Institution, 186
canals, 365
Canning College, 188
capitalism, 256. *See also* investments; swadeshi

Index

caste, 5, 11–12, 62–63, 73, 75, 82, 97, 102, 104, 108–109, 180, 182, 190, 247, 282, 334, 337, 350; Agarwals, 97, 250; Aroras, 97, 250, 256; Banias, 214–15, 319–20; Banjaras, 311; Bhatias, 320; Brahmans, 9, 17, 35, 63, 74–75, 97, 102, 104, 142, 189–90, 193, 214–15, 257–59, 261, 265–66, 277, 280, 287, 289, 300, 306, 319, 332–34, 338–39, 341–46, 348–52, 356; Chamars, 311; Chandals, 348; Dosadhs, 311; Gujars, 257; Haridasis, 346, 352; Jats, 250, 281–82; Julahas, 321; Kayasthas, 84, 97, 109, 190; Khatris, 97, 190, 250, 256, 282; Komatis, 321; Kunbis, 257; Lavannas, 320; Marathas, 257–58, 320–21, 350; Nairs, 56, 231; Nats, 311; non-Brahmans, 9, 56, 63, 102, 104, 190, 259, 300, 350, 352; Rajputs, 190–91, 223, 316; Suburnabaniks, 190; Telis, 190

Central National Muhammadan Association, 106

Central Provinces, 71, 146–47, 182n, 183, 187, 274, 286–87, 306, 309

Chambers, William, 43

Chand, Lala Lal, 251n

Chandavarkar, N. G., 47, 53, 54n, 161–62, 166, 266

Chandra, Bipan, 256n

Chapekar, Balkrishna, 346–59

Chapekar, Damodar, 18, 66–67, 153, 332, 343–59, 362

Chapekar, Wasudeo, 354–55, 362

charity, 199, 206–208, 228–29, 241, 283

Charlu, P. Ananda, 46, 54, 68, 112, 131–32, 134, 145, 155, 161, 171

Chatterji, Bankim, 337–38

Chaudhuri, Asutosh, 205

Chaudhuri, J., 214

Chaudhuri, Nirad C., 267

Chettiar, P. Somasundaram, 221

China, 23, 198

Chintamani, C. Y., 207

Chisti, Muharram Ali, 113–14, 252n, 254, 293–94

Chitnavis, G. M., 71, 161, 206

Chowdhury, Raja Surjakanta Acharea, 232

Christians, 17–18, 128, 272, 281, 284, 290–91, 344, 350–51; Indian, 41, 74; missionaries, 12, 30, 78, 283

Churchill, Lord Randolph, 48, 228n, 229n

civil disobedience, 152, 158, 366

civil service: employment, 24–27, 105–108, 155, 203, 272; inefficiency and morale, 33–36, 43. *See also* Indian Civil Service

class conflict, 180–83, 215, 266–67. *See also* land alienation; landlords; tenancy legislation

Cobden, Richard, 115

Cochin, 144, 199

Colvin, Sir Auckland, 221, 296

Comilla, 364

commercial classes, 8–9, 142, 190, 296–97, 341

communal integration, 11–12, 365

communalism, 11–18, 31, 110–111, 248–49, 271ff; dynamics of, 274–75; entry to politics through, 5, 334–35; increase, 9; lull, 329; stimulated by competitive institutions, 272, 288–89; weaker than intracommunal conflict, 271. *See also* cow protection; Hindus, martial revival; Muslims

communications, 4, 98–99, 102–103, 321; cartoons, 302, 312; chapatti-passing, 327–28; Dayananda's tours, 282–84; durbar, 294; in legal profession, 62; magic, 302; letters and postcards, 4; newspapers, 4, 93, 135–39, 319; railway, 4, 319; *shastrarths*, 284; telegraph, 319; tree-daubing, 327–28; vernacular pamphlets, 115–18, 140–41, 145, 284, 312

conciliation committees, 313, 326

Congress: aculturalism, 5, 14–15, 89, 93; affective nationalism absent, 5, 15, 359; attendance, 91–92, 118, 171; avoids class conflict, 254, 257, 266–67; avoids appearance of communalism, 359; censors Hume, 121;

Congress (cont.)
censors Paranjpe, 153–54; constitution, 16, 139, 152–75, 220, 367; and cow protection, 110–11, 273, 294–308, 321–31; crisis in, 130ff; decline, 146–51, 170–75; democracy in, 128, 156, 168–70, 172; economic ideas, 130, 212–17; in England, 47–49, 51–53, 118–19, 132–40, 164–65, 208, 218; Englishmen in, 123–29; finances, 134–46, 222–23, 228, 241; flanking movement, 132–40; founding, 43–44, 48–49, 89, 93–96, 244; general secretary, 44, 69, 89, 92, 95–96, 129, 131–32; goals, 7, 21, 24–26, 48–50, 89, 93–94, 96, 105–107, 114, 152; Gokhale's role, 171–72; Hume's role, 43–50, 89ff, 119–21; Indian Congress Committee, 162–65; joint general secretary, 126, 131, 139, 140n; and landlords, 179–83, 187, 197–202, 205–207, 220ff; leadership dispute, 166–74; and lower classes, 14, 98–99, 114–21, 242; loyalty to government, 99–100; Mehta's role, 166ff; minority role, 110–11, 304; and money lenders, 244–57, 260–61, 266–67; and Muslims, 5, 105–15, 130, 140, 152, 252, 254–57, 273, 307–308, 321–28, 330–31; and native states, 199–200; occupations of delegates, 200–201; officials attend, 144; organization, 11, 50–51, 58, 80–81, 130ff; pays delegates to attend, 97; and Permanent Settlement, 223–31; presidents, 75, 99ff, 128, 161–62, 166; and Punjab Land Alienation Act, 251–57; Reception Committee, 53n, 96, 98–99, 127, 134–35, 140, 143–47, 165, 194, 197, 221n, 232, 286, 307, 367; regionalism in, 163–66; revived, 362–67; seeks consensus, 50; self-interest in, 7, 90, 157, 180–81; social boundaries of, 332; and social reform, 28, 348–49; split in, 18, 118–21, 124–25, 127–29, 150, 154, 163, 175, 366–69; suspension suggested, 92, 171;
swaraj, 175; and tenancy rights, 178–80; untouchability in, 102; weaknesses, 5, 15–18, 90–94, 359–60.
See also leaders of Congress
Conservative Party, 134, 169, 197
Constitution of India, 275
conversion, religious, 15, 336
Cooch Behar, 205, 222n
Corn Law League, 115
Cotton, Sir Henry, 40, 43, 123
courage, 15, 332ff
Court of Wards, 183–86, 203
cow protection, 12–13, 18, 28, 130, 245, 271ff, 333–34, 344, 348, 361–62; and Congress, 294–308, 321–31; decline of, 326–27; and M. K. Gandhi, 276; and health, 285–87, 297; and Kuka sect, 280–82; and law courts, 291–97, 304; motives for, 274, 285–88, 307, 309; in native states, 278–79; notables support, 285; official policy toward, 290–94, 307, 313–15, 324, 326; organization, 282ff; origin, 276; riots, 309ff; and *sadhu*s, 298–303; and Swami Dayananda, 282–86; taxes for, 310; unites reformers and orthodox, 282
cow slaughter, and Islamic law, 279; legislative ban on, 273, 275, 282–85, 296, 307–308, 326
cows, markets, 305, 317; purifying effects, 289; symbolism, 275–76, 280, 288–89, 298, 326, 331
cricket, 347
Crooke, William, 289
cultural identity, 14–15, 271–72, 288, 329, 334. *See also* cow protection; leaders of Congress; martial, revival
Curzon, Lord, 26–28, 32, 33, 36n, 37n, 39, 40, 42–43, 92, 137, 151, 161, 174, 188, 229–30, 243, 249, 252–53

Dacca Adult Female School, 80
dakoits, 354
danda, 344–45, 357
Dar, Bandit Bishan Narayan, 54, 55n, 307, 333, 334

Index

Darbhanga, Maharaja of, 117, 124, 136, 141, 144, 145n, 184, 189, 203–204, 206n, 209, 222, 228–29, 232, 233n, 240–41, 287, 301, 303, 309, 317, 329, 367
Darbhanga Gaurakshini Sabha, 304
Das, Bhagwat Ishar, 250
Das, C. R., 61, 76
Das, Lala Ram Charan, 307
Das, Madhusudhan, 63–64, 104
Das, Seth Lachman, 294
Dayananda, Swami, 70, 282–86, 318
Deb, Raja Benoyakrishna, 206–207, 222
Deb, Maharaja Kumar Nilkrishna, 221
Deb, Raja Rajendranarain, 221
Debi, Sarala, *see* Sarala Debi Dutt
Debi, Svarnakumari, *see* Svarnakumari Debi Ghosal
Debs of Sovabazar, 190
debt, agrarian, 245, 247–53, 255–56, 258–59
Deccan Agriculturists Relief Act, 183, 258
Deccan Education Society, 55, 83, 213
Deccan riots of 1875, 246, 257–59
Deccan Sabha, 150
Delhi, 399; durbar, 39–40, 43, 165n, 193, 199, 202, 278–79, 287
Deoband, 113, 271
Dhar, Bansi, 74
Dhar, Lala Murli, 251–53, 255, 305
Dharam Sabha, 334
Digby, William, 48, 125–27, 133
Dipchund, V., 142
divide and rule, 68, 72–73, 106, 108–109, 187, 239–40, 256–57, 324–25, 334, 362
Dogras, 277
Dravid brothers, 354–55
Dreyfus affair, 343
Dufferin, Lord, 27, 92, 100, 116–17, 123, 126, 221, 243
Dumont, Louis, 190
Dumraon, 207, 222, 304, 317
Dupernex, H., 314
Durand, Sir Mortimer, 125
Dutt, Aswinikumar, 54, 158, 206

Dutt, Rambhuj, 80
Dutt, Romeshchandra, 15, 52–53, 54n, 56, 66, 67, 73–74, 138–39, 160, 166, 173n, 194, 206, 224, 229–31, 338
Dutt, Sarala Debi, 80, 98, 222n

East and West, 157
East India Association, 52, 208
East India Company, 207, 277
economic: drain, 22–24, 47–49, 155, 242, 267, 360; inequality, 212–13, 216; interests, 11, 17, 22–23, 116, 179ff; liberalism, 213–17
Education Commission, 10, 106, 186
Edward VII, 196, 198
egalitarianism, 186, 200
elections, 84–85, 94, 96, 105–109, 111–13, 156, 162–63, 180, 217, 231–41, 294–97
Elgin, Lord, 26, 31–33, 240
elites, conflict, 13–14, 108–109, 267; integration of, 179ff, 211; links with non-elites, 29–31; rivalries, 6–7, 10, 14, 81–85, 272; separation from non-elites, 14, 26, 28
England, Indians in, 52–53. *See also* Congress, in England; leaders of Congress
English, anti-Congress policy, 26–28, 100, 117; attitudes toward India, 21ff, 239–40; complacency, 22, 33; and cow killing, 277–78; economic interests, 21–23, 50; extravagance, 42–43; frustration with legal system, 248; illusions, 42; isolation, 34–38; protection of poor, 239, 243–50, 259. *See also* leaders and racism
English education, 3–5, 9–10, 51ff
estate management, 183–85, 202–205, 209
European, role in Hindu cultural revival, 44–47
excise duties on Indian cotton, 134
extremists, 91, 152–75, 362–69

factionalism, 8–9, 80–88, 146, 154, 161

Index

family life, 75–78, 82, 84, 330
famine, 29–32, 43, 45, 70–71, 93, 130, 149, 151, 199, 224, 258–59, 262–63, 290
Famine Commission, 182, 258
fatwa, 113
Finucane, Michael, 236
Fitzpatrick, Sir Dennis, 324, 328
Fraser, Sir Andrew, 41, 196
French Revolution, 120

Ganapati, 15, 157–58, 339–43, 356
Gandhi, Indira, 275
Gandhi, Kasturbai, 79–80, 102
Gandhi, M. K., 55, 56, 61, 66–67, 76, 79–80, 94, 100, 168, 202, 212–13, 276n, 280, 330, 369
Ganguli, Dwarkanath, 80, 149
Ganguli, Kadambini, 80
Garibaldi, 236
Gau Rakshaha Mandali, 306–307, 320
Gaurakshini Sabhas, 308ff
gaushalas, 310
George V, 198
Gerard, Sir Montagu, 41
Ghazipur, 315
Ghazni, Mahmud of, 319
Ghosal, Janakinath, 54, 66, 132, 148, 205, 222n
Ghosal, Sarala Debi, 80, 98, 222n, 338
Ghosal, Svarnakumari Debi, 80, 205n, 222n
Ghose, Aurobindo, 67, 157–58, 194, 360, 368n, 369
Ghose, Lalmohan, 43, 48, 52–53, 54, 170, 308n
Ghose, Manomohan, 47, 52–53, 54, 66, 69, 124, 170n, 348
Ghose, Motilal, 76, 83–85, 101–102, 124–25, 225
Ghose, Norendranath, 155
Ghose, Rashbehari, 99, 368
Ghose, Shishirkumar, 125
Gidhur, 222n
Gladstone, William, 24, 33, 123
Gokhale, G. K, 54–55, 66–67, 83, 99–100, 102, 140, 150, 158–59, 169, 171–72, 213, 261–62, 265
Gondal, 143

goondas, 70–71, 85
Gopal, Lala Nand, 285–86
Gujarat Sabha, 144
Guni, Nawab Abdul, 222n
Gupta, Lal Behari, 73
Gupta, Nagendranath, 102
Gupta period, 276
Gwalior, 198, 208, 277
Gya, 300, 303, 310, 316–17

Hamilton, Lord, 161
Hanuman, 347
Hardwar, 282, 284, 289, 298–301, 303, 327, 329
Hatwa, 301, 317
Hedgewar, Dr. Keshav Baliram, 335n
Henderson, P. D., 117
High Courts, 55–62, 67, 71, 85, 114, 131, 151, 161, 197, 235, 292–93, 301, 304–305, 307, 334
Hindoo Patriot, 201, 221, 233–34, 236
Hindu, 126
Hindus: conciliation with Muslims, 326, 330; cow protection, 271–331; deficiencies, 333–35, 346–47; martial revival, 332–58; nation, 336; raj, 338; revitalization, 6, 12–16, 46, 93, 271, 332, 361; unity through communalism, 334, 336. *See also* communalism; cow protection; cultural identity; orthodox Hindus; social reform
Hindustan, 307
Hindustan Review, 157, 173
Hindustani, 207, 295, 397
honors system, 195–99, 201–202
Howard, J. E., 225, 226n
Hume, Allan Octavian, 3, 16, 43ff, 89ff, 130–33, 136–37, 140, 152, 168–69, 225, 226n, 244, 325, 348; autocracy of, 45; calls for sacrifices, 173–74; career and character, 44–46; Congress depends on, 44; departure of, 118–23, 130–31; leaders' views of, 121–23; Muslim and peasant strategies, 90, 104–18; rebuffed by Congress leaders, 117–18; relations with Indians, 48; warning of peasant rebellion, 118–21, 220–21

Index

Hume, Rev. R. A., 111
Husain, Fazl-i-, 113
Husain, Sajjad, 113
Hutchins, Francis, 21
Hutwa, Maharaja of, 222
Hyderabad, 108, 192, 194–95, 354

Ibbetson, Denzil, 244
Ilbert, Bill, 38–39, 43–44, 48–49, 60, 167
India, 133, 135–40
Indian Association of Calcutta, 95, 116, 148–49, 219–20, 304
Indian Association of Lahore, 11, 83, 146–47, 251
Indian Civil Service, 23–27, 36–38, 52–53, 67, 73, 124, 133, 159, 183–84, 229, 249n, 295
Indian Congress Committee, 162–65
Indian Factory Act, 216
Indian League, 219
Indian National Congress, *see* Congress
Indian Parliamentary Committee, 133
Indian People, 207
Indian Political Agency, 125–27
Indian Society of Calcutta, 11
indigo, 218–19
individualism, 85
Indore, 194, 208
industrial exhibitions and conferences, 98, 144, 200
industrialists, 142, 144
industrialization, 6, 11, 22, 213–14, 216, 360
inequality, 236, 240, 360
intermediate loyalties, 14–15
investments, 212, 238–39, 246–47, 250–51, 253, 256, 260–61, 341–42
Ireland, 24, 137, 143n, 173, 229
Iyengar, V. Bhashyam, 60, 128
Iyer, G. Subramania, 54, 170, 206, 360, 365
Iyer, P. S. Sivaswami, 57, 61, 170, 197
Iyer, S. Subramania, 54, 56, 128, 145, 197, 206, 226
Iyer, V. Krishnaswami, 57, 170

Jaipur, 191, 199n, 283
Jan Sangh, 280
Japan, 171, 364
Jassawala, Seth, 251
Jeejeebhoy, Sir Jamsetjee, 48
Jenkins, Sir Lawrence, 71
Jinnah, Muhammad Ali, 61, 113
Jodhpur, 283–84, 302
Joshi, M. V., 306
Junagadh, 142, 272, 319–20, 340, 350, 353

Kal, 93, 153–54
Kali, 317, 338
Kapur, Ban Bihari, 197
Karve, Anandibai, 259n
Karve, D. K., 76, 79
Kashmir, 125–26, 192, 279
Kasim, Abdul, 113, 206
Kasimbazar, 189–90, 205–206, 226
Katju, K. N., 57
Kavyavisharad, Pandit Kaliprasanna, 83
Kelkar, N. C., 260
Kennedy, Pringle, 227n
Kesari, 93, 98, 121, 152, 339, 360
Khan, Afzail, 153, 343
Khan, Haji Muhammad Ismail, 295, 322
Khan, Hamid Ali, 113–14, 295
Khan, Kunwar Muhammad Faiyaz Ali, 294
Khan, Nawab Muhammad Hayat, 253
Khan, Nawab Reza Ali, 221
Khan, Sayyid Ahmad, 72, 106–10, 112–13, 293, 296, 307, 323–24, 336
Khare, Daji Abaji, 261, 266, 348
Khartoum, 48
Khilafat, 280n, 330–31, 369
Khimji, Lakhmidas, 320
Khoja sect, 105, 307
Khoti Settlement Act of 1880, 265–66
Kimberley, Lord, 324
kingship, 192
Kishore, Munshi Newal, 202
Kitchener, Lord, 23
Kolhapur, 55, 77, 142, 338
Krishna, 289
Krishnaswami, S., 319

kshatriya, 191, 208
Kuka sect, 274–75, 280–82, 305
Kumbh Mela, 298, 327
Kutch, 208

labor, *see* workers
Laha, Maharaja Durgacharan and family, 190, 209, 221
Lahore, 30, 64, 83, 103, 147, 283
Lal Jaiprakash, 207
Lal, Lala Harkishan, 53–54, 64–65, 83, 147, 250, 251n, 255
Lal, Lala Kanhaiya, 253
Lal, Munshi Madho, 140
Lal, Munshi Roshan, 307
land alienation and transfer, *see* alienation of land
landlords, 17, 107, 135, 140, 179ff, 211ff, 284–85, 288, 296–97, 302–303 316, 362; associations, 200–201, 217–21; charity, 206–208; and Congress, 3, 28, 107–109, 144–46, 200–201; deference of professionals to, 208–10; education, 185–88, 209–10; elections, 231–41; and legislative councils, 234–39; oppression, 149, 218–20, 238; pressure from government, 240–41; publicists, 201–202; and small landholders, 182; and tenants, 26–28. *See also* aristocracy; tenancy legislation; tenants
language, 8–9, 11–15, 34, 211, 235, 280, 283, 288, 330, 361; Bengali, 70, 74, 103; Gujarati, 169; Hindi, 305, 329, 336, 362; Hindi-Urdu dispute, 12–15, 283, 334; Marathi, 77–78; Persian, 13, 194n; Sanskrit, 12, 336, 361; Urdu, 13–15, 194n, 297, 329, 334
Lansdowne, Lord, 26, 32, 126–27, 229n, 273
Latif, Nawab Abdul, 110
law courts, 247–56, 291–97, 311–12. *See also* High Courts
Lawrence, Sir Walter Roper, 41–42, 188
lawyers, 9, 97, 179, 182, 187, 204–205, 210, 232–39, 247–49, 254–55, 309, 337
Leader, 207
leaders of Congress, 16–18, 43ff; achievement ethic, 62–67; affluence, 54–55, 360; anglicization, 51ff, 98; and aristocracy, 179ff; arrested, 368–69; dependence on Englishmen, 21, 44, 51, 55–58, 68, 89–90, 123–29, 159; elitism, 62–73; fear of violence, 72; "inner circle," 53–54; isolation, 68–79; lack of cooperation among, 80–85; lawyers, 53; orthodox Hindu pressure on, 70; privileged position, 360; professions, 51ff
legal profession, 52ff; elitism in, 62–63; overcrowding, 61, 80; racial barriers, 58–61
legislative councils, 115–16, 126, 128, 134, 159, 166–67, 172, 179, 183, 192, 201, 209–11, 220, 227n, 231–41, 253, 261–63, 265–66, 273, 293–95, 301, 308, 329, 363, 369; reforms of 1892, 25–26, 132–33, 217, 231–32, 234, 237, 294–95, 322, 327; reforms of 1909, 5, 18
Levi-Strauss, Claude, 291
Liberal Party, 24–25, 32, 48, 118, 125, 133–36, 170n, 173
literacy, 4, 34, 98
local politics, 7–15, 81–85
Local Self-Government, Resolution on, 10
Lok Sabha, 275
Lokhandi, Narayan Maghaji, 350n
London Indian Society, 138, 153–54
Long, Rev. James, 219n
Lucknow, 41, 185–86, 188, 202, 294–95, 333
Lytton, Lord, 183

MacDonnell, Sir Anthony, 223, 229n, 244–45; 258
Mackenzie, Sir Alexander, 240–41
Maclean, James M., 121
Madras, 34–35, 47, 59–61, 97, 106–107, 121, 127–28, 144–46, 149, 170–71,

182n, 185–87, 190, 194, 231, 234–35, 238–39, 364–65
Madras, University of, 194
Madras Landholders' Association, 145n, 221, 227
Magh Mela, 327
Mahabharata, 276–77, 344
Mahajana Sabha, 11, 149
Maharashtra, 97, 332, 336, 338–59. *See also* Bombay
Mahmud, Justice, 293, 304
Mahomedan Anglo-Oriental Defense Association, 328
Mahratta, 260
Maine, Henry, 24
Majithia, Sirdar Dyal Singh, 146, 207, 223, 250, 251n, 306
Malabar, 238
Malabari, Behramji, 157, 169, 338
Malaviya, Pandit Madan Mohan, 15, 53, 74, 100–101, 202, 214, 216, 227n, 230, 307
Mandlik, Vishnu Narayan, 64–65
marriage, age of, 5, 11, 14, 28, 81, 130–31, 169, 297–99, 301, 330, 338, 361; Congress attitudes toward, 127; inter-racial, 249n; reform, 76–80
martial: games, 347; races, 68, 72, 107; revival, 18, 332ff, 363; tradition, 191. *See also* Hindus, martial revival
Martin, Briton, 46
Marwaris, 257, 309
Mau, 314–15
Mazumdar, Ambicacharan, 148, 206
Mazzini, 236, 337
meat-eating, 76, 274, 284, 287, 348
Mehta, Pherozeshah, 17, 52–53, 56, 58–59, 62, 64–65, 69–70, 89, 112, 123, 131, 142, 150, 156, 159, 164, 165n, 166–72, 194, 206, 213, 367–68
military expenditure 47–49. *See also* army
military security, *see* army; security of English
Mill, John Stuart, 226
Minto, Lord, 42

Mitra, Krishnakumar, 83
Mitra, Rajendralal, 197, 217, 221
Mitter, Kalinath, 233
moderates, 33, 49, 233–34, 366–69; attitudes toward violence, 354; and extremists, 6, 18, 52, 152–75, 362
money-lenders, 17, 182, 201, 215–16, 244ff, 296
Monteath, James, 262
Moplahs, 238
Morley, Lord John, 23, 36n, 37n
Mudaliar, C. Jambulingam, 238
Mudaliar, Sabapathy, 145
Mudaliar, Sir Savalai Ramaswami, 47, 57, 73, 145, 221
Mudholkar, R. N., 53–54, 166, 214, 227
Mughals, 29, 198–99, 277–78
Muhammad, 282
Muhammad, Nawab Sayyid, 105, 113, 197, 223
Muhammadan Educational Conference, 106, 114
Muharram, 312, 339–40
Mukherji, Dakhinaranjan, 201
Mukherji, Jaikrishna, of Uttarpara, 190, 209
Mukherji, Jogendranath, 206
Mukherji, Raja Pearymohan, 221, 236
Mukherji, Sambhuchandra, 201n
Müller, Max, 361
municipalities, 217, 232–35, 330; and cow protection, 292, 296–97
Murlidhar, Lala, 172
Murshidabad, Nawab of, 222n
Muslim League, 5–6, 18, 114, 322–23, 326, 331, 362–64
Muslims, 70–71, 223, 257, 277–81, 309, 311ff, 332–43, 348, 351; anxieties, 5, 105ff, 273, 278–79, 293–97, 307–308, 322, 361–62; compared with Hindus, 333–36; and Congress, 3, 28, 51, 90, 96–97, 105–15, 152, 252, 254, 256–57, 294–308, 321–28, 330–31, 369; divisions among, 271; imperial legacy, 334; indebtedness, 246–49; integration of, 278;

Index

Muslims *(cont.)*
  and language question, 11–15, 283, 334; revival, 271–72; separatism, 106–107, 111
Mutiny of 1857, 38, 40–41, 45, 47, 68–69, 100, 106, 159, 183, 192, 194, 196, 246, 278, 290, 302, 315, 327
Mysore, 35, 127, 144, 192, 195, 199–200, 221

Nagpur, 286, 319, 335n, 367
Nagpur Gaurakshini Sabha, 286–87, 298, 304, 306
Naidu, C. Narayanswami, 286
Naidu, P. Rangia, 145, 238
Nair, C. Sankaran, 53n, 54, 56, 57, 60, 102, 104, 168, 206, 231
Namdhari sect, *see* Kuka sect
Namjoshi, Mahadev Ballal, 46, 123, 142n
Nana Sahib, 302
Naoroji, Dadabhai, 52–54, 62n, 67, 68, 118, 122–23, 133–34, 137, 139, 142–43, 154, 169, 172–73, 194, 208, 367
Narain Munshi Prag, 202n
Nasik, 335n
Nath, Bishambar, 161
Nath, Pandit Ajudhia, 53–54, 55n, 68, 122, 126, 131, 293
Nath, Pandit Shambhu, 334
nation building, 3–16, 50–51, 70, 93–94, 157, 180, 208, 212, 231, 266–67, 332, 336–37. *See also* communications; leaders of Congress
national education, 6, 364, 367–68
native states, 43, 125, 135, 142, 144–45, 179–80, 188–200, 278–79, 281, 284, 291, 346–47, 350
Natore, Maharaja of, 222n, 232
Natu, Bala Sahib and Tatia Sahib, 31, 150, 261, 263, 341–43, 353, 356
Nehru, Jawaharlal, 65
Nehru, Motilal, 65, 74, 206
Nepal, 301, 327–28
Nevinson, Henry, 63
New Delhi, 275
newspapers, 10, 31, 51, 193, 196, 207, 219, 241, 251, 260, 360; circulation, 4, 93
Nihalchand, 201
non-Brahman movement, 5, 338, 350. *See also* caste
Northcote, Lord, 260
North-Western Provinces and Oudh, 13, 44–45, 97, 105–14, 146–47, 164, 180, 182n, 183–85, 188–91, 201–202, 216–18, 234–35, 273–74, 280, 291–97, 307, 309–29
Norton, Eardley, 111, 124–25, 127–28, 145, 161, 166, 174n, 301
Nundy, Alfred, 128, 136, 137n, 139, 165n

Orissa, 63, 148, 183–84
Oriyas, 104
orthodox Hindus, 70, 73-80, 271–72, 274–75, 280, 282–86, 288–92, 296, 298–308, 328–30, 332ff, 356, 359, 360–61
Oudh, Nawab of, 334
Oudh Punch, 113
Oudh Taluqdars' Association, 201n

Paisa Akhbar, 252
Pakistan, 364
Pal, Bipinchandra, 54–55, 75–76, 123, 158, 369
Pal, Kristodas, 185, 201, 217
panchayats, 251, 311, 341
Pan-Islam, 29, 31, 271
Pantulu, P. Chentsal Rao, 221
Paranjpe, Shivram Mahadeo, 153–54, 261, 356, 366
Parekh, Gokhuldas, 160–61
Parliament, 24–25, 44, 47–49, 67, 73, 94, 96, 111, 115, 118, 121, 125, 128, 132–37, 143, 152, 169, 173–74, 197, 208, 218, 229n, 249, 284–85, 294–96, 322, 343
Parliament of Religions in Chicago, 208
Parsis, 69–70, 73, 89, 113–15, 142, 167–69, 293
Pathans, 320, 323
Patiala, 194, 296

Index

Patna, 316–17
patron-client relationships, 8–9, 82, 181, 288
Patwardhan, Wasude Balwant, 349
peasants, 3, 90, 189n, 218, 243ff, 360, 365
Pennell, T. L., 41
Permanent Settlement, 145n, 218, 220, 223–31, 242
Perraju, K., 231
Petit, Sir Dinshaw Manackjee, 287, 306
Phule, Jotirao, 338, 350
Pillai, Chidambaran, 365
Pillai, P. Ratnasabhapati, 238
Pillai, Peter Paul, 227
Pioneer, 72, 233, 301
plague, 29, 71, 130, 150–51, 263, 342–43, 351
planters, 217–18
Police Commission, 155
Poona, 28–31, 70, 131, 142n, 153–54, 263, 282, 306, 332, 338–59
post office, 4
poverty, 29, 242–43, 266, 285–87, 308, 357, 360
Prabhas Patan, 319–21, 339
Prarthana Samaj, 75, 161, 284
Prasad, Raja Shiva, 96, 197
professional associations, 11, 58–61
provincial conferences, 147–50, 160, 162, 367–68
Prussia, 214
public commissions, 25
Public Service Commission, 10, 36, 73n, 106
Punjab, 83, 97, 105, 146–47, 207, 246–57, 274–75, 277–83, 291, 301, 305–306, 317–18, 329, 334, 355, 365–66
Punjab Land Alienation Act of 1900, 114, 246–57
Punjab National Bank, 251
Punjabee, 360
Punjabis, 73, 163–66
Puranas, 344
Puranic Hinduism, 6, 12, 271, 282–84, 361
Pyarelal, 137

racism, 21–22, 37–45, 49, 357
Rafiq-i-Hind, 113, 252n, 293
Rahim, Hafiz Abdul, 113
Rai, Lajpat, 15, 55, 67, 83, 99, 134, 147, 155, 157, 214, 250, 255, 267, 287, 335–37, 357, 360, 365, 367, 369
railways, 4, 41–42, 64–65, 198
Rajputana, 282, 300
Rajputs, 72, 109, 190–91, 223, 277, 316
Ram, Bakshi Jaishi, 53, 147, 163, 250, 251n, 255
Ram, Lekh, 337
Ram, Swami Ala, 305–307
Rama, 347
Ramakrishna Mission, 361
Ramayana, 276–77
Ramdas, 339
Ramnad, Raja of, 144–45, 208, 222n, 223, 226
Ranade, M. G., 52, 54–55, 64, 69, 70, 74–80, 95, 102–104, 112, 123, 131–32, 168, 227n, 265, 284–85, 338–39, 348–49, 356; economic ideas, 213–16
Ranade, Mahadeo (terrorist), 153, 355
Ranade, Ramabai, 76–80, 103–104
Rand, Mr., 140, 151–54, 343–44, 351–55
Rangoon, 273, 318n, 321
Rao, Baji, 341, 347
Rao, Dinkar, 197
Rao, Sir T. Madhava, 68, 194, 197, 211, 221
Rashtriya Swayam Sevak, 335n
Rasul, Abdul, 113
Ratnagiri, 265–66
Ravanna, 347
Rees, J. D., 37
regionalism, 93–94, 101–104
renunciation of wealth, 64, 67, 157–58, 213
representative institutions, 105–14, 121. *See also* legislative councils; municipalities
Ripon, Lord, 10, 38, 43–45
Risley, H. H., 239–40
Rivaz, Sir Charles, 255

Index

Roberts, Lord, 68
Rohilkhand, 280
Roy, Kaliprasanna, 147, 155, 255
Roy, Prithwischandra, 206
Roy, Raja Sashi Sekhareswar, of Tahirpur, 110, 221
Roy, Sitanath, 221, 233n
Royal Commission on Indian Finances, 68
Rubbani, Nawab Ghulam, 221
Russia, 23, 31, 125, 153, 364

Sadharan Brahmo Samaj, 149
sadhus and *sannyasis*, 41, 274, 283, 299–303, 308–309, 317, 327, 337, 340
samitis, 337, 363–64
sanatan dharma sabhas, 12–14, 329
Sanatanists, 271
Sandhurst, Lord, 160
Sandhya, 360
Sapru, Tej Bahadur, 194, 206
Saran, 316
Saraswati, Swami Brahmanand, 302
Sarda, Harbilas, 283
Sarvadhikari, Rajkumar, 221, 232
Sarvajanik Sabha, 11, 29–30, 83, 116, 142, 150, 153, 261, 264, 341
Sarvarkar, Vinayak Damodar, 335n
Sastri, Seshia, 82
Satara, 160
Sayani, Muhammad Rahimtullah, 53n, 113
Schmitthener, Samuel, 57n
sea voyage, 73–75, 124, 133
Seal, Anil, 7, 9, 110
secularism, 326, 330
security of English, 23, 29–32, 244, 246–48, 290, 356
sedition law, 31–32
sedition trials, 153
Sen, Baikuntanath, 205, 228
Sen, Guruprasad, 205, 207, 232
Sen, Keshabchandra, 284
Sen, Narendranath, 46, 55n, 236
separate electorates, 5, 112, 363
Servants of India Society, 172
Shahabad, 304
Shameshad Dowla, Nawab, 221

Sharfuddin, Sayyid Muhammad, 113–14
Shastras, 79, 284, 330, 333, 346, 357
Shepherd, Horatio, 56
Shivaji, 15, 153, 157, 285, 341–43, 347–48, 353, 356
Shuddi, 336
Sikhs, 274, 277–82, 365
Simla delegation, 112, 322, 363–64
Singh, Ajit, 365
Singh, Mahatma Koot Hoomi Lal, 46
Singh, Raja Rampal, 207, 223, 307
Singh, Saligram, 205, 234n
Singh, Sir Harnam, 253
Singh, Sirdar Uttam, 221
Sinha, Sachchidananda, 54, 55n, 157
Sinhas of Raipur, 205
Sinhji, Ranjit, 67
Sita, 347
social reform, 11–12, 73–81, 127–28, 161, 271, 274–75, 280, 282, 332–34, 336–38, 342, 348, 357, 359–61
Social Reform Conference, 28, 79, 90, 131, 306, 348–49
South Africa, 35, 55
Sriman Swami, 287, 301–302, 318
Stephen, James Fitzjames, 24
Strachey, Sir John, 34, 72
strikes, 363, 365–66
Stuart, Mr., 128
students, 30, 362–63; income of, 187–88
Sudharak, 349
Sudharaks, 271
subnationalism, 12–18, 275
Suez Canal, 37
Suntharalingam, R., 9
Surat split, 91, 163, 169, 175, 367–68
Swadesamitran, 360
swadeshi, 6, 140–41, 144, 213–14, 251, 302, 341, 362–67
Swadeshi Cotton Mills, 286
Swadeshi Steam Navigation Company, 364–65

Tagore, Debendranath, 80, 205, 222, 284
Tagore family, 190, 205n, 209, 222

Index

Tagore, Maharaja Jatindramohan, 124, 185, 221
Tagore, Rabindranath, 338
Tahirpore, Raja of, 110, 308
taluqdars, *see* landlords
Tamils, 102, 104
Tata, J. N., 142–43
tax boycott, 29–30, 157, 259, 263–64
Tejpal, G. G., 142
Telang, Kashinath, 46, 52, 55n, 142, 213, 226, 307, 339
temperence, 69–70
tenancy legislation, 17, 27–28, 116, 182–83, 203, 209ff, 221n, 223, 236, 238–41, 243, 265–66
tenancy rights, 95, 149, 224ff
tenants, 180–83, 203, 247, 259, 265–67, 288, 316; occupancy, 182; supported by Congressmen, 236
terrorism, 29, 196, 227n, 332, 338, 343–59, 368. *See also* assassinations
Thagi and Dakoiti, Department for Suppression of, 117
Theosophical Society, 45–46, 286, 361
Thorburn, S. S., 246–49
Thurston, Edgar, 34
Tilak, Bal Gangadhar, 15, 29, 31, 54–55, 83, 99, 101, 120–21, 131, 140, 142n, 150–51, 157–58, 160–61, 168, 171–72, 202, 206, 313–14, 265–67, 306, 336, 339, 342–44, 348, 353–54, 356–57, 360, 366–68
Tilak, Lakshmi, 76, 77n
Tinnevelly, 365
Tippera, 222n
Travancore, 144, 194, 199
tree-daubing, 327–28
Trevelyan, Justice, 85
Tribune, 147, 207, 251, 306
Triplicane Literary Society, 11
trusteeship, Gandhi's theory of, 213
Turkey, 29, 31
Tuticorin, 364–65
two nation theory, 3, 109, 323
Tyabji, Badruddin, 52–53, 54n, 55n, 59, 66, 71, 92, 105, 109–11, 113–14, 227n, 325, 348

Udaipur, 284

ulama, 113
unemployment, 9–10, 93
United Indian Patriotic Association, 106–109, 296, 303
universalism, 12, 112, 231, 337, 359
Universities Commission, 155
U.P. Hindu Sabha, 334
urban professionals, relations with landlords and chiefs, 179ff
Utkal Union Conference, 104
Uttarpara, 203, 209

vakil raj, 188, 200–201
vakils, *see* lawyers
Varma, Ganga Prasad, 54, 307–308, 334
Varma, Shyama Krishna, 194
Vedic Hinduism, 6, 276, 284
Venkatigiri, Raja of, 145, 189, 221–22
Vernacular Press Act, 167
Victoria, Queen, 42, 74, 299n, 343, 351
Vijayaraghava Chariar, C., 238
violence, 29, 85, 107, 152–54, 243, 332ff; agrarian, 182, 209, 246–47, 257–59; anti-British, 30, 175, 196, 278, 301, 337, 365, 368; anti-reformer, 338, 349–50, 357; communal, 18, 70–71, 111, 114n, 158, 167, 238, 249, 272–81, 284–85, 291–97, 299–300, 303–305, 308–35, 340, 361, 364; English, 39; fear of, 68, 158–59; intracommunal, 283–84, 300; lower-class, 70–72, 119–21; statistics, 316; at Surat Congress, 169, 368; threat of, 144–45
Viraraghava Chariar, M., 115, 145, 168
Vivekananda, Swami, 208, 338
Vizianagram, 144–45, 184, 189, 198, 206–208
voluntary associations, 3, 10–15, 81, 146
Volunteer Corps, 46–48

Wacha, D. E., 53n, 54, 69, 100, 118, 123, 131, 139, 142, 150, 155, 164–65, 168, 172, 213, 225, 227n

Index

Wahabhis, 271, 321
Wai, 351
wards' institutions, 185
Webb, Alfred, 99, 123, 128
Wedderburn, William, 43, 45, 52, 55, 99, 119, 123, 132–34, 136–38, 140, 161, 173, 227n
Welby, Lord, 68, 72
widow re-marriage, 349
Wolpert, Stanley, 353

women, education of, 77–80
Wordsworth, Professor, 43
workers, 23, 216–17, 320n, 321, 350n, 363, 365

Yule, George, 43, 96, 99, 123, 133

Zamindari Panchayat, 237
zamindars, *see* landlords

Library of Congress Cataloging in Publication Data

McLane, John R.   1935-
   Indian nationalism and the early Congress.

   Bibliography: p.
   Includes index.
   1. India—Politics and government—19th century.
2. Indian National Congress.   3. Nationalism—India.
I. Title.
DS479.M32   320.9′54′035   77-72127
   ISBN 0-691-03113-4
   ISBN 0-691-10056-X pbk.

DATE DUE			
FEB 27 1997			
DEC 1 5 1997			

DEMCO 38-297